MAC OS X
HACKS

MAC OS X
HACKS

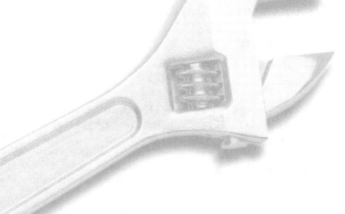

Rael Dornfest and Kevin Hemenway

O'REILLY®

Beijing · Cambridge · Farnham · Köln · Paris · Sebastopol · Taipei · Tokyo

Mac OS X Hacks

by Rael Dornfest and Kevin Hemenway

Copyright © 2003 O'Reilly & Associates, Inc. All rights reserved.
Printed in the United States of America.

Published by O'Reilly & Associates, Inc., 1005 Gravenstein Highway North, Sebastopol, CA 95472.

O'Reilly & Associates books may be purchased for educational, business, or sales promotional use. Online editions are also available for most titles (*safari.oreilly.com*). For more information, contact our corporate/institutional sales department: (800) 998-9938 or *corporate@oreilly.com*.

Editor:	Rael Dornfest
Series Editor:	Dale Dougherty
Production Editor:	Brian Sawyer
Cover Designer:	Edie Freedman
Interior Designer:	David Futato

Printing History:

March 2003:	First Edition.

ISBN: 0-596-00460-5

[C]

Contents

Credits

About the Authors

Rael Dornfest is a maven at O'Reilly & Associates, Inc., focusing on technologies just beyond the pale. He assesses, experiments, programs, and writes for the O'Reilly Network and O'Reilly publications. Rael has edited, coauthored, and contributed to various O'Reilly books. He is program chair for the O'Reilly Emerging Technology Conference and O'Reilly Mac OS X Conference, chair of the RSS-DEV Working Group, and developer of Meerkat: An Open Wire Service (*meerkat.oreillynet.com*). In his copious free time, Rael develops bits and bobs of freeware and maintains his raelity bytes weblog (*http://www.raelity.org*).

Kevin Hemenway, better known as Morbus Iff, is the creator of *disobey.com*, which bills itself as "content for the discontented." Publisher, developer, and writer of more home cooking than you could ever imagine (like the popular open source syndicated reader AmphetaDesk, the best-kept gaming secret Gamegrene.com, the popular Ghost Sites and Nonsense Network, the giggle-inducing articles at the O'Reilly Network, a few pieces at Apple's Internet Developer site, etc.) he's an ardent supporter of cloning, merely so he can get more work done. He cooks with a Fry Pan of Intellect +2 and lives in Concord, NH. You can contact him at *morbus@disobey.com*.

Contributors

The following people contributed to this book:

- Michael Brewer (*http://mbrewer.dyndns.org/macosxhacks/*) is a developer based near Charlotte, North Carolina. He has written several OS X–related articles for O'Reilly Mac DevCenter. His interests include web development of various flavors (primarily Java) and database design. When the weekend rolls around, those tend to disappear and he focuses on mountain biking.

- James Duncan Davidson (*http://www.x180.net/*) is a freelance author, speaker, and software consultant focusing on Mac OS X, Java, and XML technologies. He regularly presents at conferences all over the world on topics ranging from open source to programming Java effectively. He was the original author of Apache Tomcat and Apache Ant and was instrumental in their donation to the Apache Software Foundation by Sun Microsystems. While working at Sun, he authored two versions of the Java Servlet API specification, as well as the Java API for XML Processing specification. He currently resides in San Francisco, California.

- Edd Dumbill is Managing Editor of XML.com. He also writes free software, and packages Bluetooth-related software for the Debian GNU/Linux distribution. Edd is the creator of XMLhack (*http://xmlhack.com/*) and WriteTheWeb (*http://writetheweb.com/*).

- Rob Flickenger was born the son of a pig farmer in Bucharest. This young ne'er-do-well had few ambitions above mucking out the slop stall before dinner. But that was just at the dawn of the digital age. Who would have thought that five years later the same boy who thought cow tipping shouldn't go above 10% would go on to invent the Internet and eventually become the first living human with an ADSL line surgically attached to his spinal column. Now, in these increasingly untethered times, he has eschewed his former 6Mbit neural I/O port for an 11Mbit, encrypted, wireless version. It certainly makes it easier to leave the house without the need for miles of extension cord. In his spare time, he also writes; Rob is the author of *Building Wireless Community Networks* and *Linux Server Hacks*.

- brian d foy (*http://www.panix.com/~comdog/*) has been a dedicated Mac user since a Quadra 650, which he still uses. Seven Macs later, most of them still in use, he deals almost exclusively with Mac OS X for his Perl development work, even if he has to use Virtual PC to cheat. He is also a Perl developer and trainer who maintains several Perl modules on CPAN and publishes *The Perl Review*, all from his PoweBbook.

- Alan Graham's (*http://homepage.mac.com/agraham999/*) mission, using wit sharp as an electric razor and a modicum of grammatical skill, is enabling users to explore what's possible with straight talk and as little techno-babble as possible. He has worked in prepress, digital video and film, interactive, software development, and web development for a wide spectrum of clients that include Apple Computer, Sausage Software, Mattel, Better Homes & Gardens, OpenMarket, PresenceWorks.com,

Paramount, and Excite@home to name a few. When he's not writing for O'Reilly, you can find him doing R&D for *Mac OS X: The Missing Manual*, running errands for his pregnant wife Dana, and working on the great American novel. You can find more of Alan's writing via his blog, Trial and Eror (*http://homepage.mac.com/agraham999/iblog/*).

- Brian Jepson (*http://www.jepstone.net/*) maintains a keen focus on the sparks that fly where two cutting edges meet. Some of his favorite intersections are Mac OS X (where a solid Unix core meets the pioneering Apple user interface), Mono and Portable.NET (where Open Source meets Windows), and Rotor (where Microsoft shares a bunch of code with y'all). Brian is also an O'Reilly editor and coauthor of *Mac OS X for Unix Geeks* and *Learning Unix for Mac OS X*.

- Wei-Meng Lee (*http://www.oreillynet.com/pub/au/944*) teaches at the School of Information and Communications Technology, NgeeAnn Polytechnic, Singapore. He is an experienced author, trainer, and developer specializing in Mac OS X and Microsoft .NET technologies. Wei-Meng is also a writer for the O'Reilly Network and a contributing author to *SQL Server Magazine* and *DevX.com*.

- Jason McIntosh (*http://www.jmac.org/*) lives and works in and around Boston. He has coauthored two O'Reilly books, *Mac OS X in a Nutshell* and *Perl & XML*, and writes occasional columns and weblog entries for the O'Reilly Network.

- Bruce W. Perry is an independent software developer and writer. Since 1996, he has developed web applications and databases for various non-profits, design and marketing firms, ad agencies, and digital-music specialists. Before working in the web field, Perry remained tethered to his portable and desktop Macs while writing environmental law books and newsletters. When not hacking or writing, he loves cycling and climbing mountains in the U.S. and Switzerland. He lives in the Newburyport, Massachusetts area with his wife Stacy LeBaron and daughter Rachel.

- Erik T. Ray has worked for O'Reilly as a software developer and XML specialist since 1995. He helped to establish a complete publishing solution using DocBook-XML and Perl to produce books in print, on CD-ROM, and for the new Safari web library of books. As the author of the O'Reilly bestseller *Learning XML* and numerous articles in technical journals, Erik is known for his clear and entertaining writing style. When not hammering out code, he enjoys playing card games, reading about hemorrhagic fevers, practicing Buddhist meditation, and collecting toys. He lives in Saugus, MA with his wife Jeannine and seven parrots.

- Matthew Sparby (*http://www.obzorg.org/*) is a technology consultant and Macintosh hobbyist from Orlando, Florida. He publishes the Mac-centric web site Obzorg.org and contributes material to other technology publications and user groups

- Chris Stone is a Senior Systems Administrator (the Mac guy) at O'Reilly and coauthor of *Mac OS X in a Nutshell*. He's written several Mac OS X–related articles for the O'Reilly MacDevCenter (*http://www.macdevcenter.com*) and contributed to *Mac OS X: The Missing Manual*. Chris lives in Petaluma, California with his wife Miho and two sons, Andrew and Jonathan.

- Derrick Story (*http://www.storyphoto.com/*) is the coauthor of *iPhoto: The Missing Manual* and author of the *Digital Photography Pocket Guide*. His day job is managing editor of O'Reilly Network and the Mac DevCenter (*http://www.macdevcenter.com/*). Derrick's experience includes more than 15 years as a photojournalist, a stint as the managing editor for *Web Review*, and speaker at CMP and IDG tech conferences. He also manages his online photo business, Story Photography.

- Jon Udell (*http://udell.roninhouse.com/*) is lead analyst for the InfoWorld Test Center. He is the author of *Practical Internet Groupware*, published in 1999 by O'Reilly, and an advisor to O'Reilly's Safari Tech Books Online.

- David E. Wheeler (*http://david.wheeler.net/*) is President of Kineticode (*http://www.kineticode.com/*), an enterprise content management and software development consulting company based in San Francisco. He also serves as the maintainer and lead developer for Bricolage, an open-source content management system built on Apache, mod_perl, and PostgreSQL. An active member of the Perl community and a speaker at the O'Reilly Mac OS X Conference (*http://conferences.oreilly.com/macosxcon/*), David has contributed an appendix introducing Bricolage to O'Reilly's *Embedding Perl in HTML with Mason*, as well as several articles addressing the needs of the serious Mac OS X–based Perl and Unix developer. David lives in San Francisco with his wife, Julie, and their two cats.

Acknowledgments

We would like to thank all those who contributed their ideas and code for Mac OS X hacks to this book.

Rael

First and foremost, to Asha and Sam—always my inspiration, joy, and best friends.

My extended family and friends, both local and virtual, who'd begun to wonder if they needed to send in a rescue party.

I'd like to thank Dale Dougherty for bringing me in to work on the Hacks series; working from the other side of the page has been a learning experience and a half. The O'Reilly editors, production, product management, and marketing staff are consummate professionals, hackers, and mensches. They've helped me immeasurably in my fledgling editorial stint. Extra special thanks goes out to my virtual cube-mate, Nat Torkington, and Laurie Petrycki for showing me the ropes.

Kevin

Thanks to Derrick for suggesting the O'Reilly Network article that eventually cascaded into my current tech writing position, as well as Aaron for the good word he may or may not have put in for me.

To Katherine for putting up with my absent-minded "I'm busy!," and to Philip for getting me into Perl, Linux, and "bullets! lots of bullets!!" To Sean for picking the berries from my jam, and to Deb, who has watched me blossom into the handsome young stallion I am now, while I have merely watched her grow older and older. Don't forget my discount.

Foreword

From one perspective, Mac OS X is heresy. It's an Apple operating system with a command line. It doesn't hide its innards from tinkerers and hackers. It's not a closed box with a sticker that says, "NO USER SERVICEABLE PARTS INSIDE," like all previous Mac operating systems.

In short, it's a shocking and flagrant violation of everything the Mac has ever stood for.

As it turns out, nobody much cares. Newbies plug along, clicking Dock icons and dragging things to the Trash, without ever suspecting that only a thin shell of shiny pixels separates them from the seething, thrashing Unix engine beneath.

And power users are on Cloud 9.

So here they come, out of the woodwork: a nation of once marginalized Unix geeks, embracing the Mac, hailing Apple as the world's largest manufacturer of Unix boxes. These people are the pure of heart, the superusers who cluster at computer conferences with their PowerBook G4s and shoot bits of code at each other over the wireless network. Apple may have lost the battle for the corporate desktop, but with Mac OS X, it's picked up a new constituency of its own.

Part of the pleasure of reading this book comes from the hacks themselves: controlling iTunes with Perl scripts, using a Bluetooth cellphone as a wireless modem for your laptop, downloading files from the command line, and other preposterous stunts.

But much of the pleasure, too, comes from the pure, geeky fun the authors seem to be having. These are not serious adult males at the peaks of their writing careers—they're five-year-olds stomping in puddles, laughing their heads off. These are people who don't for a moment question the value of turning the Mac into an Internet radio station powered by iTunes. Hey—it's *cool*, and that's the greatest value of all.

These guys will lead you to favorite shareware programs, shine light on clever Unix command-line hacks, and show you how to turn off the brushed-metal window look of iChat and iSync. (Why? Because you *can*!)

This book might occasionally be over the head of many Mac fans. (If you want more general, less technical, everyday operating tips, try *Mac OS X Hints, Jaguar Edition.*)

But some people get as much a kick out of putting a computer through its paces as they do from everyday issues like productivity. Part of the spirit of hacking is doing things that the product's developer didn't quite imagine, finding the new and creative uses that only are possible to those who are willing to leave the beaten path. For the hackers among us, it's all about the thrill of discovery. If you're one of them, put on your backpack; you're about to go on quite a ride.

—David Pogue
Creator of the Missing Manual series

Preface

Mac OS X is a marvelous confluence of the user-friendly and highly customizable Macintosh of yesteryear and the power and flexibility of Unix under the hood. Those coming to Mac OS X from previous incarnations of the operating system, while recognizing much of the friendly face of the Macintosh, are plunged into a whole new world where things are almost like they were, but not quite—not to mention all that Unix command-line stuff lurking in the Terminal application. Unix converts to Mac OS X find a familiar FreeBSD-like operating system at the core and many of the command-line applications they're familiar with either already installed or a package or compile away. On the front end, however, much that is second nature to an old Mac hand is strange and new, at once fascinating and confounding to those used to the likes of X Windows and GNOME.

This presents a unique opportunity for combining traditional Unix hacking and Mac OS know-how. *Mac OS X Hacks* goes beyond the peculiar mix of manpages and not-particularly-helpful Help Center, pulling the best tips, tricks, and scripts from Mac power users and Unix hackers themselves.

The collection reflects the real-world experience of those well steeped in Unix history and expertise, sharing their no-nonsense, sometimes quick-and-dirty solutions to administering and taking full advantage of everything a Unix desktop has to offer: web, mail, and FTP serving; security services; SSH, Perl, and shell scripting, as well as compiling, configuring, scheduling, networking, and hacking. Add to that the experience of die-hard Macintosh users, customizing and modifying their hardware and software to meet their needs: System Preferences, GUI mods and tweaks, hardware tips, vital shareware and freeware, AppleScript, AppleTalk and equivalents, keyboard modifiers, and general Macintosh-style tomfoolery.

Each hack can be read easily in a few minutes, saving countless hours of searching for the right answer. *Mac OS X Hacks* provides direct, hands-on solutions that can be applied to the challenges facing both those meeting the Mac for the first time and longtime users delving into Mac OS X and its Unix underpinnings. The collection should appeal to home users and corporate IT personnel alike.

How to Use This Book

You can read this book cover-to-cover if you like; but, for the most part, each hack stands on its own. If there's a prerequisite you ought to know about, there'll be a cross-reference to guide you on the right path. So feel free to browse, flipping around whatever section interests you most.

How This Book Is Organized

Mac OS X is remarkable enough to bring together, on one desktop, long-time Mac devotees and Unix hackers of old. It does so by rebuilding the renowned Mac look-and-feel on the shoulders of a best-of-breed Unix operating system. OS X's flexibility, customizability, and extensibility mean there's just about nothing you can't do if you set your mind to it. This book goes beyond the simple tips and tricks, click here and drag there, to the more interesting hacks—bite-sized bits of truly useful functionality you can manage in just a few minutes with the help of a trusty friend. The book is divided into several chapters:

Chapter 1, *Files*

The Mac OS X filesystem is a blend of powerful, ancient Unix underpinnings and the candy-coated shell known as the Macintosh Finder. The hacks in this section poke and prod at the seams, revealing some useful techniques for backing up your system, tweaking files and folders, bending aliases to your will, and understanding how it all fits together—even dumpster diving in the Trash a little.

Chapter 2, *Startup*

At startup, there's an awful lot going on behind the scenes to bring your Mac to life. This section takes a peek beneath the surface at just what's making all that noise. We'll show you how to boot from another device, turn your Mac into a FireWire hard drive, get OS X running on that old Power Mac in your closet, and lock up your Mac good and tight.

Chapter 3, *Multimedia and the iApps*

Apple has positioned the Mac as a digital hub, the nexus for the otherwise disparate components of your iLife. This section provides tips and techniques for getting the most out of the iApps and third-party multimedia applications. Going beyond what the iApps provide out of the box, we'll also glue together audio, video, text, and photos in some unexpectedly useful and fun combinations.

Chapter 4, *The User Interface*

Mac users have a long history of tweaking the Mac OS graphical user-interface. We provide a collection of inspiring hacks and pointers to third-party applications for tweaking the look-and-feel, extending the functionality that's already there, and teaching your Mac to behave "just as it should."

Chapter 5, *Unix and the Terminal*

Beneath the sleek, elegant, Technicolor candy coating of Mac OS X's graphical user-interface beats the heart of an honest-to-goodness Unix operating system. This chapter provides a gentle introduction to the command-line environment, showing how to move around and manipulate files and folders. With that under your belt, we'll show you how to thread some of the built-in Unix applications and functions together to create new functionality.

Chapter 6, *Networking*

Where OS X really shines is in its networking, being able to connect to just about anything with an IP heartbeat. Communicate as easily with Windows and Unix machines as with other Macs. Share your Internet connection via Ethernet, WiFi, or FireWire or connect one-to-one with another computer even when there is no network to be found. This chapter highlights just some of the limitless possibilities for inter-networking with just about anything, just about anywhere.

Chapter 7, *Email*

More than just a choice of excellent mail applications, OS X's powerful Unix underpinnings provide access to an array of the most popular and versatile mail servers and filtering systems on the planet. This chapter takes you through turning your Mac into a personal intranet mail server, as well as teaching you a little more about some of the mail applications you may be using and how to get the most out of them.

Chapter 8, *The Web*

Mac OS X is a web powerhouse, both in terms of its web-serving capabilities and wide range of web browsers from which to choose. Beneath the understated Personal Web Sharing is the ubiquitous, flexible, and industrial-strength Apache web server—just click the Start button. By the end of this chapter, you'll be serving up dynamic content, running CGI applications, scripting PHP pages, and putting together server-side include–driven pages with the best of them.

Chapter 9, *Databases*

Long the backbone of just about any open source–driven web site, the MySQL and PostgreSQL database engines are just as at home on your Mac as they have been in the more traditional Unix shop. This chapter walks you through the installation and exploration of these two remarkable database applications, on both the command line and the Desktop.

Conventions Used in This Book

The following is a list of the typographical conventions used in this book:

Italic

Used to indicate new terms, URLs, filenames, file extensions, and directories and to highlight comments in examples. For example, a path in the filesystem will appear as */Developer/Applications*.

`Constant width`

Used to show code examples, the contents of files, commands, or the output from commands.

`Constant width bold`

Used in examples and tables to show commands or other text that should be typed literally.

`Constant width italic`

Used in examples and tables to show text that should be replaced with user-supplied values.

Color

The second color is used to indicate a cross-reference within the text.

↵

A carriage return (↵) at the end of a line of code is used to denote an unnatural line break; that is, you should not enter these as two lines of code, but as one continuous line. Multiple lines are used in these cases due to page width constraints.

Menu symbols

When looking at the menus for any application, you will see some symbols associated with keyboard shortcuts for a particular command. For example, to open an old chat in iChat, you would go to the File menu and select Open... (File → Open...), or you could issue the keyboard shortcut, ⌘-O. The ⌘ symbol corresponds to the ⌘ key (also known as the "Command" key), located to the left and right of the spacebar on any Macintosh keyboard.

You should pay special attention to notes set apart from the text with the following icons:

This is a tip, suggestion, or general note. It contains useful supplementary information about the topic at hand.

This is a warning or note of caution.

The thermometer icons, found next to each hack, indicate the relative complexity of the hack:

 beginner   moderate   expert

How to Contact Us

We have tested and verified the information in this book to the best of our ability, but you may find that features have changed (or even that we have made mistakes!). As a reader of this book, you can help us to improve future editions by sending us your feedback. Please let us know about any errors, inaccuracies, bugs, misleading or confusing statements, and typos that you find anywhere in this book.

Please also let us know what we can do to make this book more useful to you. We take your comments seriously and will try to incorporate reasonable suggestions into future editions. You can write to us at:

O'Reilly & Associates, Inc.
1005 Gravenstein Hwy N.
Sebastopol, CA 95472
(800) 998-9938 (in the U.S. or Canada)
(707) 829-0515 (international/local)
(707) 829-0104 (fax)

You can also send us messages electronically. To be put on the mailing list or to request a catalog, send email to:

info@oreilly.com

To ask technical questions or to comment on the book, send email to:

bookquestions@oreilly.com

The web site for *Mac OS X Hacks* lists examples, errata, and plans for future editions. You can find this page at:

http://www.oreilly.com/catalog/mcosxhks

For more information about this book and others, see the O'Reilly web site:

http://www.oreilly.com

Hack on! at:

http://hacks.oreilly.com

Files
Hacks 1–12

The Mac OS X filesystem is a blend of powerful, ancient Unix underpinnings and the candy-coated shell known as the Macintosh Finder. To make this a reality, Mac OS X pulled off quite a switcheroo! It yanked the filesystem of Mac OS 9 and earlier out from underneath the Finder's feet, replacing it with the utterly foreign world of the Unix filesystem and all that goes with it.

While all but invisible to the casual user, there are some cracks in the façade, visible upon closer inspection. Some are useful, others a little irritating, and still others simply fascinating and quite hack-worthy.

The hacks in this section poke and prod at the seams, revealing some useful techniques for backing up your system, tweaking files and folders, bending aliases to your will, understanding how it all fits together—even dumpster divingin the Trash a little.

HACK #1 Understanding and Hacking Your User Account

Before Mac OS X was released, there wasn't really a concept of a user or account in the Macintosh environment. This hack introduces you to what it means to have an account and what this business of a Home directory is all about. We'll also show you how to rename an account—a nonobvious task indeed.

When Mac OS X first appeared, a lot of people were aghast at the concept of user accounts, especially when they were the only ones using their computer. "Why go through all the hassle when only I exist?" they asked. The complaints only intensified as users were asked to enter an administrator password [Hack #50] for access to certain files, sometimes even denied access to settings and files on their very own computers—the gall of it!

The reasoning is two-fold: to protect you from yourself and to support Mac OS X's multiuser environment.

The concept of protecting you from yourself may at first blush appear intrusive, but we've all had an instance where we've deleted an innocent file from our OS 9 System Folder, only to discover our idiocy when our system didn't reboot, our printer didn't print, or our modem didn't sizzle. In this regard, OS X has your back; crucial files necessary for everyday operation are protected from overzealous removal.

The multiuser environment of OS X is based on technology that's been around for a while in the Unix world: a system of checks and balances that stop your kid sister from gleefully deleting that Photoshop file you've been working on all weekend. Whether you're the only user isn't a concern; protection from the inside (yourself, your kid sister) and protection from the outside (malicious crackers, viruses, and trojans) becomes paramount.

While a determined user can delete any file on their OS X machine with enough effort (the easiest way being to boot into OS 9), Apple has wisely made it difficult to do so through Mac OS X.

What's in a Name?

When creating an account (System Preferences → Accounts → New User...) —either the initial account upon installing Mac OS X, or an additional account—you'll be prompted for both your Name (e.g., John Jacob Jingleheimer Schmidt) and something called a Short Name (see Figure 1-1).

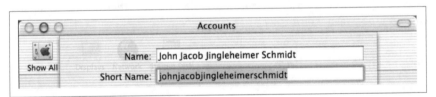

Figure 1-1. Selecting a Name and Short Name

Your Short Name is your actual username, or *login name*, the name by which your computer knows you. It is usually three to eight characters long, composed of letters or numbers. While OS X attempts to choose a Short Name for you based upon what you entered as your Name, it doesn't do a particularly good job if your name isn't as simple as Sam Smith. And, trust me, you don't want to spend your days being known by your computer as johnjacobjingleheimerschmidt. Choose something short and quick to type, like john, johnj, or schmidt. Here's why...

Your Home Directory

Your home directory is where you'll be keeping all your stuff (see Figure 1-2). In it you'll find special directories for your documents, pictures, movies, and settings (that's what the *Library* is). Of course, you're not forced to organize your stuff this way, but it is a good convention. Feel free to settle in, create new folders, and shuffle things about. It's generally a good idea not to throw out the special folders, as the operating system and its applications often make use of them and expect them to be there. In particular, don't touch your *Library* folder; it's the home of your preferences, settings, and other pieces used by particular applications.

Figure 1-2. Finder view of a typical home directory

If you chose john as your Short Name, then your home directory will be *Macintosh HD → Users → john*. By creating a central place for all your important data, OS X ensures easy backup or deployment on other machines. Instead of having to single out your favorite control panels or extensions from OS 9, you can simply backup your home directory. When you're ready to restore, simply copy it over to the same location, and your environment (iTunes music library, desktop pictures, added software tweaks, etc.) will take effect the next time you log in.

From the command line's [Hack #48] point of view, your home directory—again, assuming your Short Name is john—is */Users/john*. You'll sometimes see it referred to on the command line as ~. It's a shortcut that saves you from having to type out your full login name when referring to your home directory. So *~/Documents* actually refers to */Users/john/Documents* (*Macintosh HD → Users → john → Documents* in the Finder).

Who's the Boss?

As the primary user of your computer, you're automatically afforded administrative privileges [Hack #50], which means that you can install just about any software, modify settings affecting how OS X functions, and create and delete other accounts. Needless to say, if you don't want your kid sister messing up your computer, you shouldn't make her an administrative user. Give administrative access only to those people (read: accounts) that truly need it.

Renaming an Account

While OS X makes it easy to create new accounts, alter their capabilities, or change and delete their passwords, it's less than helpful when it comes to renaming an account (i.e., changing its Short Name). In fact, there's simply no way to do so from the GUI side of things. To do so, you'll have to do some of the work on the command line.

For example, let's fix our earlier johnjacobjingleheimerschmidt bungle, renaming the account (a.k.a. Short Name) to john.

First, create a brand-new account (System Preferences → Accounts → New User). OS X won't allow you to enter the same Name, so change it slightly for now; you're always able to change the full name. As shown in Figure 1-3, I chose John Jacob Jingleheimer Schmidt II as a placeholder. For Short Name, choose something reasonable. Again, I chose the more sensical john, since I know he'll be the only John using my computer and I don't expect much confusion about who's who.

Next, you'll need to pull a switcheroo, giving a copy of johnjacobjingleheimerschidt's home directory to john to use as his own. Since you'll be making a copy rather than permanently pulling johnjacobjingleheimerschidt's home directory out from underneath him, you'll be able to verify that all is as it should be before deleting anything potentially valuable.

 Before moving on, you should make sure that you have enough hard drive space to hold both copies. Compare the size of the home directory to the amount of available space on your drive using Get Info (File → Get Info) on each.

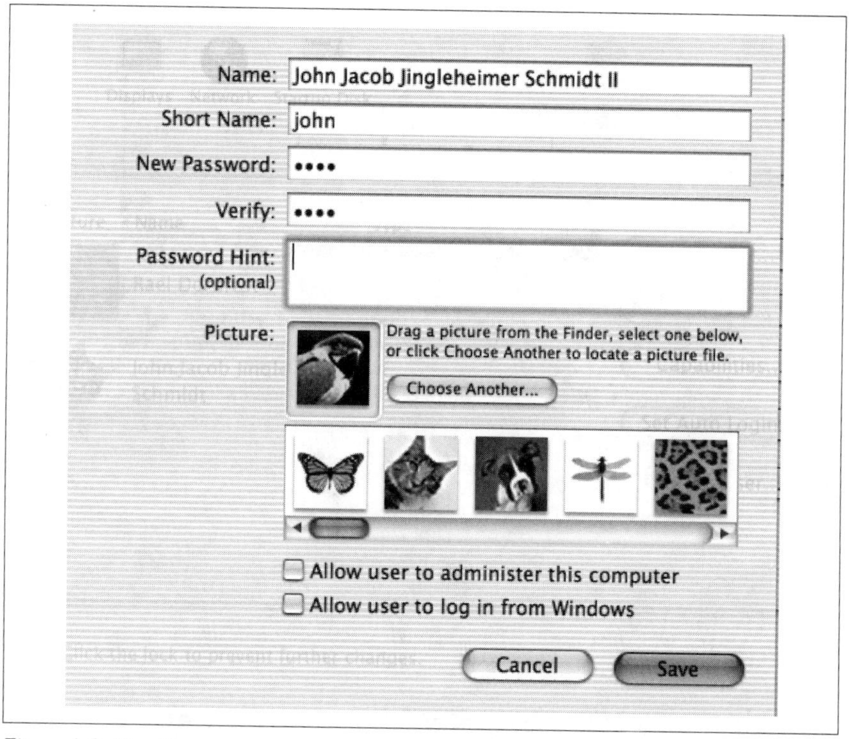

Figure 1-3. Creating a new account

All of this must be done as the administrative (or root) user, as you'll be manipulating files belonging to two other accounts. If you have not already done so, enable the root user [Hack #50] and log in as root.

Navigate in the Finder to *Macintosh HD → Users*.

First, you'll remove john's home directory; don't worry, since it's brand new, it doesn't contain much of any worth. Drag the *john* folder to the Trash.

That out of the way, duplicate the *johnjacobjingleheimerschmidt* directory by Control-clicking it and selecting Duplicate from the context menu, as shown in Figure 1-4, and rename it to *john*, as shown in Figure 1-5.

john and johnjacobjingleheimerschidt now own identical home directories.

About the only bit you don't want to be identical is the keychain, still named *johnjacobjingleheimerschmidt* in john's new home directory. Navigate to *Macintosh HD → Users → john → Library → Keychains* and rename the file *johnjacobjingleheimerschmidt* to *john*, as shown in Figure 1-6.

Understanding and Hacking Your User Account

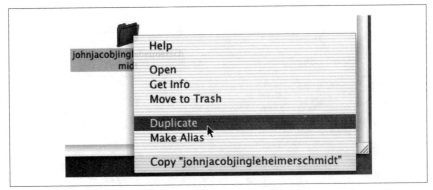

Figure 1-4. Duplicating johnjacobjingleheimerschmidt's home directory

Figure 1-5. Renaming the copy of johnjacobjingleheimerschmidt's directory to john

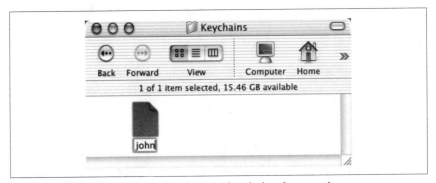

Figure 1-6. Renaming johnjacobjingleheimerschmid's keychain to john

Speaking of ownership, while john now has a new home directory, if you took a close look at the permissions, you'd see that he still doesn't actually own the directory or anything in it—everything's owned by the root user (since he requested the duplication, he owns the files). To fix the permissions, launch the Terminal [Hack #48] (*Applications → Utilities → Terminal*) and use the chown command, like so:

```
[HappyMac:/Users] root# chown -R john.staff john
[HappyMac:/Users] root# ls -l
total 0
drwxrwx---  4 root    admin   136 Feb  6 23:07 Deleted Users
drwxrwxrwt  3 root    wheel   102 Jul 13 2002 Shared
```

```
drwxr-xr-x  11 john      staff   374 Feb  6 23:08 john
drwxr-xr-x  11 johnjaco  staff   374 Feb  5 17:48 ⌐
johnjacobjingleheimerschmidt
```

Notice that the *john* directory is now owned by the john account and is in the right (staff) group.

> You'd think you could do this via the Get Info dialog box. It does, after all, allow you to change permissions on a folder and "Apply to enclosed items…", but it just doesn't work as expected. You can apply some changes recursively to the contents of a folder, but you can't change the ownership in this way.

Log out as the root user and log back in again as yourself. Disable the root user [Hack #50] and you're done.

Give the new john account a try by logging in and fiddling about. When you're sure all's as it should be, go ahead and delete the old johnjacobjingle-heimerschmidt account and alter john's Name (System Preferences → Accounts → Edit User) as appropriate—in this example, we dropped the II bit.

Deleting an Account

Deleting an account under Mac OS X is simple using the Accounts System Preferences panel (System Preferences → Accounts → Delete User). This will remove the account and disable the associated home directory.

Deleted accounts, however, are gone but not completely forgotten. If you take a moment to actually read the confirmation dialog shown in Figure 1-7, you'll learn that the contents of the now-deleted account's home directory are archived as a disk image in *Macintosh HD → Users → Deleted Users*.

Figure 1-7. Confirming account deletion

When and if you're ready to permanently delete the contents of an archived home directory (see Figure 1-8), simply drag its disk image to the Trash.

Figure 1-8. A deleted account's archived home directory

Taking the Bite Out of Backup

HACK #2

With a confusing array of backup solutions for Mac OS X, we pick out a couple of our favorites: Apple's Backup and the open source, Perl-based psync.

Backup is the bane of anybody's computer existence. You know it's an integral part of data hygiene—not unlike flossing, in fact. But it's late, you have a presentation in the morning, and you're too busy creating data to bother finding a CD or some extra hard drive space to shove a backup set onto. Not that you'd know what and how to back up in the first place.

Many of the available software applications don't work as advertised, are complicated when they shouldn't be, don't restore as one would hope during your time of need, and are often expensive to boot. Online backup always sounds like a good idea; and it is, for reasonably sized data sets, meaning not mine and probably yours.

Backup proves such a pain that you never really think about it until it's too late—again, much like flossing.

So what's a data hog to do?

.Mac's Backup

Backup (*http://www.mac.com/1/iTour/tour_backup.html*), .Mac's free personal backup software, has the simplicity you've been craving in a backup application.

It sports an intuitive iApp-style interface and an intelligent QuickPicks feature to help you identify important files and locate them on your hard drive for you rather than the hunt-and-peck of lesser backup programs. You can back up to CD or DVD, even spanning multiple CDs or DVDs should your important data be just that much. If you're a .Mac member ($99.95 per year), you have 100 megabytes of iDisk space (upgradable up to 1 gigabyte for a fee) that can be used for remote backup. That 100 megabytes isn't much and will be gobbled up pretty quickly if used as your primary backup space, but it's useful for backing up your address book, keychain, Internet Explorer settings and favorites, Quicken financial data, and a few other vital files while you're on the road.

> Disappointingly, Backup doesn't allow you to back up to an internal or external hard drive, meaning that my 20-gigabyte external FireWire simply can't be used by this utility. Otto Moerbeek has a nice hack for running Apple's Backup without a .Mac account (*http://www.drijf.net/dototto/*).

Backup is also covered in "Backing Up on the Go" [Hack #3].

psync

Dan Kogai's psync (*http://www.dan.co.jp/cases/macosx/psync.html*), part of the MacOSX::File (*http://search.cpan.org/dist/MacOSX-File/*) Perl module distribution is a rather nice, free, open source backup solution. It will back up Mac volumes, synchronize directories, and create bootable backups but cannot yet make an incremental backup of only changed files. It plays nicely with just about any media you throw at it, including NFS and Samba for remote backup.

psyncX

psyncX (*http://sourceforge.net/projects/psyncx*) is an Aqua front end to the psync command. psyncX's Package Installer guides you gently through installation of both psyncX and the underlying psync Perl bits. It includes a handy backup scheduler (see Figure 1-9), so you can archive your data while you snooze—just so long as your computer isn't asleep as well.

Backing up. If you forego psyncX's GUI interface and would rather run psync from the command line or regularly out of cron [Hack #53], go ahead and start up the Terminal [Hack #48]. Run the psync command specifying a source directory to back up and a destination directory for the backup. Here I back up everything in my *Documents* directory to my FireWire drive:

```
% psync ~/Documents /Volumes/Fire
```

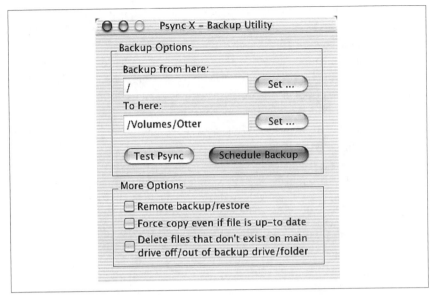

Figure 1-9. The psyncX Aqua interface

The destination directory should be on another disk or at least another partition; otherwise, it won't do much good if the original partition or drive goes under.

To back up anything but your own home directory, you need superuser privileges **[Hack #50]**; after all, you can't back up what you don't have permission to access. Use the su command to temporarily (for this command only) become the superuser. For example, the following backs up everything on the local drive (the / directory and below) to another mounted volume, */Volumes/BackupDisk*:

```
% sudo psync / /Volumes/BackupDisk
```

By the time you next back up the same source directory to the same destination directory, you may well have removed some of the original files—that project was over and you wanted to be rid of all traces of it. If you really don't want them in your backup directory, tell psync to delete those files that exist in the destination but not in the source, using the -d switch like so:

```
% psync -d ~/Documents/Projects /Volumes/Fire
```

Testing backup. To test psync to make sure it does the right thing without actually copying any files, use the -n switch to turn on simulation mode. The psync command reports what it would have done, but does nothing otherwise.

```
% sudo psync -n / /Volumes/BackupDisk
```

Remote backup. To back up to a filesystem other than a mounted hard drive, use the -r switch to turn on remote backup mode:

```
% psync -r ~/Documents /Volumes/Windows_Share
```

Since remote filesystems do not behave in quite the same manner as a local hard drive, psync stores some extra information in a file called *.psync.db*.

Restoring from backup. To restore your data, simply reverse the source and destination directories—you're only synchronizing/copying, after all. The psync command automatically turns into remote restore mode if it finds the *.psync.db* file in the source directory, and allows it to restore file ownership and permissions.

See Also

- Retrospect Express Backup (available at *http://www.dantz.com/index. php3?SCREEN=reb_mac*) ($49) is probably the most well respected commercial backup solution for Macintosh.
- "Using CVS to Manage Data on Multiple Machines" [Hack #60]

—brian d foy

HACK #3 Backing Up on the Go

Combining .Mac services with 802.11b connectivity provides some vital protection for current projects while on the road.

Generally speaking, I'm pretty good about backing up my PowerBook data. But sometimes a few days go by between sessions. I used to think that such a span was acceptable, but these days, when every hour of work is as precious as gold, I'm rethinking my old habits.

I don't want to replace my existing system. I like it. What I really want to do is add the capability to temporarily back up work files to protect me between archiving sessions. As I was mulling over this situation, I noticed a nice convergence of technologies that presented me with a solution.

Backup as Part of .Mac Membership

After I upgraded my .Mac membership, I took a look at the new tools available. At this point, the one that interests me the most is the Backup (*http:// www.mac.com/*) application. Clearly, I didn't see this as a total solution to my archiving needs, especially with a measly 100MB iDisk, but I thought that Backup had some potential as a temporary container for my work in progress.

The appealing aspect of this new application is that I can designate particular folders on my hard drive to be copied to my iDisk whenever I have a network connection. At the end of each work session, for example, I simply click the Backup Now button, and the latest version of my designated files is copied to my iDisk (see Figure 1-10). That means instead of risking 24 hours or more between archiving sessions, I'm constantly saving my most important documents many times a day.

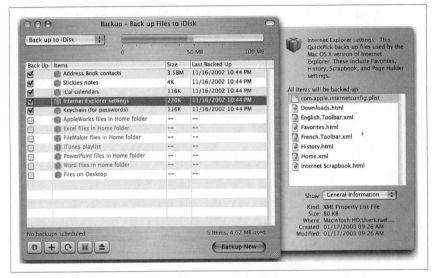

Figure 1-10. Backup

The log files for Backup are very accessible and help me keep track of the success of my sessions. I recommend that you use the Show Toolbar view of Backup, enabling you to access your log files directly from the main interface. Also, to keep this system as efficient as possible, don't designate too many items to back up—your sessions will run too long and defeat the purpose of having an easy-to-use safety net during the course of your workday.

For the most part, the application's behavior has been steady. Every now and then I get a strange pop-up notice that I need to join .Mac to use Backup. I just click the Quit button, and Backup continues to go about its business uninterrupted.

If you want to restore a file—in other words, copy it from your iDisk back to your computer—simply select Restore from iDisk from the View menu. Backup will ask you if you're sure you want to replace your existing file with the iDisk version before copying it to your hard drive. This function worked well in my testing.

AirPort, Unwiring Backup

More and more I'm writing outside of the office or home. Travel means that I find myself working on documents in Starbucks, airports, and other remote locations. Since I'm using a laptop, I've been concerned about protecting my work while I'm away from the auxiliary FireWire drive I use at home for archiving.

Fortunately, 802.11b networks are appearing everywhere. For example, Starbucks has contracted with T Mobile HotSpot (*http://www.t-mobile.com/hotspot/*) to provide wireless Internet access in most of their U.S. locations. You can sign up (without a contract) and use the service for $2.99 for a 15-minute session, which is more than enough time to check your email and run Backup. If you want more time, you can sign up for a monthly program too.

This type of connectivity changes everything. If I'm on the road working on a project for an hour in Starbucks, then as soon as I finish sipping my tall Americano, I can run Backup and send updates of all the changed files to my iDisk drive, and that includes new browser bookmarks and scrapbook pages.

Heaven forbid if my PowerBook ever suffered an ill fate while on the go, but if so, I won't lose a single hour of work as a result.

Using Other Media Too

You can use Backup to save to CDs also, which does have some merit for larger archiving sessions. For my purposes on the road, I'm not as interested in this feature, because if I lose my laptop, chances are that the CDs in the case are gone too.

Obviously, CD archives offer some protection from hard-drive failure. But for the most part, I think my existing archiving system covers that base just fine.

The Cost of Protection

This nifty system I've discussed is flexible and, so far, has proved reliable. But it's a convenience that comes with a price tag. The upgrade to my .Mac membership was $49 (annual fee), and next year I'll have to pay the full $99. Wireless access on the road runs from $2.99 a session to as much as $10, depending on the service you use. Every now and then you may happen upon a free access point, but generally speaking, you should be prepared to pony up a few bucks for the connection.

Final Thoughts

The individual technologies are not groundbreaking in and of themselves, but what I find interesting is that I can string these services together to fill a need. These days, the thought of losing even one hour of productive work is disheartening. Now, by combining .Mac services with 802.11b connectivity, I'll keep my projects safe, even when I'm on the road.

—Derrick Story

HACK #4 Dealing with Archives of Many Colors: .img, .sit, .tar, .gz

Back in the innocent days of OS 9, one compression format reigned supreme: Stuffit from Aladdin Systems. With OS X and its BSD Unix foundation, there's a whole slew of compression technologies available, all built into your default installation.

Stuffit Expander, DropStuff, and their Aladdin ilk have long been stalwarts of the Mac OS, included on Apple CDs and preinstalled machines. The same can be said for Unix utilities like gzip, bzip2, and compress, also included with OS X and available through the Terminal. Throw in Apple's disk-image technology, which creates archives that look and act like removable disks, and you've got a veritable cornucopia of compression and archival technologies.

.dmg and .img

Apple has been providing disk image technology in the shape of its Disk Copy utility for years now. Creating a disk image is a mindless task—simply open Disk Copy, drag a folder over the floating window (see Figure 1-11), decide if you want encryption, and choose where to save the resultant file (see Figure 1-12).

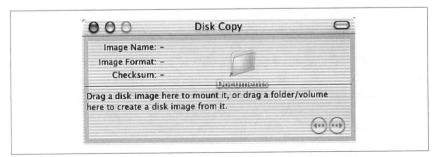

Figure 1-11. Dragging a folder into Disk Copy

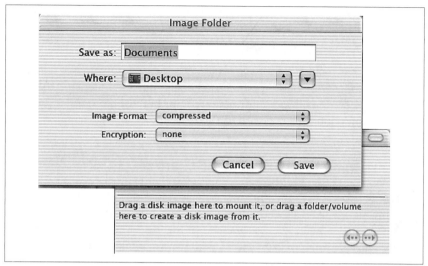

Figure 1-12. Setting Image Folder options

Creating image files, however, doesn't offer much compression, and you'll see a lot of *dmg.gz* extensions on your new downloads. That leads us into gzip and tar. gzip is as much of a Unix standard as Stuffit has been for the Mac. By itself, it's only a compression utility—it doesn't bundle and archive multiple files like Aladdin's DropStuff (also included in OS X). For that ability, it's most often combined with another utility called tar or with the generated disk images from Apple's Disk Copy. If you want to compress a *.dmg* file you've just created, you'd jump into the Terminal [Hack #48]:

```
gzip -9 filename.dmg
```

This command will automatically compress *filename.dmg* into *filename.dmg. gz*, at maximum compression. If we don't include the -9, then gzip will finish slightly faster, but at the expense of a slightly larger file size (-6 is the default). Alternatively, if we're going to use tar (very common when it comes to Unix downloads), we could bundle up our entire *~/Documents* directory this way:

```
tar -cvf filename.tar ~/Documents
```

The c is to create a new archive, the v is to keep us informed of its progress, and f indicates the name of the final archive—in this case, *filename.tar*. Finally, we indicate what we want to archive, which is *~/Documents*. We could easily archive more directories (or individual files) by adding them after our initial *~/Documents*. Unlike gzip, tar only archives the files—it compresses nothing itself, much like Apple's Disk Copy. To compress our new *filename.tar*, we'd used gzip as shown earlier. Because tar and gzip are so often intertwined, we can combine two commands into one:

```
tar -cvzf filename.tar.gz ~/Documents
```

Notice that we've added a z flag, which tells tar to automatically compress the final archive with gzip. We've also changed our final filename to reflect its compressed status. More information about both of these utilities can be accessed from your Terminal with man gzip and man tar.

bzip2

Whereas gzip uses a compression technique called Lempel-Ziv, bzip2 takes a different approach with the Burrows-Wheeler block-sorting text-compression algorithm. It's a little slower compressing than gzip, but it often returns a smaller file size (see Table 1-1 at the end of this hack). Its use (and combination with tar) is similar to gzip, always preferring maximum compression:

```
tar -cvf filename.tar ~/Documents
bzip2 filename.tar
```

Other Compression Techniques

While gzip is more popular than bzip2 for Unix downloads, bzip2 has been making headway due to its stronger compression. Stuffit Expander can readily extract either format. Still more compression flavors exist, however. I've briefly outlined their usage here—you can find more information about their usage and specific abilities by typing man compress, man zip, or man jar in your Terminal.

```
# using the compress utility
tar -cvf filename.tar ~/Documents
compress filename.tar

# the same as previous
tar -cvZf filename.tar.Z ~/Documents

# now, zip at maximum compression
zip -r -9 filename.zip ~/Documents

# and jar (useful for Java applications)
jar cf filename.zip ~/Documents
```

Don't Forget Stuffit

Aladdin Systems realized there would be a need for a simple drag and drop utility that could compress in other formats besides its own—that's why you'll see DropTar and DropZip utilities in your */Applications/Utilities/Stuffit Lite* (or *Stuffit Standard*) directory. Using these is as you'd expect—simply drag and drop the files and folders you want to archive over its icon (or drag to its window), and you're set. DropTar even has the capability to compress in multiple formats: bzip2, compress, gzip, and the native Stuffit format.

In Table 1-1, we've compressed a 100MB directory using each of the utilities, with maximum compression. If you're looking for the smallest file, then bzip2 should be your first choice, but gzip could be more compatible with every computer your archive lands on (if you're worried only about OS X, then bzip2 is a good bet). Be forewarned: the types of files you're archiving will give you different results with each utility—the source directory in this case was filled with an equal amount of text, image, and binary files, but you'll notice fluctuating results with large text files, multiple tiny files, and so on.

Table 1-1. Compression techniques and resulting file sizes

Compression technique	File size (in bytes)
compress	45,264,549
DropTar (compress)	45,032,503
jar	30,322,992
zip	30,232,529
DropTar (gzip)	30,069,414
gzip	30,042,941
DropZip	29,877,021
DropTar (bzip2)	26,072,415
bzip2	25,825,723

HACK #5   A Line Break Is a Line Break

A line break is a line break is a line break, except when it's not. Surprisingly, there are three different types of line breaks in the modern computing world, and OS X uses two of the three.

One might think the innocent line break, that docile whitespace that tells us when paragraphs begin and end, would be a relatively simple piece of computer engineering. Unfortunately, there's more to the line break than meets the eye.

There are three different types of line breaks, all originally unique to the major operating systems: Windows/DOS, Macintosh, and Unix. A document using Mac line breaks would look horrid on a Windows system, and a document using Windows line breaks on Unix also wouldn't be interpreted correctly. The cause for this is how the line break is actually created. The Mac, by default, uses a single carriage return (<CR>), represented as \r. Unix, on the other hand, uses a single linefeed (<LF>), \n. Windows goes one step further and uses both, creating a (<CRLF>) combination, \r\n.

To make matters still more interesting, until OS X came along, OS-specific line breaks stayed in their own environment and didn't play nicely with others. Windows understood only its brethren, Unix cackled madly at anything else, and the Mac just grinned knowingly. OS X, however, understands both the original Mac line break and Unix line breaks.

This can cause confusion very easily, especially considering that most Mac applications (i.e., most anything that runs through the GUI of OS X) read and save using Mac-style line breaks, while anything used through the Terminal (like the common text editors [Hack #51]: vi, pico, and Emacs) enforces the Unix variety.

Thankfully, it's pretty easy to solve problems caused by this dual mentality. The first step is identifying that you have an issue. Say you have a text file you saved with SimpleText or a default installation of BBEdit. If you try to open that file in a shell editor like vi, you'll see this instead of what you'd expect:

```
This should be line one.^MThis should be on line two.
```

See that ugly ^M character stuck in the middle of our two sentences? That's the best vi (and most Unix applications) can do in an attempt to display a Mac linefeed. Likewise, if you open a text file crafted in vi with SimpleText, you'll see square boxes where there should be line breaks. Obviously, this wreaks havoc with any attempt at poetry—or system administration, for that matter.

There are a few solutions, depending on your skills and desires. The most obvious is to change your text editor to match what you'll be needing most frequently. If you're constantly going to be writing files that will be used in the shell, then set your text editor to save as Unix linefeeds. A must-have editor, BBEdit (*http://www.barebones.com/*) from Bare Bones Software, allows you to do this quite easily, both on a file-by-file basis (see Figure 1-13) and globally through BBEdit's ultraconfigurable preferences (see Figure 1-14).

If Terminal-based text editors are more your cup of tea, a stronger version of vi called *vim* (for vi, improved) is flexible and infinitely configurable when it comes to editing files of varying formats. *http://vim.sourceforge.net/htmldoc/usr_23.html* provides more than enough detail on choosing your own line break.

If you want a less permanent option, a single command line can save you some hassle. Here, we've listed two simple Perl one-liners. The first translates Mac linefeeds to their Unix equivalent, and the second does the reverse. You'll notice that the linefeeds are represented by the same characters we mentioned before:

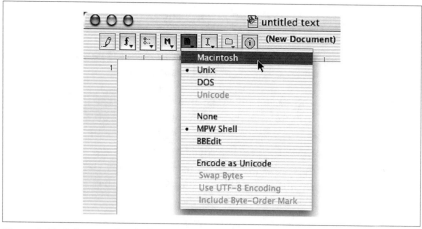

Figure 1-13. Selecting a linefeed style in BBEdit

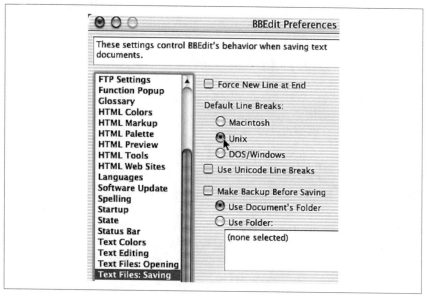

Figure 1-14. Setting default linefeed style in BBEdit preferences

```
perl -pi -e 's/\r/\n/g' file_with_mac_linefeeds.txt
perl -pi -e 's/\n/\r/g' file_with_unix_linefeeds.txt
```

On the flip side, if you ever run across a file with Windows linefeeds, you can easily convert them to your preferred format with the following examples:

```
perl -pi -e 's/\r\n/\n/g' file_with_win_linefeeds.txt
perl -pi -e 's/\r\n/\r/g' file_with_win_linefeeds.txt
```

Using the examples presented in this hack, you'll be able to piece together the code needed to convert to Windows linefeeds from either Mac or Unix.

HACK #6 Fiddling with Type/Creator Codes and File Extensions

Mac OS X uses a combination of type and creator codes and file extensions to determine the application with which a file is associated.

Every file in OS X and earlier versions of the Mac OS usually have both a *type* and *creator* attribute that help determine which application should open them. For example, a *.html* file may have a type and creator that say it should be opened in Microsoft's Internet Explorer, while a *.mov* file would have different attributes that suggest it should be opened by QuickTime. Files also have other attributes, like stationary, locked or unlocked, and timely information like creation and modification dates.

Unlike Windows, however, a Mac file doesn't need an extension to determine association with an application. A file named *webcam* could be a JPEG image, a text file to be opened by BBEdit, or even an HTML file associated with Internet Explorer. The type and creator codes rise above petty naming distinctions.

Normally, you'd need special software to set or change these types and creators, making the task more difficult (or expensive) than you'd hope. Long-time users of the Mac OS would often use the venerable ResEdit to perform the dirty deed, perhaps also tweaking other application strings in a fit of mirth and because they're there.

Thankfully, if you've installed Apple's Developer Tools, you can do this easily with the Terminal [Hack #48].

The easiest way to change a file's type and creator codes is to find a file you want to mimic and use its type and creator codes as a guide for your changes. For example, if you had a copy of Apple's home page (*http://www.apple.com*) saved as an HTML file named *Apple Home.html*, you'd enter the following into a Terminal [Hack #48] window to find its type and creator:

```
% /Developer/Tools/GetFileInfo "Apple Home.html"
```

The output would look something like this:

```
file: "Apple Home.html"
type: "TEXT"
creator: "MSIE"
attributes: avbstclinmed
created: 08/08/2002 19:12:46
modified: 08/08/2002 19:12:46
```

With this, we know that a file associated with Internet Explorer needs to have a type of TEXT and a creator of MSIE. If you check other files, you'll notice that types and creators are always four letters in length, often creating ungodly combinations of whimsy, like DBSE and FTCH, which have nothing to do with what you might think they do (an Extensis Portfolio database).

To associate some other file with Internet Explorer, you'd enter the following:

```
% /Developer/Tools/SetFile -c MSIE -t TEXT some_other_file
```

Because Mac OS X has a Unix underlayer, some files utilized by the Unix side of things may have no type and creator. GetFileInfo, in those cases, would show blank values for those fields:

```
% /Developer/Tools/GetFileInfo /usr/bin/vi
file: "/usr/bin/vi"
type: ""
creator: ""
attributes: avbstclinmed
created: 11/11/2002 18:28:56
modified: 11/11/2002 18:28:56
```

What's interesting is how a file with no associated type or creator codes might still be associated and opened with a particular application. Take, for example, an archived copy of the source code for Perl 5.8, freshly downloaded off the Net:

```
% /Developer/Tools/GetFileInfo perl-5.8.0.tar.gz
file: "perl-5.8.0.tar.gz"
type: ""
creator: ""
```

With no file type and creator, you may be confounded by the fact that *tar.gz* is nonetheless associated with Stuffit Expander when you look at it from the Finder's point of view, as shown in Figure 1-15.

Figure 1-15. tar.gz is associated with Stuffit Expander

The reasoning is simple: if a file has type and creator codes, they're used. Otherwise, Mac OS X takes a look at the file extension—much like Windows does—with an eye to figuring out what it belongs with. Rename *perl-5.8.0.tar.gz* to just *perl-5.8.0* and Mac OS X will be lost; the Stuffit Expander icon changes immediately to a blank sheet.

Armed with an understanding of setting types and creators, you can easily fix this. A gzipped file has a type of Gzip and a creator of SITx; alter the codes on the command line and all's as expected:

```
% /Developer/Tools/SetFile -c SITx -t Gzip perl-5.8.0
```

With type and creator set, you can rename that file to your heart's content, appending whatever extension you like, and it'll remain associated with Stuffit Expander.

See Also

- For details on GetFileInfo and SetFile, at the Terminal [Hack #48], type man GetFileInfo and man SetFile, respectively.

HACK #7   Locking and Unlocking Files

For years, the Macintosh operating system has allowed you to lock a file or folder to protect against accidental deletion or modification. In OS X, you have that same ability, either through the Finder or the shell.

If there's one thing that friends and family know, it's how to find that one file you've been spending an inordinate amount of time on and then delete it in a fit of gleeful innocence. For many years in Mac OS 9 and earlier, the first line of defense for this behavior has been locking a file, making sure that it can't be changed or deleted unless it is specifically unlocked.

This ability remains in Mac OS X and applies even to the root user (locked files can't be deleted without being unlocked first, period). Longtime Mac users are familiar with the following process for locking a file or directory in the Finder:

1. Select the file or directory you want to lock.
2. Choose Get Info from the File menu or press ⌘-I.
3. Place a check in the Locked checkbox.

Either of the following two shell commands do the same thing under OS X:

```
% chflags uchg filename.txt
% /Developer/Tools/SetFile -a L filename.txt
```

The chflags utility is part of a default OS X install and changes the uchg flag of a file, representing the immutable bit (literally, "this file is not subject to change"). chflags can be performed only by a superuser or the file's owner. SetFile is a utility that comes with the Developer Tools and operates on a file's attributes (attributes and flags can be considered equivalent). In this case, you're saying the locked attribute (-a L) of the file should be set.

Via the Finder, you can tell when a file is locked because it'll have a padlock icon superimposed over the lower left of its normal icon, as shown in Figure 1-16.

Figure 1-16. A locked file

In the Terminal [Hack #48], you can type ls -ol (o to show the file flags, and l for long listing). Any file with the uchg flag is locked:

```
% ls -ol filename.txt
-rw-r--r-- 1 morbus staff uchg 0 Dec 4 01:07 filename.txt
```

Unlocking is a simple matter of reversal. Either uncheck the locked checkbox in the file's Get Info inspector or enter one of the following shell commands:

```
% chflags nouchg filename.txt
% /Developer/Tools/SetFile -a L filename.txt
```

Nothing really surprising there. To unset a uchg or any other file flag using the chflags utility, simply prefix the flag name with no. When using SetFile, simply reverse the case of the attribute letters; uppercase letters always add the flag to the file, and lowercase letters remove the flag.

See Also

- For details on chflags and SetFile, at the Terminal [Hack #48], type man chflags and man SetFile, respectively.

HACK #8 Stubborn Trash, Stuck Images, and Jammed CDs

Every so often it takes a little know-how to empty the Trash or eject a CD; learn when and how.

There are times, rare as they may be, when OS X goes a little haywire and simply won't spit out a CD or DVD, unmount a disk image, or empty the Trash. Often things have a way of sorting themselves with a little patience, with a Finder restart, by logging out and back in, or (heaven forbid) by rebooting your Mac. Sometimes, however, that stuck CD/DVD or image doesn't budge or the Trash simply refuses to empty.

Stubborn Trash

It does the heart good to do some occasional housekeeping. One such activity is emptying the Trash folder to free up more disk space for your Mac. This is usually as simple as Finder → Empty Trash... or ⌘-Shift-Delete. Every so often, though, a file or folder refuses to leave.

First a little background on the mystical Trash can. Every file you delete is moved into a folder called *.Trash* in your home directory:

```
% ls -al
total 48
drwxr-xr-x 20 weimengl staff 680 Dec 14 12:35 .
drwxrwxr-t 8 root wheel 272 Dec 10 09:30 ..
drwx------ 6 weimengl staff 204 Dec 14 12:55 .Trash
...
```

To dip into the Trash, simply open a Terminal [Hack #48] window, navigate to the *.Trash* directory, and list files:

```
% cd .Trash
% ls -al
```

Emptying the Trash is nothing more than deleting all the contents of your *.Trash* folder.

In use. Despite having been placed into the Trash, a file may still be in use by an application (see Figure 1-17).

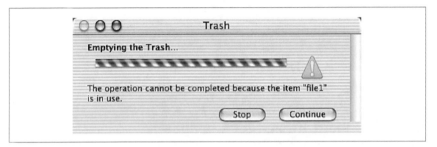

Figure 1-17. Trashed file still in use

The remedy is to guess which application is using it and close the file or shut down the application if you're no longer using it. Try emptying the Trash again and, assuming that was the problem, it should empty without incident.

If you aren't able to figure out what application is using the file and have shut down just about anything you can find, launch the Terminal and use the fstat (file status) command to ascertain which is the offending program:

```
% fstat .Trash/file1
USER     CMD        PID   FD INUM    MODE      SZ|DV R/W MOUNT NAME
weimengl LaunchCFMA 2070  30 347708 -rw-r--r-- 31974 rw  / .Trash/file1
```

Notice the PID (process ID) of the application holding the file hostage. Let's see what application that corresponds to by using the ps (process status) command. The -p 2070 argument specifies the process ID, and -w displays the first 132 characters of the process name rather than just as much as can fit on one Terminal line.

```
% ps -wp 2070
PID  TT STAT      TIME COMMAND
2070 ?? S      23:47.77 /Applications/Microsoft Office X/Microsoft Word /
Applications/Microsoft Office X/Microsoft Word -psn_0_18
```

There we are! It's Microsoft Word. Get it to release the file and try emptying the Trash again.

Locked. Another problem that crops up occasionally is locked files [Hack #7] in the Trash. While you shouldn't be able to put a locked file into the Trash in the first place, sometimes one sneaks by. Look in your *Trash* folder via the Finder and see if the offending file is locked (the icon is overlaid by a small lock), as shown in Figure 1-18.

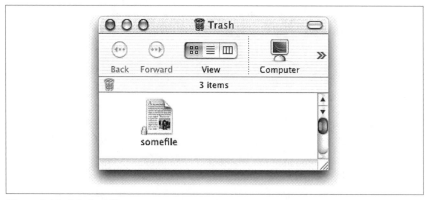

Figure 1-18. A locked file

To unlock the file, select File → Get Info or press ⌘-I for the File Info inspector (see Figure 1-19). If the Locked checkbox is checked, click it to unlock the file.

If the file refuses to unlock, try one of the techniques covered in "Locking and Unlocking Files" [Hack #7].

Permissions. Another possibility is that a file in your Trash may not belong to you. You'll need to alter the permissions or take ownership [Hack #49] of the file before you're able to empty it from the Trash.

rm. It's still there and refusing to budge? Try simply removing the offending file(s) using the rm [Hack #48] command, like so:

```
% rm ~/.Trash/file1
```

If that has no effect, or if OS X complains about something else, force it with the -f option:

```
% rm -f ~/.Trash/file1
```

Figure 1-19. A locked file

If there's a whole hierarchy of folders and files causing you trouble, you can recursively delete all the files in your Trash using sudo to get around permissions issues, -i to ask for confirmation before deleting each, and -r to recurse through the hierarchy:

```
% sudo rm -ri ~/.Trash/*
remove /Users/weimengl/.Trash/file1? y
```

Be forewarned! Most books on Unix will warn you of the disastrous outcome if you are not careful with the rm -r combination, and I'm going to say it again. Imagine the effects of inadvertantly adding a space like so: sudo rm -rf ~/. Trash; you'd remove all the contents of your home directory. Before deleting anything, think twice before you hit the Return key.

Stuck Image

You've pressed ⌘-E and dragged that mounted disk image to the Trash until you're blue in the face, but still it won't disappear. No complaints, no errors, nothing; it simply ignores your every attempt to eject it.

This is usually one of those situations best cleaned up by a logging out and back in, relaunching the Finder, or rebooting. It's safer and less likely to mangle the data on the disk image if you avoid resorting to brute force tactics.

Jammed CD/DVD

CD/DVD loading and unloading on all recent Macintoshes are done through the operating system rather than the physical eject buttons you usually find on other systems. Windows users are often caught looking nervously about for the CD eject button—I have to admit I've done so myself. What to do if that CD/DVD gets stuck?

Your first course of action is to pull out your handy-dandy paper clip, the tool of choice for the Mac generation. Oh, you don't have one? Shame on you! All right, so there's actually another way to do it that will work, just so long as there's nothing physically wrong with the drive that's keeping it from ejecting your CD/DVD. Launch the Terminal and use the df command to find the filesystem ID of your CD/DVD:

```
% df -l
Filesystem    512-blocks    Used   Avail Capacity Mounted on
/dev/disk0s9  120091280 31348032 88231248    26% /
fdesc                 2        2       0   100% /dev
/dev/disk1s1s2   614256   478912  135344    77% /Volumes/A CD
```

In my case, the CD is mounted as disk1s1s2. To eject the CD, use the disktool utility, handing it the filesystem ID:

```
% disktool -e disk1s1s2
disk1s1s2 device will attempt to be ejected ...
***Notifications Complete for type 1
***Disk Unmounted('disk1')
***Disk Unmounted('disk1s1s1')
***Disk Unmounted('disk1s1')
***Responding yes to unmount - disk1s1s2
***Disk Unmounted('disk1s1s2')
***Responding yes to eject - disk1
***Responding yes to eject - disk1s1s1
***Responding yes to eject - disk1s1s2
***Responding yes to eject - disk1s1
***Disk Ejected('disk1')
***Disk Ejected('disk1s1s1')
***Disk Ejected('disk1s1s2')
```

Your CD/DVD should pop right out.

—Wei-Meng Lee and Rael Dornfest

HACK #9 Aliases, Symlinks, and Hard Links

Poking about with aliases, symlinks, and hard links reveals some interesting entanglements in the merging of the Mac GUI and its Unix underpinnings.

Aliases (shortcuts, if you're from the Windows world) are indispensable for those of us who insist upon filing things in more than one place or like to have access to particular groupings of applications, files, and whatnot within easy reach. An alias provides a trail of bread crumbs to the original item aliased, keeping track of it no matter where it might reside. It was common in OS 9 to add aliases for your oft-used applications and folders either right on the desktop or in the Apple menu, or, indeed, both. Now, thanks to the Dock and some Dock alternatives [Hack #36], there's little need to clutter your Apple menu or Desktop with aliases.

That's not to say that OS X doesn't have aliases; it does indeed. Simply select a file, folder, application, or whatnot and select File → Make Alias or press ⌘-L (in OS 9 it was ⌘-M, which now, sadly, minimizes the current window instead).

OS X being a hybrid of the Mac and Unix worlds causes some interesting entanglements when it comes to keeping track of the locations of things and their aliases. Mac OS X does a seamless job of glossing over the details. That doesn't mean, however, it's not worth poking about a bit.

The Unix world's aliases—actually called links—come in two flavors: hard and soft (symbolic). With a hard link, two or more filenames point to the same data on disk; think *my house, our house,* and *the house where I live.* A symbolic link (a.k.a. soft link or symlink) is a different file from the original, holding nothing but a link to the original's filename; think *address book, signpost,* or *bank account number.* Remove one of two hard links and your data still exists. Remove the last remaining hard link and a symlink doesn't do you a bit of good, holding no real data itself.

The ln command creates and alters links on the command line via the Terminal [Hack #48]. Figure 1-20 shows me creating a file, *original,* then hard linking, and symlinking to it. Note that the original alias was created on the desktop via the Finder's Make Alias option.

As the Info box shows, OS X sees no difference between a symlink created on the command line and an alias created via the Make Alias command. However, from the command-line point of view, this is not the case; the original alias is an entirely different file. Edit it and you'll find you've not touched the original, nor does it have any effect on the GUI view of the original alias itself at all. Mac OS X appears to care only about knowing it's an alias from the GUI side, leaving the Unix side to treat it as a regular file.

Touching the original (touch original) again to alter its timestamp affects only the original and hard link as expected, since they are indeed the same file.

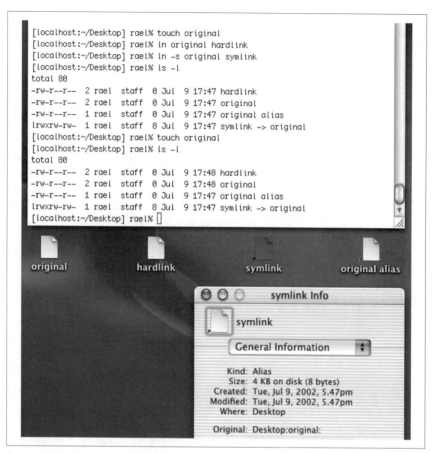

```
[localhost:~/Desktop] rael% touch original
[localhost:~/Desktop] rael% ln original hardlink
[localhost:~/Desktop] rael% ln -s original symlink
[localhost:~/Desktop] rael% ls -l
total 80
-rw-r--r--  2 rael  staff  0 Jul  9 17:47 hardlink
-rw-r--r--  2 rael  staff  0 Jul  9 17:47 original
-rw-r--r--  1 rael  staff  0 Jul  9 17:47 original alias
lrwxrw-rw-  1 rael  staff  8 Jul  9 17:47 symlink -> original
[localhost:~/Desktop] rael% touch original
[localhost:~/Desktop] rael% ls -l
total 80
-rw-r--r--  2 rael  staff  0 Jul  9 17:48 hardlink
-rw-r--r--  2 rael  staff  0 Jul  9 17:48 original
-rw-r--r--  1 rael  staff  0 Jul  9 17:47 original alias
lrwxrw-rw-  1 rael  staff  8 Jul  9 17:47 symlink -> original
[localhost:~/Desktop] rael% []
```

original   hardlink   symlink   original alias

```
  ○ ○ ○         symlink Info
    symlink

  General Information        ◆

       Kind: Alias
       Size: 4 KB on disk (8 bytes)
    Created: Tue, Jul 9, 2002, 5.47pm
   Modified: Tue, Jul 9, 2002, 5.47pm
      Where: Desktop

   Original: Desktop:original:
```

Figure 1-20. Creating an alias on the command line

HACK #10 Recent Filenames

Mac OS X has some tricky ways of remembering which files were used recently.

Did you know that OS X applications don't actually remember the names of recent files you've opened? That's not to say that they don't recall what you've been editing; after all, Open Recent does work rather nicely.

What the application remembers is the location of the file on disk. Rename that file. Change its file extension. Move it somewhere else entirely. Just as long as it's still on the same disk (inodes don't transfer from disk to disk), your app should be able to find it the next time you choose Open Recent.

Just how this is implemented varies from application to application. Starting with a file called *somefile.txt* on my Desktop, I did a little experimenting.

Move, rename, and tamper with it as I might, BBEdit continued to list it as *Hard Drive:Users:rael:Desktop:somefile.txt.* Preview noticed a rename of *somefile.tiff* to *someotherfile.tiff.* Microsoft Word, like BBEdit, insisted *somefile.doc* was still *somefile.doc*, despite its being renamed *someotherfile. doc* and moved elsewhere.

Why's this useful? Let's say you've created a marvelous piece of poetry, saved it to the Desktop in a hurry as your plane lands, later renamed it to something more appropriate than *Untitled1.doc*, and moved it somewhere or other. Sure, Sherlock may be able to find it if you search by content, date changed, or document type. Or you could simply relaunch the app you believe you were using at the time, select it from the list of recent files, and you're off to the races.

Inspecting the Contents of an .app Package

HACK
#11

If you were an OS 9 fiddler, tweaker, or deviant, there was one piece of software you simply had to have: ResEdit, Apple's venerable, unsupported, use-at-your-own risk utility. ResEdit is no longer applicable under OS X, but package editing is.

In earlier versions of the Mac OS, files could have data forks and resource forks. The data fork was the gooey inside, and the resource fork was the fluffy outside—whether it be image thumbnails, saved editing data from applications like BBEdit, or application widgets, like window layouts, user interface images, and so forth. With Apple's ResEdit, you could easily access this resource fork and change the fluff—it wasn't easily possible to change the coding of an application, but it was certainly mindless to change interface elements.

In OS X, with its grounding in the BSD operating system, resource forks are rarely used for applications, effectively making ResEdit useless. Instead, we've got packages or, less jargony, files that end in *.app.* You've got *.app* files spread all over your OS X system already—you just may not know it. Take, for instance, Apple's popular Mail program. It sits innocently in your *Applications* folder, acting as if it were a single file. Instead, it's really called *Mail.app*; the *.app* is hidden from view (you can confirm its existence by examining the Get Info properties).

The magic of these *.app* files is that they're really a special kind of folder called a package; they contain a good portion of the same fluff available in an OS 9 application's resource fork. Even better, you don't need an extra utility like ResEdit to start fiddling; simply Control-click on a file you know is an *.app* and choose Show Package Contents, as shown in Figure 1-21.

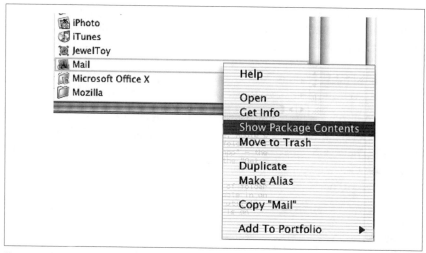

Figure 1-21. Revealing package contents via Control-click context menu

Once inside the package *Contents* folder, you'll see a subfolder called *Resources* (see Figure 1-22). If you needed yet another hint that this is similar to ResEdit hacking, then this naming choice is it. In the case of Apple's Mail, we can see a decent number of image files, representative of various visual elements you see during normal use of Mail, as well as a few *.plist*, *.toolbar*, and *.nib* files.

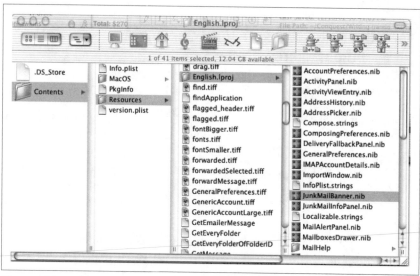

Figure 1-22. Package resources

The *.tiff* and *.icns* files are obvious; modify them in your preferred graphic editor, restart Mail, and you'll see your changes. *.plist* files are the equivalent of preferences; there are usually frontends to these settings via the program itself (not always though—in Mail's case, you can edit *urlPrefixes.plist* to add more clickable bits of text in mail messages, or *Colors.plist* to edit two more levels of quote coloring).

The *.nib* and *.string* files, located under *English.lproj* for English-speaking users, are where you can find some user-interface aspects of the program in question. You won't see these for every package you open (like iTunes), but in the case of Mail, you can go nuts editing warning messages, like this one in *Prefs.strings* (perhaps to the more ferocious "Ya Screwed Up, Idiot!"):

```
/* Title of panel shown when the user tries to enter an empty hostname for
an account */
"INVALID_SMTP_HOST_TITLE" = "Invalid SMTP Hostname";
```

On the other hand, if you know your way around Apple's Interface Builder (available if you have the Apple Developer Tools **[Hack #55]** installed), you can open up one of the many *.nib* files and further tweak display elements.

As with the typical warnings when using ResEdit, be sure to make a backup before doing anything more than exploring (and exploring is when the best discoveries are made, like the ability to peel the annoying chrome **[Hack #47]** from a shiny iApp, add new boards and pieces to Chess, or change the default search engine in Internet Explorer).

H A C K
#12 Opening Microsoft Word Documents Without Microsoft Word

The text of any Microsoft Word document is readable with the greatest of ease thanks to a tiny, free utility and a little open source know-how.

You open an innocent email from some long-lost relative, and she's sent you a vitally important document. "Open now!" the email shouts, comical in its attempt to disguise the friendly spam it really is. Even worse, the attachment is a Microsoft Word document, and you've yet to pony up the dough for Office under OS X. How do you read it? Run out and get some large Word equivalent like AbiWord or AppleWorks, or download a free, 300K utility?

Crafty, experimental users realize that every file or document ever created can be opened up in a plain-old text editor. Whether you actually get something useful is up for grabs, but more times than not, you can recover a bit of meaning from a Word document by dropping it into your friendly neighborhood text editor, as shown in Figure 1-23. In some cases, you can actually learn information the sending user didn't intend for you to know—like the location on her hard drive where it was originally saved.

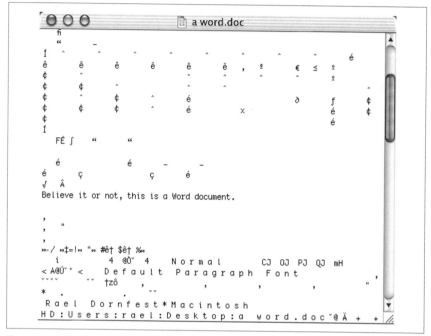

Figure 1-23. A Word document in TextEdit

But I digress. Opening Word documents in BBEdit or TextEdit (or even vi, pico, or Emacs for shell **[Hack #48]** lovers) is a hack at best—one we could certainly do without in our beloved OS X. That's where AntiWordService (*http://www.devon-technologies.com/*) from DEVONtechnologies comes in. It's a very small and easy-to-install piece of freeware that will give any Cocoa application the ability to open Microsoft Word documents. Download, drop into your *~/Library/Services* directory, log out and back in, and drag that dastardly *.doc* to TextEdit. Bingo! Instant plain text. It's not perfect, as the documentation confesses: only plain text is preserved, no images and no formatting. But in most cases that's more than enough, since you're opening up a Word document; naturally, you should be interested only in the words.

One thing of note about AntiWordService is how it's a perfect marriage of the OS X ease of use and the power of Unix, now part of Apple's OS for the next fifteen years. In actuality, AntiWordService is just an OS X wrapper around an open source shell utility called *antiword* (*http://antiword.cjb.net/*), available for ten different operating systems. You'll also find two other OS X utilities based on antiword: the *antiword port* (*http://www.ronaldo.com/projects/antiword/*) by Ronaldo Nascimento and *DOCtor* (*http://www.stone.com/DOCtor/*) from Stone Design. Of the three OS X variants, AntiWordService integrates best with your day-to-day work, making the translation effort invisible.

## CHAPTER TWO

Startup
Hacks 13–17

As you stare admiringly at that elegant white-on-gray Apple logo and are mesmerized by that spiraling progress spinner, you may notice the quiet ticking, grinding, and plinking emanating from your Mac's innards. Before fading to a brilliant blue and filling your screen with colorful icons and that familiar menu bar, there's an awful lot going on behind the scenes to bring your Mac to life.

And it isn't all that pretty.

This chapter takes a peek beneath the surface at just what's making all that noise. We'll show you how to boot from another device, turn your Mac into a FireWire hard drive, get OS X running on that old Power Mac in your closet, and lock up your Mac good and tight so that only those with the right key can get to your stuff.

HACK #13 Getting a Glimpse of the Boot Process

A lot goes on behind the scenes whenever you restart your Macintosh; verbose booting provides a unique glimpse of the Unix underpinnings of Mac OS X.

A lot goes on behind the scenes whenever you restart your Macintosh. In pre–OS X days, we couldn't really tap into this knowledge; at most, we knew what control panels and extensions had been started, but that was about it. Nicely, OS X gives us a few ways we can turn on *verbose booting*, providing more esoteric knowledge for our coffers.

Being able to see exactly what goes on when you start your computer is easier than you may think. Longtime OS 9 users may recall the Shift or spacebar keyboard tricks: hold one down during bootup and you'll disable, or interactively choose, your extensions, respectively. The same principle lies behind verbose booting in OS X: simply hold down the ⌘ and V keys.

When you do this during startup, your screen should turn black and you'll see tiny text instead of the normal happy Mac or Apple logo. Most of this text may not make much sense to you, but some messages about your hardware will appear as OS X tries to figure out what you've got plugged in or installed.

You may find that the text scrolls by too fast for your inquisitive mind to handle. No worries, though; since OS X is based on Unix, nearly everything gets written down. Once you're logged into the Finder, open a Terminal window and enter the following command:

```
dmesg
```

This displays the system message buffer and covers everything before the OS X logging daemon boots up (called *syslogd*, it's common across Unix installations). The output from your dmesg will contain most of the hardware lines I mentioned before, as well as a few other nitpicks here and there; what you see will be unique for your combination of hardware and equipment.

Once the OS X logging daemon comes into play, the rest of your data is saved into */var/log/system.log*, the normal place for messages like these. If you open that file up in any text editor (like vi or Emacs), you'll see the output from dmesg (as the buffer is flushed to the *system.log*), as well as a few other ConsoleMessage lines—which should be the same as what you'd see right before the OS X login screen (or Finder, if autologin is enabled).

If you want to see the verbose messages for each and every bootup, there's an easier way then holding down the two keys, and that's by modifying your computer's nonvolatile RAM to remember your preference. Enter the following command:

```
sudo nvram boot-args="-v"
```

With this, your computer will always restart with verbose booting and will continue to do so until the PRAM is zapped or you boot into OS 9. To stop the verbosity manually, simply leave boot-args empty:

```
sudo nvram boot-args=""
```

See Also

- For details on dmesg and nvram, at the Terminal [Hack #48], type man dmesg and man nvram, respectively.
- Booting and Logging In (*http://developer.apple.com/techpubs/macosx/ Essentials/SystemOverview/BootingLogin/index.html*).

Booting from Another Device

**HACK
#14**

Boot and run your Mac from another device, whether it's an internal hard
drive or an external FireWire drive.

I was thrilled to have the chance to try out a seed build or two of Mac OS X
10.2 (Jaguar) before final release. That is, until yet-unnoticed bugs with the
Quartz rendering engine turned my screen to mush and compatibility problems with some of my old settings rendered an application all but unusable.

Thank goodness I'd not actually installed the prerelease on my iBook's hard
drive, but was running it from an external FireWire hard drive. A quick
reboot and I was back to my trusty 10.1.5 partition running on my internal
drive.

Macintosh makes it easy to boot from another device. No need to fiddle
with a BIOS or horrid *boot.ini* files. And absolutely no need to unplug one
drive to have the Mac recognize and use another.

To boot from another device, make sure it's plugged in, is recognized by
Mac OS X, and has a bootable partition containing a usable operating system. Shut down your Mac (Apple menu → Shut Down). While holding
down the Option key, turn on your Mac. You'll be greeted with the screen
shown in Figure 2-1.

Figure 2-1. Booting from another device

I have only one partition listed, despite having an external FireWire drive
plugged in; the FireWire drive doesn't have a viable operating system on it at
present, so it is excluded from the list of possibilities. Were I to have more
than one usable device/operating system, they would be listed alongside
Macintosh HD.

Your mouse pointer will probably look like a watch for a time as your Mac
scans attached and internal hardware for possible boot devices. You can

force a rescan—perhaps after plugging in another device—by clicking the button with the semicircular icon on the left.

When you're ready, choose a device by clicking on it. Macintosh HD, in my case, is already selected. Click the button with the right arrow on the right to boot.

Of course, if you just want to boot from another partition on your local hard drive—you want to pop into Mac OS 9 for a moment, for instance—you should use the Startup Disk preference pane (*Applications → System Preferences → Startup Disk*). Select the system you wish to boot and click the Restart... button, as shown in Figure 2-2.

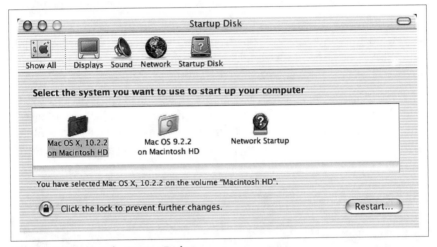

Figure 2-2. Selecting the Startup Disk

 ## Turning Your Mac into a Hard Drive
HACK #15
Boot your Mac in target mode and treat it like just another FireWire drive.

I got my brand-spanking-new 800MHz iBook the other day. I was short on time—finishing this book, in fact—but couldn't wait to make the switch from my existing Mac to my sleek, snappy bundle of OS X joy. How could I move all of my applications and home directory (*/Users/rael*)? I could do without the eternity I'd have to wait transferring it over the network. I didn't relish the number of CDs I'd have to burn to bring across all 3 gigabytes. And the idea of picking through the clutter on my external FireWire drive to make room left me ill.

If only I could mount my old machine's hard drive alongside the new one without tools and duct tape. Surely I could just treat my old Mac as a hard drive somehow. I sure could, and did.

It turns out you can mount one Mac's hard drive onto another Mac over FireWire quite easily. You simply tie them together with a FireWire cable and reboot one of them with the T (for target) key held down.

> This assumes, of course, that you have a FireWire-capable Mac on both ends.

After just a few seconds, my old machine booted into what's known as target mode, the screen blinking a FireWire logo where usually there'd be a Mac OS X login screen. A click, spinup, and whirr later, my old hard drive showed up right on my new Mac's desktop.

Thanks to Macintosh's tradition of not spreading installed software all over the hard drive, I was able to drag over individual applications from my *Applications* folder. I dragged my home directory over and logged out and back in again and I was moved in, preferences and Desktop as I'd left them on the other machine. And all that in around 23 minutes, from boot to enjoy.

When you're done, eject the mounted drive by dragging it to the Trash or selecting it and pressing ⌘-E. As far as the target machine's concerned, just turn it off or reboot it when you're finished; it'll come back up as if it were all just a dream.

Using Open Firmware Password Protection

Password-protect your Mac, blocking circumvention by booting from another device, booting into single-user mode, and more.

There are times when you want nary a finger but your own fiddling with your computer. No sister, no boss, no mother looking for porn, no husband reading chat logs. With the Open Firmware built into newer models of the Mac (iBooks, G4s, some iMacs, etc.), you have access to a strong, low-level way of password protecting your Mac from meddling interlopers and innocent wanderers.

Before we go any further, you'll have to check whether your computer has the necessary firmware. To do so, open the Apple System Profiler (under */Applications/Utilities/*) and look under the System Overview section for the Boot ROM version (which also represents your Open Firmware version), as shown in Figure 2-3. On my dual 450MHz G4 running 10.2.2, you can see Boot ROM info with a value of 4.2.8f1. To be eligible for password protection, you'll need later than 4.1.7 or 4.1.8 (firmware upgrades are available at Apple's web site).

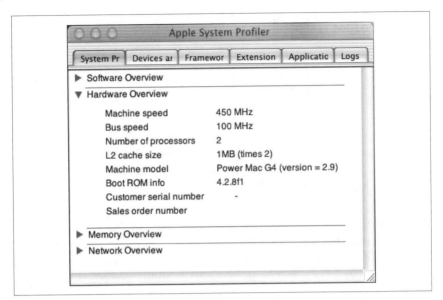

Figure 2-3. Apple System Profiler

Once we've met the version prerequisites, what exactly does this password protection prevent? Longtime users of the Mac OS may recall such pre–OS X hacks as holding down the Shift key or customizing your extensions with the spacebar, as well as the ability to boot from a CD. While extensions don't exist under OS X, Open Firmware blocks all other avenues that do, including booting up with the C, N, or T keys depressed, in single or verbose mode, or zapping the PRAM. It'll also require a password if you try to edit its settings or get into the Startup Manager.

As with most technology, there's more than one way to set the password, depending on your skills. Apple provides a utility that will do all the magic for you in a pretty GUI (see the link in the "See Also" section of this hack). Simply download the installer, run the single screen configuration, and reboot your machine to solidify your password protection.

But what if you wanted to do everything by accessing Open Firmware manually and having complete control over the process? No problem! First off, boot into Open Firmware by holding down the ⌘, Option, O, and F keys during startup. You'll be dropped into a blank screen with a mere prompt for typing commands. Next, set the firmware password by typing password and entering your password twice (for verification). Once you've done that, set the security level with setenv security-mode *<mode>*, where *<mode>* can be one of three words: none (no security), command (restricts usable Open Firmware commands), or full (which does the same thing as Apple's downloadable utility). Finally, to reboot the computer with your changes saved, enter reset-all.

Disabling the password protection can be done with Apple's provided utility or by booting into Open Firmware (as before), typing setenv security-mode none, entering your password, and then rebooting the computer with reset-all.

Hacking the Hack

The inevitable has happened: you've forgotten the password you've set in Open Firmware. Luckily, there are a couple of alternatives: booting into OS 9 (and optionally zapping the PRAM) or removing some memory DIMMs. But if you're lucky enough to still be logged into the Finder (before a worrisome reboot), you can download an OS 9 utility called FW Sucker. With a simple double-click, it'll display the current firmware password, from which you can then disable the protection or change it to something more suitable (via the earlier instructions).

See Also

- How to Set Up Open Firmware Password Protection (*http://docs.info.apple.com/article.html?artnum=106482*)
- Open Firmware Password 1.02 Download (*http://docs.info.apple.com/article.html?artnum=120095*)
- Open Firmware Password Protection (*http://www.securemac.com/openfirmwarepasswordprotection.php*)
- FW Sucker 1.0 (*http://www.msec.net/software/index.html#fwsucker*)

HACK #17 OS X for This Old Mac

Give your legacy Mac hardware a nudge into OS X with the XPostFacto hack.

Wait, don't throw out that old Power Mac or Umax clone; it may just be up for a little Mac OS X sprucing. Some of those old Macs will actually run Mac OS X 10.2 (Jaguar)—with a little help from an unassuming-looking control panel.

I recently gave an old 7500 a G3 upgrade card from Sonnet (*http://www.sonnettech.com/*), a quad-port FireWire card, and a dual-port USB card (only $37, combined). Mac OS 9 ran rather snappily and the machine served quite nicely as a USB print server. Then I stumbled across a little something called XPostFacto (*http://eshop.macsales.com/OSXCenter/XPostFacto/*), which is open source and free.

XPostFacto is a little hack that brings Mac OS X, OS X Server, and Darwin to older, unsupported, and forgotten Mac models—those draped in the unfashionable beige of times past.

Before you think of giving XPostFacto a whirl, be sure to consult the compatibility chart at:

> *http://eshop.macsales.com/OSXCenter/XPostFacto/framework.*
> *cfm?page=XPostFacto.html#preparing*

Also, make sure your machine has been recently backed up. You're dealing with an unsupported hack here.

You can find XPostFacto site's comprehesive documentation at:

> *http://eshop.macsales.com/OSXCenter/XPostFacto/framework.*
> *cfm?page=XPostFacto.html*

The procedure in a nutshell is:

1. Boot into Mac OS 9.
2. Insert your standard-issue Mac OS X installation CD.
3. Run the XPostFacto application (icon shown in Figure 2-4).
4. Point XPostFacto at the install CD and target volume.
5. Click the Install button.
6. Follow the usual installation instructions.

XPostFacto

Figure 2-4. The XPostFacto utility

It'll take a while, mind you. Have some coffee, read *The New York Times*, watch a movie, and have a good meal. When you return, if all's gone according to plan, OS X should be humming away on your old throwaway Mac.

> Other World Computing does offer XPostFacto support for a one-time $10 fee. If you're going to be running OS X on a legacy machine in a real production environment—as opposed to just seeing if it can be done—making the investment in some help may just be worthwhile.

## CHAPTER THREE

Multimedia and the iApps
Hacks 18–32

Apple has positioned the Mac as a digital hub, the nexus for the otherwise disparate components of your iLife. It has more than backed up this claim with a suite of simply powerful applications: iPhoto, your digital shoebox; iTunes, your personal audio jukebox; iMovie and iDVD, for the budding independent filmmaker; iCal to keep track of where you're supposed to be next; and iSync to keep all your devices in sync.

Add to this Apple's .Mac online service, ever more integrated into your Mac's online life. Back up your Mac's preferences and those important documents you have with you on the road. Check your mail, consult your address book, and share your calendar through any ordinary web browser.

It's all coming together rather nicely. That doesn't mean there isn't room to hack. This chapter provides tips and techniques for getting the most out of the iApps and third-party multimedia applications. Going beyond what the iApps provide out of the box, we'll also glue together audio, video, text, and photos in some unexpectedly useful and fun combinations.

HACK #18 Top iChat Tips

iChat is more than just a great instant messenger client. Here is a collection of tips to get the most out of this fabulous addition to the iApp family.

The moment it became available, just about every Mac geek I knew dropped their AIMs, Adiums, Fires, Jabbers, and Proteuses and made the switch to iChat, Apple's iApp-flavored instant messaging client. What's not to love? It's colorful, friendly, and decidedly Mac. But there's more beneath the candy-coated surface than just another instant messenger (IM) application.

This hack is all about getting the most out of iChat through a few useful tips and delightful surprises discovered between "Up late?," "We're moving that meeting to Friday," and "Dinner's ready!"

Into the Well

Before you do anything else, be sure to put a face to your IM name. There's nothing quite as distancing as a conversation with a generic AIM (AOL Instant Messenger) icon. Whether you choose a cartoon character close to your heart or a recent promo snapshot you were badgered into, simply drag an image into the buddy icon well at the top right of the iChat buddy list window (see Figure 3-1) and it'll appear along with your name or IM handle in your buddies' buddy lists.

Figure 3-1. Dragging a picture into the buddy icon well

As shown in Figure 3-2, iChat's Buddy Icon dialog allows you to scale and position your preferred image until it's just right. Slide the little blue ball left and right to scale the image. Drag the image itself around until it's where you like it. Click Done when you're done.

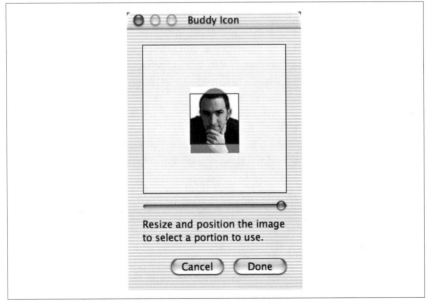

Figure 3-2. Resizing and positioning a buddy icon

Change your buddy icon any time you wish, depending on mood, interest, or just randomly to confuse and delight your friends.

Rendezvous

Rendezvous (*http://www.apple.com/macosx/jaguar/rendezvous.html*), Apple's branding of a larger standardization effort called Zeroconf (*http://www.zeroconf.org/*), allows for devices to broadcast their existence and discover others on a local network, peering and making use of each other's available services—all with zero configuration. iChat has Rendezvous baked right in. It'll notice other iChat users coming and going on the local network, keeping track of the transient population in a Rendezvous buddy list (see Figure 3-3).

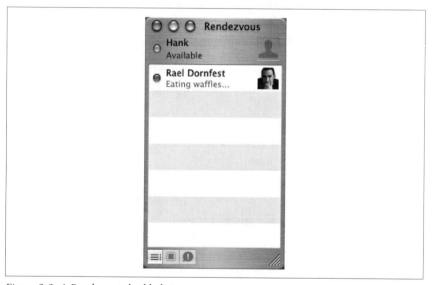

Figure 3-3. A Rendezvous buddy list

To enable Rendezvous in iChat, select iChat → Log Into Rendezvous or press Option-⌘-L. To display the special Rendezvous buddy list (separate from your personal IM buddy list), select Window → Rendezvous or press ⌘-2.

Even if you're not connected to the Internet, you can chat on your local Ethernet or AirPort network through the wonders of Rendezvous. Rather than IM messages flowing between two buddies via AOL's Instant Messenger servers, they flow directly, peer to peer. This means too that file transfer over iChat is much faster, limited by the speed of your local network rather than your connection to the Internet and responsiveness of AOL's servers.

iChat Rendezvous is just perfect for a home network, intermittently connected (to the Internet) classroom network, and at meetings for ad hoc collaborative online note taking and side conversation. Where the Rendezvous/iChat combo really shines is at WiFi-enabled conferences, participants keeping in touch with one another through the course of the day and discovering people they didn't know were attending.

File Transfer

You're chatting with a buddy about some latest bit of shareware and want to pass it along. Perhaps you're checking in with a coworker a world away about the latest copy of that report you're both suppposed to have finished already. Simply drag that shareware installer, PowerPoint report, or any other file to the name or icon representing someone in your buddy list. He'll be notified that you've initiated a file transfer, confirm receipt, and away that file goes. No need for uploading the report to your enterprise server for download by your coworker. No need for turning on Apache, figuring your your IP address, and providing your buddy with a URL.

iChat's perfect when you want to copy a file quickly from one machine to another. No need to set up a separate IM name; Rendezvous will take care of the introductions for you. Just drag the file onto your alter ego's name in your Rendezvous buddy list and roll your chair across the floor to the other machine to accept the file transfer.

If you have multiple files to transfer, unfortunately, iChat won't simply allow you to drag them all onto a buddy's name. What you can do, however, is put the files into a folder and drag and drop the folder to your buddy.

File transfer works regardless of operating system or IM application, just as long as you're both using an AOL Instant Messenger– or *@mac.com*-enabled IM client. Your firewall will also need to be liberal enough to allow peer-to-peer file transfer.

Screenshot Sharing

Here's a variation on the file-transfer theme. Trying to help a family member with something on her Mac and having trouble picturing what exactly it is that she's doing? Get her to take a screenshot [Hack #41] (⌘-Shift-3) of her screen just as it is at that moment and drag the *Picture x.pdf* file to your name in her buddy list. It's amazing what a time saver this can be. If you're a customer-support person dealing with a Mac user, try this with that customer who doesn't appear all that adept at describing what he's doing.

Whereabouts

Even when I don't chat with the gaggle of buddies winking in and out of existence in my buddy list, it's nice to see them passing through. Sometimes I even get a slightly more detailed glimpse of what they're up to and where they're going, thanks to buddy status messages. Set your status by clicking the existing status message below your name at the top of your Buddy List window, as shown in Figure 3-4.

Figure 3-4. Setting availability status

The defaults aren't particularly descriptive: Available, Away, and Offline. But you can set a custom status associated with either a red or green status light. Instead of choosing a status from the list, select Custom... associated with either a red (unavailable) or green (available) status light. Type in a short message—10 to 15 characters is about right—and press your Return key. The result should look something like Figure 3-5.

Figure 3-5. Creating a custom status

Your custom status will be reflected wherever you appear in someone's buddy list (see Figure 3-3).

If you ever want to remove old status messages en masse, select Edit List... from the status list.

> Selecting a red status light means that anyone who doesn't notice that you're unavailable and tries to initiate a chat will receive your status message as an autoreply. You'll still have their incoming message waiting for you when you return.

Chatrooms

iChat allows more than just one-to-one IM chats. You can create a new ad hoc chatroom and invite buddies to join you, all chatting together in a secluded little online space. There are actually two types of chat space: invite-only and a more traditional chatroom where people can pop in at will—assuming they know of its existence.

To start an invite-only chat space, select File → New Chat (⌘-N). This creates a chat space just as with any other one-to-one conversation. The differences are that you are currently the only participant and a Participants pane is attached to the side of the chat window. To invite someone, click the plus sign (+) in the Participants pane and select a buddy. Do this for as many buddies as you like.

Actually, any one-to-one chat can be turned into an invite-only chat space by clicking the person icon (that's the leftmost button on the bottom of a chat window) to open the Participants pane and then proceeding as before.

The second type of group chat is a more traditional AOL-style chatroom. To create or join an existing chatroom, select File → Go To Chat... (⌘-G), as shown in Figure 3-6.

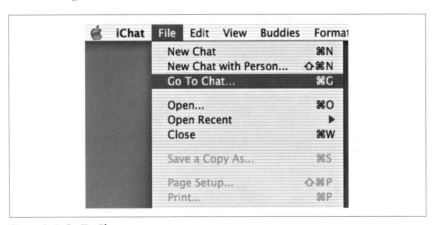

Figure 3-6. Go To Chat...

In the Go To Chat... dialog, leave the AOL Instant Messenger service selected and type the name of an existing chatroom or whatever you'd like to name a new one in the Chat Name field, as shown in Figure 3-7. Click Go and you'll be whisked away to your chatroom after a few seconds.

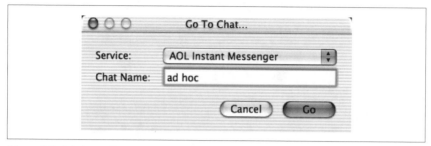

Figure 3-7. Joining a chatroom

To leave a chat space, simply close the chat window. Your buddies can continue chatting as if you'd never been there.

Buddies

Unfortunately, at the time of this writing, iChat doesn't have any easy way to add someone you've been chatting with to your buddy list. You'd think it'd just be a matter of dragging his buddy name from the chat window to the buddy list, but that simply doesn't work.

To add a buddy, click the plus sign (+) button on the bottom left of your Buddy List window (see Figure 3-8).

Figure 3-8. The add buddy button

You'll be offered the opportunity to search for or select someone from your Address Book. If she is in your Address Book but doesn't yet have an AIM or @mac.com handle associated with her, enter one in the supplied field and you're done. If she's not already one of your contacts, click New Person and fill in the form to create an entry in the Address Book and add her to your buddy list simultaneously (see Figure 3-9).

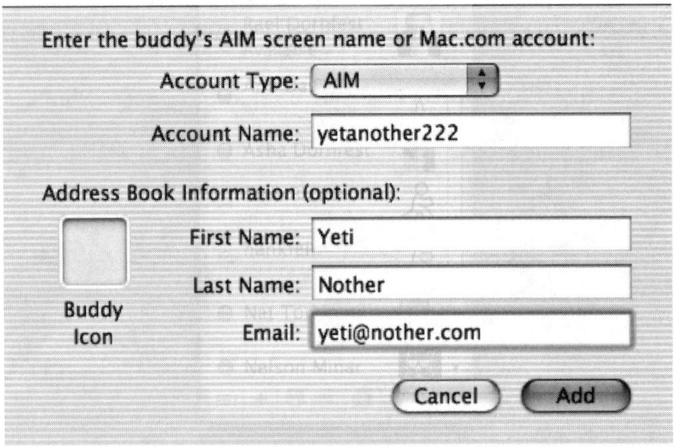

Enter the buddy's AIM screen name or Mac.com account:

Account Type: AIM

Account Name: yetanother222

Address Book Information (optional):

First Name: Yeti

Last Name: Nother

Buddy
Icon

Email: yeti@nother.com

Cancel   Add

Figure 3-9. Adding a buddy

Logs

Unless you've chanced upon them in your *Documents* directory, you probably don't know that iChat keeps logs of every chat you have. You'll find them all in *Documents/iChats*. They're listed by buddy (full name or buddy handle) and number, starting with 1 (e.g., *Steve Jobs #7.chat*). Don't bother trying to read them in a text editor; they're serialized objects (noise to you and me) viewable either programmatically or from within iChat.

Open an old chat by selecting File → Open... (⌘-O) and selecting it from the list, as shown in Figure 3-10.

Figure 3-11 shows an exact replica of an earlier chat, replete with buddy icons and smileys.

Of course you can remove old logs at any time by simply deleting them from *Documents/iChats*.

HACK
#19   AIM Alternatives

There are various feature-packed alternatives to the default AOL Instant Messenger client for Mac OS X.

When people started discovering AOL's Instant Messenger taking up a large portion of their CPU for seemingly menial (or nonexistent) tasks, the proverbial chad hit the fan; people wanted something better and they wanted it

Figure 3-10. Opening an iChat log entry

Figure 3-11. Reading an iChat log entry

now, regardless of what silly or pointless features they may end up missing. Let's take a brief look at some of the alternatives that have gained popularity:

iChat (http://www.apple.com/ichat/)

Since Apple ships iChat with its OS X 10.2, there's a very good chance that iChat will become the reigning champ of AIM imitators. Created with the blessing of AOL itself, iChat supports chats, file transfers, and buddy icons and uses a GUI that manifests messages into cartoon-style balloons (which don't look as bad as they sound). It has strong support for Mail (a column that tells you if the sender of the email is online) and the Address Book, along with the ability to customize which actions will be performed for a number of common events (buddy logging in, buddy typing, etc.).

Adium (http://www.adiumx.com)

Adium has been gaining a strong following for guerrilla AIM users, mainly due to its immense customization and its low system requirements. It has a clean and refined interface, as well as being minimal for those worried about screen real estate. It's free and is built using Cocoa (and thus gets a number of things for free: spellchecking, antialiasing, etc.).

Fire (http://www.epicware.com/fire.html)

Fire is the granddaddy of instant messengers for OS X; it's been around as long as OS X has and has consistently been improved from version to version. It's open source and it shows, offering langauge localizations contributed by others, hearty amounts of bug fixes, soundsets, icons, and more. While its interface may not be the prettiest, its ability to hook into AIM, Yahoo!, MSN, ICQ, Jabber, and IRC is a clincher for those with multiple service needs.

Proteus (http://www.indigofield.com/)

Proteus, my current favorite, is much like Fire in that it hooks into a number of providers: AIM, Yahoo!, MSN, ICQ, and Jabber. It benefits by having a strong amount of customization, with the interesting ability to run shell scripts at various points (such as when messages are received, so that, for instance, you could make your own logging system), along with the ability to choose themes, icons, soundsets, and so on. Its GUI is a little more refined than Fire's.

If these AIM alternatives don't satisfy your messaging itch, don't hesitate to browse the excellent VersionTracker (*http://www.versiontracker.com*) for more possibilities. You may also want to take a look into Jabber messenging systems, which can hook into any IM protocol that the Jabber server supports. The best way to find these XML-based alternatives is to search Sourceforge (*http://www.sourceforge.net/*) or VersionTracker.

Printing to PDF or Bitmapped Image
#20

Printing to PDF or bitmapped TIFF image under OS X is built right in, available to almost any application with Print functionality.

OS X's reliance on PDFs for everything from the Dock to Print Preview presents quite a boon when it comes to PDF viewing support and the creation of simple PDFs. While it's something that ordinarily requires specialized software, printing to PDF or bitmapped TIFF image under OS X is built right in, available to almost any application with the ability to print.

From your application, choose Print—almost always File → Print or ⌘-P. In the Print dialog, select the application-specific settings from the pull-down menu (Copies & Pages should be selected by default) and make any adjustments you wish. These range from simple font selection to Internet Explorer's wide-page handling and control over the inclusion of headers and footers, images, and backgrounds. Some applications make their options available outside of the Print dialog via an Option button. When you're ready, rather than being tempted by the pulsating Print button, click Preview (see Figure 3-12).

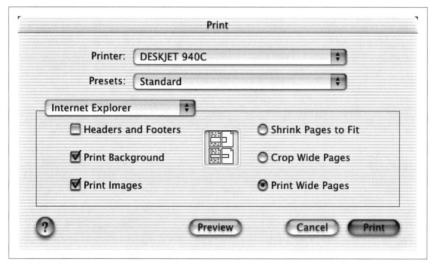

Figure 3-12. Internet Explorer's Print dialog

If Print Preview's more visual way of adjusting options is more your game—and is available to you in the application at hand—go right ahead. When you're finished, click Print in the Print Preview dialog followed by Preview in the Print dialog and you're back with the class.

Previews are handled, appropriately enough, by the Preview application, the lightweight PDF viewer that comes with OS X. You'll see a fresh, piping hot PDF of whatever it was you were printing. To save the PDF, select File → Save As PDF…, rename Preview of *whatever.pdf* to something nicer, select your preferred save location, and click the Save button. Don't worry about that *.pdf* file extension [Hack #6]; if you lop it off, OS X will kindly stick it back on for you.

If you prefer to save the preview as a bitmapped TIFF image, select instead File → Save As... or the key combination Shift-⌘-S.

Of course, using a specialized application like Adobe Acrobat for your PDF creation and editing needs provides much more fine-grained control over text formatting, image scaling, margins, indenting, and the like. If, however, you just want to quickly package up a web page for offline viewing **[Hack #86]** or a rough cut of your latest brochure for a friend without needing anything but a PDF viewer, Save As PDF in Preview sure does the trick.

H A C K
#21 Image Conversion in a Pinch
The ability to convert images from one format to another with minimal retouching and manipulation is built right into Mac OS X.

Every so often—but not often enough to warrant shelling out for a full-scale draw or paint program—I find myself needing to convert an image from one format to another. Perhaps I have a photo in TIFF format I'd like to incorporate into my web site as a JPEG or GIF. Or I need to share a screenshot with a Windows user who prefers BMP to PNG.

Thankfully, OS X users have some minimal functionality for image conversion and alteration built right into their OS.

Preview

Preview takes me back to the days when a web browser became a launchpad for a plethora of helper apps, specialized viewers for images, movies, or sounds. It's the helper you always wished for for all things image, able to open, save, and convert PDF, JPEG, TIFF, PNG, and others, as well as to export a Photoshop image as a GIF, a Windows BMP to Quicktime, or a fancy new PNG to old faithful MacPaint.

Open an image via File → Open, ⌘-O, or double-clicking an image file or dragging and dropping it to Preview's Dock or Finder icon. Choose File → Export..., pick an output format, and save. For a mite more fine-tuning, click the Options... button in the Save sheet to set color depth, simple filtering, interlacing, and the like, as shown in Figure 3-13.

Now, don't expect much more than open and save. Preview has some minimal flipping and rotating, but that's about it. Most notably lacking is the ability to crop, a must-have when creating screenshots or a doing a quick hack job on an unduly large image before forwarding it via email.

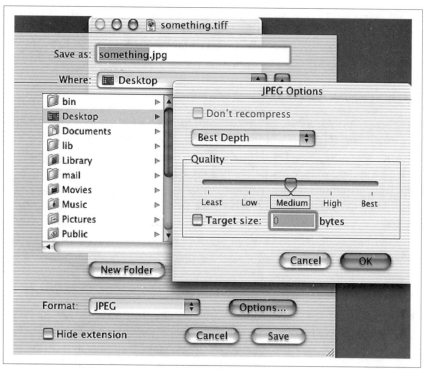

Figure 3-13. Exporting to a different image format

iPhoto

iPhoto (*http://www.apple.com/iphoto/*), while best suited to its primary role of digital shoebox, does provide some useful conversion facilities in a pinch. It's far more limited than Preview in the image formats it supports (JPG, TIFF, and PNG) but has a good deal more features up its sleeve: scaling, simple brightness and contrast controls, red-eye reduction, rotation, cropping, one-click enhance, retouching, and converting to black and white.

Launch iPhoto. Drag one or more images into its window or select files via File → Import… iPhoto will import your specified images and add them to its library. Click the Last Import roll in the lefthand pane to narrow your view to only what you just imported. If you'd like to do some editing, select an image and click Edit at the bottom of the Preview (righthand) pane.

Most apropos to what we're trying to accomplish is iPhoto's ability to convert multiple files at once. When you're ready to save, go back to the organize view by clicking Organize at the bottom of the preview pane, select (#)

the images you wish to save, and choose File → Export... or press ⌘-E. Choose the File Export tab, make any size adjustments you wish, pick a format, and click Export. iPhoto will prompt you with the standard OS X Save dialog for a preferred export location.

Graphic Converter

The venerable Graphic Converter (*http://lemkesoft.com/us_gcabout.html*) shareware app (U.S.$30 in Europe, U.S.$35 in the rest of the world at the time of this writing) makes the transition over from OS 9 to carbonized OS X. It's been the Swiss Army knife for images on the Mac as far back as 1993, importing around 160 image file formats and exporting to around 45. Graphic Converter supports batch conversion, is AppleScript-aware (*http://lemkesoft.com/us_scripts.html*), and sports a comprehensive toolset including: rotation, comprehensive level adjustment, sharpen and blur, cropping, and lots more.

More

Of course if you need more advanced image manipulation and drawing tools, you may be in the market for something like Photoshop or Illustrator. The major drawback is, of course, price; comprehensive commercial packages do come rather dear. A free, open source alternative is The Gimp (*http://gimp. org/*), the GNU Image Manipulation Program (read: Photoshop-alike); although it runs only under X11 for Mac OS X (*http://www.apple.com/macosx/x11*) or XonX (*http://mrcla.com/XonX/*) (that's X Windows on OS X), you certainly can't beat the power/price combination.

HACK #22   Top 10 iPhoto Tips

Yes, at first glance, iPhoto appears deceptively simple. But there's a Unix-compatible database lurking beneath that beautiful Aqua surface.

At first glance, Apple's iPhoto (*http://www.apple.com/iphoto*) appears deceptively simple. You plug in your digital camera, iPhoto grabs all the pictures, and you play with them on your computer screen.

This process is so easy, in fact, that the next thing you know you have hundreds, if not thousands of images annexing real estate on your hard drive. At some point sobriety settles in, and you realize that you need to back up those iPhoto images. Or you may want to move them to another computer or free up space on your hard drive for even more pictures.

So, you open your *iPhoto Library* folder, which has grown to more than a gig in size, and figure you'll just grab logical parts of it and burn a few CDs.

Problem is, there appears to be nothing logical about the contents of this folder. All you see are numbered directories, which when you open them contain more numbered directories. Suddenly you realize that sorting all this out isn't going to be so easy.

This scenario is based on the premise that you've figured out the best way to shoot your pictures in the first place. You've heard some recommendations here and there about how to take good digital images, but you're still not sure about things such as: Do you always shoot at the highest resolution? How do you take flattering portraits of people outdoors? And how the heck do you prevent red eye?

By now you may be thinking, "Hey, I thought iPhoto was going to solve all my problems. I'm more confused than ever. You're bringing me down, man."

The truth is, iPhoto is really quite powerful (and complicated), even though it appears simple on the surface. The following 10 tips will put you on the fast track to avoiding the iPhoto "gotchas" that lurk beneath its Aqua surface.

Data In: Taking Better Pictures

I refer to this first section (the first five tips) as "Data In" because iPhoto is really just another database. As with all databases, the higher the quality of the information going in, the better your output will be. Taking good pictures is key to an enjoyable iPhoto experience.

Tip #1: Buy a bigger memory card for your camera. Forget about that cheesy 8MB card that came with your digicam and buy yourself some real memory. Pony up for at least 32MB for 1.3-megapixel cameras, 64MB for 2-megapixel models, 128MB for 3-megapixel digis, and 256MB for 4-megapixel shooters—anything less will force you to shoot at low resolution, tempt you to pass on creative pictures, or send you constantly running to your hotel room to upload images because your memory card is full again. Stick the 8MB card in your pocket for emergencies and go with the big guns in your camera.

Tip #2: Shoot at your camera's highest resolution. You'll need a decent-sized memory card to do this, but it's worth the investment many times over. You may think that you only want vacation photos for your web site, but what if one turns out to be a real winner? Wouldn't it be nice to have it as an 8-by-10-inch print too? You'll need all the resolution your camera can muster to make a photo-quality print that size. Remember, you can always scale high-resolution images down for other uses, but you can't go the other way without loss of quality.

To get the most out of your camera, look for settings such as SHQ (super-high quality) and avoid anything marked as standard resolution—which is really camera-company lingo for substandard.

Tip #3: Get closer. Casual photographers tend to stand too far away from their subjects. Sure you can crop the image later in iPhoto, but that's like turning your pricey 3-megapixel camera into a run-of-the-mill 2-megapixel model. Get close to your subject, frame it in your viewfinder, then get even closer. Your shots will require less cropping and have more personality.

Tip #4: Find the fill flash setting and use it. Fill flash means that the camera's flash fires every time, even in broad daylight. You see, just because it's light outside doesn't mean that the light is good on your subject's face. By turning on the fill flash and getting within 10 feet of your model, you illuminate his handsome features and add a nice twinkle to his eyes.

Look for the flash icon that's usually a plain lightning bolt. Remember that your flash will most likely return to the default autosetting when you turn off the camera, which means your camera, not you, will decide when to use the flash.

Tip #5: Avoid red eye when possible. This monsterlike countenance that appears in otherwise innocent subjects is the bane of compact cameras. Red eye is caused by the flash reflecting off the subject's retinas. This usually happens in dimly lit rooms when a subject's eyes are dilated.

You can help avoid red eye by having the subject look at a lamp or an open window (that is, if it's light outside!) right before the shot. Other tricks include turning up the room lights or shooting from a slight angle so that the subject isn't looking directly into the camera.

If all else fails, iPhoto does include a red-eye-removal tool that can help with this problem, but it's best to avoid postproduction work as much as possible.

Data Out: Managing iPhoto Files

This section (the last five tips) focuses on managing the mountain of data you'll be loading into your computer in the form of JPEG files. With just a little foresight, and by adding a couple of free (or really inexpensive) tools, you'll never suffer from the iPhoto backup blues.

Tip #6: Limit library size to 650MBs. Every time you upload a photo, your iPhoto library grows a little more. Before too long it can easily swell to a gigabyte or more. Unless you own a DVD burner or you have lots of spare space on a FireWire hard drive, you're going to have a hard time fitting libraries onto standard CDs for backup and portability. Plus, if you hang out in the iPhoto discussion groups, you know that performance tends to slow down as libraries grow in size.

You can check the size of your iPhoto library by following this path: *Macintosh HD → Users → Your Name → Pictures → iPhoto Library*. Click once on the folder to highlight it, then choose Show Info from the File drop-down menu (or press ⌘-I). If your library is approaching 650MB, burn it onto a CD, then pull it out of your Pictures folder. The next time you launch iPhoto, it will create a brand-new library.

Tip #7: Use iPhoto Library Manager to switch between libraries. Brian Webster's nifty piece of freeware enables you to select the iPhoto library you want to view before you launch the program. If you have three different libraries on your hard disk (each 650MBs or less!), then simply launch iPhoto Library Manager first and select the library you want to load, as shown in Figure 3-14. You can download Brian's software at *http://www.versiontracker.com*.

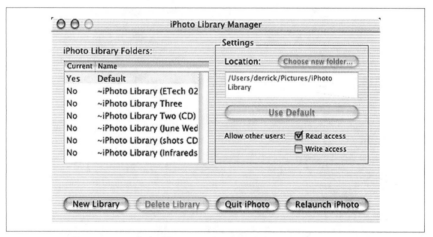

Figure 3-14. Choosing an iPhoto library with iPhoto Library Manager

I recommend that you keep all your iPhoto libraries in your *Pictures* folder. I give each library a descriptive name such as *iPhoto Library (Vol 2)* to help me keep track of them. I also like to put a ~ at the beginning of the filename, so the iPhoto libraries show up at the top of the window when I open my *Pictures* folder in list view.

Tip #8: Create custom albums for better organization and retrieval. Not only will this help you manage your pictures within iPhoto, but it also forces the application to create readable data that can be retrieved by CD-cataloging applications. Figure 3-15 shows a selection of iPhoto albums.

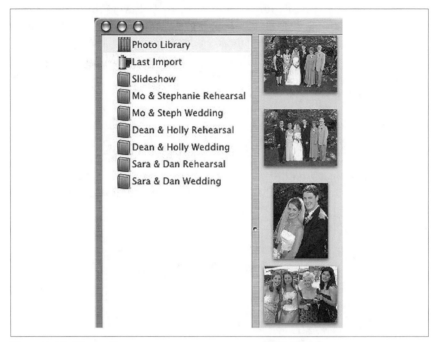

Figure 3-15. iPhoto albums

> To create an album in iPhoto, just click the + button in the lower-left corner.

By creating custom albums in iPhoto, you force the application to create data that can be retrieved quickly by cataloging applications such as CDFinder.

Over time, you'll probably end up with dozens of iPhoto libraries stored on dozens of CDs. If you use cataloging software such as CDFinder (*http://www.cdfinder.de/*), it will capture all of those album names you created within each iPhoto library (see Figure 3-16). When you need to find out which CD (iPhoto library) a group of photos resides on, such as European Vacation 2001, then just use the Find command in your CD-catalog program, and it will tell you which iPhoto library contains those images.

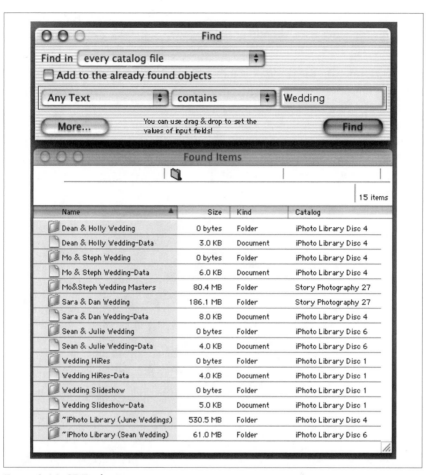

Figure 3-16. CDFinder in action

Tip #9: Duplicate photos before editing. When preparing a picture in iPhoto for printing or other specific output, you may want to duplicate it before you start editing. This allows you to keep the pristine, original image for future use right beside the edited version. To duplicate a photo, click on the thumbnail once to highlight it, then press ⌘-D or choose File → Duplicate.

If you forget to duplicate and want to restore an edited photo back to its original state, you can select File → Revert to Original.

Tip #10: Add titles to important photos. Digital cameras are user-friendly in many ways, but the files they produce are not. iPhoto can help you create logical names for your pictures that replace the alphanumeric system the cameras use. This functionality is particularly nice for images that you want to export for other uses outside of iPhoto, such as creating web pages, email attachments, and CD libraries.

First, click once on the iPhoto thumbnail to highlight it, then enter the information you want to use as the filename in the Title field, as shown in Figure 3-17. You have to enter each photo's title individually unless you want to opt for one of iPhoto's batch options: Roll Info, File Name, or Date/Time. To use one of these labels to replace the existing filenames for an entire batch of photos, Shift-click all the images you want selected, and choose Set Title To under the Edit drop-down menu.

Figure 3-17. Adding a descriptive title to a photo

Most likely though, you're going to want to add filenames that are more descriptive, such as Eiffel Tower, Big Ben, or Crazy Taxi Driver. In that case, highlight the thumbnail, enter the descriptive name in the Title field, and press the Return key.

You may want to enlarge the size of your thumbnails using the slider bar on the lower-right side of iPhoto's application window. This will make it easier to identify the picture.

Once you have all of your new titles entered the way you want them, create a new album (by clicking on the + key in the lower-left side of iPhoto and drag all the newly named images into the album. Then click once on the album to highlight it, and click on the Share button to reveal the Export icon in the lower-right corner of iPhoto. Click on Export and choose File Export from the tabbed dialog box.

In the File Export dialog box, be sure to click on the Use Titles radio button under Name. Once you've decided the other parameters you want, click the Export button. iPhoto will ask you where you want these images placed on your hard drive. Navigate to the desired folder, click OK, and iPhoto) will export the entire album and include the names you wrote in the Title field as the new filenames for the pictures.

Now here's something really cool: if you want to build an iPhoto library that has all descriptive filenames for your JPEGs, and then include them in your Title field too, follow these easy steps:

1. Create a fresh iPhoto library as described in Tip #6.
2. Choose Import from the File menu.
3. Navigate to a folder with renamed images.
4. Import the entire folder.

All of your pictures will retain their descriptive filenames in iPhoto, and those names will also be displayed in the Title field.

Editor's note: Since the time of this writing, Apple has released its much-anticipated upgrade, iPhoto2. Nevertheless, all of the information in this hack still holds true. For a quick run-down of some of the changes, upgrade guidelines, and initial impressions, see "iPhoto—It's Mostly Good News" (*http://www.oreillynet.com/cs/weblog/view/wlg/2691*).

—Derrick Story

Make Your Own Documentary

HACK #23

Using only digital photographs, music, a $10 app, and what the iApps provide, you can put together a rather nice documentary.

A lot has been going on in the video industry lately. Emmy winner and master of the documentary film, Ken Burns, has rereleased a digitally remastered copy of his epic film *The Civil War*. The Digital Hollywood conference has come and gone. And someone named Chris Meyer has released a $10 application called Photo to Movie (*http://lqgraphics.com/software/phototomovie.html*), which I consider a milestone in video production.

Editor's note: Apple's newly released iMovie3 actually incorporates much of the functionality of Photo to Movie as a "Ken Burns Effect." Still, Photo to Movie offers more control over movement and key frames.

Basically, this small app (approximately 1MB) allows you to take a photo or image and do a panning motion effect across it (Pan & Scan), a la Ken Burns. This caused me to have a strange time-warp experience; all of a sudden I thought about my old studio. I remembered editing video and doing animation on my $100,000 Mac Media 100 workstation (with a $15,000 10GB drive array, $20,000 in software, a blazing fast 8100 running at 110MHz, an unheard-of 256MB of RAM, etc.).

Then it dawned on me that I can now do more advanced video work than I could with that system, with a $1,600 laptop and a $9.95 program. Heck, you don't even need a video camera to use iMovie.

Thanks to Apple, more and more people are exploring digital video, but I wasn't sure if people realized how far we've come in such a short time. The whole art form has been liberated and simplified. I recently set up a Bryce server farm in my house to render animation between three Macs and a PC. It took about 30 minutes of setup time. Six years ago, that type of computing power would have been nearly impossible without several SGI machines and $1,000,000. Apple has opened the door to new filmmakers who have no idea how lucky they are.

Anyway, Photo to Movie inspired me to experiment with making a documentary movie. And although I can't promise that our work will ever measure up to that of Mr. Burns, it doesn't mean we can't aspire to do great work! This is not a highly technical piece on editing video. This is just a fun exercise to get your feet wet.

What You'll Need

- Scanner or digital camera
- iPhoto or Photoshop
- iMovie
- Some music
- A piece of freeware called Audio In (optional)
- Photo to Movie ($9.95)
- Stopwatch or watch with second hand
- A few spare gigs of drive space (or an iPod)

Photos and Music

When making our documentary video, we need to decide what it will be about. Remember, video is story/concept driven, so pick items that have a narrative thread. I thought that I would use some photos from my childhood on the farm.

My first decision was about how many photos I planned to use. Part of this decision had to do with the length of the audio track. So, if you plan on setting your movie to music, you need to do a quick-and-dirty calculation of time per shot. So, let's get our audio piece lined up, shall we?

As a source of audio, you can use any MP3 file or even pull a CD track right from your CD-ROM while in iMovie. I decided to use an audio track from one of the selections up on iDisk. There is a folder in *Software → Extras* called *FreePlay Music*. Inside, you'll find hundreds of royalty-free MP3 audio clips for use in your movies. The clips' lengths range from 10 seconds to several minutes.

> If you view the tracks in column view, you can sample the audio before you download.

Now, take the length of the audio track and divide it by the number of images you've selected. My audio track was 2:03, so I converted that to seconds and dropped the extra three seconds in order to work with a simple number. Later, I could always fudge (trim) the length of my clips to accommodate the extra three seconds. I took 120 seconds and divided it by the number of photos I was using. In my case, I decided on six photos, which gave me 20 seconds per clip. Now, I know that 20 seconds doesn't sound like a lot of time, but go over to your TV and count to yourself for 20 seconds. How many shot changes do you see in the typical commercial?

Image Prep

I scanned my six photos onto one sheet. This saved me a great deal of scanning time. If you're using iPhoto, you can mimic Photoshop's editing abilities by importing the image several times and then cropping each copy or just scan individual photos. Let's not forget you can use any images for this, not just scanned photos.

Let's talk about image resolution for a moment. Later, when we get to the Photo to Movie application, we want to avoid getting artifacts in our video (the same goes for iMovie), so when I scanned my image, I opted for a minimum of 300 dots per inch (dpi) to prevent unwanted distortions. You can get away with 72-dpi images for video, but when zooming in and out of an image, it is best to start with a higher resolution.

Since the look of the video we are trying to mimic is that of a Ken Burns black-and-white documentary, I decided to alter my photos by converting them to grayscale (change them to Black and White), adjusting the curves (play with the Brightness and Contrast, as shown in Figure 3-18), and adding some grain and imperfections to each image. I didn't want the photos to appear perfect, or the illusion of time would be lost.

Figure 3-18. Altering a photo's brightness and contrast in Photoshop

Go ahead and save the file as a JPEG or Photoshop file, and duplicate this process with each additional photo.

Storyboard

To save time, it is smart to plan out your movie before you begin to edit it. For me, I took the original photos and laid them out in the order in which I wanted them to appear. If you are planning to add narration to your movie, you may want to take this time to write the script that will go with each photo, and then time how long it takes for you to speak it (this is where the stopwatch comes in handy). You may want to use little sticky notes beneath each image (and I'm referring to actual pieces of paper). If you're using purely digital images, you can insert them into a Word doc, type the text there, and then print it out.

Originally, I thought of doing a narration for my movie, but I changed my mind because I thought the power of the music and the images would be diluted with words.

Photo to Movie

It is rare to find an application that does what it should in such a simple and straightforward way. And although Photo to Movie is missing a few features (which I hear are coming) that, as a professional video editor, I would like to see, it does such a respectable job for the price that I hardly miss them.

Begin by dragging your first image into the image well of the application. You'll see two squares. The green square is the start frame, or where your camera is when the movie begins. You can adjust the scale of this frame to give the illusion of zooming in a camera lens. Move the start frame to where you want the clip to begin and the end frame (the red box) to where you want the clip to end. Then set the duration of the clip; in Figure 3-19, I set mine to 20 seconds.

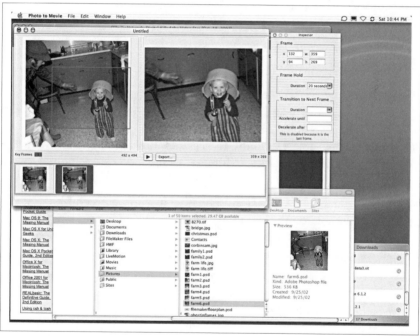

Figure 3-19. Photo to Movie in action

A word about artistic interpretation; since the world of art is a subjective one, I can't really tell you how to line up your camera shots for this. I can, however, give you some advice. I suggest that you place your end frame at a point that holds some significance or is the most powerful point in the image. This is the image that your viewer will ultimately be left with. Whatever you decide to do, just remember each image will have its own special meaning, so try to decipher that when making each clip.

Once we've set the start and end frames, we can preview the clip by using the Play button. If we're happy with the preview, we can go ahead and render this clip.

Advanced Options

Under the File menu, you'll find a menu item called Advanced Options (this drops down a hidden drawer). Here we have the option of changing the duration of the clip to a more specific time frame, but we also have some control over the acceleration/deceleration of the clip and the option to hold the camera at the start frame/end frame for a period of time to lend more impact to the image.

For example, say the clip is set to:

- Duration: 20 seconds
- Acceleration: 10 seconds
- Deceleration: 15 seconds
- Hold start: 2 seconds
- Hold end: 2 seconds

The camera will first hold the start frame in position for 2 seconds. It will go slow initially, speeding up until 10 seconds into the clip, then track over the image at the same rate until 15 seconds into the clip. Finally, it will slow down until it reaches the end frame, where it will stop and hold for 2 seconds.

For my own images, I went ahead and selected a four-second hold at the start frame, no hold on the end frame, and no acceleration or deceleration. I have plans to use a certain transition (cross-dissolve) in iMovie, so holding the camera at the end frame won't be necessary.

Once you are happy with the clip, go ahead and click Make Movie (see Figure 3-20). Name the video clip and save it to a location, such as the *Movies* folder. Be careful to select the DV Stream format, and if you live in North America, select NTSC as the Video Standard. Finally, if this video is going to tape, you should select high-quality rendering.

Narration

I decided to skip a narration, but I want to discuss a few points for those that decide to use it. There are a few ways to record your narration; one solution is to record the audio directly into iMovie, as shown in Figure 3-21.

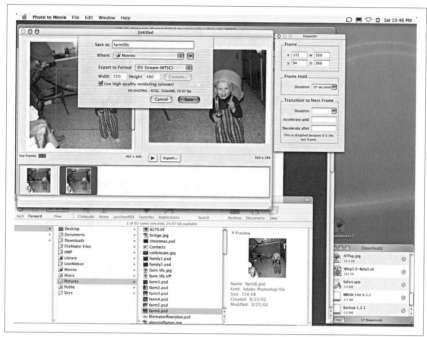

Figure 3-20. Make Movie

If you take a peek in the iMovie application, you'll see a button called Audio. Here you'll find a line-level meter and, if your microphone is connected, you may see the meter spike as it detects sound. The problem with recording here is that you may run into a problem of iMovie having difficulty recording audio because of disk speed. It may not be able to keep up. If this happens to you, you'll need another third-party solution to record your audio. A good free solution, called Audio In, can be found on Version-Tracker. The interface needs some work, but the price is right and it does a respectable job.

I recorded a few samples and found that iMovie wouldn't recognize the AIFF format of the Audio In files. I'm not sure why this is, but in case this happens to you, I have a fast workaround. When you record your narration tracks with Audio In, it saves them to the desktop. Drag the files into the Library of iTunes. Then, from iTunes, select Advanced → Convert Selection to MP3. Then just export the MP3 file to a folder.

iMovie, You Movie

Step one is to locate and import all of the video clips we made with Photo to Movie, and let's not forget our audio tracks (see Figure 3-22).

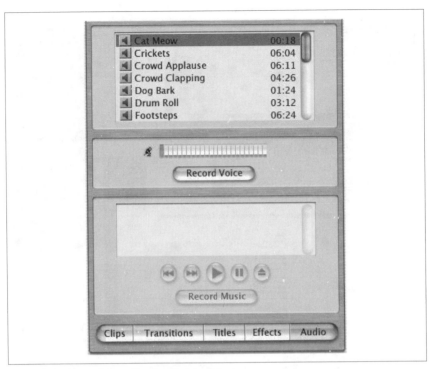

Figure 3-21. Recording audio directly into iMovie

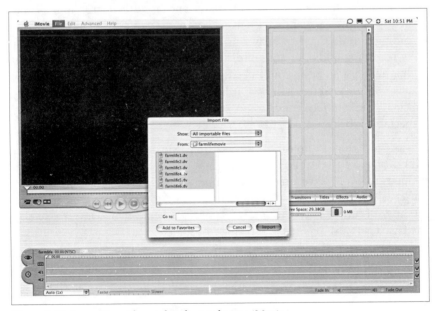

Figure 3-22. Importing video and audio tracks into iMovie

Drag the imported clips down to the time line in the order in which you would like them to appear. I suggest you use the tab with the little eyeball (as shown in Figure 3-23), which gives you a visual representation of the story narrative.

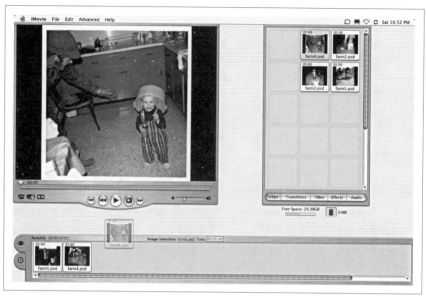

Figure 3-23. Adding tracks to the time line

Transitions

A *transition* is the change from one scene to the next. It can be a straight cut or an effect. In iMovie, the transitions are effects that bring two different scenes together. You don't have to use transitions; good examples of some of the best straight cuts ever can be found in the movie *Lawrence of Arabia*. In one scene, Lawrence has a lit match in his fingers and the moment he blows it out, there is a straight cut to the sun rising in the desert. Stunning!

However, transition effects can add a lot of substance to the images. The trick when using transitions in a short piece is using them sparingly and limiting the variety. In publishing, the rule of thumb is to limit your font choice; the same applies here. One of my biggest pet peeves when I see a Power-Point presentation is when someone has used every available type of transition. Sometimes, less is more.

I used three transitions in my movie. The first, fade in, was applied at the beginning of the first clip. It gave me a nice, slow entry into my movie, which fit the style of the music. The second transition, cross-dissolve, was used between each pair of clips. One of my favorites, this transition dissolves one clip out while fading the next clip in. The blend of the two clips has a nice, soft, and soothing feeling. Finally, my last transition was at the end of the movie. I used a fade out just as the last chord of music started to fade.

Can I Have the Envelope, Please?

The whole point of this hack was to give you some sense of the power you have right there in your computer. You don't need the best equipment and you don't need a $1,000 video camera to get some value out of iMovie. A scanner or digital camera, a $10 shareware app, and an OS X Mac, and you're making movies.

In total, this movie took approximately one and a half hours to complete, and by using the video out on my iBook, I was able to transfer it to VHS with very little effort.

See Also

- An Introduction to iMovie (*http://www.macdevcenter.com/pub/a/mac/ 2002/10/11/imovie.html*) by N.D. Woods
- *iMovie 2: The Missing Manual* (*http://www.oreilly.com/catalog/ imoviemm2/*) by David Pogue

—*Alan Graham*

From Slideshow to Video Presentation

#24

Make a slideshow into a video presentation using the combined power of iMovie, iPhoto, and iTunes.

The so-called media iApps—iMovie, iPhoto, and iTunes—actually form an ad hoc integrated development environment (IDE) for creating digital content. You probably didn't realize this because Apple's marketing focus to consumers is simplicity, not integrated environments. But there's certainly more to the iApps than initially meets the eye.

This hack shows you how these components work together by making an iPhoto slideshow into a full-fledged video presentation. All you need is a decent digital camera, a stack of music CDs, and Mac OS X.

Using Just One Leg of a Three-Legged Stool

During a recent iPhoto workshop, I learned that many of the participants hadn't opened iMovie or played much with iTunes. When I asked, "Why not?" I heard responses such as, "I don't own a DV camcorder or an iPod, so why would I need those apps?"

I realized that many creative people have been influenced by Apple's consumer marketing that aims to keep things simple in order to appeal to the greatest number of potential customers. But the iApps are better than that. Beneath their tantalizing GUI lurk powerful tools capable of producing professional quality media, especially when used as a group. So, let's take a look at how to get some serious work done with this trio of digital media programs.

Get Your Toolbox in Order

If you don't have Jaguar (10.2) yet, that's job number one. You need all the performance you can get when working with digital media, and Jaguar is the best Apple has to offer.

Next, make sure you have iMovie, iTunes, and iPhoto accessible, because you'll be opening them a lot. I keep them in the Dock. Put them wherever you want, but make sure they're easy to get to.

If you haven't upgraded to QuickTime Pro, Version 6 (*http://www.apple.com/quicktime/download/*), now's the time to do it. The player version is fine for playback, but you'll need the pro tools to do serious work. And for $29.95, it's not a bad deal, especially since the iApps come bundled with the operating system.

Finally, you may want to grab a couple of enhancement applications to expand the capabilities of the media iApps. Here are my favorites:

BBEdit (http://www.barebones.com/products/bbedit_lite.html) (Lite Version 6.1 is free)
> Serious Mac power users typically have the full version of this versatile text editor. If you haven't snagged your own copy yet, you can use the free version until you're ready to upgrade. This tool is necessary for editing code for tasks such as embedding QuickTime movies into web pages.

PixelNhance image editor (http://www.caffeinesoft.com/products/pnh/) (free)
> It's like the folks at Caffeine Software looked at iPhoto and created an application to fill its gaps. You'll need this freebie for sharpening, color adjusting, and levels control.

iPhoto Library Manager (http://www.versiontracker.com/moreinfo. fcgi?id=13532&db=mac) (free)
> This application enables you to create multiple iPhoto libraries, store them on hard drives, then switch between them as necessary. It gives iPhoto the flexibility you need for managing thousands of pictures without bogging down the application.

CDFinder (http://www.cdfinder.de/) (shareware)
> This nifty application allows you to catalog the archive CDs and external drives where your collection of iPhoto libraries and other media reside. If you can't remember in which iPhoto library the NY Times Square images reside, CDFinder will help you locate them.

How the iApps Can Work Together

Now it's time to look at how the iApps can work together. First, let's explore the two database applications: iTunes and iPhoto. This is where your music and still images are stored and organized. You can tap these databases from other applications or through the Finder. If you configure them properly, you can easily find the content you're looking for when you're outside the cozy confines of the application interface.

What do I mean by this? Let's say you want to find a song in iTunes to accompany a slideshow (as we're going to do later in this hack). If all of your songs in iTunes have their database records completed (artist, album, song, etc.), then you'll be able to find what you're looking for quickly when searching your music DB via iPhoto (yes, iPhoto can talk to iTunes) or when looking for a particular tune via the Finder. If you haven't completed those iTunes records, then all you'll see is Unknown Artist and Track 01—not much help. More on this later.

I'm assuming that you have data in iTunes and iPhoto. If you haven't used these two programs much, go upload some pictures and rip a few CDs so you have media in there to play with. You'll be surprised at how often you'll tap this information after it's in there.

Once you have content in your databases, then you can use QuickTime Pro, iMovie 2, and BBEdit to assemble and enhance your media. The basic process looks like this:

1. Upload music and images into the database apps (iPhoto and iTunes).
2. Organize the content and make sure the database records that accompany the media are accurate.
3. Output raw content from the databases.
4. Assemble and enhance the raw content with iMovie, QT Pro, and BBEdit.
5. Share the finished product with coworkers, clients, friends, and family.

Obviously, there are many variations on this theme of iApps working together. If you're shooting digital video, for example, you may think you never have to leave the iMovie environment. But what if you want to import still images into your movie (iPhoto)? How about adding music (iTunes)?

Why continue to shuffle through music CDs when you have your entire library sitting there in iTunes? Once you understand the iApp relationships, you'll find that you can create better productions in less time, regardless of which medium you're primarily working in.

To work with this example, you'll need a decent digital camera and some good music on a CD. We're going to build a better slideshow. iPhoto enables you to export pictures and music to QuickTime, but the final product is a little rough around the edges. By enhancing the core slideshow with iMovie, iTunes, and QT Pro, you can transform your humble iPhoto slideshow into a polished presentation.

After a few minutes of work, you'll see how the iApps function as a full-fledged development environment. This is only one scenario. There are many other exciting ways to use these tools.

So, let's start by digging into the two database applications: iTunes and iPhoto.

iTunes. I probably don't have to say this, but you need to have a good variety of music in your iTunes library. So, take a stack of your favorite CDs and rip them. Before doing so, however, remember two things:

- Encode at 192 kbps to capture as much fidelity as possible. You can always sample down specific tracks later if you need to reduce their size. But in terms of file size, music tracks are actually relatively small compared to video and images. There's no need to scrimp on sound quality unless you're serving on the Web, which is a different animal altogether.

- Connect to the Internet before ripping. Prior to encoding your CD tracks, go to the Advanced menu and select Get CD Track Names. By doing so you'll populate all the vital data fields associated with your music including song title, artist, and album. Remember, iTunes is your *music database*. If you're to use it efficiently, you need to have your records filled out properly. This is the easiest way to do so. You'll see how this plays out soon.

When you first load a CD in iTunes, you see only the most basic data, such as Track 01. If you were to rip the music at this point, you wouldn't have much data to accompany the MP3 files, which makes it difficult to use them outside of iTunes later on. If you're online, you can access the CDDB resource to automatically populate the important fields in your songs' database records. Select Advanced → Get CD Track Names to have them filled in for you.

Now, after accessing the CDDB, you have much richer song records, as shown in Figure 3-24. iTunes will use this information to build a logical folder structure on your hard drive (as long as you have "Keep iTunes music folder organized" checked in the Advanced preferences).

Figure 3-24. CD in iTunes showing richer song records

iPhoto. Now it's time to get your image database in order. As with iTunes for music, there are a few details to tend to when populating your database that will make your workflow smoother later on:

- Capture your images at high quality and full resolution. I don't mess much with saving pictures in TIFF or Raw formats because they are unwieldy (even though the quality is great!), but I do recommend that you use the highest quality JPEG settings. You want the best data possible in your iPhoto libraries, because you never know how you're going to want to use that information down the road.

- Check your camera's date and time settings to make sure they are correct. When you capture a picture, your camera also writes valuable metadata to the file header. But your settings have to be on target for this information to be accurate. For more information about the value of picture metadata, see "Use Metadata to Improve Your Pictures" (*http://www.macdevcenter.com/pub/a/mac/2002/11/14/photo_metadata.html*).

- Create descriptive custom albums in iPhoto to organize your various shoots. Every time you create one of these custom albums, iPhoto writes valuable data to your library file. This data makes it easy to search specific images across many libraries and will save you lots of time as your image collection grows. When you name your iPhoto albums, think in terms of keywords, such as Paris Vacation 2000, Annie's Graduation 1999, or Southwest Images 2002.

- Keep your iPhoto libraries to 650 MBs or less. Use iPhoto Library Manager to switch between libraries as needed. By limiting the size of your libraries, iPhoto will perform better and you can easily archive your images to CD.

- Add descriptive information to the Title and Comments fields. Again, the time you spend adding data to this image record will come back to you positively in the future when you're trying to find in which iPhoto library those images reside.

iPhoto also lets you add valuable data to your digital content. The four key areas are: custom albums (e.g., Tues Uploads in Figure 3-25), Title, Date, and Comments. When you add information in these record fields, iPhoto stores it in the iPhoto library with the image files. Now you can search for images across many iPhoto libraries using catalog apps such as CDFinder.

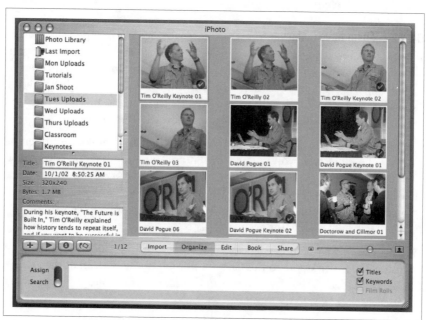

Figure 3-25. Added data associated with a picture in iPhoto

Working Example: Use iMovie and iTunes to Add Professional Touches to Your Still Images

One of the most powerful methods I have for presenting still images is the QuickTime slideshow. The pictures seem to come to life as they are organized by story line and accompanied by music. For example, in my photo business I now show these two-minute shows at the beginning of wedding appointments before I hand over the actual prints. The combination of pictures and music telling the story of their marriage makes a tremendous impact on clients, and the rest of the appointment always seems to go well.

But like everything else good in life, there's an art to making a persuasive presentation, whether it be for clients, coworkers, friends, or family. My best slideshows use iPhoto to create the core presentation, iTunes for the music, iMovie for the titles, and QuickTime Pro to stitch everything together.

I'm going to breeze through a couple of techniques to give you a feel for how these apps can cooperate with one another. If you don't have experience working in iPhoto, iMovie, and QuickTime Pro, you may wish to refer to my tutorials in the Digital Photography (*http://www.macdevcenter.com/pub/a/mac/collections/iphoto.html*) and QuickTime and iMovie (*http://www.macdevcenter.com/pub/a/mac/collections/qt_imovie.html*) collections on MacDevCenter.com.

Create opening titles in iMovie. Start by exporting your core slideshow from iPhoto to QuickTime. (Highlight the album that contains the frames for your slideshow, click the Share button, then click on Export, then select the QuickTime tab.) At this point, you don't need to export the music with the slides, even though I usually include it so I have a feel for the raw presentation. You'll actually end up adding a different soundtrack later in this process.

Here's where iMovie comes in handy for this project: to build your opening title for the slideshow you created in iPhoto and exported to QuickTime. Open iMovie and create a new project. Then build your opening title using the Titles palette, shown in Figure 3-26. This is an amazing tool. Even though you can create just about any opening sequence possible using Titles in iMovie, keep it simple for now.

Once you have an opening that you like, you need to render it by dragging it from the Titles work area to the Clip Viewer bar at the bottom of the iMovie interface. iMovie will now take a few seconds to build your opening sequence.

Export your sequence by choosing File → Export Movie. Then select To QuickTime, and choose Expert in the Format drop-down menu. Here's where you set a few parameters, such as dimensions, compression, and frame rate. Make sure your sequence has the same dimensions as the core slideshow you created in iPhoto, usually 640×480 or 320×240. Photo JPEG is a good compression setting, and 12 or 15 fps will do for frame rate. Click

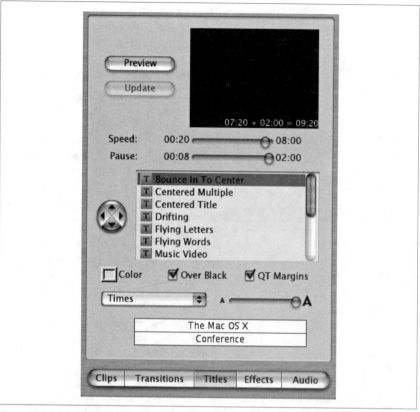

Figure 3-26. The iMovie Titles box is a gold mine for digital moviemakers

OK, then Export. You now have a QuickTime opening sequence for your iPhoto slideshow.

This is where you need QuickTime Pro to stitch them together. You're going to select the entire contents of your core slideshow (exported from iPhoto), copy it, then add it to the opening sequence you created in iMovie, then exported to QuickTime.

Click on the core slideshow, then grab its content by choosing Select All, then Copy. Now click on the opening sequence movie and select Add. QuickTime will add the core slideshow to wherever you have the playback indicator positioned. In this case, it should be at the end of the clip. Now you have a slideshow with an opening sequence.

If you have QuickTime Pro, you can stitch various QT clips together by copying the clip from one player, then adding it to the other (Don't use

Paste, or one clip will replace the other!). In Figure 3-27 I'm adding the soundtrack I exported from iMovie to my QuickTime slideshow.

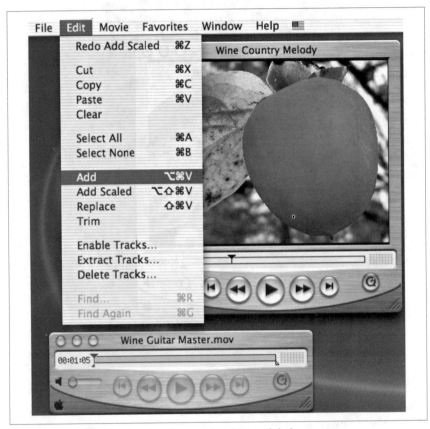

Figure 3-27. Adding the soundtrack to my QuickTime slideshow

You can create as many sequences as you want in iMovie and add them to your QuickTime presentations. I usually stick with opening and closing titles, but I'm not limited to them.

Fine-tune your music track. Once you have all of your image sequences stitched together, it's time to add the soundtrack. You probably want to clean out any existing soundtracks in your presentation. This is easy in QuickTime Pro. Go to Edit and select Delete Tracks. You'll see a number of video tracks (don't touch those!) and a couple of soundtracks. Delete all of the soundtracks.

Note the length of your movie. Hopefully it's not longer than a couple of minutes. Now open iMovie again and select Import File from the File menu.

Navigate to your *Music* folder where iTunes keeps all of your audio assets. If you've been conscientious about filing out your song records, then you'll see a list of folders by artist, with their respective albums inside. But it gets even better. Open the album folder, and you'll see all of the MP3 files with the song titles as the filenames. Sweet.

Import the song you want to use for your presentation into iMovie where it will be placed on the audio portion of the Clip Viewer. Move the endpoints of the track to make it the same length (or a tad shorter) than your slideshow. (For example, if your slideshow is 2 minutes long, then you might move the audio endpoints to create a music track that is 1 minute, 55 seconds in length.) Then, check the Fade In and Fade Out boxes so your music doesn't begin and end abruptly. Fade Out is especially important and worth using iMovie just for that function.

Now export your edited music track to QuickTime just as you did your title clip. I usually choose no compression for my music unless I plan on serving it on the Web.

When you open the music track in QuickTime, you'll see that it also has an unnecessary video track. Use Delete Tracks to get rid of it, then Select All, Copy, and Add to your slideshow. Now you have a custom soundtrack that is the perfect length for your show and fades at the end.

If you want, you can add many soundtracks at various points throughout your presentation. And, for that matter, you can add voiceover too.

Pulling It All Together

Once you have your presentation the way you want it, save it as a self-contained movie. This will put all of your parts in one container that you can play off your hard drive, burn onto a CD, or attach to mail (if it's not too big!). You can serve it on the Web too, but there are some issues involved, such as compression (to reduce download times) and authorization for the music. You can bypass these issues for now by sharing your presentations in person.

Once you've finished your work of art, be sure to use the Save As command and click the "Make movie self-contained" radio button, as shown in Figure 3-28. By doing so, QuickTime will place all the movie elements in one portable container that you can burn to CD or share with friends.

Of course, there are many ways to refine your presentation, but even with these few simple techniques, you can see how well the iApps work together and what great potential they have as a harmonious group.

—*Derrick Story*

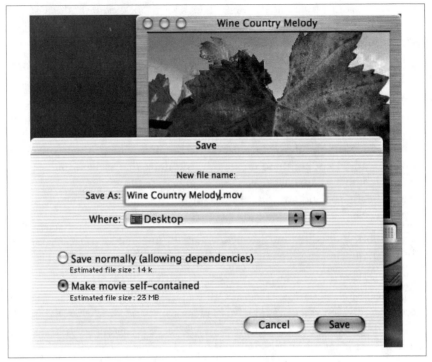

Figure 3-28. Saving as a self-contained movie

Hijacking Audio from Mac Apps

HACK #25

Audio Hijack grabs the audio output of any Mac OS X Cocoa or Carbon application for your listening pleasure.

Rogue Amoeba's Audio Hijack (*http://www.rogueamoeba.com/audiohijack/*), as its name suggests, hijacks the audio of any Mac OS X application for doctoring and recording. Billed as an audio enhancer with DSP effects and an equalizer to beat all others, it's the audio recording that's of most interest to me. Figure 3-29 shows the Audio Hijack interface.

Launch Audio Hijack, select a target application, and launch it with the Launch button. Audio Hijack will attach itself—this is why you must launch the target app from the inside—and pass through all sound generated by the app. You can begin and end recording at any time using the Start Recording/ Stop Recording button. You can forego setting a maximum duration if you're not sure what it should be, but I found setting it and letting it record unattended far more relaxing than remembering to check back every so often for fear of the audio filling up my hard drive.

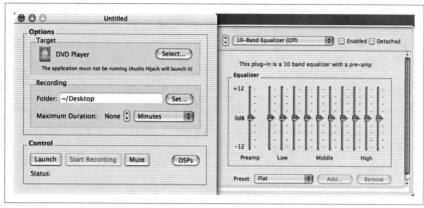

Figure 3-29. Audio Hijack interface with equalizer

Click the DSPs button and you can apply all manner of sound effects to the sound output and recording. Add flange or reverb, alter the bass and treble levels, display a pair of VU meters, or treat yourself to a 10-band equalizer with savable presets, as shown in Figure 3-29.

A friend pointed out that Audio Hijack is the perfect utility for recording live audio streams delivered via Real Audio. The application's timers act as an audio VCR of sorts, launching Real Audio and recording for a specified amount of time. Drop the recording of NPR's *All Things Considered* onto iTunes and sync with your iPod, and you have your favorite public radio on demand and portable.

Finally, I can grab the audio tracks from my yoga class video, allowing me to take my practice anywhere my iPod goes.

Audio Hijack is available for a 15-day free trial, after which it's only $16 for a fully licensed version.

HACK #26 Running Your Own Web Radio Station

Create private playlists you can stream 24/7 to almost any web-enabled device, inside or outside the home.

If you've been paying attention to what's happened with the deregulation of the airwaves, you may have noticed that most of the dial is owned by a few media conglomerates that control most of what you hear. Many of us turned to the Internet to find a tasteful alternative to all of the FM noise. And while the future of webcasting is currently tied up in the muck of figuring out fair music licensing fees, there is no doubt in my mind that the Internet is the last bastion for music.

If the idea of having your own radio webcast, for fun or profit, intrigues you, then you've come to the right place. Even if you don't plan on sharing your musical tastes with the world, you can have a lot of fun creating private playlists you can stream 24/7 to almost any web device in your home. Or maybe you just want to be able to tune into your music anywhere, anytime, on any machine. Well, guess what? You've probably got most of what you'll need sitting on your home machine. Moreover, setting up your own station is easy to do and costs nothing to get running.

What you'll need:

- A DSL or cable connection
- Music (MP3)
- QuickTime Streaming Server (free from Apple's web site)
- Promo music and microphone
- iMovie
- iTunes

Step 1: Calculate Bandwidth

The first thing you need to do is calculate the adequate server bandwidth for your station. If you figure to provide your stream at the same rate to all visitors, the basic calculation for this (via Apple's Knowledge Base) is to multiply the maximum number of users you expect by the bit rate you plan to stream. So, for your own private use, if you plan on serving up to three connections at 128 kbps over the Internet, you need an upload connection speed greater than 384 kbps to keep a stutter-free connection. If you plan to run your station over a LAN connection (streaming playlists to multiple terminals in your home), you could probably sustain as many as 50 to 60 connections on a 10Mbps network (not taking network traffic into consideration). As you can see, if you plan on running a commercial or nonprofit station for the public, you'll need a fat pipe.

A DSL or cable connection isn't fast enough to support a lot of visitors, but it is usually adequate for serving your personal use. Before you start streaming, be sure that it doesn't violate the service agreement with your ISP.

Step 2: Install/Configure QuickTime Streaming Server

The next thing you need to do is download the QT Streaming Server (QTSS) from Apple's site (*http://www.apple.com/quicktime/products/qtss/*) and install it. Once the install is complete, you'll find the installer placed an icon in your *Applications* folder that looks like Figure 3-30.

Figure 3-30. Apple's QTSS icon

Since the server can be configured and controlled through a web browser, this icon will always take you there. Go ahead and configure the server for the first time with the defaults in place. You may need to make some adjustment based on your own network settings or personal preferences. Figures 3-31, 3-32, and 3-33 show various settings being changed in the Setup Assistant.

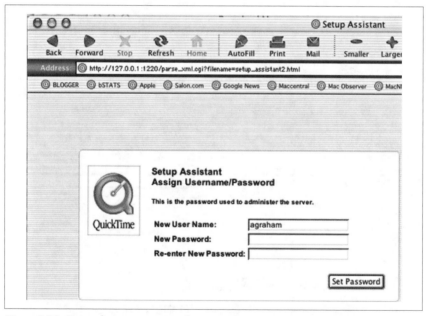

Figure 3-31. Your admin username and password

The QTSS requires that you use one folder as the main source of your media. Most people use iTunes and the music is located in the *Music* folder. You may wish to change the default location, because moving all your media (as shown in Figure 3-34) isn't practical. The path to your iTunes folder should resemble this: */Users/yourusername/Music/iTunes/iTunes Music*. Figure 3-35 shows a setting that could interfere with Apache or other web servers running on your machine.

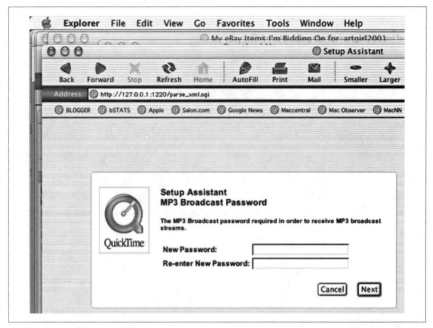

Figure 3-32. Setting an administrator password

Figure 3-33. For most people, a SSL connection won't be necessary

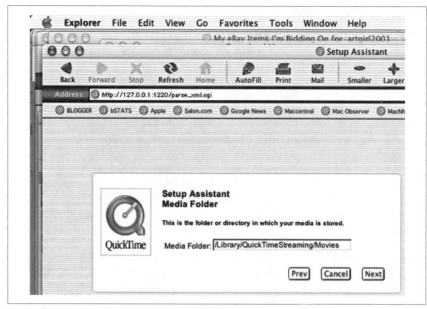

Figure 3-34. The location of your music files

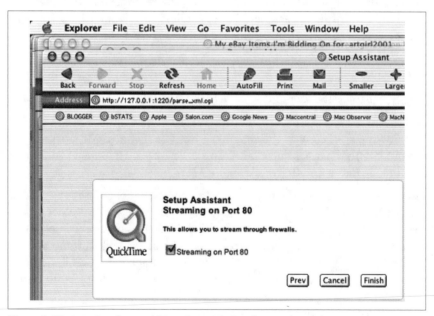

Figure 3-35. A setting that could interfere with Apache or other web servers running on your machine

Step 3: Create a Promotional Spot

Depending on the level of professional spit and polish you want on your station, you may want to put together a promo spot to let people know who you are. There is a really simple way to pull this off using some royalty-free iMovie music, a microphone, and iMovie.

You can use some of the free music Apple provides in your iDisk, but of course you must have a .Mac subscription for that. If you don't belong to .Mac, all you really need is a short piece of music in MP3 format, or you can skip the music portion of your spot completely.

Open iMovie and import your music clip, then head over to the Audio tab of iMovie (shown in Figure 3-36) and record the vocals of your promo spot. Since I don't have any call letters, I settled for, "You're listening to O'Reilly Radio."

Drag the music clip into one of the music tracks down below. Your vocal spot should already be waiting for you. Then just move the two tracks so that they fit together in a manner that sounds good to you (see Figure 3-37).

Once you're done editing your audio track, export the movie as Quick-Time. We need to make some changes to our file as we export it. When you choose to export the file as QuickTime, you'll get an option to alter the format. Select the Expert setting in this menu (see Figure 3-38).

Now click Prepare for Internet → Quicktime Streaming Server (see Figure 3-39).

Finally, change the compression settings to MPEG-4 and export (see Figure 3-40).

You now need to convert the movie file from MPEG-4 to MP3 before you can use it with the other music files. This is very easy. First open iTunes and drag the file into your library (see Figure 3-41).

The next step is to edit the promo spot song information, so that when you convert this file to MP3, it will automatically create a promo folder where we can collect future files. Simply highlight the file and select File → Get Info. At the top of the window, type a title for this spot, like Promo Spot 1. Under Artist, type something like My Promotional Spots. In the Album field, name it Promo Spots, and now you have a folder in which to place all future promo files.

To convert the file to MP3, highlight it and select Advanced → Convert Selection to MP3. Now you can delete the old file from the library and move on to getting your station up and running.

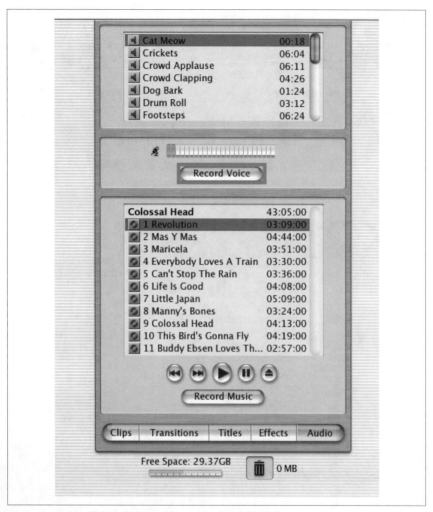

Figure 3-36. You'll find the record button in the Audio tab

Step 4: QTSS General Settings

Open the server and jump on over to General Settings. Here we want to double-check that our media directory matches our *iTunes* folder. You can set your maximum number of connections and your maximum throughput. Remember to calculate your required bandwidth. When your traffic exceeds the maximum throughput, the server will not allow any more connections. If you want to run the server 24/7, check "Start Server at System Startup," as shown in Figure 3-42.

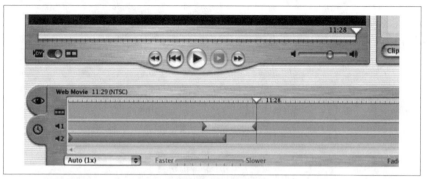

Figure 3-37. Fitting the audio tracks together

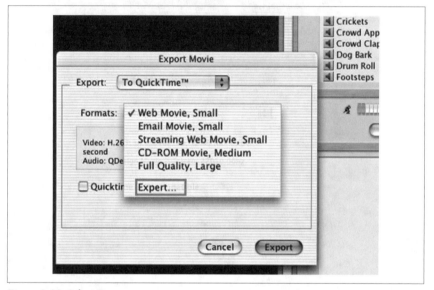

Figure 3-38. Select Expert

Step 5: Build a Playlist

You can create playlists using most text editors, but most people will find it easier to create a playlist through the server's web interface. Our main QTSS screen looks like Figure 3-42.

Jump to the Playlists link to the left. At the Playlists screen, click on the button to create a new MP3 playlist, as shown in Figure 3-43.

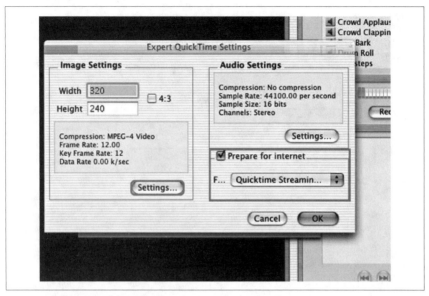

Figure 3-39. Prepare for Internet…

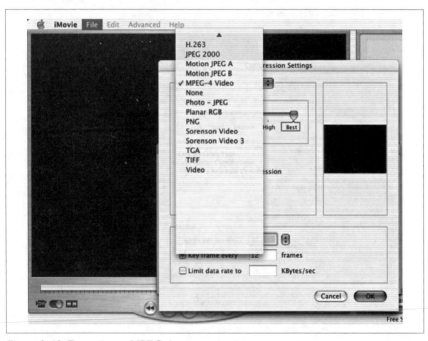

Figure 3-40. Exporting as MPEG-4

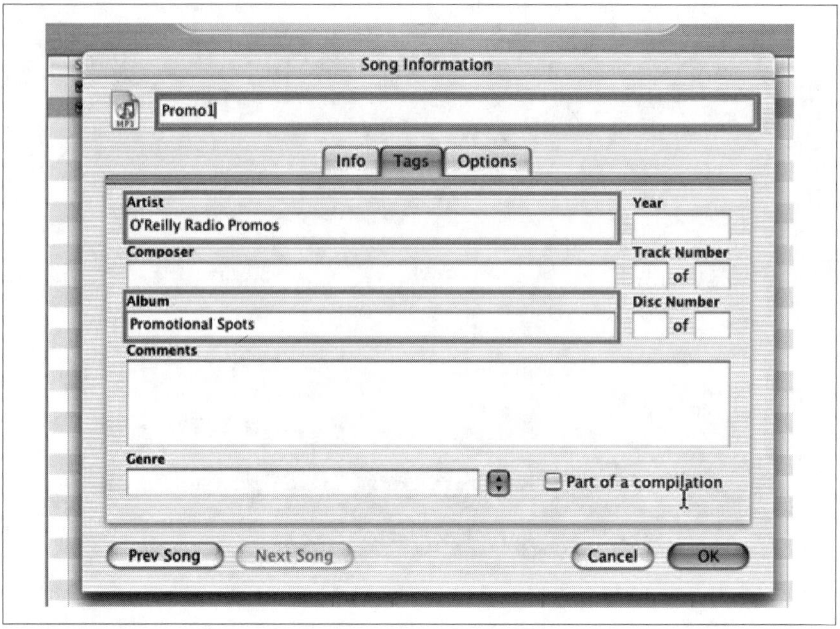

Figure 3-41. Time to edit the promo song information

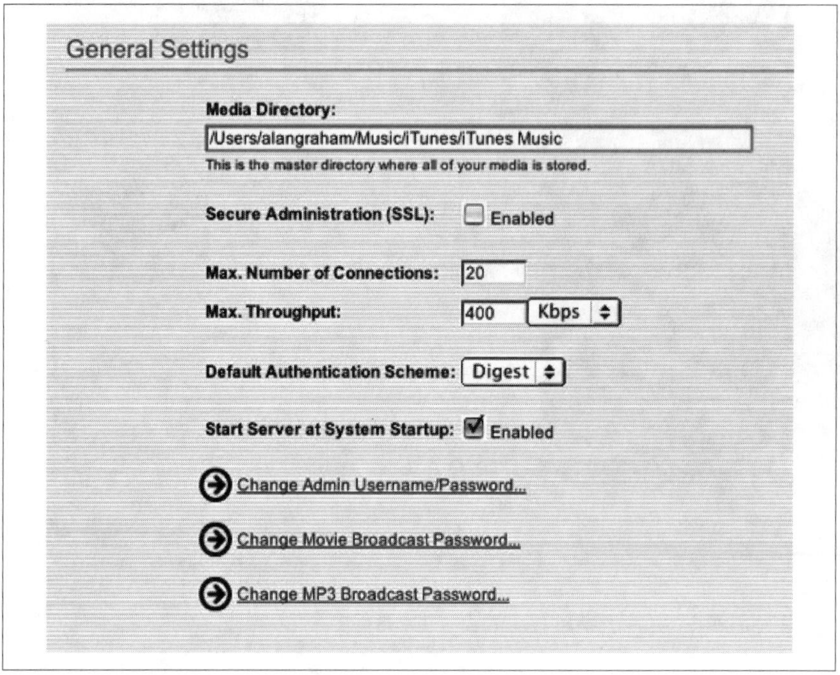

Figure 3-42. QTSS General Settings

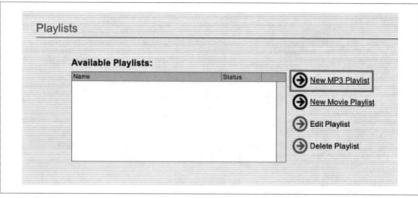

Figure 3-43. Playlist

Creating the actual playlist (see Figure 3-44) is quite simple, although there are a few quirks:

Name

Enter the name of your station: whatever name you enter here will be displayed in the client's music player.

Mount Point

Part of the URL location that your users will use to tune into your station. By entering different mount points for different playlists, you could run more than one active playlist for different genres and listeners could listen to different types of music.

Genre

Simply the genre of the music.

Play Mode

The order in which to play the media. You can specify the following options:

Sequential

Plays the media in the order they appear in the playlist. When the last file is done playing, the broadcast stops.

Sequential Looped

Streams media in the order it appears in the playlist file. When the last file is done, the playlist restarts in the same order.

Weighted Random

Streams media in random, using the specified weights to decide how often to play an item. The higher the weight number, the more the item is played. The media plays until you stop it.

Repetition

Sets the number of files that play before a file repeats.

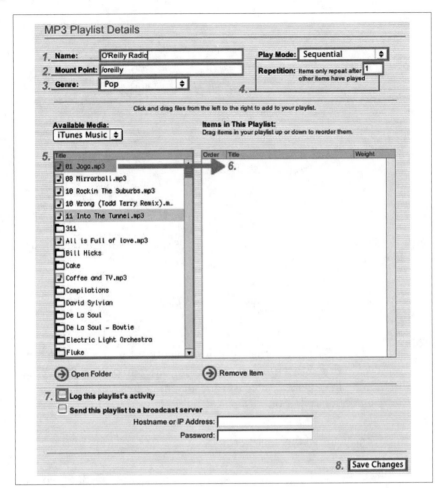

Figure 3-44. Creating the playlist

Available Media

Select the tracks you want to appear in your playlist and drag them over to the Playlist column (labeled "6." in Figure 3-44) to the right. You can Shift-click items, but unfortunately you cannot ⌘-click them. You can enter any folder in the media list by double-clicking. Also in this listing you will find the folder with your promo spots in it. After creating your playlist, drag and drop your promo spots wherever you wish for it to play.

Log this playlist's activity

Select if you want to keep a log of this playlists activity.

Save Changes

Save your settings and we're almost ready to tune in.

Step 6: Finish Up

You have a few small items to finish up before you are ready to go. First, go back to the main Playlists menu using the link to the left. Now, make sure that your QTSS is running by clicking the Start button in the upper-lefthand corner (see Figure 3-45).

Stop Server
Server is Running

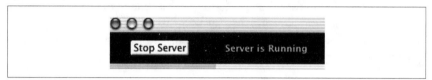

Figure 3-45. The QTSS server is running

Next, you need to start the playlist. Click on the Play button in the Playlist window (see Figures 3-46 and 3-47).

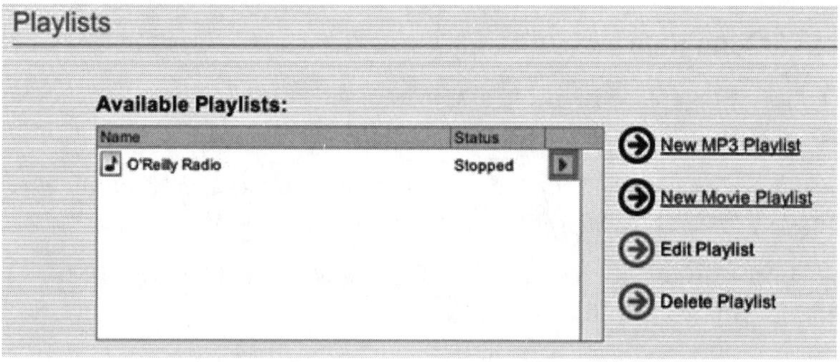
Playlists
Available Playlists:
Name
Status
O'Reilly Radio
Stopped
New MP3 Playlist
New Movie Playlist
Edit Playlist
Delete Playlist

Figure 3-46. Just press the button…

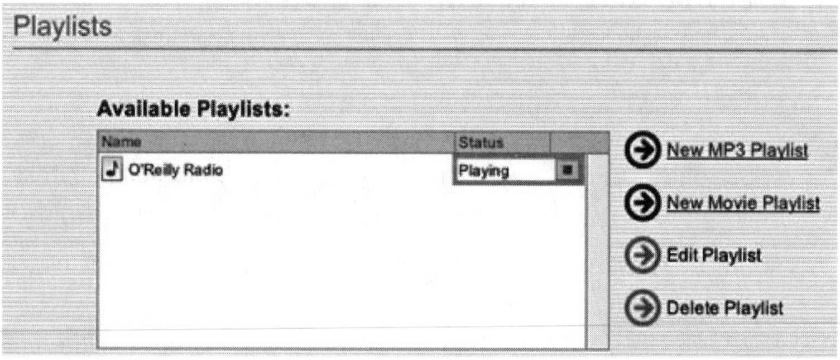
Playlists
Available Playlists:
Name
Status
O'Reilly Radio
Playing
New MP3 Playlist
New Movie Playlist
Edit Playlist
Delete Playlist

Figure 3-47. Notice the change in status…

Step 7: Tune In

We've installed our server, created our promos, configured our server, built our playlists, and started our server. Now it is time to test our station by tuning in.

Open up iTunes and select Advanced → Open Stream (⌘-U). Enter your IP address or URL followed by the port number and finally the mount point. It should look something like 192.168.2.9:8000/oreilly (where the IP address or URL is your own). If everything goes well, you should hear some tunes blasting from your speakers.

Step 8: Administer Remotely

One handy feature of the QTSS is remote administration. You can make changes to the server or your playlist regardless of your location. Access the server by typing your IP address or URL and specifying port 1220.

Step 9: Getting Help

Apple has an extensive help file associated with QTSS. You can access it via the server's interface, but you can also find it here:

> *http://helpqt.apple.com/qtssWebAdminHelpR4/qtssWebAdmin.help/*
> *English.lproj/QTSSHelp.htm*

There are tons of exciting things you can do with the QTSS and Mac OS X. Streaming can be a complicated task, but hopefully this will get you started.

—Alan Graham

HACK #27 Sharing Your Listening Preferences

iTunes and a little hackery make sharing your currently playing track a snap.

Listening to music while you work is a given for a large portion of the computing populace. Without music, the halls and cubicles seem a little lonelier, the days seem a little slower, and eating is more lifeless than usual. Music is a part of our computing lives, and being without it can be traumatizing.

Just as we enjoy listening, we also lust after more music to whet our auditory ensembles. Hearing an unknown artist, falling in love, and then orchestrating a search for MP3s or used CDs is a part of many of our lives as well. Suggestions from friends is a crucial part of our discovery process.

With iTunes, telling people what you listen to is easier than you think. Utilities like the donationware Kung-Tunes (*http://www.kung-foo.tv/itti.html*)

publish information on your currently playing iTunes track on your web site, allowing the world to tune in to your musical enjoyment. Alternatively, use the freeware Moa Tunes (*http://beam.to/woodenbrain*) to alter the signature of your Entourage or Eudora email messages with the music that accompanied your response. Even Inter-Relay Chat (IRC) programs are getting into the act, as the shareware Snak (*http://www.snak.com/*) provides a MusicalOSX script that will display tracks in IRC channels.

If that's not enough, and you want iTunes integration with every instrument you use daily, check out the following piece of AppleScript, which will put the currently playing song, artist, and album into the clipboard. Simply run, paste, and seduce!

```
tell application "iTunes"
    set iname to name of current track
    set iartist to artist of current track
    set ialbum to album of current track
end tell

tell application "Finder"
    set music to "\"" & iname & "\" by " & iartist & " on the album \"" ⏎
    & ialbum & "\"."
    set the clipboard to the music
end tell
```

Figure 3-48 shows the result of running this script.

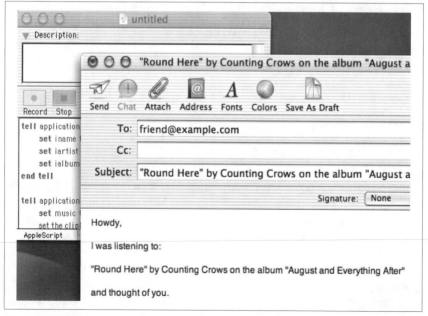

Figure 3-48. Passing on your listening preferences

If you're not an AppleScript roadie, you could use a bit of Perl to *ftp* the last 10 songs you've heard to your web site. The following code uses the MacOSX::iTunes (*http://sourceforge.net/projects/brian-d-foy*) module:

```perl
#!/usr/bin/perl -w
use strict;
use Mac::iTunes;
use Net::FTP;

# rather self-explanatory settings
my $itunes_library = "/Users/morbus/Music/iTunes/iTunes 3 Music Library";
my $itunes_playlist = "Recently Played";
my $ftp_host = "ftp.disobey.com";
my $ftp_username = "anonymous";
my $ftp_password = "morbus\@disobey.com";
my $ftp_path = "/incoming";
my $ftp_file = "itunes.html";

# data collector
open(FILE, ">$ftp_file") or die "couldn't create temp file: $!";
print FILE "<html><title>iTunes, $itunes_playlist</title>";
print FILE "<body><h1>iTunes, $itunes_playlist</h1><ul>";

# our library object
my $itunes = MacOSX::iTunes->read ( $itunes_library );
die "could not load the iTunes library" unless ref $itunes;

# and our playlist. We loop through tracks, adding to output.
my $playlist = $itunes->get_playlist( $itunes_playlist );
foreach my $track ( $playlist->items ) {
  print FILE "<li>", $track->as_string, "</li>";
}
print FILE '</ul></body></html>'; close FILE;

# and now send to our FTP site.
my $conn = Net::FTP->new($ftp_host) or die "could not connect to host: $!";
$ftp->login($ftp_username, $ftp_password);
$ftp->mkdir($ftp_path, 1);
$ftp->cwd($ftp_path);
$ftp->put($ftp_file) or die "could not upload file: $!";
$ftp->quit;
```

iTunes has struck a chord with many music lovers, and these hacks can help others get in on your groove. (Yes, we know. There were far too many musical innuendos in this hack for it to be considered good taste. Blame the composer, not the maestro.)

Controlling iTunes with Perl

The Mac::iTunes module means that controlling iTunes from across the room or across the world is only a Perl script away.

I created the Mac::iTunes Perl module to control iTunes from my scripts and from other machines. Everything that I present in this hack comes with either the Mac::iTunes or Apache::iTunes distribution (*http://search.cpan. org/author/BDFOY/*), available on the Comprehensive Perl Archive Network (CPAN).

Once I have a back end, I can create almost any interface to iTunes that I like—and I do.

iTunes Is AppleScriptable

Apple's MP3 player, iTunes (*http://www.apple.com/itunes/*), has been Apple-Script-aware since Version 2 (the latest version is 3.0.1). This gives me a lot of freedom to control how I use iTunes.

I can use Script Editor to create a script, but I can also use the osascript command-line tool from a Terminal window. I can use the -e switch to run a short script on the command line:

```
% osascript -e 'tell application "iTunes" activate'
```

Or, I can store the script in a file and pass it to the osascript on the command line:

```
-- iTunes script "quit_itunes"
-- run as "osascript quit_itunes"
tell application "iTunes"
quit
end tell
% osascript quit_itunes
```

Once I liberate myself from Script Editor, I have more flexibility.

Scripts for iTunes can automate a lot of my common tasks. Apple has a collection of scripts (*http://www.apple.com/AppleScript/itunes/*), and Doug's AppleScripts for iTunes & SoundJam (*http://www.malcolmadams.com/ itunes/scrxcont.shtml*) has several more good ones.

iTunes and Perl

Although I like AppleScript for very simple things, I think it gets tedious for complicated scripts. The language is verbose and does not have a good extension mechanism. Perl, on the other hand, does, but at the moment it does not have good access to Aqua applications, even though it can control the usual Unix applications in Mac OS X, just as it can on other Unix platforms.

When I started to work with iTunes AppleScripts, I wanted it to be as easy to do as writing Perl scripts, even though it was not. After a while, I decided to fix that by writing a Perl module to handle the AppleScript portions of iTunes. I already had a MacOSX::iTunes Perl module that I used to parse the binary format of the *iTunes Music Library* file. I needed to add AppleScript support to it.

On the suggestion of Chris Nandor, the caretaker of MacPerl and author of Mac::Carbon, I changed the name of my distribution to Mac::iTunes and added the Mac::iTunes::AppleScript module, which wrapped common AppleScripts in Perl functions. The meat of the module was the _osascript routine, which creates an AppleScript string and calls osascript just as I did earlier:

```perl
sub _osascript
{
  my $script = shift;

  require IPC::Open2;

  my( $read, $write );
  my $pid = IPC::Open2::open2( $read, $write, 'osascript' );

  print $write qq(tell application "iTunes"\n), $script, qq(\nend tell\n);
  close $write;

  my $data = do { local $/; <$read> };

  return $data;
}
```

The Mac::iTunes::AppleScript works much like the osascript command-line tool. Indeed, the first version simply created a script string (called osascript), and captured the output, if any, for parsing. About the same time I finished the first version, Nathan Torkington needed Perl access to AppleScript and convinced Dan Sugalski to write Mac::AppleScript. With that module, Perl could work with AppleScript without calling an external program. I replaced the _osascript routine with tell(), which uses the RunAppleScript function from Mac::AppleScript:

```perl
sub tell
{
  my $self = shift;
  my $command = shift;

  my $script = qq(tell application "iTunes"\n$command\nend tell);
```

```
my $result = RunAppleScript( $script );

if( $@ )
{
  carp $@;
  return;
}

return 1 if( defined $result and $result eq '' );

$result =~ s/^"|"$//g;

return $result;
}
```

Once I have tell( ), I simply feed it an AppleScript string, which it runs and then returns the result. For example, iTunes can play Internet streams. The AppleScript way to say this uses open location:

```
tell application "iTunes"
  open location "http://www.example.com/streaming.mp3"
end tell
```

In Mac::iTunes::AppleScript, I wrapped this little script in a method, named open_url( ), which takes a URL as an argument and uses tell( ) to run it:

```
sub open_url
{
  my $self = shift;
  my $url = shift;

  $self->tell( qq|open location "$url"| );
}
```

Most of the AppleScript commands for iTunes have a corresponding method in Mac::iTunes::AppleScript. Now I can use the full power of Perl, even though I am really using AppleScript behind the scenes.

iTunes, Perl, and Terminal

Just as I ran AppleScripts from the Terminal window with osascript, I can now run Perl programs that interact with iTunes. I want to play streaming media with very few keystrokes and without going to the iTunes Open Streaming… menu item; it's just too much work when I do not want to switch applications. I created a simple program, named stream, using Mac::iTunes. I create an iTunes controller object, then call the open_url( ) method with the first command-line argument. Perl tells iTunes to play the MP3 stream, and even though iTunes starts to do something, it stays in the background while I continue whatever I am doing. I can even use this program from shell scripts.

```
#!/usr/bin/perl
use Mac::iTunes;
my $controller = Mac::iTunes->controller;
$controller->open_url( $ARGV[0] );
% stream http://www.example.com/streaming.mp3
```

Small scripts do not have much of an advantage over the equivalent Apple-Scripts, but as things get more complex, Perl starts to shine.

iTunes, Perl, and Apache

I have been using Apple's AirPort for a while. We swear by it in my household, and my guests like to bring their laptops and wireless cards when they visit. The AirPort has raised our computer expectations; we want to be able to do any task from anywhere in the house. However, when it comes to playing music, we have a problem. Which computer is hooked up to the stereo? I do not like listening to music on the built-in speakers of my laptop, so I have another Mac hooked up to my stereo and a very large external hard drive filled with MP3s.

With all of that, I cannot carry that computer around my apartment. Even if I could, I want it to just play music and perhaps perform other silent tasks. I should not have to interrupt my music because I decide to change something on the Mac I am working on. I want the music to keep playing even if I restart the iTunes on my laptop, which I do frequently while developing Mac::iTunes.

I need to control this central MP3 player remotely. I could create a command-line tool to control iTunes and then log in the machine with ssh, but not everyone who wants to control iTunes likes using the Terminal. I need a more pleasing interface. Since Mac OS X comes with the Apache web server (which runs by default), I can write a CGI script to control iTunes:

```
#!/usr/bin/perl
use strict;

use CGI qw(:standard);
use Mac::iTunes;
use Text::Template;

my $Template = '/Users/brian/Dev/MacOSX/iTunes/html/iTunes.html';

=head1 NAME

iTunes.cgi - control iTunes from the web

=head1 SYNOPSIS

=head1 DESCRIPTION
```

This is only a proof-of-concept script.

=head1 AUTHOR

brian d foy, E<bdfoy@cpan.org>

=head1 COPYRIGHT

Copyright 2002 brian d foy, All rights reserved

=cut

```perl
my $controller = Mac::iTunes->new( )->controller;

my $command = param('command');
my $playlist = param('playlist') || 'Library';
my $set_playlist = param('set_playlist');

if( $command )
{
  my %Commands = map { $_, 1 } qw( play stop pause back_track);
  $controller->$command if exists $Commands{$command};
}
elsif( $set_playlist )
{
  $controller->_set_playlist( $set_playlist );
  $playlist = $set_playlist;
}

my %var;

$var{base} = 'http://10.0.1.2:8080/cgi-bin/iTunes.cgi';
$var{state} = $controller->player_state;
$var{current} = $controller->current_track_name;
$var{playlist} = $playlist;
$var{playlists} = $controller->get_playlists;
$var{tracks} = $controller->get_track_names_in_playlist( $playlist );

my $html = Text::Template::fill_in_file( $Template, HASH => \%var );

print header( ), $html, "\n";
```

On the first run without input, the script creates an iTunes controller object, sets the starting playlist to Library (the iTunes virtual playlist that has everything iTunes knows about), then asks iTunes for a lot of state information, including the names of tracks in the playlists, the names of the playlists, and what iTunes is currently doing (e.g., playing or stopped). The script uses Text::Template to turn all of this into HTML, which it sends back to a web browser. The template file I use is in the *html* directory of the Mac::iTunes distribution, and those with any sort of design skills will surely want to change it to something more pleasing. The code is separated from the presentation. Figure 3-49 shows the iTunes Web Interface.

Figure 3-49. iTunes Web Interface

I have a small problem with this approach. To tell an application to do something through AppleScript, the telling program has to be running as a logged-in user. The web server is set up to run as the unprivileged pseudouser nobody, so this CGI script will not work from the stock Apache configuration. This is not much of a problem, since I can make Apache run under my user. On my machine, I run a second Apache server with the same configuration file, except for a couple of changes.

First, I have to make the web server run as my user, so I change the User directive. Along with that, I have to choose another port, since only the root user can use port numbers below 1024, and Apache expects to use port 80. I choose port 8080 instead. I will have to pass this nonstandard port along in any URLs, but my CGI script already does that. As long as I use the web interface without typing into the web browser's location box, I will not have to worry about that.

```
User brian
Port 8080
```

I also have to change any file paths that Apache expects to write to. Since Apache runs as my user, it can create files only where I can create files.

```
PidFile "/Users/brian/httpd-brian.pid"
```

Once everything is set up, I access the CGI script from any computer in my home network, Mac or not, and I can control my central iTunes.

iTunes, Perl, Apache, and mod_perl

CGI scripts are slow. Every time I run a CGI script, the web server has to launch the script and the script has to load all of the modules that it needs to do its work. I have another problem with Mac::iTunes, though. The first call to Mac::AppleScript's RunAppleScript() seems to be slower than subsequent calls. I pay a first-use penalty for that. To get around that, I want to keep my iTunes controller running so I do not have to pay this overhead over and over again.

I created Apache::iTunes to do just that. I could run my CGI script under Apache::Registry, but I like the native Apache interface better. I configured my web server to hand off any requests of a URL starting with *iTunes* to my module. I use PerlSetEnv directives to configure the literal data I had in the CGI version.

```
<Location /iTunes>
SetHandler perl-script
PerlHandler Apache::iTunes
PerlModule Mac::iTunes
PerlInitHandler Apache::StatINC
PerlSetEnv APACHE_ITUNES_HTML /web/templates/iTunes.html
PerlSetEnv APACHE_ITUNES_URL http://www.example.com:8080/iTunes
PerlSetEnv APACHE_ITUNES 1
</Location>
```

The output, shown in Figure 3-50, looks a little different from the CGI version because I used a different template that included more features. I can change the look-and-feel without touching the code.

I tend to like the mod_perl interface more. Instead of passing variables around in the query string, the URL itself is the command and is simple, short, and without funny-looking characters:

```
http://www.example.com/iTunes/play
http://www.example.com/iTunes/stop
```

Figure 3-50. Apache::iTunes interface

iTunes, Perl, and Tk

As I was working on Apache::iTunes, I was also working on a different project that needed the Tk (*http://www.lns.cornell.edu/~pvhp/ptk/ptkFAQ. html*) widget toolkit. I was programming things on FreeBSD, but I like to work on my Mac. That's easy enough, since I have XonX (that's the combination of XDarwin (*http://www.xdarwin.org*) and OrobosX (*http://oroborosx. sourceforge.net/*)) installed. Under Mac OS X 10.2 these work without a problem, although if you use 10.1 you have to perform a little bit of surgery on your system, following Steve Lidie's instructions (*http://www.lehigh.edu/ ~sol0/Macintosh/X/ptk/*). Since I had been away from the Tk world for awhile, I was referring to O'Reilly's *Mastering Perl/Tk* quite a bit. As I was flipping through the pages on my way to the next thing I needed to read, I noticed a screenshot of iTunes. It was not really iTunes though—Steve Lidie had taken the iTunes look-and-feel as a front end for his MP3 player example.

I already had all of the back-end stuff to control iTunes and none of it was tied to a particular interface. Even my CGI script could output something other than HTML, like plain text or even a huge image. I could easily add a Tk interface to the same thing—or so I thought.

Controlling iTunes is easy. Controlling it from a web page is easy. Controlling it from Tk, which has a persistent connection to whatever it hooks up to, was harder. Since I had the persistent connection, I could reflect changes in iTunes instantaneously. In the web versions, if somebody else changed the state, like changing the song or muting the volume, the web page would not show that until I reloaded. The Tk interface (shown in Figure 3-51) could show it almost instantaneously. In reality, I could get the Tk interface to poll iTunes for its state only every three and a half seconds or so before it took a big drop in performance, but that is good enough for me.

Figure 3-51. Tk iTunes interface

The *tk-itunes.pl* script comes with Mac::iTunes. Someday I might develop a skins mechanism for it; all I, or somebody else, need to do is make the colors configurable. The script already uses a configuration file, although I can configure only a few things at the moment.

Final Thoughts

Perl can interact with Aqua applications through AppleScript. With Mac::iTunes as a back end, I can create multiple interfaces to iTunes that I can use on the same computer or on other computers on the same network. Everyone in my house, or within range of my AirPort, can control my iTunes.

—*brian d foy*

iCal Calling iTunes

Wouldn't it be nice to choose tracks from iCal, reminding yourself to exercise with the inspiring theme from Flashdance?

You give people an inch, they'll want to take a mile. In this corner, Apple's iTunes, MP3 player supreme with smart playlists, XML exports, ratings, play count, ID3 support, and more. And in the other, Apple's iCal with alerts, multiple calendar coloring, web-based subscriptions, to-do lists, and drill-down views. Both free, powerful, and useful. Are people happy with the birds on their doorsteps? "Not without integration," they sing, and integration comes in the form of a free AppleScript from Doug Adams.

There's no installation; just stick the application any place you'd like (as is typical of most AppleScripts). With proper configuration, iCal Calling iTunes can trigger the start of any iTunes playlist, shuffle that playlist, or likewise stop that playlist at any date or time.

Configuration is simple. First, create a new calendar called iTunes. It's here that you'll configure all your sound events (you can configure other events, but as we'll see, their status will be marked as Tentative). To integrate iCal with iTunes, define an event named after one of your iTunes playlists, and configure the dates as you would normally. After that, simply double-click the iCal Calling iTunes AppleScript, and it'll resolutely play tracks from the matching play list when the event triggers.

To stop a playlist, set the To date of the event for when you want the litany to halt, and change the status to Confirmed. Other status changes also exist: if the iTunes playlist could not be found, the event's status will change to Tentative, and skipping events is as easy as changing the status to Cancelled. Shuffling playlists can be accomplished by appending an asterisk to the event name.

The possibilities of this integration are widespread: configure a day's worth of music, starting with slow-tempo progressive, speeding up to DJs in the afternoon, overtaking with digital hard-core in the evening, and then easing into mindlessness with nighttime trance. Or trigger a playlist of romantic songs on your anniversary, a pinch to grow an inch on your birthday, and a wee bit o' shamrockery on St. Patrick's Day.

See Also

- Doug's AppleScripts (*http://www.malcolmadams.com/itunes/*)

Publishing and Subscribing to iCal Calendars

Publish your own iCal calendars on .Mac or any WebDAV-enabled web server for subscription.

iCal, Apple's calendaring application for Mac OS X, is already being used by hundreds of people who are publishing their own calendars for subscription. Apple's site has a bunch of calendars for obvious things like sporting events, television season premieres, and state and religious holidays. iCalShare (*http://www.icalshare.com*) has even more.

Publishing

Publishing a calendar to a WebDAV server [Hack #95] is just about as simple as publishing to .Mac, since the latter, in fact, uses WebDAV. Choose the calendar you wish to publish in the top-left iCal pane and select Calendar → Publish... In the Publish Calendar dialog box (shown in Figure 3-52), select "Publish on a web server" rather than "Publish on .Mac"; the box will expand to accomodate three new fields: URL, Login, and Password. You'll need to fill in the appropriate location and authentication information specific to your WebDAV [Hack #95] setup. In the URL box, be sure to put only the path where the calendar should be kept on the WebDAV server; iCal will fill in a filename for you (e.g., *Home.ics* for a calendar called Home). If you'd like to have your published calendar updated live each time you make an alteration to the local copy, be sure to check the "Publish changes automatically" box. When you're ready, click the Publish button and away your calendar goes.

> The path on your WebDAV-enabled web server will differ. I've used a path and account created in "Turning on Web-DAV" [Hack #95].

If you decide not to enable autoupdating, you can always manually push the latest using Calendar → Update. And if you decide to take the calendar down after an event has passed or the local theater season is over, simply select Calendar → Unpublish.

Subscribing

You subscribe in the same way to a published calendar, whether it was published to .Mac, pushed to a WebDAV server, or exported to an *.ics* file made available on a web server.

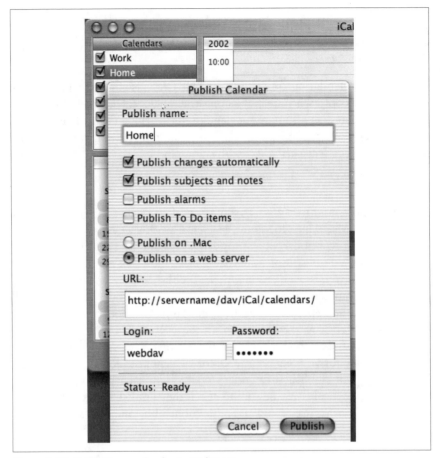

Figure 3-52. Publishing a calendar to WebDAV

Select Calendar → Subscribe… to bring up the Subscribe to Calendar dialog box. Type or paste the published calendar's URL, including the filename (ending in *.ics*). If you believe the calendar will be updated regularly, check Refresh and select an appropriate frequency at which iCal should revisit the calendar and grab the latest. It's up to you whether or not you want to remove alarms and to-do items from the published calendar; simply click the associated checkbox to check or uncheck it.

If the calendar has restricted access, click the disclosure triangle next to "Advanced options", check the "Needs authentication" checkbox, and fill in an authorized login and password. The screenshot in Figure 3-53 shows authenticated access to a password-protected calendar in action.

Click the Subscribe button and you should see the calendar slot itself nicely into your own iCal view of the world.

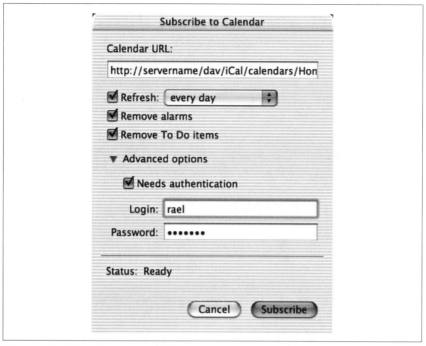

Figure 3-53. Subscribing to a calendar

You can make subscription easier on your audience by providing a link directly to the *.ics* file, available via email or on
your web site, allowing them to simply click on a link to
launch iCal and subscribe.

—*Erik T. Ray*

H A C K
#31

Using Bluetooth for SMS and Phone-Call Handling

With Bluetooth-enabled cell phones and Mac OS X's Bluetooth support, you
can send and receive SMS messages and handle cellphone calls right from
your keyboard.

Apple is popularizing Bluetooth (*http://www.apple.com/bluetooth/*) much as
it did USB, 802.11b, and FireWire technologies.

Although Apple has done a good job supporting Bluetooth technology—
and, indeed, baking it right in—not much has been done to educate users
about what it can do. Recently, I was pleasantly surprised to see that the

nifty little Address Book in Mac OS X has built-in Bluetooth functionality that allows you to send and receive Short Message Service (SMS) messages through your Bluetooth-enabled phone, all via your computer!

If you've ever hammered out an SMS note using the buttons on your tiny cell phone, then you know it would be much easier to use your full-sized computer keyboard instead. In this hack, I will show you how to use Mac OS X to send SMS messages easily.

You will need a Bluetooth adapter, such as the D-Link USB Bluetooth Adapter (available at *http://store.apple.com/1-800-MY-APPLE/WebObjects/ AppleStore?productLearnMore=T4728G/B*), for your Mac, and a Bluetooth-enabled phone, such as the Ericsson T68i (*http://www.ericsson.com/ mobilityworld/sub/open/devices/t68i/index.html*).

Pairing Up Your Phone with Address Book

With your Address Book powered up, the first thing to do is to pair it up with your Bluetooth-enabled mobile phone. To do so, you need to turn on the Bluetooth radio on your phone, and then click on the Bluetooth icon on the Address Book (see Figure 3-54).

Figure 3-54. The Bluetooth icon connects to your Bluetooth-enabled phone

If the pairing is successful, you should see the icon in blue; otherwise, it will appear grayed out.

Sending SMS Messages

With the pairing done, you are now ready to send an SMS message! To send someone in your Address Book an SMS message, select the name and click on the phone number of the user. Three options will be displayed, as shown in Figure 3-55.

You can display the number in huge fonts, send the person an SMS message, or make a call to him. If you select SMS Message, you can key in the message (maximum of 160 characters) and click Send (see Figure 3-56). Tired fingers are now a thing of the past!

Figure 3-55. Sending an SMS message using Address Book

Figure 3-56. Typing an SMS message on the Mac

Receiving SMS Messages

Besides sending SMS messages, your Address Book will also inform you of incoming SMS messages, as shown in Figure 3-57.

When an incoming message is received, Address Book will prompt a window displaying the message. You can save the message to the Address Book (more on this later) or reply to the message. Address Book will automatically match the number of the caller (supplied by your mobile phone, which requires caller ID service) with its name list and display the person's name.

To reply to the message, simply click the Reply button. You can now reply to a SMS message directly on the Mac, as shown in Figure 3-58.

Figure 3-57. Receiving an incoming SMS message on your Mac

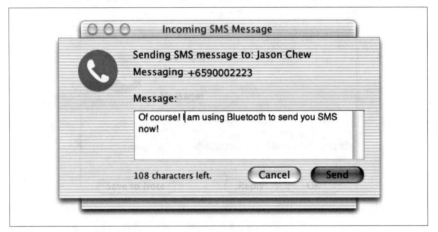

Figure 3-58. Replying to a SMS message from the Mac

Handling Incoming Calls

When your phone rings, Address Book will notify you and provide three options (as shown in Figure 3-59): reply to the caller via SMS, activate voice mail on the mobile phone (the phone will then stop ringing), or simply answer the call.

If you click SMS Reply, you can then send an SMS message to the caller, perhaps to inform him that you will call him later.

Figure 3-59. Incoming call displayed on the Mac

Saving Incoming Messages

When you receive an incoming message, you can save it to your Address Book for archiving. Clicking on the Save to Note button in the Incoming SMS Message window will append the message to the contact information, as shown in Figure 3-60.

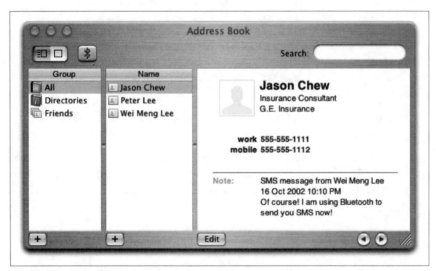

Figure 3-60. SMS messages can be archived in Address Book

—Wei-Meng Lee

iSync via Bluetooth

Bluetooth means never having to plug in a cable when synchronizing your phone or PDA with your Mac.

Apple's iSync, the synchronization software based on the SyncML protocol (*http://www.syncml.org/*), synchronizes the contact and calendar information on your mobile devices with your Macintosh. In addition, if you have more than one Mac, it will also help to synchronize the information in your Address Book and iCal calendars (.Mac (*http://www.mac.com/*) membership is required).

The mobile devices supported by iSync include the latest GPRS, Bluetooth-enabled (*http://www.apple.com/bluetooth/*) phones (such as the popular Ericsson T68 and the Sony Ericsson T68i) and Palm OS devices (such as the Palm m515). iSync even synchronizes the information on your iPod with your Mac.

To download iSync, go to *http://www.apple.com/isync/*. The download is about 7MB. You need to have the latest Mac OS X 10.2 Jaguar running.

Installing iSync

Installing iSync is a snap, provided you already have iCal installed. iCal is required for iSync to work. You can download a free copy of iCal from *http://www.apple.com/iCal/*.

iSync contains two packages: iSync and iSync_Palm. The latter is required for synchronization with Palm devices.

For this hack, I have tried iSync using my Ericsson T68 and my Palm m515. I will walk you through the steps to get the devices connected as well as to set up Bluetooth on your Mac so that the synchronization can be done wirelessly.

Adding the T68 Using Bluetooth

For Bluetooth connectivity on my Mac, I used the Billionton USB Bluetooth adapter. Another popular adapter is the D-Link.

With built-in Bluetooth or a plugged-in USB Bluetooth adapter, you should see a Bluetooth icon in your System Preferences window, as shown in Figure 3-61.

Clicking on the Bluetooth icon reveals the four tabs for configuring Bluetooth access. As I wanted to establish a connection between my Mac and my Ericsson T68, I went to the Paired Devices tab (see Figure 3-62) and clicked on New....

Figure 3-61. Bluetooth icon in System Preferences

Figure 3-62. Paired Devices tab

You also need to turn on the Bluetooth radio on your phone and set it to be Bluetooth Discoverable. This allows your phone to be seen in the Bluetooth ether; an undiscoverable phone is an invisible phone.

Once your Mac finds the phone, click Pair to establish a relationship between the phone and the Mac (see Figure 3-63). Each side of the pairing needs to be sure that the other is authorized to pair. This is accomplished by a throwaway passkey (read: one-time password). Anything will do, even 1234. You should be prompted by both your Mac and your phone to enter the same passkey. If all goes to plan, the devices should be paired and handle all further authentication and so forth without needing anything more from you.

Once the devices are paired, you will be prompted with another screen, allowing you to choose the services that you can use with this phone (see Figure 3-64).

Figure 3-63. Pairing a newly detected device

Figure 3-64. Choosing the services to use with the phone

Once this step is completed, you should be able to see your T68 icon in the iSync window (see Figure 3-65). To start syncing, simply click on the Sync button, shown in Figure 3-66. To customize synchronization, click the phone icon and select the relevant syncing options (see Figure 3-67).

iSync will synchronize the Contacts and Calendars information on the T68 with the Address Book and iCal on your Mac, respectively.

Figure 3-65. The phone appears in the iSync window

Figure 3-66. The Sync button

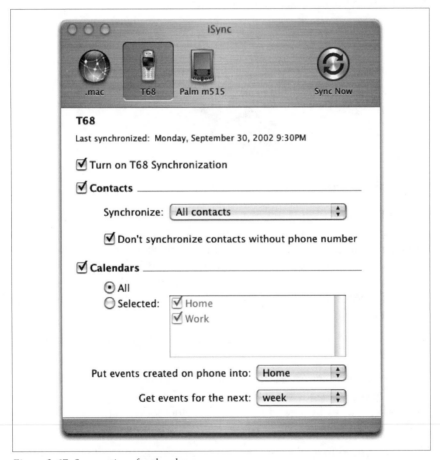

Figure 3-67. Sync options for the phone

I found that if you have an awful lot of data, iSync can get stuck trying to synchronize all the data from both the Address Book and iCal on the first sync. This is exasscerbated if you insist (as I do) on keeping two weeks' worth of data on your phone. A workaround is to skip your contacts the first time (uncheck the Contacts box in sync options for your phone), adding it back in after the initial large sync.

Adding the Palm m515

The Palm used for this hack is an m515, shown in Figure 3-68. It comes with a Secure Digital (SD) slot for SD cards. I use the SD Bluetooth card (made by Toshiba) with the m515 for Bluetooth connectivity.

Figure 3-68. Palm m515 with SD Bluetooth card

Adding Palm devices to iSync is not as straightforward as adding a phone, with three extra steps along the way. The first step is to install Palm HotSync Manager for Mac OS X (*http://www.palm.com/software/desktop/ mac.html*). It works in concert with iSync to keep your Palm up-to-date. With that installed and tested—make sure you can HotSync in the standard Palm way before proceeding—you should install the second iSync package, *iSync_Palm.pkg*.

As with the phone, you'll need to pair up your Mac and Palm device via Bluetooth.

Next, you need to inform HotSync Manager that you want to use the Bluetooth connection as a serial port for syncing purposes in addition to using the cradle. Do so by checking both the bluetooth... and USB boxes in HotSync's Connection Settings dialog box, shown in Figure 3-69.

Now you'll need to alter your Conduit Setting (from the HotSync menu) so that HotSync's default is to do nothing with the Address Book, Date Book, and To Do List, leaving these up to iSync to handle:

1. Set the action for Address book to Do Nothing.

Figure 3-69. Enabling the Bluetooth serial port for syncing

2. Set the action for Date Book to Do Nothing.

3. Set the action for To Do List to Do Nothing.

Figure 3-70 shows the resulting settings.

Figure 3-70. Configuring Conduit Settings

Finally, configure the setting for iSync Configuration so that iSync knows which items to synchronize with your Palm device. With iSync Conduit selected, click the Conduit Settings button at the top-left of the window. In the resulting dialog box (see Figure 3-71), check both Synchronize Contacts and Synchronize Calendars (To Do Lists are part of Calendars) and click OK.

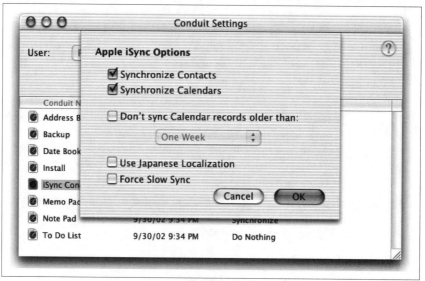

Figure 3-71. Selecting items to synchronize using iSync

You should now see the Palm device in iSync, as shown in Figure 3-72.

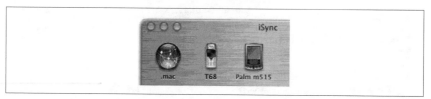

Figure 3-72. The Palm shows up in the iSync window

When you've completed all the preceding steps, the next time you use HotSync to synchronize your Palm device the Address Book, Date Book, and To Do List will be synchronized with the Mac's Address Book and iCal, respectively. To test this out, I set up some items in iCal (see Figure 3-73) and used iSync to sync it with my Palm m515. To sync, just click iSync's Sync Now button. As a precaution, you will be alerted to any changes you make to your devices (see Figure 3-74), so that you can decide to proceed or to cancel the operation.

Note that there are two ways to sync your Palm devices. You can either use the Bluetooth connection (in which case you have to use the HotSync icon on the device) or you can use the cradle. If you are using the cradle, you need to press the HotSync button on the cradle. Clicking on the syncing button on iSync does not synchronize Palm devices.

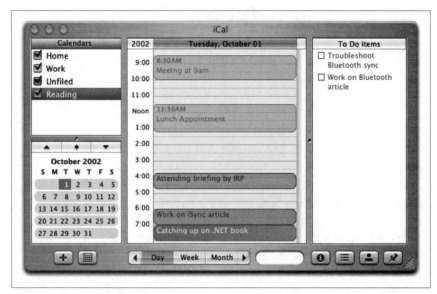

Figure 3-73. My calendar in iCal

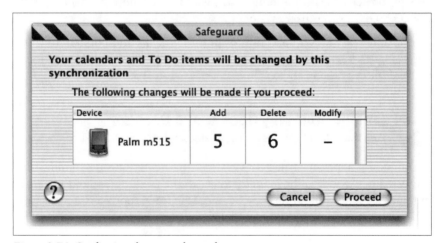

Figure 3-74. Confirming changes to be made

iSync will synchronize the Address Book, Date Book, and To Do List on Palm devices; it won't, unfortunately, touch the Notepad.

—Wei-Meng Lee

CHAPTER FOUR

The User Interface
Hacks 33–47

Mac users have a long history of tweaking the Mac OS graphical user interface. Some regard the Mac OS X GUI as a panacea for all the ills of interface design over the years, a breath of fresh air in a world dominated by dusty windows and quivering mice. Some find OS X just enough like Mac OS 9 to get by, perhaps even grow to love. Then there are those who find it an abomination, fixable by sheer will and determination, something to bend, spindle, and hack until it looks "just as it should."

Regardless of which of these camps you find yourself in, there's more than enough power beneath the hood and myriad tools and tricks to customize the OS X GUI to your heart's content.

This chapter provides a collection of inspiring hacks and pointers to third-party applications for tweaking the look-and-feel, extending the functionality that's already there, and teaching your Mac to behave just as it should.

HACK #33 Finding Your Way Back to the Desktop
Push that clutter of windows aside and get yourself back to your Desktop.

A common complaint of new OS X users (particularly those coming from the Windows world) is the inability to get to the Desktop without having to minimize or hide applications one by one. Mac OS X sports a couple of ways to hide a handful of applications and their associated windows in one fell swoop.

Mac OS 9 users will probably be familiar with Application Name → Hide Others, where Application Name is the name of the currently active application. The Finder is considered an application like any other, so this works as expected. To hide everything but the Desktop and any open Finder windows, Control-click on the Desktop or Finder icon in the Dock and select Finder → Hide Others.

Modified Dock clicks abound, providing various subtleties when switching or launching applications. Option-click (holding down the Option key while clicking on a Dock icon) hides the application previously in the foreground. Option-⌘-click hides all but the selected application.

The second-shortest but best path I've found to the Desktop (introduced in Mac OS X 10.2, Jaguar) is to click on the Desktop and press Option-⌘-H for Hide Others. The absolute shortest path is to Option-⌘-click the Finder (Mac OS smiley-face logo) in the Dock; while this hides all applications other than the Finder, it does have the unfortunate side effect of opening a Finder window right in the middle of the Desktop.

Show Desktop (*http://www.everydaysoftware.net/system/*), as its name suggests, is a popular piece of freeware serving to hide all applications and show your Desktop at the click of an icon. Show Desktop can live in either your menu bar or Dock, as shown in Figure 4-1.

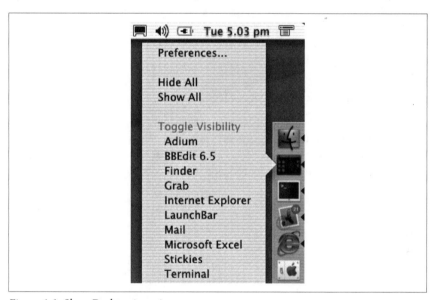

Figure 4-1. Show Desktop in action

 ## Alt-Tab Alt-Ternatives

#34 While Mac OS X Jaguar markedly improved ⌘-Tabbing your way between applications, there's still plenty of room for enhancement.

It's such an innocent key combination: ⌘-Tab. Easy to say, easy to do, easy to type. Innocent it may be, but embroiled with controversy is this little key command; sure, it switches you to the next open application (and ⌘-Shift-Tab sends you to the previous one), but still people clamor for more. They want a smart switcher—one that goes in order of application usage, not Dock order, or even one that understands individual windows within a single application.

> In previous versions of OS X, it was easy for software to override the ⌘-Tab behavior, allowing previous usage order to be mimicked with third-party software. To add more fat to the fire comes this warning from Keyboard Maestro's latest release: Apple has disabled Keyboard Maestro's (and any other third-party application's) ability to override the ⌘-Tab keystroke from the Dock and replace it with other functionality.

In fact, it's not the Alt-Tab, per se, that's at issue. It's the Mac concept of windows belonging to applications rather than existing semiautonomously that causes unrest. While hopping from Mail to Internet Explorer (IE) to BBEdit is a snap, it's simply impossible to alternate between, say, Google residing in its own IE windows and *Document1* in Word. Some applications do provide their own local keyboard shortcut—⌘-~ in both IE and Mail— but this is a rarity and varies from application to application. Other applications assign windows to ⌘-# keys, but who the heck can bear all that in mind while actually trying to get some work done.

At heart, there are two issues: Jaguar (but not previous releases of OS X) allows you to ⌘-Tab to go to your previously used application, and applications, not the windows within them, are ⌘-Tab destinations. Some attempts have been made to alter ⌘-Tab behavior. Here are a few of the highlights:

LiteSwitchX (http://www.proteron.com/liteswitchx/)
    LiteSwitchX, from Proteron software, is a freeware application switcher (via ⌘-Tab in 10.1.x and below, or a configurable combination) and comes with window layering controls, allowing the user to duplicate previous versions of the Mac OS. One such option (there are four) is Classic Finder Windows, which makes all of the Finder windows come forward together (i.e., click on the Desktop and have all your Finder windows pop to the front). Along with window layering, the ⌘-Tab application overlay (which looks similar to the Microsoft Windows overlay) can be resized up or down and supports drag-and-drop and contextual menu items.

AppSwitcher (http://www.uwm.edu/~mikeash/appswitcher/)
    AppSwitcher, by Michael Ash, is no longer being activitely developed and is usable only under 10.1.x and below. It brings up a horizontal overlay window (like Microsoft Windows and LiteSwitchX), which shows your applications sorted by front to back, in usage order. Like LiteSwitchX, it's free.

Keyboard Maestro (http://www.keyboardmaestro.com/)

>Keyboard Maestro comes in a limited Lite edition and a full version at $20. It's more than a simple application switcher, as it allows multiple clipboards and hot keys with multiple actions. Like the other software listed earlier, it can sort running applications in usage order, but also includes the ability to define applications that should *always* or *never* be allowed in the list. You can also tweak the overlay window to display vertically, as opposed to the more common horizontal display.

QuicKeys (http://www.cesoft.com/)

>Finally, there's the popular QuicKeys from CESoft, which does far more than mere application switching, allowing you to define macros, hot keys, text insertion, new floating palettes—the list goes on and on. Available for $79.95, it includes the ability to switch applications, giving you the opportunity to set up a hot key (other than ⌘-Tab) that can switch forward, backward, or to the previously running application. Pricey to some, it encompasses the abilities of a number of other utilities.

Putting Things in the Apple Menu

HACK #35

The FruitMenu haxie restores the ability to add favorite applications, folders, and other things to the Apple menu—and more.

Although Mac users are a tried-and-true bunch, stalwart to the end, there are often outcries when something doesn't function exactly as users expect. Such moaning was heard when OS X was released: "Where are my beloved Apple menu items?"

Prior to OS X, the Macintosh had a feature that many of us enjoyed: the ability to put items into the Apple menu, be they folders, files, AppleScripts, or what have you. Thankfully, Unsanity has (re)delivered this functionality with an excellent piece of software called FruitMenu (*http://www.unsanity.com/*) that's just the ticket (see Figure 4-2).

FruitMenu is a small download but packs a decent wallop, immediately becoming a part of many a user's essential software downloads. Just as it suggests, FruitMenu allows you to customize the Apple menu, including customization of contextual menus. And we're not just talking about files and folders, either.

The latest version of FruitMenu supports adding AppleScripts and shell scripts to your menus, the ability to show your IP address (and upon selection, to copy it to the clipboard, which is an immense time saver for dial-up users), the ability to show currently running applications (much like the System menu from previous OSs), in-menu picture previews (like OS X's Preview pane), as well as a Move To option, allowing easy organizing across

Figure 4-2. Choosing items for your FruitMenu

folders you define. To top it off, you can also assign hot keys to most of your FruitMenu options.

The similarities to the excellent FinderPop from OS 9 don't end there either; much as you could order the menu items of FinderPop by naming your files and folders a certain way, FruitMenu supports the same syntax, allowing you to organize your power any way you wish.

For only $7, FruitMenu—along with the many other haxies that Unsanity develops—is an excellent addition to the power user's arsenal.

HACK #36   Keeping Your Snippets Organized

DropDrawers is one of those applications you have to try to believe. It'll keep all those bits and bobs littering your Desktop neatly tucked away until you need them and helps stamp out stickies proliferation.

Are you one of those people whose desktop, both real and virtual, is littered with colorful sticky notes too numerous to actually see much of anything else? While Jaguar's stickies (*Applications → Stickies*) provide disposable spaces into which to drop thoughts, URLs, phone numbers—anything you can paste—it's not particularly well integrated with your other applications. A URL pasted into a sticky can't, for instance, be double-clicked and opened in your web browser. Even an alias to a folder dragged into a sticky doesn't mean the folder is just a double-click away.

DropDrawers (*http://www.sigsoftware.com/dropdrawers/*) ($20; fully functional demo available for download) by Sig Software provides much-needed cubby holes for stowing and organizing those bits and bobs that otherwise clutter up your Desktop, browser's bookmark list, or proliferation of yellow stickies: file and folder aliases, URLs, scripts, snippets of text, and what have you. If you can drag and drop it, you can stuff it in a DropDrawer.

Install DropDrawers and you're provided some sample drawers to get you going:

- A Processes drawer (see Figure 4-3) displays all the applications that are currently active.
- The Launcher holds application shortcuts.
- Web Sites contains a collection of URLs.
- Text Clips is a clipboard for blocks of text.
- Miscellaneous is a repository for miscellaneous text snippets, sound clips, and the like.
- An onboard tutorial provides quick-start help for using DropDrawers.

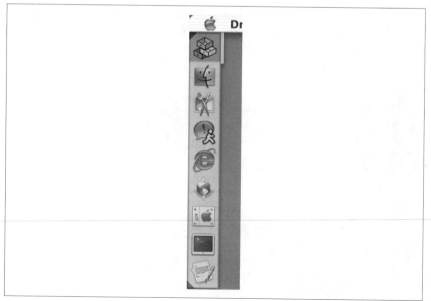

Figure 4-3. The Processes drawer in the Dock

The drawers can be positioned anywhere on the four edges of the screen. They're opened by clicking on or moving your mouse (configurable) over their tabs. Figure 4-4 shows the tabs for other sample draws.

Figure 4-4. The other sample drawers

Launcher Drawer

The Launcher provides shortcuts to commonly used applications, as shown in Figure 4-5. To create a shortcut, drag an application icon onto the drawer. To launch an application, just click the alias icon.

Figure 4-5. The Launcher

Processes Drawer

The Processes drawer displays a list of applications currently running. You can switch to an app by clicking its icon. Control-click (or right-click) the icon and select Reveal, as shown in Figure 4-6, to display the folder containing the application.

Figure 4-6. Switching to an app with the Processes drawer

The Launcher and Processes drawers together provide a decent stand-in for the Dock—for those who dislike the Dock, that is.

Creating More Drawers

If you run out of drawer space, you can create additional drawers at any time by selecting File → New Drawer, as shown in Figure 4-7.

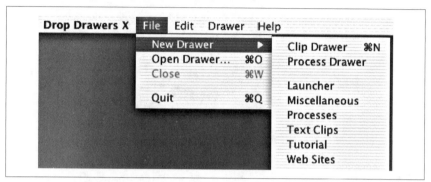

Figure 4-7. Creating a new drawer

Every new drawer you create will be saved in the *Drawers* folder, *Library/Preferences/Drawers* in your home directory.

Everything's Active and Configurable

The magic of DropDrawers is that everything's active and double-clickable. Sounds and movies play, shortcuts open their targets, URLs launch in your default browser, and text can be copied, pasted, edited, and styled using the built-in editor.

DropDrawers is also configurable to the nth degree. Every drawer has its own Drawer Options... (see Figure 4-8) and Arrange Drawer... context menu.

—Wei-Meng Lee

LaunchBar, a Dock Alternative
HACK #37

LaunchBar puts just about anything else you might want within easy reach from your keyboard.

More than simply a Dock alternative, LaunchBar (*http://www.obdev.at/products/launchbar/*) is an integral part of any alpha geek's tricked-out OS X desktop. You're just a keystroke or three away from your files, apps, favorite web sites, email addresses, and just about anything else you might want

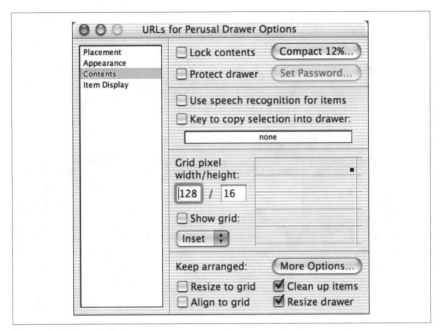

Figure 4-8. Drawer Options... menu

within easy reach. IE launches Internet Explorer, M switches me to Mail, NYT directs my browser to *The New York Times* on the Web.

LaunchBar's engine suggests closest matches according to a combination of its own innate sense (read: adaptive algorithms) of what your keystrokes might mean and what you've ended up choosing on previous occasions. IM might suggest NetInfo Manager as the top choice the first time you give it a whirl, but choose iMovie from the list and you've taught LaunchBar not to make the same mistake twice. Figure 4-9 shows the LaunchBar in action.

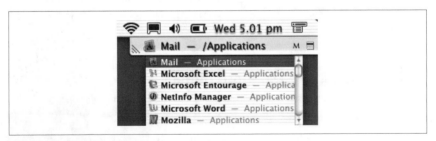

Figure 4-9. LaunchBar in action

Beyond what its name suggests, LaunchBar is quite the Alt-Tab stand-in, affording fast switching between running apps. Assign single character shortcuts to your oft-used apps—M for Mail, O for OmniWeb, A for AIM, X for Excel—and you'll never visit the Dock between applications again.

Feeding LaunchBar's suggestions is a default set of folders and files to peek at upon startup; each is associated with particular file types or attributes to memorize: all applications in *Applications*, HTML links in *Internet Explorer Favorites*, sound files in your *Music* folder, and anything in your home directory. You can, and indeed should, alter this list to suit your fancy and aid LaunchBar in its powers of suggestion (see Figure 4-10).

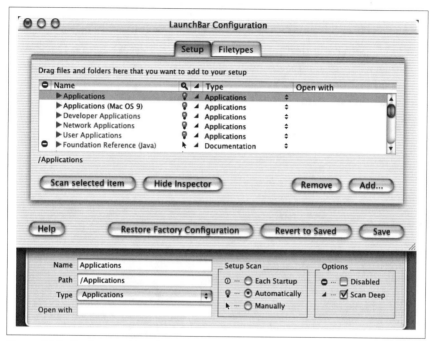

Figure 4-10. Configuring LaunchBar

LaunchBar is a commercial application ($19.95 for personal use, $39.00 for business at the time of this writing) yet sports a liberal evaluation license, the only constraint being the number of different items accessed via Launch-Bar per session. While seven's the limit, you can actually go a little further if you don't mind the occasional nags. That said, it doesn't take long to decide that LaunchBar is a must-have application.

DockSwap, Another Dock Alternative
Avoid Dock bloat with multiple configurable Docks.

Whether you love it or hate it, OS X's Dock has been lambasted for being a user interface nightmare (by an ex–Apple interface designer, no less), while at the same time receiving hearty cheers from fans of tabbed folders from OS 9.

Either way, you may find yourself falling victim to Dock bloat, a sin many consider worthy of a few chuckles.

Myself, I'm a fan of the Dock. I've got my recently used Internet applications first, then text editors, followed by my file-sharing programs, then graphics, utilities, games, and folder pop ups. What I'd really love would be to get some more of those vertical lines in there so that I can more clearly differentiate which applications are in what category. As you can imagine, my Dock is pretty full, pretty small, and magnifies gratuitously.

Needing a better solution for my Dock madness, I cracked open DockSwap (*http://www.pidog.com/OSX/*) from piDog Software and immediately started having a blast organizing. You simply create a new Dock, switch to it, and add and remove items at will until it's just the way you want it (see Figure 4-11).

Figure 4-11. The DockSwap main window

Switch Docks via context menu (⌘-click on the DockSwap Dock icon, as shown in Figure 4-12) or key command (Control-Esc).

With DockSwap, you can have a Dock for every occasion, and multiple Docks I soon did have. Here's my current setup, switchable with a mouse click or key command:

Figure 4-12. Switching Docks using the context menu

Internet Tweakery

Includes all my browsers (for testing web designs and accessing non-standard sites), BBEdit, various file-sharing programs (like Hotline, Carracho, Acquisition, xNap, Fetch, etc.), diagnostic utilities (the OS X Network Utility, shell files for tcpdump, etc.), and various other applications (iCamMaster, Snak, MT-NewsWatcher, etc.).

Writing

Contains various text editors—like BBEdit, Microsoft Word, and Text-Edit (with AntiWordService **[Hack #12]**)—and a healthy dose of bookmarks for dictionaries, thesauri, clichés, word meanings, and so on. It also includes Sherlock for those quick encyclopedic/knowledge-of-the-Net searches.

Games

Rarely used because my extra time is nonexistent, but contains such favorites as Snood, iColumns, JewelToy, Solitaire Till Dawn, and more. It includes a few bookmarks for quick searching at *gamers.com*, *gamefaqs.com*, and MobyGames. Having these out of the way in a separate Dock helps me resist the temptation to procrastinate accidentally.

I could go on and on about my Development, Miscellany, and EveryDay Docks, but I think you get the picture. DockSwap is yet another excellent RealBasic utility, available for a suggested shareware fee of $12.

Tinkering with Your User Interface

HACK
#39

Beautify your Mac's look-and-feel with the freeware TinkerTool Preference Pane.

Despite the plethora of built-in customizations, tweaks, beautifications, and alterations to the look-and-feel of your Mac, there are times when you want to take things just that little bit further.

TinkerTool (*http://www.bresink.de/osx/TinkerTool2.html*) (freeware) gives you much to tinker with. While some of its functionality has been subsumed into Mac OS X 10.2 (Jaguar), there's still much you can do with TinkerTool that simply can't be done otherwise. The latest version has, in turn, pulled in some more of Jaguar's functionality, providing a one-stop customization shop for your Mac GUI.

TinkerTool's Preference Pane Installer (see Figure 4-13) drops the app into place simply and cleanly, allowing you to choose whether it's available to all users or just you.

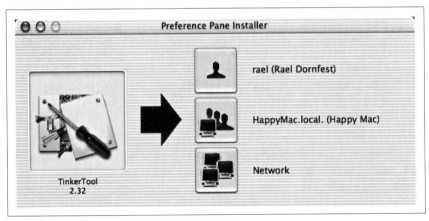

Figure 4-13. Running the Preference Pane Installer

There are several areas of settings that TinkerTool allows you to customize:

- Features related to the Finder, such as the effects of opening files, number of lines shown for filenames, and so forth (see Figure 4-14)
- Dock placement, drop-shadows, transparent hidden applications
- General positioning of scrollbar arrows, startup/login language
- Fonts and font smoothing used by the system and applications

> Some of the TinkerTool features are grayed out in Jaguar, since they're applicable only to those still running Mac OS X 10.1.

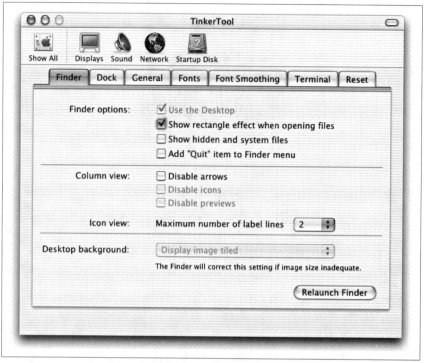

Figure 4-14. Using TinkerTool

Some features require you to restart the Finder, while others require you to restart the application before you can see the changed effect. Fortunately, the handy Relaunch Finder button makes it easy to restart without needing to log out and back in again.

Here's an overview of a few of the more interesting TinkerTool features.

Dock Position

While Jaguar allows you to place your Dock on the left, right, or bottom (default) of your screen, TinkerTool lets you define whether it's anchored in the middle, start, or end of the screen. Figure 4-15 is a screenshot of my Dock tied to the top right.

Removing Arrows

When you view a folder in column view, Jaguar displays an arrow next to each item. If these arrows bother you—as they do some users—you can ask TinkerTool to remove them (see Figure 4-16).

Figure 4-15. Docking the Dock

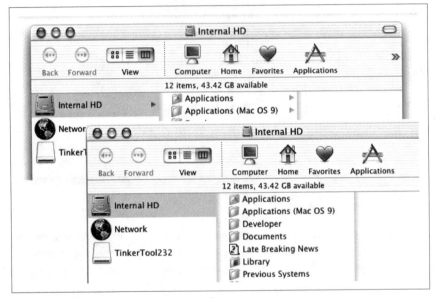

Figure 4-16. Removing folder arrows in column view

Displaying Multiple Lines of a Filename

By default, the Finder displays a maximum of two lines for filenames. Tinker-Tool allows you to display up to three lines, as shown in Figure 4-17. This is useful if you tend to use rather long filenames.

Figure 4-17. Displaying long filenames

Shadowing the Dock

While windows in Jaguar have nice drop-shadows, interestingly enough, the Dock does not. If this confuses your sense of perspective, go ahead and let TinkerTool add a shadow to your Dock (see Figure 4-18).

Figure 4-18. Giving the Dock a nice shadow

Changing the System Fonts

Tired of the system font? You can change the fonts used by the system as well as your applications, as shown in Figure 4-19.

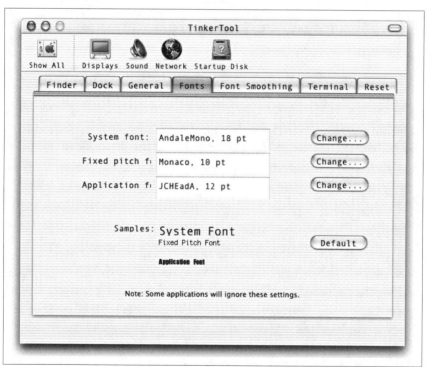

Figure 4-19. Changing fonts

Be careful with the fonts you choose; inappropriate fonts can yield some unpredictable results, such as cropped sentences, as shown in Figure 4-20.

—*Wei-Meng Lee*

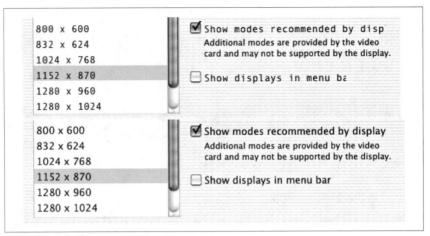

Figure 4-20. Inappropriate choice of fonts

Extending Your Screen Real Estate with Virtual Desktops

Stretch your screen real estate up to 100 times its size and organize different views of your workspace with virtual desktop software.

Ever wish that you had a larger monitor? While not everyone can afford the 23-inch Apple Cinema HD Display (*http://www.apple.com/displays/acd23/*), you can actually achieve the same effect (wow! factor not included) for as little as $0 to get...well...near to unlimited screen real estate!

CodeTek VirtualDesktop

The CodeTek VirtualDesktop (*http://www.codetek.com/php/virtual.php*) ($40; trial available) is an application that enhances your screen real estate through software emulation. It does so by creating virtual desktops, each containing whatever you put into it and organized how you left it last. Keep your writing (Word, BBEdit, Sherlock Thesaurus, and a browser window) on one screen, your mail on another, and coding (Application Builder, Interface Builder, Script Editor, Terminal windows) in still another. Switching between them is just a matter of a mouse click.

While the trial version allows for only two virtual screens, it's more than enough to get the idea. Pay for VirtualDesktop and you can have up to 100 virtual screens!

Installing CodeTek VirtualDesktop is straightforward. Simply double-click on the application icon and you are ready to go. The first thing you'll notice is a miniwindow known as the pager. The pager displays the virtual desktops available to you, organized on a grid, as shown in Figure 4-21. You'll notice that the desktop on the left holds a browser window while the one on the right is still empty.

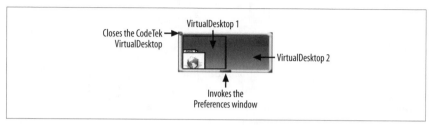

Figure 4-21. The VirtualDesktop pager

You can change the skin (appearance) of the pager by creating one yourself or downloading one from CodeTek's site (http://www.codetek.com/php/virtual_skins.php).

There are so many ways to switch desktops, one or more of them will likely appeal. Click on a window in the pager and you're transported there instantly. Mouse between one desktop and the other by moving off the edge of the screen in the direction (according to the grid layout) of the destination desktop. Hot-key left, right, up, or down between screens. Or use the handy menu-bar icon to switch between open application windows or hop to another desktop, as shown in Figure 4-22.

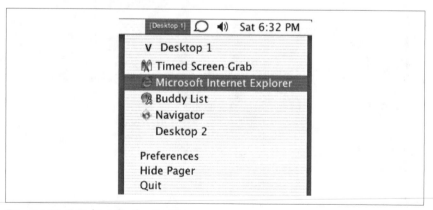

Figure 4-22. Switching via the menu bar

Not only can you move yourself from one desktop to the next, you can also drag applications between desktops. Either grab the window you want and mouse over to the appropriate desktop. Or drag and drop the icon representing the application in the pager, as shown in Figure 4-23.

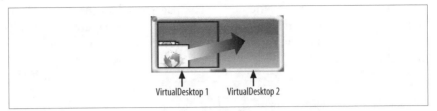

Figure 4-23. Moving a window from one virtual desktop to another

CodeTek VirtualDesktop is ultraconfigurable. Pin particular applications down so that they appear on every desktop; I do this with iChat and iPulse [Hack #42]. Alter the pager's appearance, set hot keys, and configure the layout of your virtual desktop grid (see Figure 4-24).

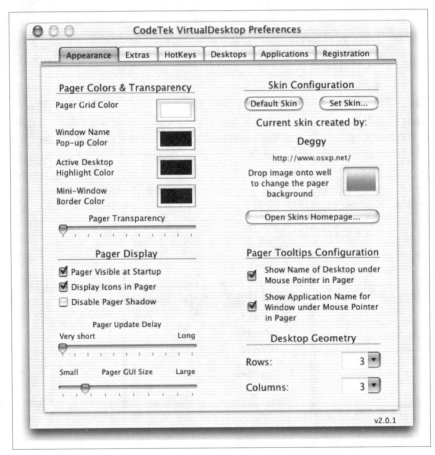

Figure 4-24. Tweaking preferences

VirtualDesktop is a must-have for the multitasking geek in you.

Project Space.app

If you are not up for paying $40 for CodeTek VirtualDesktop, or if you are willing to settle for something simpler without all the bells and whistles, then Space.app (*http://sourceforge.net/projects/space/*) is a decent alternative. It is free for personal and commercial use and distributed under the open source GPL license.

Space.app offers a user interface similar to that of the CodeTek, offering up to 16 workspaces (nameable) and a floating pager (see Figure 4-25).

Figure 4-25. The Space.app pager showing nine workspaces

Rather than creating actual virtual screens, Space.app operates by remembering which application is shown or hidden in each view (a.k.a. screen). While it's a decent stand-in for VirtualDesktop and the price can't be beat, the difference in feel and functionality is substantial. You cannot, for instance, have two windows from the same application open in two different spaces; it's the entire app or nothing at all. The refresh when switching from screen to screen is also a little jerky, as applications are hidden and shown before your very eyes.

—Wei-Meng Lee

Top Screenshot Tips

These screen-capture tips provide built-in and add-on solutions to just about anything you might wish to snap.

Capturing good screenshots in Mac OS X requires some experimentation. If you simply want to capture the screen for reference later on, you can do it easily with the built-in screen-capture tool. However, if you are a professional writer or a student preparing that term paper and need great-looking screen shots, you have to spend a little more time exploring your options.

These screen capture tips provide built-in and add-on solutions to just about anything you might wish to snap.

Built-Ins

Mac OS X Jaguar comes with a built-in capability for capturing screenshots. To capture the entire screen, simply press ⌘-Shift-3 and a PDF grab of your current view will appear on your desktop. Screenshots are numbered sequentially, such as *Picture 1.pdf*, *Picture 2.pdf*, and so on.

To capture a particular region of the screen, type ⌘-Shift-4 and highlight— using click-and-drag—whatever portion of the screen you'd like, as shown in Figure 4-26.

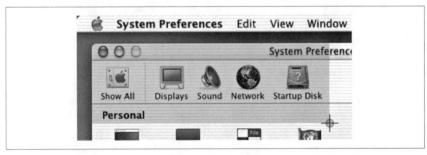

Figure 4-26. Capturing a portion of the screen

An extension to region grabbing is snagging a picture of a particular window or dialog box. Press ⌘-Shift-4, then the spacebar; any window you run your mouse over will be highlighted. Click to capture it. You can toggle back and forth between region and window modes by pressing the spacebar.

 To change your mind and cancel screen capture, press the Escape (Esc) key on your keyboard.

While the built-in screen-capture tool is good enough for just about all purposes, it has a couple of drawbacks. It doesn't capture the mouse pointer in any of the screenshots—not even optionally (see Figure 4-27). This is a bust for technical writers explaining the operation of menus, buttons, and so forth. Second, while PDF is the be-all and end-all of all things GUI under Mac OS X, I need my screenshots in PNG or TIFF. Sure, I can convert them using Preview or the like [Hack #21], but that's an extra step I simply shouldn't have to take.

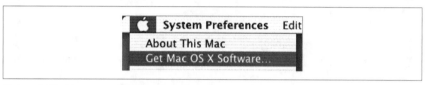

Figure 4-27. *The cursor is not captured using screen capture*

Grab

Mac OS X bundles a little utility called Grab (*Applications → Utilities → Grab*) which supports three modes of screen capture: screen, selection (a.k.a. region), and timed screen (captures the entire screen after a specific time interval). Unlike its built-in counterpart, Grab saves to TIFF format and optionally includes mouse pointers in its captures; it even allows you to specify a preferred pointer (Grab → Preferences), as shown in Figure 4-28.

There is one problem that I noticed with the selection capture. In order to capture an active window using the selection mode, you need to switch to Grab first. Yet doing so makes the window inactive and fall to the background. Now, when I do a selection grab, I want to capture the window in its active state.

The selection grab will also display the size of the image you are capturing at the bottom right corner of the selection region. This is useful if you need to capture images of an exact size. One gripe though: you can't create a region of a particular size and then move it about.

> Oddly, while Capture → Window is listed, it's grayed out and doesn't appear to be functional.

Using Snapz Pro X

The ultimate screen-capture utility is Snapz Pro X ($29, $49 with movie-capture support; 30-day demo available) from Ambrosia Software Inc. (*http://www.ambrosiasw.com/utilities/snapzprox/*). It sports customizability

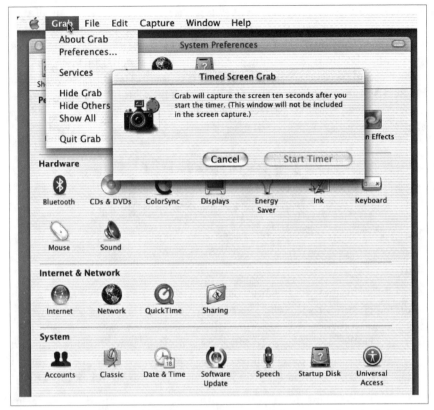

Figure 4-28. Using the timed screen mode to capture action, mouse pointer included

and multiple output formats, and it grabs the screen as you see it, including or excluding that pesky mouse arrow, at will.

Set up your shot and press ⌘-Shift-3 (customizable) to freeze the screen and take care of the details, as shown in Figure 4-29. You can choose the entire screen, objects (windows or icons), or a region, even during Quicktime and DVD movie playback (the built-in screen capture featrure is disabled while DVD Player is active).

Selection capture, coming after you've set up your screen just the way you like it (see Figure 4-30), allows you to take your time to mark out and alter the region before double-clicking it to take the final shot.

Snapz Pro X can even capture the drop-shadows beneath a window. Simply change the Border option under Image Options to Drop Shadow. Prior to Snapz Pro X, I'd always have to switch the background to white to capture the nice shadow around the window without including a slice of my desktop image.

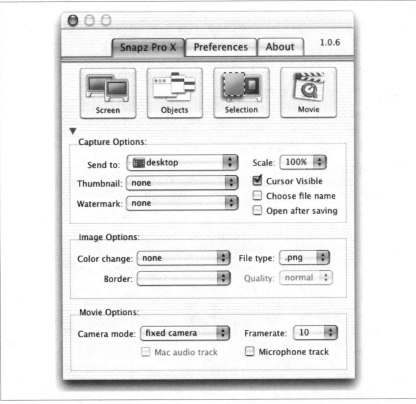

Figure 4-29. Taking care of SnapZ Pro X screenshot details

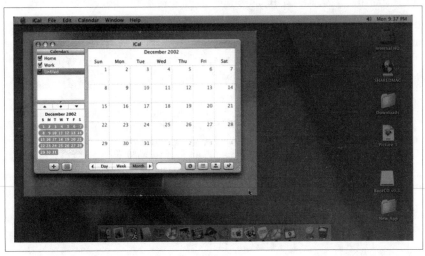

Figure 4-30. Capturing a portion of the screen

There's so much more to Snapz Pro X—like recording screen activities as a QuickTime movie for purposes such as product demos—that it's difficult to do it justice in this quick overview. Download the 30-day trial and give it a whirl yourself.

Screen Capture with Terminal

Terminal **[Hack #48]** comes with a command-line version of the built-in screen-capture utility, aptly named screencapture. For usage instructions, simply invoke it on the command line:

```
% screencapture
screencapture: illegal usage, file required if not going to clipboard
usage: screencapture [-icmwsWx] [file] [cursor]
  -i    capture screen interactively, by selection or window
            control key - causes screen shot to go to clipboard
            space key   - toggle between mouse selection and
                          window selection modes
            escape key  - cancels interactive screen shot
  -c    force screen capture to go to the clipboard
  -m    only capture the main monitor, undefined if -i is set
  -w    only allow window selection mode
  -s    only allow mouse selection mode
  -W    start interaction in window selection mode
  -x    do not play sounds
  file  where to save the screen capture
```

To capture the entire screen, type screencapture ~/Desktop/image.pdf, where *~/Desktop/image.pdf* is the path and filename to which you wish it saved. To capture the screen interactively in regional or window mode, use screencapture -i image.pdf, as shown in Figure 4-31.

If you prefer the output to go right to the clipboard rather than an image file, use screencapture -c. Of course, you can use these various command-line options in tandem; screencapture -ic, for example, is an interactive screen-capture session, sending the result to the clipboard.

> You can grab a screenshot of a remote Mac's desktop—or even the login screen—thanks to screencapture and some not-so-fancy remote access footwork **[Hack #71]**. Simply log in to the other Mac remotely, run screencapture on the command line, and copy the resulting screenshots back over to your local Mac.

—Wei-Meng Lee

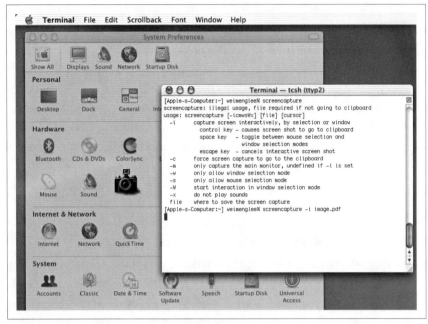

Figure 4-31. Using screencapture on the command line

 ## Checking Your Mac's Pulse

#42

iPulse provides a quick, colorful overview of what's going on with your Mac's CPU, memory, drives, and network activity under the hood.

The Iconfactory's (*http://www.iconfactory.com/*) iPulse (*http://www. iconfactory.com/ip_home.asp*) ($9 shareware) provides a visually appealing view of your Mac's vitals as your drives hum, memory churns, and network flows away under your fingertips (see Figure 4-32).

Figure 4-32. System monitoring with iPulse

Yes, it does strike us as a little esoteric and more than a little unnecessary at first blush. However, it's well worth the few minutes it takes to decipher its interface and the few cycles it takes to leave it running in an unused corner of your desktop.

iPulse's gauges (refer to Figure 4-32) monitor:

- CPU utilization (inner blue circle), both user and system space
- Memory usage (middle ring between nine and three o'clock) in percentage used/unused and page swapping in/out (outermost ring between nine and three o'clock)
- Disk-space usage (middle ring between three and nine o'clock) with disk-full warning
- Network traffic (outermost ring between three and nine o'clock), both in (red) and out (green)

Each gauge, along with its graphical representation, displays an absolute value numerically for quick perusal.

iPulse even sports a nifty analog clock with second hand (that black dot in Figure 4-32) and day of month (that "9" at the top of the clock face).

iPulse is fully configurable via a set of preference panes, from which you can turn particular guages on and off, alter their degree of granularity, and fine-tune the overall display. You can even choose not to show iPulse as a floating window, using instead its tiny mirrored display in the Dock icon.

Don't dismiss iPulse out of hand as no more than eye candy. Having spent five years as a system administrator, I've done my share of system monitoring via a plethora of Terminal windows running top, netstat, df, and the like—not to mention the countless monitoring scripts firing email messages at me day and night like so many party favors. Figure 4-33 gives you just a mild taste.

Blech! I sure could have used iPulse for a quick update on how a particular machine was faring.

Here's a neat idea for those with a Mac-based server farm: place iPulse at the center of your desktop and use Jaguar's fabulous screen zoom accessibility to zoom it to full screen for a passing glance at how your web, mail, or other server is coping. Option-⌘-8 turns on screen zooming; Option-⌘-= zooms in on the mouse pointer and Option-⌘-– (that's a minus sign) zooms back out again.

 It also makes one heck of a stand-in for counting sheep. ;-)

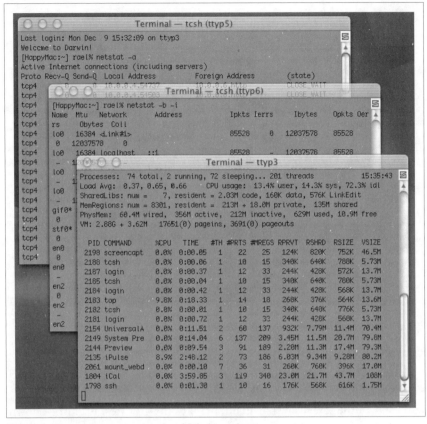

Figure 4-33. System monitoring the old-fashioned way

HACK #43 Screensaver as Desktop

Drive yourself to distraction by turning your Desktop into a flurry of color or an active slideshow.

Some hacks are just too cool to bother rationalizing. This is just such a hack.

Type the following into a Terminal **[Hack #48]** window:

```
% /System/Library/Frameworks/ScreenSaver.framework/Resources/
ScreenSaverEngine.app/Contents/MacOS/ScreenSaverEngine -background
```

Now lean back, press the Return key, and prepare to be amazed. No, you're not imagining things; that is indeed your preferred screensaver running right smack dab on your Desktop, behind and between your running applications (see Figure 4-34).

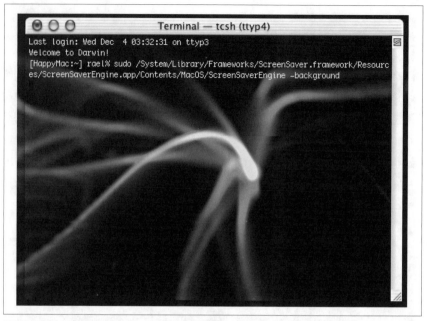

Figure 4-34. The screensaver running as desktop

Probably the most useful part of this hack is turning it off and returning your Desktop to its unchanging self. To do so, type Control-C in the same Terminal window from which you started the screensaver running.

While any of the screensavers will do, perhaps the grooviest is Flurry, shown in Figure 4-34. More serene, but no less impressive, is one of the slide-shows: Forest, Cosmos, or Abstract. Of course, a homemade slideshow composed of snapshots in your *Pictures* folder will keep those near and dear to you even nearer.

> This hack is not for the faint of CPU and RAM. While it's possible to keep the screensaver running while getting things done—aside, of course, from the utter distraction it causes— it'll eat up quite a bit of your computer's brainpower, slowing things to a crawl on anything but the latest hardware with plenty of memory.

As you might expect, there are a number of freeware apps (*http://www. versiontracker.com/mp/new_search.m?productDB=mac&mode=Quick&OS_ Filter=MacOSX&search=screensaver+desktop*) available to turn the desktop screensaver on and off without needing a visit to the command line.

Dipping Your Pen into Inkwell
HACK #44

Inkwell, Apple's handwriting-recognition technology, has the potential to put some of the joy back into writing by hand.

The recent launch of the Microsoft Tablet PC was accompanied by major fanfare, hailing writing as a whole new way of using the computer. The Tablet PC is basically a notebook equipped with a graphics tablet built in to allow users to scribble notes on it. Behind the hardware is the Microsoft Windows XP Tablet PC edition, a souped-up version of Windows XP with handwriting-recognition capabilities.

Unknown to many, surprisingly enough to any longtime Apple devotee, Apple also possesses similar handwriting recognition technology, dating from the days of the now-discontinued Newton message pad (*http://www. panix.com/~clay/newton/*). In Mac OS X Jaguar, Apple has quietly shipped the handwriting-recognition technology known as Inkwell (*http://www. apple.com/macosx/jaguar/inkwell.html*). Let's dip our pens into Inkwell and see how it measures up and how you can make use of it.

First and foremost, to use Inkwell you need a graphics tablet; unfortunately, you cannot use a mouse to simulate handwriting strokes. Perhaps this is one reason why Inkwell has not been widely used, as not everyone has a graphics tablet. For my experimentation, I used the Intuos2 graphics tablet from Wacom (*http://www.wacom.com/*), shown in Figure 4-35.

Figure 4-35. A graphics tablet

The package comes with a tablet, a pen, and a mouse. For most of the stuff that I am going to show you, using the pen is sufficient. But you may want to consider using the bundled mouse; it's wireless and glides nicely on the tablet.

To invoke Inkwell, you need to plug in your tablet and install the drivers provided by Wacom. A required restart and you should find a new Ink icon under the Hardware section of your System Preferences, as shown in Figure 4-36.

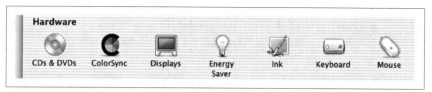

Figure 4-36. The Ink System Preferences icon

Before you start using Inkwell, you need to do a little configuration. Click the Ink icon.

Under the Settings tab (see *Figure 4-37*), you can configure Inkwell to let you write anywhere on the screen or only within InkPad (more on this in a moment). You can also set your handwriting style and fine-tune your writing style by clicking the Options... button. *Figure 4-38* shows the Ink options.

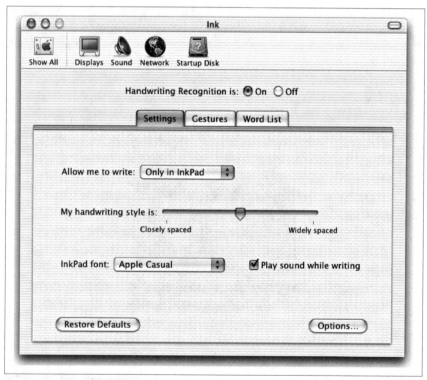

Figure 4-37. Ink Settings

In my test, I found that if you are a slow writer, it is useful to increase the delay for handwriting recognition.

The next tab, Gestures, contains support for gestures. Anyone who's used a PDA—particularly a Palm—will find these familiar. They're essentially

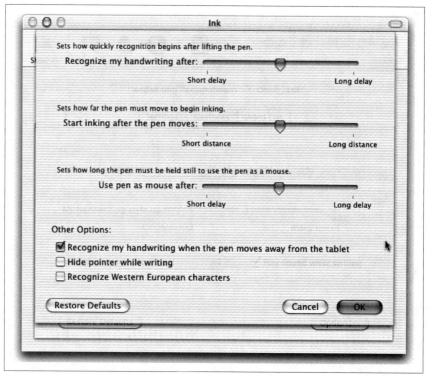

Figure 4-38. Ink Options

scribbled shortcuts for common actions you'd normallly find under the menu bar's Edit menu: Cut, Copy, Paste, Undo, Select All, and so forth, as shown in Figure 4-39.

The last tab is Word List (see Figure 4-40), which allows you to enter unusual words that you use often. Inkwell uses a built-in dictionary, comparing words that you write against known common words and exceptions you've added yourself. To speed up the process, you should add words that are not found in the dictionary on the fly (Inkwell will tell you if a word is found in the dictionary).

With configuration out of the way, let's get down to work. Make sure that you have turned on handwriting recognition, as shown in Figure 4-41.

Whenever handwriting recognition is turned on, the InkBar (Figure 4-42) will be floating about somewhere on your screen.

Of interest are the four icons: Command, Shift, Option, and Control. These icons allow you to input special characters or commands without using the mouse. For example, if I want to cut out a specific segment of text, I can

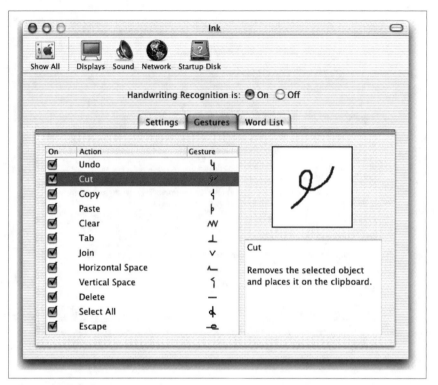

Figure 4-39. Ink Gestures

highlight the text (using the other tip of the pen) and tap on the Command icon, then write x.

You can input text into your application with the pen in two ways: using the InkPad or writing directly on the application. To use the InkPad, click on the InkPad button and start writing on your tablet, as shown in Figure 4-43.

The InkPad is a temporary writing space, not unlike a sticky. In Figure 4-43, I have opened a TextEdit document and used the InkPad for writing. When you are done with the writing, you can transfer your writing to the application by clicking the Send button at the bottom of the window. The Clear button clears the content of the InkPad.

To create a drawing, you can click on the Drawing button (see Figure 4-44).

This is useful for signatures or when you want to insert drawings into your documents, as shown in Figure 4-45.

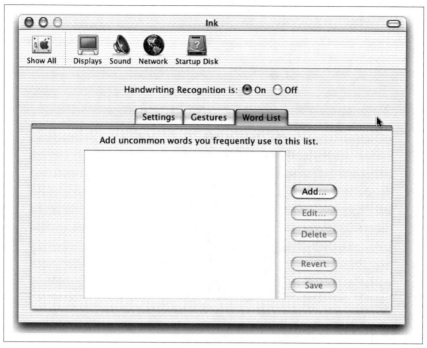

Figure 4-40. Ink Word List

Figure 4-41. Handwriting recognition

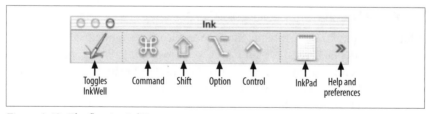

Figure 4-42. The floating InkBar

Besides using the InkPad, you can also write directly onto the document. In this case, you need to set Inkwell to write anywhere, as shown in Figure 4-46. When you move your pen into your application and start writing, a yellow writing pad will be shown. The writing pad will expand as you write to accommodate the text that you are entering.

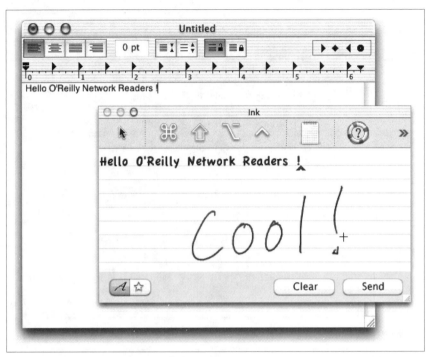

Figure 4-43. Start writing on the tablet

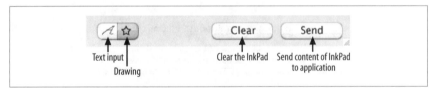

Figure 4-44. Creating a drawing

Makes You Wonder...

While the ability to write directly into my application sounds cool, I am quite skeptical of its practical use. I am better at typing using my keyboard, as it is definitely much faster than scribbling onto a tablet. Furthermore, the hand-writing recognition requires you to print the characters in order to achieve the best result. If you write like a doctor (read: illegibly), Inkwell is going to have a lot of trouble deciphering your handwriting. In my test, it works quite well when I print slowly. Cursive writing is definitely not recommended.

While Inkwell has the potential to bring back some of the joy of writing to the keyboard-addicted geek, as yet it is of limited practical use.

—*Wei-Meng Lee*

Figure 4-45. Signatures

Speakable Web Services
#45

Explore Mac OS X's speech recognition and its suitability for building useful, voice-driven commands that invoke external as well as local web services.

When Scotty tried to talk to a Macintosh through its mouse in *Star Trek IV* (1986), the joke was on Apple. Why couldn't this famously easy-to-use computer accept the most natural form of input? Over the years, I dabbled now and then with voice command systems, but they never seemed worth the trouble—until now. I've been exploring the speech technologies in Mac OS X on an 800MHz TiBook, and I'm really impressed. Apple has done a marvelous job with the recognition and control systems, and now that you can script the Internet so easily in OS X, it's straightforward to build useful voice-driven commands that invoke external as well as local services. Consider this dialog:

Me: "Temperature"

Computer: "36 degrees"

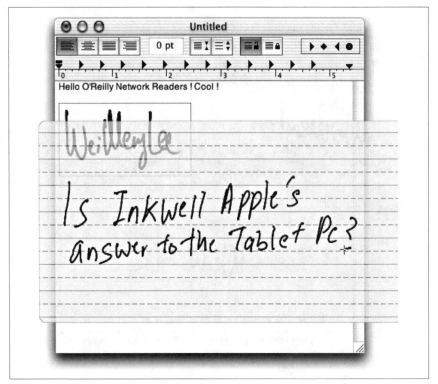

Figure 4-46. Writing anywhere

There are, of course, a million ways to look up the temperature on the Web. Most of them start with the browser. You fire it up and go to a bookmark, which in my case is *http://www.weather.com/weather/local/03431*. There are at least two problems with this scenario. First, you have to translate the request into an application context (the browser) and a procedure (go to bookmarks, select Local Weather). Second, you destroy your original context. For example, I'm typing these words in the Emacs Terminal-based text editor. I'd like to keep on typing, and reading what I am writing, even as I ask for and receive the temperature. Speaking the request and hearing the response is an ideal solution. Here are a few ways to implement it.

Perl and AppleScript Working Together

I started with a Perl script that uses SOAP::Lite to hit a web service at XMethods (*http://www.xmethods.com*), like so:

```
#! /usr/bin/perl -w
use strict;
use SOAP::Lite;
my $temp = SOAP::Lite
```

```
-> service('http://www.xmethods.net/sd/2001/TemperatureService.wsdl')
-> getTemp('03431') . " degrees";
`osascript -e 'say "$temp"'`;
```

Here, we're using Perl's backtick evaluation to run a command-line tool, osascript, which runs AppleScript code—in this case, to speak the result of the SOAP call. Use of the text-to-speech engine introduces some fascinating subtleties. For example, if you omit the leading space in degrees, the answer will sound like:

> three six period zero dee eee gee are eee eee ess

It would be handy if you could just save this as a file called *Temperature* in the *Speakable Items* folder (for example, */Users/john/Library/Speech/ SpeakableItems*) and launch it by speaking the name "temperature." But so far as I've been able to determine, scripted speakable items (as opposed to those that invoke key-driven commands) have to be written in AppleScript and, further, saved from the script editor as type *application* (not *text* or *compiled script*). Fortunately, AppleScript can invoke the Unix shell, which can invoke the Perl script. Let's refactor slightly, and have the Perl script simply return a bare value, suitable for downstream use in any kind of application, whether voice-enabled or not:

```
#! /usr/bin/perl -w
use strict;
use SOAP::Lite;
print SOAP::Lite
-> service('http://www.xmethods.net/sd/2001/TemperatureService.wsdl')
-> getTemp('03431');
```

I saved that script as */Users/jon/Temperature* and then saved the following AppleScript application as */Users/jon/Library/Speech/SpeakableItems/ Temperature*:

```
set theResult to do shell script "/Users/jon/Temperature"
say theResult & " degrees" as string
```

Now, the textual result of the Temperature script is spoken by AppleScript. You can, alternatively, do the whole thing in AppleScript, like so:

```
tell application "http://services.xmethods.net:80/soap/servlet/rpcrouter"
  set theResult to call soap {method name:"getTemp", \
    parameters:{zipcode:"03431"}, method namespace \
    uri:"urn:xmethods-Temperature", SOAPAction:"/TemperatureService"}
end tell
```

```
say theResult & " degrees" as string
```

This is easier in one way, harder in another. It's easier if you're not a Perl programmer or if you haven't added SOAP::Lite and its required substrate (expat, XML::Parser) to the Perl kit that comes with Mac OS X. But when a web service is described by a Web Services Description Language (WSDL) file, it's easier to use SOAP::Lite than AppleScript, since the former can use the WSDL file to simplify access.

It's ideal when there's a web service that will give you the answer you're looking for, but when that's not the case, there's always good old HTML screen-scraping. In that case, a language like Perl or Python will run rings around AppleScript. Here's a script that speaks my weblog's current rank and page-view count for today:

```
! /usr/bin/perl -w
use strict;
use LWP::Simple;
my $res = get "http://www.weblogs.com/rankingsByPageReads.html";
$res =~ m#(.+)Jon's Radio</a></td><td><td align="right">(†+) #;
my $preface = $1;
my $count = $2;
$preface =~m#>(†+)` </td><td>#;
my $rank = $1;
'osascript -e 'say "Rank $rank, count $count"'';
```

In this case, it's more trouble than it's worth to return raw results from Perl and format them for speech output in AppleScript.

I have to confess I'm still tempted to dismiss this speech stuff as an amusing parlor trick. But it may finally be reaching a tipping point. Look, Dad's talking to the computer, my kids snickered. When I showed my son he could play GnuChess using voice commands, though, he was riveted. It's a case-by-case thing, but when an application has a limited control vocabulary ("pawn a2 to a4"), the Mac's speaker-independent speech recognition can give you hands-free control that's accurate and more effective than mouse control. Well, to be honest, mostly accurate. I'm having a little trouble getting GnuChess to distinguish between "d" and "e"—a problem that could be solved by also supporting "delta" and "echo."

Not many of the XMethods services are likely candidates for voice treatment. Complex inputs and outputs don't make much sense. You can build IVR-style (interactive voice response) menus, like so:

```
tell application "SpeechRecognitionServer"
  local choices
  set choices to {"Temperature" "BlogStats"}
  set thePrompt to "What do you need to know?"
  try
    set theResult to listen for choices with prompt thePrompt giving ⏎
    up after 10
    say (do shell script "/Users/Jon/" & theResult)
  end try
end tell
```

Unless you really want to inflict voice trees on yourself, though, you'll probably soon tire of this approach, once the novelty wears off. Complex output is a nonstarter as well. It's faster to read than to hear more than a word or short phrase, the Mac's synthesized voices work best on short snippets, and there's no way for the computer to usefully speak structured output.

Namespace Management

The namespace mode of the files in the *Speakable Items* folder is active system wide. There are separate per-application namespaces. For example, the *Speakable Items/Internet Explorer* subfolder defines voice commands just for MSIE. You can, in fact, extend that namespace in a hands-free manner, using the "make this page speakable" voice command. If the current page is *http://news.google.com*, for example, then "make this page speakable" prompts with the page's HTML doctitle, Google News. When the prompt is active, the valid speech commands are "save" and "cancel." If you say "save," you will create a voice-activated bookmark triggered by the phrase "Google News." Pretty darned slick! It's IE-specific, though, and that's a shame because I prefer Mozilla on the Mac to the IE version (5.2) that came with the TiBook.

The per-application namespaces are segregated from one another, but as you extend the main namespace, you'll start to run into conflicts. New commands that sound too much like existing ones will cause misrecognition. The problem is easily solved, though. Just open the *Speakable Items* folder and rename files—either preexisting items or your new items—in order to step around these conflicts.

As you build up vocabularies, it's easy to forget that the recognition engine is speaker-independent, not language-dependent. For example, I've been enjoying Brent Simmons' Huevos **[Hack #85]**, a nifty little tool that can float in a small window and send a search term to any of a user-defined set of web sites. The voice command to launch it—"switch to Huevos"—works best when I anglicize the name as "Hoo-eee-vos." Apple's site says that a Spanish recognizer is available but, for now, I'm still trying to decide whether to mangle the pronunciation of "Huevos" or rename it for speech purposes.

Speech control of computers is mainly considered to be an assistive technology. In my case, there's certainly an element of that. After too many years of typing and mousing, my wrists are chronically sore, and I'm happy to avoid all keystrokes and mouse clicks that I can. Most of that wear and tear is from writing and programming, though, so until I can come to terms with dictation (as, I'm told, the prolific author David Pogue has done), voice control won't help much. But Apple's implementation has made me rethink the mixed-mode user interface. Consider, for example, the mechanism for picking one of the 50 U.S. states in a web form. Some sites ask you to type the two-letter abbreviation, but most offer a picklist. Scanning a list of 50 items is unproductive. I can use completion to skip to the N section of the list, but adding an H takes me to Hawaii, not New Hampshire. Here's a well-defined namespace that could probably be accessed using speech more quickly and naturally than by any other method. I suspect the same holds true for many multiple-choice situations in data entry forms and elsewhere.

Consider another Brent Simmons application, the popular RSS newsreader NetNewsWire [Hack #87]. It's already more usefully speakable then most OS X apps I've tried. Along with menu navigation, you can speak the crucial commands "next unread," "mark all as unread," and "open in browser." These are more mnemonic than their keyboard equivalents (⌘-G, ⌘-Shift-K, and ⌘-B) and, especially in the case of ⌘-Shift-K, more accessible too. An interesting refinement would be to voice-enable random access to feeds, just as MSIE allows spoken random access to items on the Go and Favorites menus. I've got 128 subscriptions, for example. It would be cool to say "Sam Ruby" and jump straight to Sam's blog. Or to say "Jeremy" and jump to a completion list showing Allaire and Zawodny, and speak one of those surnames to finalize the selection.

As software services multiply, so do their control vocabularies. XML manages this proliferation using namespaces. Per-application or per-service speech-enabling can use the same strategy to reduce the hard problem of open-ended speech recognition to an easier one that can be solved in useful and practical ways.

—Jon Udell

HACK #46   Using AppleScript in Contextual Menus

Ranchero's BigCat is a plug-in to Mac OS X, allowing you to run AppleScripts via a new Scripts item in your contextual menus.

Back in the old days, there was a magical little utility called FinderPop (*http://www.finderpop.com/*). FinderPop was pre–OS X, and many users saw that it was good…very good, in fact. Along with a healthy dose of other features, you could add a number of new abilities to your contextual menu, including the abilities to browse compressed archives, change file types, run AppleScripts, and more. FinderPop, sadly, won't ever exist for OS X, but what else do we have?

Enter BigCat from Ranchero Software (*http://www.ranchero.com/*). With one simple 185K free download (read that again, eh? 185K!), you can install a plug-in for OS X that will allow you to run AppleScripts via a new Scripts item in your contextual menus.

True to its purpose, BigCat operates on context. When you install the Big-Cat scripts, there are two subfolders: one for *Text*, which includes such basic examples as Copy, Google Search, and Open Selection in BBEdit, and the other called *Files*, containing Copy Path, Open in TextEdit, and Stuff (i.e., Archive with Stuffit). Even though there are two folders, you'll see only one based on—you guessed it—context. Got some text highlighted? You'll see only the scripts in the *Text* folder will be shown. Selected a bunch of files? Only those in the *Files* folder.

This is an important advantage over other utilities like ScriptMenu, now shipped by default with Jaguar. Sure, you can run AppleScripts on the current selection via ScriptMenu, but you'll also see all the scripts that have no effect on the current selection (Current Date and Time, etc.). BigCat makes hitting the right script a lot easier.

And what about changing file types and creators **[Hack #6]**? For a pure Apple-Script solution, changing a file's info to that of a common GIF is done like this:

```
tell application "Finder"
  set filelist to selection as list
end tell

tell application "Finder"
  repeat with i in filelist
    set file type of i to "GIFf"
    set creator type of i to "ogle"
  end repeat
end tell
```

Or, if you wanted to run a shell script, you could wrap it in an AppleScript as well. Here's the same script as before, only using the utilities provided with the Developer Tools CD:

```
tell application "Finder"
  set filelist to selection as list
end tell

tell application "Finder"
  repeat with i in filelist
    set macFilePath to (i as alias)
    set unixFilePath to POSIX path of macFilePath
    set command to "/Developer/Tools/SetFile -c ogle -t GIFf " & ↵
    unixFilePath
    do shell script command
  end repeat
end tell
```

HACK #47 Prying the Chrome Off Cocoa Applications

Metallifizer paints and strips the brushed-metal appearance of any Cocoa application.

There are two types of Mac users: those who find the brushed-metal look-and-feel of iTunes, Address Book, iChat, and the like just plain fab and those who wonder what some of these app designers are thinking with all this futuristic nonsense. Thank heavens for Metallifizer (*http://www. unsanity.com/download.php?product=metallifizer*) (freeware), another terrific haxie from the folks at Unsanity. Give any Cocoa application that brushed-metal appearance if you're so inclined. Or pry the default chrome right off that otherwise-favorite app.

> Perhaps a quick recap of the three Mac OS X application types is in order. Classic refers to applications built pre–Mac OS X; these run in Classic mode, effectively a Mac OS 9 emulator. Carbon applications have been modified to run under both Mac OS X and Mac OS 9; examples include: iMovie, Internet Explorer, QuickTime, and iTunes. Cocoa applications—like iChat, iPhoto, and the Address Book—are built specifically for Mac OS X. Metallifizer works only on the last category of applications.

Installation

Metallifizer is a module for Unsanity's Application Enhancer (APE) haxie (*http://www.haxies.com/ape/*). You'll need to download and install it before you can use Metallifizer. Figure 4-47 shows the APE preference pane.

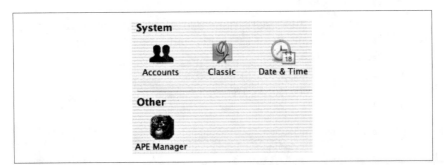

Figure 4-47. The APE preference pane

With APE installed, download and install Metallifizer by dragging it into your *Library/Application Enhancers* folder, as shown in Figure 4-48. If the folder doesn't yet exist, go ahead and create it.

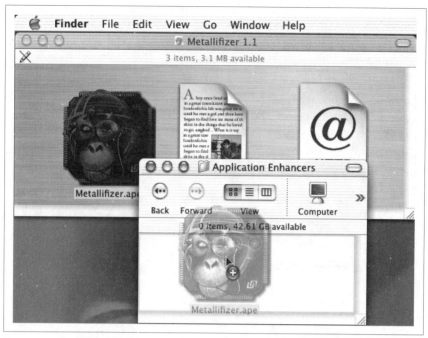

Figure 4-48. Installing Metallifizer

You'll need to log out and back in again before the Metallifizer will work. Once you've done so, open the System Preferences → APE Manager preference pane, shown in Figure 4-49.

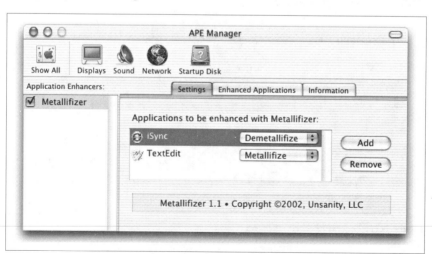

Figure 4-49. Metallifizing and demetallifizing applications

You'll notice that the Metallifizer plug-in is in operation; its checkbox should be checked. Altering the appearance of an application is then just a matter of adding it to or removing it from the APE Manager and selecting Metallifize (add the brushed-metal effect) or Demetallifize (remove the brushed-metal effect).

Figure 4-50 shows what iSync looks like before and after demetallifizing. Figure 4-51 shows a before and after composite for TextEdit, the ubiquitous Mac OS X text editor—not metallifized by default.

Figure 4-50. iSync before and after

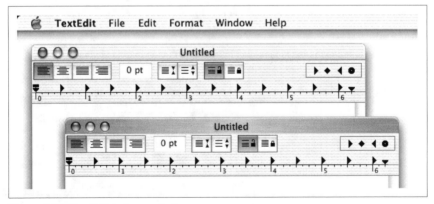

Figure 4-51. TextEdit before and after

—Wei-Meng Lee

## CHAPTER FIVE

Unix and the Terminal
Hacks 48–65

Beneath the sleek, elegant, Technicolor—and, yes, at times whimsical—candy coating of Mac OS X's graphical user interface beats the heart of an honest-to-goodness Unix operating system. It's a world of high-contrast plain text, at first blush not entirely unlike the much-maligned DOS shell of the Windows world.

While much of a Mac user's life is lived above the desktop abstraction, an occasional dip beneath the surface brings powers unimaginable and simply not possible with a point-and-click interface. There are servers to run, remote machines to manipulate, settings to tweak, events to schedule, and more. Many of the hacks in this book are best dealt with on the command line.

This chapter provides a gentle introduction to the command-line environment: how to move around and manipulate files and folders (they're called *directories* down here). With that under your belt, we'll show you how to thread some of the built-in Unix applications and functions together to create new functionality and construct command-line applications to meet your needs. You'll edit special Unix files, transfer files to and from other computers on the Internet, schedule events for regular invocation, and even become the all-powerful administrative, or *root*, user for a moment or two.

HACK #48   Introducing the Terminal

This brief tour of the Terminal introduces you to some of the more basic commands required to find out where you are, move about, manipulate files and directories, and get back out again when you've had enough.

This brief tour of the Terminal assumes you're either an old-time Mac hand who's been thanking your lucky stars you've never been near a command-line interface (CLI) or a recent Windows switcher who's been previously scared away by the complexity or unimpressed by the functionality of the rather ill-equipped DOS shell. It is meant as a quick-start guide, introducing you to some of the more basic commands required to find out where you are, move about, manipulate files and directories, and get back out again when you've had enough. Come on in, the water's fine!

Launching the Terminal

To invoke the Terminal, choose *Applications* → *Utilities* → *Terminal*, as shown in Figure 5-1.

Figure 5-1. Launching the Terminal

A few Dock bounces later and you'll have a fresh Terminal window in which to work (see Figure 5-2). The Terminal informs you about the date of your last visit and welcomes you to Darwin, the Unix core of Mac OS X.

> Need another Terminal window? Simply click File → New Shell or ⌘-N and another will make itself available to you.

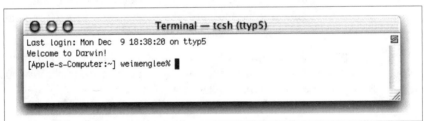

Figure 5-2. A fresh Terminal window

All that [Apple-s-Computer:~] weimenglee% jazz is known as the prompt and provides some useful information about your current working environment. The bit before the : is your computer's name (set in the System Preferences → Sharing pane). After the : is your current path, or whereabouts on your hard drive. In this case, I'm in my home directory, referred to colloquially as ~ (that's a tilde, found on the top left of your keyboard); were I in the *Applications* folder, my location would read as :/Applications. The bit just before the % is your username—weimenglee, in my case.

You'll be issuing all your commands at the prompt, with the cursor—that black block—keeping track of your typing in much the same way the I-beam does in your text editor.

Typing fingers ready? You're ready to issue your first command.

Current Working Directory

Let's make sure we know where we are, shall we? Type pwd, short for "print working directory":

```
[Apple-s-Computer:~] weimenglee% pwd
/Users/weimenglee
```

Unless you've gone anywhere since opening your Terminal window, you should be in your home directory, */Users/login*, where *login* is your Short Name [Hack #1] on the system. Again, this is the same as the ~ shortcut.

That's all well and good, but where exactly is */Users/weimenglee* with respect to the folders in the more familiar Finder? The screenshot in Figure 5-3 should help you to get your bearings.

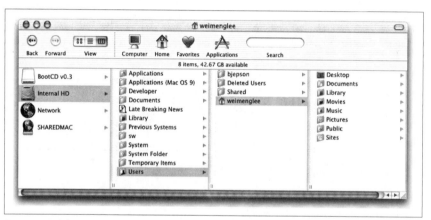

Figure 5-3. The current working directory in the Finder

While in the Finder we have *folders*, in Terminal we call them *directories*. Subdirectories are delimited by a / (forward slash) character. Switchers, note that Windows uses \ (backslash) to delimit subdirectories, as in *c:\ mydocu~1*. Remember to use / on the Mac command line.

> Backslash, under Unix, has magical properties of its own. It's used to escape or call out special characters like spaces, question marks, or the like. You'll most likely use it for dealing with files containing spaces on the command line, letting Unix know that you're still talking about the same file and haven't moved on to another. Notice the semantic difference between the file *this\ is\ one\ file* versus *file1 file2 file3*.

List Files and Folders

Now that you know your whereabouts, let's take a gander at the content of the current directory. The ls (list) command displays the content of a particular directory:

```
[Apple-s-Computer:~] weimenglee% ls
Desktop Documents Library Movies
Music   Pictures Public Sites
```

The ls command in this example displays the content of the current directory. You can also ask ls to list the contents of a specific directory and display the result in a particular format by passing it command-line options and a directory name.

In the Terminal, commands are in the format Command -options parameter. Options are prefixed by a - (hyphen); when there are more than one, they're pushed together.

As shown in Figure 5-4, ls -al Documents asked ls to list all (-a) the files using a longer (-l) listing format in the Documents directory.

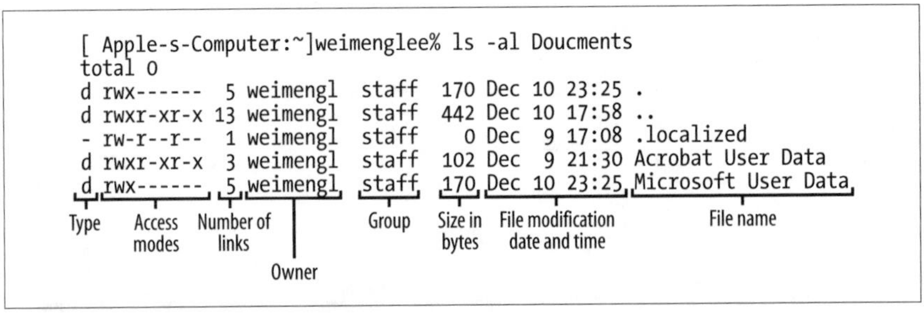

Figure 5-4. Output generated by ls -al

By default, files beginning with . (dot) will not be displayed by ls. To display them, use the -a option. The two files listed with names . and .. are special files known as the current and parent directory, respectively.

Occasionally, you may have a long file listing, with output flowing off the top of the screen. To page through, one screenful at a time, send—known as piping because of its use of the | (pipe) character—the output to the more command:

```
[Apple-s-Computer:~] weimenglee% ls -al | more
```

Clearing the Screen

After trying out these comamnds, your screen will no doubt be full of files and directories. To clear the screen, type clear or press Control-L.

Changing Directories

To move about, issue a cd, or change directory, command, specifying a directory as the parameter. This is akin to opening a folder in the Finder. For example, let's meander over to the *Public* directory:

```
[Apple-s-Computer:~] weimenglee% cd Public
[Apple-s-Computer:~/Public] weimenglee%
```

Notice how the current directory—the bit after the : in your prompt—changes to ~/*Public*. This is a constant reminder of where you are at any moment in time; no need to keep typing cwd to find out. Remember that the ~ refers to your home directory; so, in this case I'm actually in */Users/weimenglee/Public*.

There are two ways of specifying a particular directory. The first is to use the absolute or full path (e.g., cd /Users/weimenglee/Public). The second, much shorter when you're moving down the path relative to your current location, is to use the relative path (e.g., cd Public). Assuming you're in your home directory, these examples are equivalent.

Let's now turn our attention to the contents of the *Public* folder:

```
[Apple-s-Computer:~/Public] weimenglee% ls
Drop Box
```

Inside of *Public*, there is one subdirectory, *Drop Box*, and no files. Change to the *Drop Box* directory by typing cd Drop\ Box. You can also use tab completion to save yourself a little typing; simply type cd D and press the Tab key. Bingo! The directory name is automatically completed for you. This works on both files and folders, relative and absolute paths. If there's another file or folder with the same initial letter, type the second letter and press Tab—and so on, typing as much of the name necessary to distinguish it from others.

Moving On Up

To move up one step in the directory hierarchy, use .. to refer to the special parent directory:

```
[Apple-s-Computer:~/Public/Drop Box] weimenglee% cd ..
[Apple-s-Computer:~/Public] weimenglee%
```

Move up multiple levels by combining .. and /, like so:

```
[Apple-s-Computer:~/Public] weimenglee% pwd
/Users/weimenglee/Public
[Apple-s-Computer:~/Public] weimenglee% cd ../..
[Apple-s-Computer:/Users] weimenglee% pwd
/Users/
```

cd . will have no effect, changing the current directory to, well, the current directory. But . will come in handy in a moment when we start copying files.

To go to the top of the directory (known as the *root* directory), use / all by itself:

```
[Apple-s-Computer:/Users] weimenglee% cd /
[Apple-s-Computer:/] weimenglee%
```

To return to your home directory, simply use the cd command with no parameters, the equivalent of cd ~ and cd /Users/login (where login is your Short Name):

```
[Apple-s-Computer:/] weimenglee% cd
[Apple-s-Computer:~/] weimenglee%
```

Creating Directories

To create a new directory, use the mkdir (make directory) command, followed by the directory name—either relative or absolute path. Note that if your new directory name contains spaces, you need to escape them or enclose the entire directory name in "" (double quotes). Otherwise mkdir will think that you mean to create multiple directories, as the following failed attempt to create a new folder called *Temp Folder* shows:

```
[Apple-s-Computer:~] weimenglee% mkdir Temp Folder
[Apple-s-Computer:~] weimenglee% ls -al
total 0
drwxr-xr-x  6 weimengl staff 204 Dec 11 08:50 .
drwxr-xr-x 13 weimengl staff 442 Dec 10 17:58 ..
-rw-r--r--  1 weimengl staff   0 Dec  9 17:08 .localized
drwxr-xr-x  2 weimengl staff  68 Dec 11 08:50 Folder
drwxr-xr-x  2 weimengl staff  68 Dec 11 08:50 Temp
```

Either of the following two versions will work as expected:

```
mkdir Temp\ Folder
mkdir "Temp Folder"
```

Removing Directories

To remove a directory, use rmdir (remove directory), the polar opposite of mkdir. The space issue applies as expected; either of the following will do:

```
rmdir Temp\ Folder
rmdir "Temp Folder"
```

Copying Files

To copy a file, use the cp (copy) command, followed by the file to copy and its intended destination. Use either a relative or absolute path for each. For example, let's copy the file *index.html* from the directory *Sites* to *Documents*:

```
[Apple-s-Computer:~] weimenglee% cp Sites/index.html Documents
[Apple-s-Computer:~/Documents] weimenglee% cd Documents
[Apple-s-Computer:~/Documents] weimenglee% ls
index.html
```

To copy a file to the current directory, use the special . filename, like so:

```
[Apple-s-Computer:~/Documents] weimenglee% cp Sites/index.html .
```

Deleting Files

To delete a file, use the rm (remove) command. The following example deletes that *index.html* we just copied to *Documents*:

```
[Apple-s-Computer:~/Documents] weimenglee% rm index.html
```

Moving Files

To move a file from one directory to another, use the mv (move) command, followed by the space-separated name and destination path. The following example moves the file *index.html* from the directory *Sites* to *Documents*:

```
[Apple-s-Computer:~] weimenglee% mv Sites/index.html Documents
[Apple-s-Computer:~] weimenglee% cd Sites/
[Apple-s-Computer:~/Sites] weimenglee% ls
images
[Apple-s-Computer:~/Sites] weimenglee% cd ../Documents
[Apple-s-Computer:~/Documents] weimenglee% ls
index.html
```

The mv command is also used for renaming files. The following example renames the file from *index.html* to *index.txt*:

```
[Apple-s-Computer:~/Documents] weimenglee% mv index.html index.txt
[Apple-s-Computer:~/Documents] weimenglee% ls
index.txt
```

Let's put everything back, shall we? Type mv index.txt ~/Sites/index.html, and all should be as it was when we started this ride.

Viewing the Content of a Text File

At times, you may want to take a quick peek at the contents of a text file. To do so, use cat (concatenate), specifying the file or files to display, like so:

```
% cat .lpoptions
Default _192_168_254_149
```

Copy and Paste, Drag and Drop

The standard editing suite, select all, copy, and paste, works as expected in the Terminal, whether invoked with ⌘-A, ⌘-C, and ⌘-V or pulled down from the Edit menu.

A nice bit of interaction between command line and GUI is the ability to drag a file, directory, or bookmark from anywhere you may be in the Finder right onto the command line. Want to edit a file in a Terminal-based editor [Hack #51] without navigating the directory hierarchy to get to it? Type pico (or the like), followed by a space, and drag the file right into the Terminal window. It's a shortcut that comes in handy more often than you'd think.

Consulting the Manpages

There is only so much I can cover in this quick tour of the Terminal. You'll encounter a plethora of commands and applications on the command line. Whenever you need any help, try consulting the manual. Simply type man (as in *manual*, not *oh, man!*), followed by the command name. Your average manpage looks something like Figure 5-5.

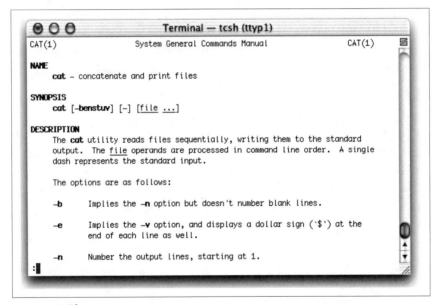

Figure 5-5. The average manpage

Getting Off the Command Line

At any point you can always close the Terminal window as you would any other. It is far more polite—not to mention cleaner—to log out of the shell session you're running by typing exit or logout:

```
% logout
[Process completed]
```

—*Wei-Meng Lee and Rael Dornfest*

More Terminal Tricks and Tips

So many commands, so little time to learn them all. Here are a few more command-line tips and tricks that you are sure to find useful.

With a plethora of commands and various ways in which to combine them and string them together, you can do virtually unlimited things on the command line. Here are a few more tips and tricks you'll find useful while working your way through some of the hacks in this book.

Of course, this crash course combined with "Introducing the Terminal" **[Hack #48]** barely scratches the surface of the powerful Unix operating system. For a more in-depth treatment, we highly recommend *Unix Power Tools* (*http://www.oreilly.com/catalog/upt3/*).

Customizing Your Terminal

Over time, you will no doubt be bored with Terminal's plain black-on-white settings. Here are some tips for adding some spice to your Terminal windows.

Longtime Unix users would be familiar with the green-on-black settings. Those were the days when dumb terminals ruled and a color monitor was more a luxury than a necessity. In Mac OS X, you can change the color of your Terminal window to mimic the good old days.

To change the color of your Terminal window, click on Terminal → Window Settings..., as shown in Figure 5-6.

The Terminal Inspector window will appear (see Figure 5-7); it's from here that you may make various changes to your Terminal window configuration.

If you simply want all Terminal windows to adopt the settings you have just created, select File → Use Settings As Defaults.

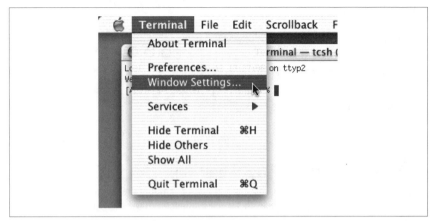

Figure 5-6. Changing the appearance of your Terminal window

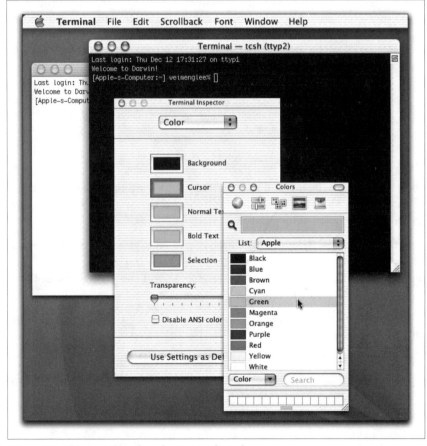

Figure 5-7. Changing the color of a Terminal window

To save your modified settings without applying them globally, select File → Save As... to save them to a *.term* preference file, as shown in Figure 5-8.

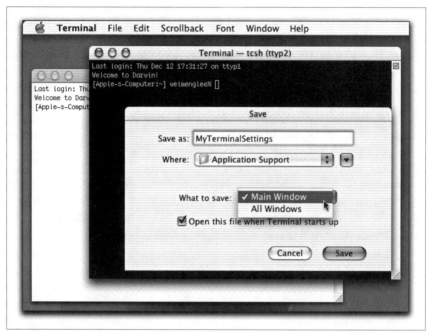

Figure 5-8. Saving Terminal settings to a .term file

You can create multiple *.term* files representing various different configurations. To open a Terminal window with a particular setting, select it from File → Library, select File → Open..., and choose the appropriate *.term* file, or drag it to your Dock and click it whenever you want a Terminal window of that type. By default, *.term* files are saved to your *Library/Application Support/Terminal* directory.

You can even have a particular *.term* file run a specific command when it opens. Open a *.term* file in your favorite plain-text editor [Hack #51] and look for this:

```
... <key>ExecutionString</key> <string></string> ...
```

Alter the value of the `<string>` element to be whatever you'd like run on the command line when the Terminal window opens. I have a shell script for port-forwarding my mail [Hack #70], called `mailforward.sh`, which I run every time I come online after being off for a while simply by double-clicking my *mailforward.term* file in my Dock. That *.term* file's `ExecutionString` looks like this:

```
... <key>ExecutionString</key> <string>~/bin/mailforward.sh</string> ...
```

Switching Terminal Windows

Often, you may have many Terminal windows lying about. Switching between them using mouse clicks can be more trouble than it's worth. Thankfully, there are a few keyboard shortcuts. Press ⌘-1 to switch to the first window, ⌘-2 for the second, and so on. If you want to loop through the open Terminal windows, type ⌘–right arrow or ⌘–left arrow for forward and backward, respectively.

Learning from History

At times, you may want to reuse the commands that you've typed previously, especially if a command has lengthy options and parameters; you wouldn't want to type everything again, now would you? You can always use the up and down arrow keys to navigate previously used commands, but when you're reaching back a number of commands ago, there's a better way than wearing away your fingerprint hitting that up arrow repeatedly. Use the history command to display the list of previously executed commands:

```
% history
1 11:34 cal 2003
2 11:34 ls -al
3 11:34 clear
4 11:34 man open
5 11:34 history
```

The history command even lists the time at which the command was executed. To reuse a particular command, type ! (exclamation point or "bang" in hacker-speak), followed by the number listed alongside the command you want to reuse, then press the Return key. Here, for example, I run the second item in the list:

```
% !2
ls -al
{a long-format listing of all files in the local directory}
```

If you have a long history list—I always do—you can also use the first few letters of the command line instead of the command number, like so:

```
% !ls
ls -al
{a long-format listing of all files in the local directory}
```

This can, however, be dangerous and unpredictable if you end up running something that started with the same letters but wasn't quite the same command you had in mind. Think about running rm * (remove all files in the current directory) when you think you're running rm notes.txt (remove the *notes.txt* file). You can get history to show you what it thinks you mean by adding a :p to the end of the history reference, whether it be by number or first few characters:

```
% !ls:p
ls -al
% !ls
ls -al
{a long-format listing of all files in the local directory}
```

You can also use :p to recall and then slightly alter an earlier command by pressing the up arrow right afterward, editing the command line, and pressing Return:

```
% !rm:p
rm a.txt b.txt c.txt
{hit the Up arrow}
% rm a.txt b.txt d.txt
```

Listing All the Commands

The man (manual) command [Hack #48] allows you to check for the usage of a command. But how do you know which commands are available to you in the first place? You can take a gander at the entire list of available commands by pressing Control-X, Control-D.

Changing Permissions with chmod

The Unix command chmod (change mode) alters permissions on files and directories, allowing you to fine-tune access control and protect files from unauthorized users or accidental deletion (hey, it happens!).

Permissions are perhaps best explained by example. First, create a new directory named *my_folder*:

```
% mkdir my_folder
```

Change into the newly created directory and list all the files therein; there shouldn't be anything aside from . (this directory) and .. (the parent directory):

```
% cd my_folder
% ls -al
total 0
drwxr-xr-x 2 weimengl staff 68 Dec 13 09:31 .
drwxr-xr-x 18 weimengl staff 612 Dec 13 09:31 ..
```

Next, create a new text file. One of the simplest ways to create a quick test file is by echoing some text to it, literally sending some text toward the file, indicating toward using the > redirection operator:

```
% echo "Some text" > file1.txt
```

Take a look at the default permissions for the file we just created; they're at the left margin associated with *file1.txt*:

```
% ls -l
total 8
-rw-r--r-- 1 weimengl staff 10 Dec 13 09:33 file1.txt
```

Permissions come in three sets of three: owner, group, and world, each with an associated read, write, and execute permission. Our *file1.txt* is readable and writeable (rw-) by the owner (that's you), readable (r--) by the group (that's anyone who's in the staff group along with you), and readable (r--) by anyone else.

We will concern ourselves only with owner permissions at this point. Let's change the permissions on *file1.txt* so that it is not writable by you, thus protecting it against accidental overwriting:

```
% chmod u-w file1.txt
```

The parameter u-w tells chmod to remove the write permission from the user (owner). To confirm, take another look:

```
% ls -l
total 8
-r--r--r-- 1 weimengl staff 10 Dec 13 09:33 file1.txt
```

Try deleting the file. You'll be prompted to override the permission settings. If you weren't the owner, however, you'd simply be denied permission altogether:

```
% rm file1.txt
override r--r--r-- weimengl/staff for file1.txt?
```

Try appending some text to the file (>> means *append* rather than *write to*). Since you've denied yourself write permission, you'll fail:

```
% echo "Some more text" >> file1.txt file1.txt: Permission denied.
```

To grant yourself write permission again, do the inverse of the previous chmod using +, like so:

```
% chmod u+w file1.txt
```

Now let's return to the home directory and examine the permission settings for the *my_folder* directory:

```
% cd ~
% ls -l
total 40
...
drwxr-xr-x 3 weimengl staff 102 Dec 13 09:39 myFolder
...
```

Try removing the execute (x) permission from the directory for yourself, the owner. Then try visiting it again using cd:

```
% chmod u-x my_folder
% cd my_folder
my_folder: Permission denied.
```

Why are you locked out? Directories are special files requiring execute permissions before allowing you into or across their borders. Since you don't have execute permission, you're barred.

Put back the execute permission while at the same time removing write permission and cd into *my_folder* again:

```
% chmod u+x my_folder
% chmod u-w my_folder
% cd my_folder
```

All appears back to normal; you should have landed just fine inside *my_folder*. Try to create another file in your now unwritable directory:

```
% echo "Some text" > file2.txt file2.txt: Permission denied.
```

As you might have guessed, while you can visit the folder thanks to executable permission, you can't alter it in any way without write permission. You can't create, move, or delete anything. You can, however, still edit *file1.txt*, since a file's permissions take precedence when dealing directly with it.

> There is also a way to refer to permissions numerically (e.g., chmod 755 script.cgi), but we'll leave that to a more advanced Unix text.

Changing Owner and Group with chown and chgrp

This is all well and good, given that all the files in your directory (presumably) belong to you. But what of files that aren't yours yet need some dealing with? That's where chown (change owner) and chgrp (change group) come in.

Take a quick look at the document directory for your onboard Apache web server [Hack #88]:

```
% cd /Library/WebServer/Documents/
% ls -al
total 376
drwxrwxr-x 38 root admin 1292 Dec 13 00:24 .
drwxrwxr-x 5 root admin 170 Dec 10 17:39 ..
-rw-rw-r-- 1 root admin 3726 Jul 27 14:31 PoweredByMacOSx.gif
-rw-rw-r-- 1 root admin 31958 Jul 27 14:31 PoweredByMacOSxLarge.gif
-rw-rw-r-- 1 root admin 2326 Apr 14 1999 apache_pb.gif
-rw-rw-r-- 1 root admin 1884 Oct 17 2001 index.html.ca
...
-rw-rw-r-- 1 root admin 1062 Jun 19 18:23 index.html.zh
lrwxrwxr-x 1 root admin 38 Dec 13 00:24 manual -> /Library/Documentation/
Services/apache
```

Notice that, by default, they're all owned by the root user **[Hack #50]** and admin group. I'm not root, but I am an admin user, as shown by the whoami and groups commands:

```
% whoami
weimengl
% groups
staff admin
```

Given the permissions on the files and the directory they're in, I should be able to create, edit, move, and remove anything I need to in order to tend this machine's web site. But what of the nonadministrative users I have helping me? There has to be some way to give them ownership of some of these files. And there must be some way to claim ownership of a file and block admin access to it—except by the root user, of course.

The chown command does just that. Perhaps you'd like to take ownership of *index.html.ca* and horde write permission:

```
% sudo chown weimengl index.html.ca
Password:
% chmod g-w index.html.ca
% ls -l index.html.ca
-rw-r--r-- 1 weimengl admin 1884 Oct 17 2001 index.html.ca
```

Now the file is owned by you, and nobody but you has write permission to it.

> Since you can't simultaneously be the owner of the file as it stands and the owner you're about to give it, chown requires becoming the root user for a moment **[Hack #50]**.

Perhaps you want to give write permission to everyone working on the web site. You could change permissions so that all the files are world writable (chmod o+w), but that's generally regarded as bad form. Instead, you could simply change the group ownership (chgrp) of the particular files you'd like them to all share, in this case, all the *index.html* files:

```
% sudo chgrp staff index.html*
Password:
% ls -al index.html.*
-rw-rw-r-- 1 root staff 1884 Oct 17 2001 index.html.ca
...
-rw-rw-r-- 1 root staff 1062 Jun 19 18:23 index.html.zh
```

> Being pedantic, it's actually best to create a new group, webadmin, for example, into which to put all those folks working on the site. This is better than giving write access to anyone you happen to let log in to your machine. But, since this was meant as a quick demonstration of chgrp, we glossed over those details.

If you have some reason to change both owner and group at the same time, you can combine these actions into one command: chown owner.group.

Counting Files

Unlike Windows (or DOS, in particular), the ls command in Unix does not display the total number of files displayed. Consider the following example:

```
[Apple-s-Computer:~] weimenglee% ls -l
total 2200
drwx------ 12 weimengl staff    408 Dec 12 11:35 Desktop
drwx------ 6  weimengl staff    204 Dec 11 20:17 Documents
drwx------ 24 weimengl staff    816 Dec  9 21:09 Library
drwx------ 3  weimengl staff    102 Dec  9 17:08 Movies
drwx------ 3  weimengl staff    102 Dec  9 17:08 Music
drwx------ 4  weimengl staff    136 Dec  9 20:36 Pictures
drwxr-xr-x 4  weimengl staff    136 Dec 11 08:53 Public
drwxr-xr-x 5  weimengl staff    170 Dec 11 09:05 Sites
-rw-r--r-- 1  weimengl staff 380235 Dec 11 15:17 foo.pdf
-rw-r--r-- 1  weimengl staff 412280 Dec 11 15:48 image.pdf
-rw-r--r-- 1  weimengl staff 328970 Dec 11 15:38 test.pdf
```

For directories with few files, this generally is not a problem. But at times you need to know the total number of files and you do not want to wade through a long list of files.

To count the files, you can use the | (pipe) character and the wc (word count) command with the -l option to count the number of lines:

```
% ls -l | wc -l
12
```

Note that the actual file count should be 11, but the count includes the line total 2200 and so is off by 1.

And if you want to count the number of directories, you can use the grep command. The grep command looks over incoming text and prints out lines that match the specified pattern. To find all lines starting with d, you'd use ^d as the pattern, the ^ signifying the beginning of a line:

```
% ls -l | grep ^d | wc -l
8
```

And if you want only regular files, you'd look for lines starting with -:

```
% ls -l | grep ^- | wc -l
3
```

If you'd like to see a listing of only PDF files, you can again use a pattern, this time grepping for the characters at the end of the line. The end-of-line pattern indicator is $:

```
% ls -l | grep pdf$ | wc -l
3
```

It found *foo.pdf*, *image.pdf*, and *test.pdf*, as it should have. One could more easily have used * (star or splat) as a stand-in for the bits of the files we didn't know and simply listed everything ending in *.pdf* like so:

```
% ls *.pdf | wc -l
3
```

Displaying a Calendar

Need to check the date for last Wednesday? Here is a quick way to do it in the Terminal. Use the cal (calendar) command:

```
% cal
December 2002
 S  M Tu  W Th  F  S
 1  2  3  4  5  6  7
 8  9 10 11 12 13 14
15 16 17 18 19 20 21
22 23 24 25 26 27 28
29 30 31
```

Without any parameters, cal will display the calendar for the current month. You can also display the calendar for the entire year. cal supports years 1 to 9999:

```
% cal 2003
2003

      January               February                March
 S  M Tu  W Th  F  S    S  M Tu  W Th  F  S    S  M Tu  W Th  F  S
          1  2  3  4                      1                      1
 5  6  7  8  9 10 11    2  3  4  5  6  7  8    2  3  4  5  6  7  8
12 13 14 15 16 17 18    9 10 11 12 13 14 15    9 10 11 12 13 14 15
19 20 21 22 23 24 25   16 17 18 19 20 21 22   16 17 18 19 20 21 22
26 27 28 29 30 31      23 24 25 26 27 28      23 24 25 26 27 28 29
                                              30 31

 ...

      October               November               December
 S  M Tu  W Th  F  S    S  M Tu  W Th  F  S    S  M Tu  W Th  F  S
          1  2  3  4                      1     1  2  3  4  5  6
 5  6  7  8  9 10 11    2  3  4  5  6  7  8    7  8  9 10 11 12 13
12 13 14 15 16 17 18    9 10 11 12 13 14 15   14 15 16 17 18 19 20
19 20 21 22 23 24 25   16 17 18 19 20 21 22   21 22 23 24 25 26 27
26 27 28 29 30 31      23 24 25 26 27 28 29   28 29 30 31
                       30
```

You can also opt to display a particular month in a particular year:

```
% cal 1 2003
January 2003
 S  M Tu  W Th  F  S
           1  2  3  4
 5  6  7  8  9 10 11
12 13 14 15 16 17 18
19 20 21 22 23 24 25
26 27 28 29 30 31
```

Or, you can display the date in Julian format:

```
% cal -j 2003
2003

January                         February
 S   M  Tu   W  Th   F   S    S   M  Tu   W  Th   F   S
              1   2   3   4                               32
 5   6   7   8   9  10  11   33  34  35  36  37  38  39
12  13  14  15  16  17  18   40  41  42  43  44  45  46
19  20  21  22  23  24  25   47  48  49  50  51  52  53
26  27  28  29  30  31        54  55  56  57  58  59

...

November                        December
 S   M  Tu   W  Th   F   S    S   M  Tu   W  Th   F   S
                        305       335 336 337 338 339 340
306 307 308 309 310 311 312   341 342 343 344 345 346 347
313 314 315 316 317 318 319   348 349 350 351 352 353 354
320 321 322 323 324 325 326   355 356 357 358 359 360 361
327 328 329 330 331 332 333   362 363 364 365
334
```

—Wei-Meng Lee

HACK #50 Becoming an Administrator for a Moment

Your Mac does its best to protect you from yourself and your family by requiring authentication, both in the GUI and on the command line, when you're about to do something potentially problematic.

OS X, being a multiuser Unix system at its heart, tries to prevent you (or your family) from doing anything that might adversely affect your Mac. It does so by denying access to particular files that keep your system running and disallowing actions that it considers potentially harmful. Every now and again, however, you need to install a piece of software or touch a vital Unix configuration file to get something done. Before it'll let you do so, OS X will require that you authenticate yourself as an administrative user, known in Unix parlance as *root*.

Desktop Root

While most applications can be installed simply by dragging them into the *Applications* folder, some require a little more tomfoolery. Application and package installers often need to create folders, drop files into place, and adjust configuration settings in restricted parts of the operating system.

At these times you're either not allowed to continue if you're not listed as an administrative user of the system (take a look at the *System Preferences →Users* pane) or prompted for your password if you are. A typical Authenticate dialog looks like Figure 5-9.

Figure 5-9. Authenticate dialog

You'll notice I've expanded the detail level by clicking on the Details arrow. In this case, the application asking for authentication is the standard Mac OS X Installer.

Type in your password and the Installer will continue. What you've done, in effect, is become an administrator with full power over your system, if only for a moment. You've then granted the Installer similar power to do what it needs to do.

> Whenever you authenticate yourself to an application, realize that it's going to be fiddling with your system and make sure you have some idea what it's trying to do. Read the notices displayed by installers carefully.

You'll also encounter times when you need to authenticate yourself to make a configuration change in the System Preferences or the like. If you find that you're unable to change some settings that seem as if they should be editable, look around the window for a little lock icon. If it's locked, you may need to unlock it (click on it) and authenticate yourself. If you feel the need to lock the settings again when you're done, click the lock again (see Figure 5-10).

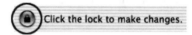

Figure 5-10. Locked settings

Command-Line Root

On the command line [Hack #48], there is no fancy dialog for authenticating you as the root user. The sudo utility (substitute-user do) allows you to gain temporary root privileges on a per-command basis. To use sudo, simply preface the command you wish to run as root with sudo and a space, and sudo will prompt you for your (not root's) password. If you have administrator privileges, entering your password will run the sudoed command as if the root user were doing it.

 Use sudo with care. You can easily make mistakes with sudo that could require a complete reinstallation of the OS to get going again. If that thought makes you queasy, it would be wise for now to use sudo only as directed in this hack.

Typical sudo use looks like this:

```
% sudo apachectl restart
```

Notes about sudo:

- The first time you run sudo, you'll see another reminder to use sudo with care.

- You'll need to enter your password only when you haven't already used sudo within the last five minutes.

- It's not necessary to activate the root account or do anything else special to start using sudo.

Enabling the Root Account

You may find a reason at some point to enable the root account on your Mac. While it's a rare hack indeed that would require logging in as the root user, it does come up (e.g., "Understanding and Hacking Your User Account" [Hack #1]).

To do so, launch NetInfo Manager (*Applications → Utilities → NetInfo Manager*) and authenticate yourself by clicking the lock icon at the bottom-left and entering your password, as show in Figure 5-11.

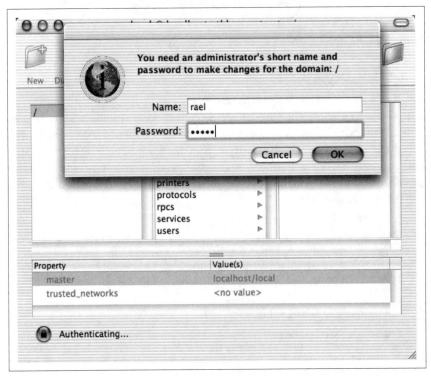

Figure 5-11. Authenticating yourself to NetInfo Manager

To enable the root user, select Security → Enable Root User from the menu bar. If this is the first time you've done this, you'll be warned that the root password is currently blank (see Figure 5-12) and you'll be prompted to set one (see Figure 5-13).

Click the lock icon again to disallow any further changes, and close NetInfo Manager. The root account is now active.

To disable the account, follow the same steps, but select Security → Disable Root User.

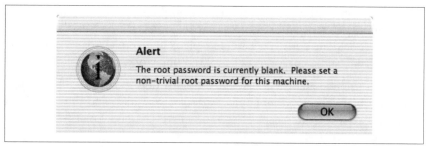

Figure 5-12. A warning about the root password not being set

Figure 5-13. Setting the root password

Logging in as Root

Log in as root just as you would log in as any other user. The only differ-ence is that root won't appear in the list of users and their associated cute icons. Click Other, enter root as the Name, and enter the password you assigned to the root account as Password.

—Chris Stone and Rael Dornfest

Editing Special Unix Files

HACK
#51

Special Unix files need special handling. You can't simply edit them in Word and expect things to work. Here's a crash course in editing using the pico command-line editor and TextEdit GUI editor.

You've no doubt discovered OS X's default text editor, the aptly named TextEdit. Hopefully, you've also heard of and downloaded the outstanding BBEdit (*http://www.bbedit.com/index.html*), favorite text editor of genera-tions of Mac users. But unless you're a Unix jock, you probably don't know that OS X ships with several other feature- and history-rich Terminal-based text editors. Veterans will tend to swear by either vi (the Visual Editor) or Emacs, but seldom both. Then there's pico, the simplest of the three, yet still more than sufficient for most simple editing work.

Here we'll provide a crash course in editing those special Unix files we talk about in this book: *httpd.conf*, */etc/inetd.conf*, *plist* files, and the like. We'll skip the two with the steepest learning curve—vi and Emacs—and stick with pico and TextEdit.

Using pico

pico was developed at the University of Washington. It is a simple but powerful Unix text editor. To fire up pico, type `pico` (by itself or followed by a particular file to edit) in a Terminal [Hack #48] window (see Figure 5-14).

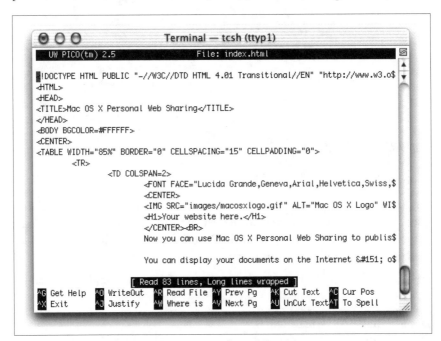

Figure 5-14. The pico interface

pico's interface, while perhaps a little Unixey for the uninitiated, is pretty straightforward. Rather than clicking buttons in menu bars, commands are issued by typing Control-character shortcuts; the bottom two rows provide a list of commonly used shortcuts. That ^ character prefixing all of the shortcuts stands for the Control key on your keyboard; thus, ^G signifies that for more comprehensive help, you should press Control-G (see Figure 5-15).

Press Control-X to leave pico help.

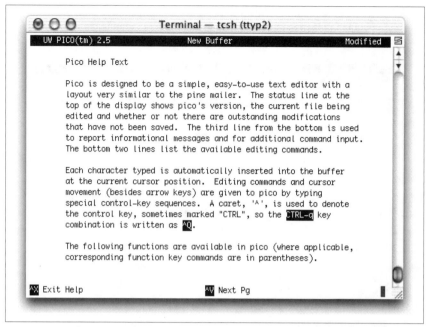

Figure 5-15. Getting help in pico

Now that you have pico warmed up, let's take it for a spin with some common operations.

Moving about. Move about within the text file you're editing, as you might expect, using the arrow keys. Beyond basic character-by-character movement, however, your old habits will fail you. None of the ⌘- sequences work here. To scroll through long text, you cannot use the Page Up and Page Down keys on your keyboard; it's Control-Y for page up and Control-V for page down. To jump to the beginning of a line, press Control-A. To jump to the end, type Control-E.

To search within the current file for a snippet of text, press Control-W, enter the text to find at the Search: prompt, and press Return. To search for the same text again, press Control-W, followed by Return. To change your mind and cancel a search, press Control-C.

Saving. To save a file (see Figure 5-16), press ⌘-O (write out—go figure!).

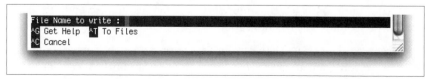

Figure 5-16. Saving a file in pico

Type a filename or fully qualified path (e.g., /tmp/test.txt) to which to save, as shown in Figure 5-17, and press Return.

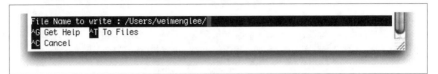

Figure 5-17. Supplying a filename or path to save to

You can also use the built-in file and directory browser (press Control-T) to locate a particular directory into which to save your file (see Figure 5-18). Use the arrow keys to move about, Return to move into a directory, .. to move up a directory, and e to select a directory and return to the File Name to write: prompt. You can also select a filename, and whatever you save will overwrite what's already there.

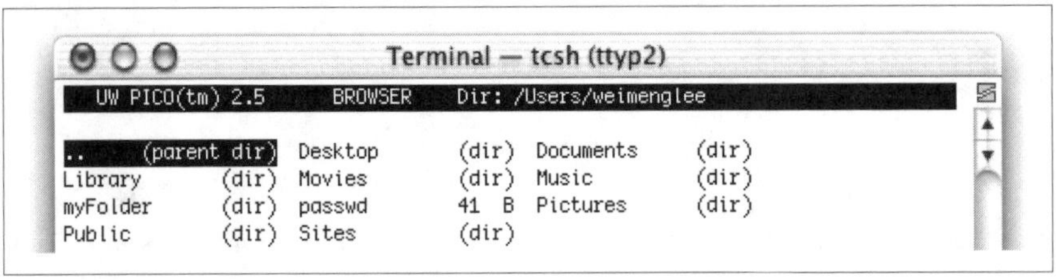

Figure 5-18. The pico directory browser

Opening. Oddly enough, pico doesn't have an Open File command. Instead, you insert the contents of a file into the editor, as shown in Figure 5-19. Press Control-R and everything's pretty much the same as it was with saving, directory browser and all. The only difference is that you use Return rather then e to make your final selection. The selected file's contents will appear in the editor, appended to anything you've already been editing.

```
Insert file from home directory:
^G Get Help  ^T To Files
^C Cancel
```

Figure 5-19. Inserting a file

Selecting text. Selecting a block of text in pico is not as straightforward as using your mouse. In fact, the mouse is utterly useless in pico and just about every other command-line application.

To select a block of text, use the arrow keys to position your cursor at the start of the text you want to select and press Control-Shift-6 (a.k.a. Control-^).

pico will respond with [Mark Set]. Move about until you've selected all the text you wish; selected text is called out in inverse colors.

To simply unselect the text, press Control-Shift-6 again.

To cut the selected block, press Control-K. To paste it somewhere, move the cursor to the right place and press Control-U. Note that there's no copy in pico. To copy, just cut and paste (Control-K, Control-U) in place and then paste again with Control-U anywhere and as many times as you wish.

Deleting. Use your Delete key as usual to delete the character before your cursor. To delete the character after the cursor, press Control-D. Delete an entire line with Control-K.

Leaving. To get out of pico at any time, press Control-X. If you've not saved what you're currently editing, pico will offer you one last chance to Save modified buffer.

TextEdit

TextEdit (*Applications → TextEdit*) is the default GUI text editor. Being more like any other application you've used than pico, TextEdit is also much more novice-friendly.

As in most Mac applications, you drag and drop selections made with your mouse. Saving, opening, cutting, copying, and pasting work as expected. Moving about with the arrow keys and ⌘-modified arrow keys also holds no surprises. Page Up and Page Down shift up and down a page.

Setting Your Default Command-Line Editor

The default command-line editor is vi—not a great choice for beginners. Commands like crontab -e **[Hack #53]** use the default as their editor of choice, rather than allowing you to use the pico editor you now know and love.

To set your command-line editor of choice to pico, create a file in your home directory called *.tcshrc* containing the following single line:

```
setenv EDITOR /usr/bin/pico
```

The next time you invoke a Terminal command that requires a default editor (and respects the EDITOR environment variable), pico will be used instead of vi.

Why Not Simply Go GUI?

Why, then, would anyone bother delving into antiquity with pico or any of the other Terminal-based editors? Good question.

One answer is that editing on the command line is far better integrated into working with special Unix files than throwing them out to a GUI text editor and jumping back to the command line when you're done. This is especially true when it comes to editing files you don't have permission to edit without becoming an administrative (root) user [Hack #50]. Just type sudo pico *special_filename*, authenticate yourself, and you're editing. Try opening that same file in TextEdit and you won't be allowed to save it once you're done editing.

That said, you can invoke TextEdit as the administrative user from the command line:

```
% sudo /Applications/TextEdit.app/Contents/MacOS/TextEdit
```

You have added a step, though, since you'll still have to open the particular file you were after from within TextEdit.

Another reason to use the command line is that some Terminal commands automatically open your default editor for you and rely upon knowing when it's done. This doesn't always work particularly well with an external GUI editor like TextEdit.

For those who regularly log in to a remote machine [Hack #71] for administrative tasks, there's no choice but one of the Terminal-based editors—either that or running a desktop-sharing app, which is overkill for editing a configuration file.

And, as mentioned, vi and Emacs are powerful editors, enabling far more than would be possible within a traditional text editor. This power takes some know-how, but it quickly becomes indispensable.

The choice is really yours. If you're more comfortable using a GUI editor like TextEdit or BBEdit (which can authenticate as an administrative user from the GUI), go right ahead. If you're using the command line quite a bit and it's starting to grow on you, pico, vi, or Emacs might turn out to be your killer editor.

—*Wei-Meng Lee*

HACK #52 Setting Shell Environment Variables

An environment variable is a magical piece of invisible data that is acted upon by shell programs and utilities that look for its existence. They're innocent enough and you rarely interact with them, but they can prove to be quite powerful and time saving when used as part of your daily lifestyle.

Smart developers who care about code integrity use something called a versioning system to ensure a system of checks and balances, easy reversion to previous code, and preventive overwriting (by an automatic or manual merging process). It's such a common part of a developer's toolkit that the popular open source web IDE Sourceforge.net provides it as a default service.

One annoyance of Concurrent Versioning System (CVS) (longtime users can find many more) is the command line—without an enviroment variable, you have to type your cvsroot each and every time you make any changes to your repository:

```
cvs -d:pserver:anonymous@cvs.amphetadesk.sourceforge.net:/cvsroot/
amphetadesk login
cvs -z3 -d:pserver:anonymous@cvs.amphetadesk.sourceforge.net:/cvsroot/
amphetadesk co AmphetaDesk
```

These two lines log you into a CVS server as the user anonymous and then check out the entire source tree of a program called AmphetaDesk. A cursory examination shows that the largest part of the command line is the -d flag; it's also repetitive, as it needs to be a part of every cvs command. It can make a person nuts when she has to worry about committing modifications to a dozen different files. Wouldn't it be great if you never had to type the -d flag and its heavy payload?

Thankfully, using environment variables, you don't. Think of an environment variable as a configuration file; the values are acted upon only by the application that knows how to handle them. Instead of being located in seperate config files, they're loaded into the shell environment. You can think of them (roughly) as preferences for your shell (as opposed to preferences for the OS X Terminal application). The environment variable you want to set is called, semantically enough, CVS_ROOT (named after what the -d flag represents).

If you haven't been fiddling with the Terminal preferences, then you're using the tcsh shell. There are lots of different types of shells, tcsh being the default on OS X (with an additional choice of bash under 10.2). Setting an environment variable will change depending on which shell you're using, but under tcsh, enter the following:

```
setenv CVS_ROOT "-d:pserver:anonymous@cvs.amphetadesk.sourceforge.net:/
cvsroot/amphetadesk"
```

If, on the other hand, you've tweaked Terminal to use bash, enter the following instead:

```
export CVS_ROOT="-d:pserver:anonymous@cvs.amphetadesk.sourceforge.net:/
cvsroot/amphetadesk"
```

With the preceding command, you'll notice that nothing seems to happen. That's because environment variables are invisible—there's only visual feedback when you've screwed up the previous command (or else use a program that uses the variable). To see your variable set properly, type printenv (for either shell). You'll see your CVS_ROOT, as well as a number of other variables already defined by OS X.

You can now enter the much smaller, and more readable, commands:

```
cvs login
cvs -z3 co AmphetaDesk
```

The problem with setenv and export are that they're both temporary; once you close the Terminal, your CVS_ROOT will be forgotten and you'll be back in the forest with a command line a mile long. What do you do? Make it permanent, of course.

Doing so again differs depending on what shell you've chosen. Each shell has the ability to read a startup file—something you create that says "hey, everytime I start this shell, do the commands within this file." These files are located in your home directory and normally are not visible to the Finder. With the tcsh shell, the file is named *.tcshrc*; under bash, it's *.bash_profile*. Creating those files, adding the matching command from before, and then starting a new Terminal window will set the CVS_ROOT at startup (you can check this with the printenv command).

Another alternative is using the *plist* preference file format. More information is available in the "See Also" section later in this hack, but creating a file at *~/.MacOSX/environment.plist* with the following contents would do it for you:

```
<?xml version="1.0" encoding="UTF-8"?>
<!DOCTYPE plist SYSTEM "file://localhost/System/Library/DTDs/PropertyList.
dtd">
<plist version="0.9">
<dict>
<key>CVS_ROOT</key>
<string>-d:pserver:anonymous@cvs.amphetadesk.sourceforge.net:/cvsroot/
amphetadesk</string>
</dict>
</plist>
```

See Also

- Setting environment variables (*http://developer.apple.com/qa/qa2001/qa1067.html*)

HACK #53 Scheduling with System Tasks and Other Events

The cron utility runs continuously in the background, taking care of scheduled system tasks and user requests at the appropriate time.

You might not know it, but your Mac does quite a bit on its own behind your back—or under your fingertips, I should say. Your system regularly purges itself of outdated, space-hogging log files, updates system databases so utilities like locate (type man locate on the command line for details) can work effectively, and performs several other maintenance tasks that keep your system running lean and mean.

It does so by means of a task-scheduling utility called cron (as in chronological). The cron command launches automatically at system startup and runs continuously in the background. It keeps a list of what needs to happen when and consults this list each and every minute of each and every day, at least while your machine is awake. When it notices it's time to perform some duty, it does so quietly in the background.

The lists are kept in *crontab* files associating a particular action with a timetable. Each user account can have its own *crontab* file. The system itself has a special *crontab*, found in the */etc* directory; it belongs to the superuser, or root, account and takes care of actions requiring the kind of system access allowed only to root [Hack #50].

The crontab File

The format of a *crontab* file might appear rather esoteric at first, but it's really rather simple. For example, Figure 5-20 shows the system's *crontab* for carrying out regular maintenance. The numbers in the circled area specify the time cron runs the scripts (there are actually three of them).

Each of the three lines (numbered 1, 2, and 3 in Figure 5-20) specifies one of the three scripts the system's cron runs by default. Each script is different, performing its own appropriate set of maintenance procedures. The daily script, on the line labeled 1, runs once each day. The weekly script, specified on line 2, runs once each week. And the monthly script, specified on line 3, runs—you guessed it—once each month.

The first five columns or fields of each line specify at exactly which interval the script will run. The fields specify, from left to right, the minute, hour (on a 24-hour clock), day of the month, month, and weekday (either short versions, MON-FRI, or numerically, with Sunday as 0 or 7). An asterisk instead of a number in a field means "every."

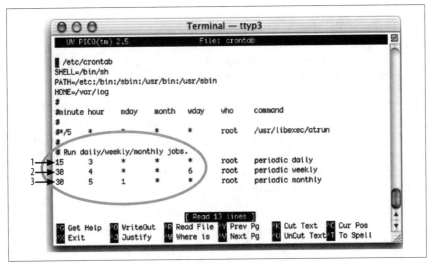

Figure 5-20. The system's crontab

For example, line 1 specifies a time of 3:15 a.m.:

```
15 3 * * * root periodic daily
```

Since the rest of the columns contain asterisks, the daily script will run at 3:15 a.m. on every day of the month, every month, and every day of the week—that is, every day at 3:15 a.m.

Line 2 specifies that the weekly script runs at 4:30 a.m. on every weekday number 6, or Saturday:

```
30 4 * * 6 root periodic weekly
```

And line 3 specifies that the monthly script runs at 5:30 a.m. on day 1 (the first) of each month:

```
30 5 1 * * root periodic monthly
```

That's about all there is to it.

Your User crontab

As I mentioned, you have your own personal *crontab* with which to have the system automatically and regularly do your bidding. To take a gander at what you've already got scheduled, open a Terminal [Hack #48] window and type: crontab -l (that's l as in *list*):

```
% crontab -l
crontab: no crontab for rael
```

crontab is not only the name of a file, it's also a command used for viewing and editing your *crontab*.

If, like me, you've not yet scheduled anything, crontab -l doesn't produce anything particularly remarkable. Let's change that by editing your *crontab* and adding something interesting.

Before doing so, you should set your default command-line editor **[Hack #51]** so that the file opens in an editor you can use. The crontab command uses this editor to edit its files. Here, I set my editor to pico and open up my *crontab*:

```
% setenv EDITOR /usr/bin/pico
% crontab -e
```

The -e option, as you might have guessed, stands for edit. pico launches and I'm editing an as-yet-empty text file. Don't worry about what file it is or where it lives; crontab takes care of all those details for you.

Using the guidelines explained earlier in "The crontab File," let's add a reminder to exercise at 4:00 p.m. every weekday. The only difference is that the who field (see Figure 5-20) doesn't apply, since this *crontab* already belongs to someone—you:

```
#minute hour mday month wday command
0 16 * * mon-fri /usr/bin/osascript -e 'say "time to get your lazy ↵
butt off that chair and do some exercise."'
```

I've taken the liberty of copying the comment from the system's *crontab* (removing the who field) to remind me what goes where. Any line prefixed with a # (hash or pound sign) is treated as a comment for a human reader's information only and is ignored.

Each entry should be contained on one line. The previous example is split only for presentation purposes and would not run. It's generally better form to push long commands out to a script and just invoke the script via cron. I might put that AppleScript invocation into a file called *exercise.sh* in a *bin* directory in my home directory:

```
#!/bin/sh

/usr/bin/osascript -e 'say "time to get your lazy butt off that chair and do
some exercise."'
```

I'd make it executable **[Hack #49]** (chmod u+x exercise.sh) and alter my *crontab* appropriately:

```
#minute hour mday month wday     command
0       16   *    *     mon-fri /Users/rael/bin/exercise.sh
```

The nice thing about cron—in this case—is that it doesn't run when the computer's asleep or shut down; it'll remind me to exercise only when I'm working at four in the afternoon, Monday through Friday.

The System crontab

Apple has preconfigured the system's *crontab* to automate various tasks you wouldn't know to do in the first place. The not-so-good news is that they've scheduled these groups of tasks to run between 4:00 and 5:00 in the morning—a time when your Mac is likely not even on! And if your Mac is never on during these times, these important tasks will never happen. If your Mac is powered on but in deep sleep, the jobs still won't run.

Let's modify the system's schedule slightly so that these tasks occur at more reasonable times. Of course, what counts as reasonable depends on your own situation, so consider these factors when deciding:

- Choose a time when your Mac is likely to be on (and not asleep).
- Choose a time when a few minutes of background activity won't disturb your work too much. On faster machines the activity is hardly noticeable, but it could cause some stuttering if, for example, you happened to be watching a DVD at the time.
- Choose a time that is unique for each script. You don't want to schedule scripts to run at the same time.

For example, these times might be good for a machine that's on only during normal work hours:

Daily
> Every day at 4:15 p.m.

Weekly
> Every Monday at 9:50 a.m.

Monthly
> The first of every month at 10:30 a.m.

Regarding the monthly job, the first of the month sometimes falls on a weekend or holiday, but for now that's the best you can do.

To modify the system's *crontab* file to reflect these new times, you'll need to open it up in pico, edit it, and save it yourself since the jobs don't belong to one user in particular, rendering crontab -e inapplicable.

```
% sudo pico /private/etc/crontab
```

First, change the 3 in the daily script line to 16:

```
15 16 * * * root periodic daily
```

Next, change the time in the weekly script line as shown here:

```
50 8 * * 2 root periodic weekly
```

Finally, change the time in the monthly script line:

```
30 10 1 * * root periodic monthly
```

Once you've made the changes, save (write out) the document by pressing Control-O. You'll then be prompted to confirm the save; just press Return to do so. Finally, quit pico by pressing Control-X.

Once you've saved the *crontab* file, the new scheduling takes effect immediately; there's no need to restart.

—Chris Stone

HACK #54   Opening Things from the Command Line

Why should you have to pop on up to the GUI to open applications, files, directories, and URLs when it's just as easy from the command line?

The open command launches applications and opens files, directories, and URLs from the command line just as if you'd double-clicked its associated icon in the Finder.

Launch applications by supplying open with their path. Here we launch Internet Explorer and Microsoft Word:

```
% open /Applications/Internet\ Explorer.app
...
% open /Applications/Microsoft\ Office\ X/Microsoft\ Word
```

> You'll notice that Internet Explorer ends in *.app* while Microsoft Word does not. Cocoa applications are postfixed with a *.app* extension. Carbon or Classic apps have no special extension.

Opening a directory is no different; to bring your *Music* folder up in the Finder, type:

```
% open ~/Music
```

Just as the Finder mysteriously figures out which application is associated with any particular files, shortcuts, or URLs, so too does open determine which application, if any, to use. The underlying magic involved comes in two flavors: type/creator codes and file extensions [Hack #6], from the Mac OS 9 and Unix worlds, respectively. The Macintosh operating system maintains a database of type/creator codes and their associated applications, quietly looking up the application best suited to deal with a file you double-click and launching it for you. The Unix world doesn't know such codes and relies instead on file extensions, like *.txt* for text files, *.doc* for Word documents, and *.url* for URL shortcuts. Being a hybrid, Mac OS X relies on both.

For example:

```
% open ~/Desktop/Apple.url
```

opens the *Apple.url* Internet shortcut [Hack #66] on the Desktop, directing my default web browser to the Apple home page, *http://www.apple.com*. In this case, the type code of LINK informs the application choice rather than the *.url* file extension.

 You can even open a URL directly using open *URL*, like so:

```
open http://www.apple.com
```

What about a file without either type/creator codes or a file extension? A little experimentation reveals much:

```
% touch somefile
% open somefile
2002-07-09 01:29:46.744 open[7344] LSOpenFromURLSpec( ) returned -10814 for
application (null) path /Users/rael/somefile.
2002-07-09 01:29:46.748 open[7344] Couldn't open file: /Users/rael/somefile
```

The open command is stumped, having nothing to go on whatsoever. Now you can advise open. The -e flag says to open the file using the default application, TextEdit. Using the -a flag, you can specify a particular application to use. Both of the following open *somefile* in TextEdit:

```
% open -e somefile
% open -a /Applications/TextEdit.app somefile
```

Perhaps you prefer to edit the file in Microsoft Word or view it in Internet Explorer:

```
% open -a /Applications/Microsoft\ Office\ X/Microsoft\ Word somefile
% open -a /Applications/Internet\ Explorer.app somefile
```

The best course of action for a file you'll be visiting again and again is to associate it with a specific application. Either fiddle with type/creator codes [Hack #6] or, as a quick fix, give the file an extension by renaming it in the Finder or on the command line:

```
% mv somefile somefile.txt
```

Or, if you're one to avoid ugly extensions, alter the "Open with application" setting in the Finder's Info inspector, as shown in Figure 5-21.

Whichever you choose will have the same effect, that of associating *somefile* (or *somefile.txt*) with the default text editor, usually TextEdit. In fact, it turns out that assigning a file extension, either on the command line or through the Finder, quietly sets the type/creator codes in the background.

To open more than one file at a time, whether with the same type or not, go ahead and list them—space-separated—on the command line after the open command. You can, of course, make use of the full complement of command-line wildcards:

```
% open ~/Desktop/Apple.url files*.txt
```

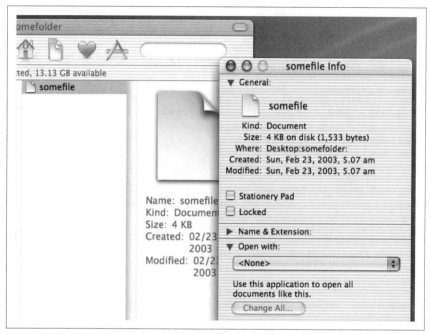

Figure 5-21. The Finder's Info inspector

This is all well and good, but why wouldn't I simply double-click the associated icon and skip all this command-line tomfoolery? The open command is really useful only when you're on the command line in the first place, deep in some directory tree somewhere, and want to open that file right there in front of you. Sure you could hop on up to the GUI level and navigate your way back down via the Finder's friendly interface, but why?

HACK #55 Introducing and Installing the Mac OS X Developer Tools

The Mac OS X Developer Tools are a treasure trove of developer applications, utilities, tools, and scripts vital to both developing for OS X and building open source applications from source.

Mac development has taken a quantum leap forward, thanks to the Mac OS X Developer Tools (*http://developer.apple.com/tools/*). Originally written for the NeXT operating system, they've been ported across to OS X. The major bundled components are: Project Builder for managing application development, writing code, and building apps and Interface Builder, a marvelous application for designing user interfaces and binding their components to application code.

So why, you may ask, should you care? After all, you're not a developer (maybe you are) and are just after a few hacks for your Mac. Alongside the main tools for building applications on Macintosh are a host of Unix commands and utilities vital for configuring, compiling, and deploying a plethora of applications and services—most open source and free for the taking. You'll need the Developer Tools installed to follow along with some of the hacks in this book, especially in the Unix, Terminal, Mail, and web sections.

Getting the Developer Tools

You may already have the Developer Tools installed (check for the */Developer* folder on your hard drive), not yet installed but on your hard drive as a package (check *Applications/Installers/Developer Tools*), or on CD in the box your Mac arrived in, assuming your system's fairly recent. If you don't have them handy, don't worry; you can download them for free from the Apple Developer Connection web site (*http://www.apple.com/developer/*), either as one large distribution (around 200 megabytes) or as 21 separate files (about 10 megabytes each). (All sizes and numbers are correct at of the time of this writing but will almost certainly be different by the time you read this.) You'll need a free ADC account; if you don't already have one, sign up online (*https://connect.apple.com/*). You'll also gain access to lots of documentation, samples, and a range of development tools and utilities.

 You'll need the right version for your operating system. If you're running 10.2 (Jaguar), use the latest and greatest. If you're running an earlier version of OS X, download an appropriate version of the Developer Tools.

Installing the Developer Tools

The Developer Tools, no matter which way you get them, come as a Mac OS X package. Double-click on the *Developer.mpkg* icon to start the standard Mac OS X Package Installer, which will lead you gently through the process.

Once you've agreed to the license conditions, the installer asks you for the destination volume and defaults to the startup hard drive. You probably want to leave that as it is because other third-party tools expect to find the *Developer* directory there.

Please be sure to install the BSD Software Development Kit (SDK), as this contains the commands and utilities for building many of the open source applications you'll find in this book and elsewhere. To be sure, on the Installation Type screen, click the Customize button and be sure the checkbox associated with the BSD SDK package is checked, as shown in Figure 5-22.

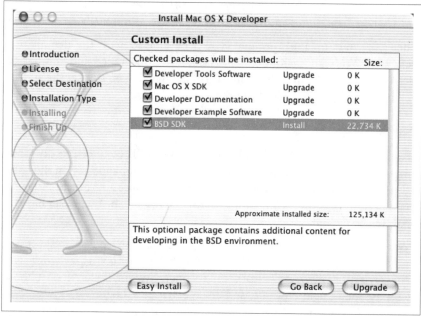

Figure 5-22. The Custom Install screen

When you're ready to continue, click the Easy Install (or Upgrade, in my case) button and the Developer Tools will be installed. It'll take a while, so now's probably a good time to go grab that coffee.

Removing the Developer Tools

To remove the Developer Tools, run the Perl script, */Developer/Tools/ uninstall-devtools.pl*, from the command line [Hack #48].

—brian d foy

Top 10 Mac OS X Tips for Unix Geeks
#56

Author Brian Jepson offers the top 10 tips he gathered while working on O'Reilly's *Mac OS X for Unix Geeks*.

These tips will show you the differences between Mac OS X and other flavors of Unix, help you find the bits that resemble the Unix you are used to, and even feather your nest with XFree86 and ports of popular open source applications.

1. Where's My Shell?

A Unix geek won't get too far without a shell, right? You can find the Terminal application by navigating to */Applications/Utilities* in the Finder. Drag the Terminal application to your Dock so you can access it quickly.

When you start up the Terminal, you'll be greeted with the default user shell, tcsh. You can customize the Terminal's appearance and settings by selecting Window Settings from the Terminal menu. You can set the startup shell by selecting Preferences from the Terminal menu.

2. sudo, Not su

By default, the root user is disabled on Mac OS X. If you need to do something as root, use the sudo command. To use this command, pass in the command and arguments you want to execute, as in sudo vi /etc/hostconfig. You'll need to be a user with administrator privileges. The main user has this capability by default.

If you need a root shell, you can always use sudo tcsh or sudo bash. If you want to enable the root user, it's as simple as giving root a password with sudo passwd root. You'll also want to open System Preferences, choose Accounts, then Login Options, and change "Display Login Windows as" to Name and Password. Then you can log out and log in as the root user.

3. Startup

Mac OS X startup [Hack #13] is nothing like other Unix systems. Most significantly, Mac OS X has nothing like the */etc/init.d* directory. Instead, it finds its startup items in either */System/Library/StartupItems* (for system startup items) or */Library/StartupItems* (for locally installed startup items).

You can use existing startup items as a template or check out *Mac OS X for Unix Geeks* for detailed instructions. At a minimum, you need to:

1. Create a subdirectory under */Library/StartupItems*. For example, if you are setting up a startup item for MySQL, you might create the directory */Library/StartupItems/MySQL*.

2. Put a startup file in that subdirectory. It should have the same name as its parent folder, as in */Library/StartupItems/MySQL/MySQL*. For an example, you can look at Mac OS X's startup item for Apache, */System/Library/StartupItems/Apache/Apache*.

3. At a minimum, add a *StartupParameters.plist* file to that subdirectory. Again, see an existing startup item for a template.

4. If you used a control variable to determine whether your daemon starts at boot (Apache uses WEBSERVER), set that variable to -YES- or -NO- in /etc/hostconfig.

After you've done these steps, you can start the service with SystemStarter, as in sudo SystemStarter start MySQL.

4. Filesystem Layout

If you open up a Finder window to the top level of your hard drive, you'll see that familiar friends like /var and /usr are missing. They are actually hidden (more on that later). If you open up a Terminal shell and do an ls /, you'll see the missing folders, as well as a few others, such as /Library and /Developer.

Table 5-1 lists some of the folders that you'll see (Appendix A of Mac OS X for Unix Geeks contains a more comprehensive list).

Table 5-1. Mac OS X files and directories

File or directory	Description
.DS_Store	File containing Finder settings.
.Trashes	Directory containing files that have been dragged to the Trash.
.vol/	Directory mapping HFS+ file IDs to files.
Applications/	Directory holding all your Mac OS X applications. Check out its Utilities/ subdirectory for lots of fun stuff!
Desktop DB, Desktop DF	The Classic Mac OS desktop database.
Desktop Folder/	The Mac OS 9 desktop folder.
Developer/	Apple's Developer Tools and documentation. Available only if you have installed the Developer Tools.
Library/	Support files for locally installed applications, among other things.
Network/	Network-mounted Application, Library, and Users directories, as well as a Servers directory.
Shared Items/	Used by Mac OS 9 to share items between users.
System Folder/	The Mac OS 9 System Folder.
System/	Support files for the system and system applications, among other things.
Temporary Items/	Temporary files used by Mac OS 9.
TheVolumeSettings Folder/	Tracks details such as open windows and desktop printers.
Trash/	The Mac OS 9 trash folder.
Users/	Home directories.

Table 5-1. Mac OS X files and directories (continued)

File or directory	Description
VM Storage	Mac OS 9 virtual memory file.
Volumes/	All mounted filesystems.
automount/	Handles static NFS mounts.
bin/	Essential system binaries.
cores/	If core dumps are enabled (with tcsh's `limit` and bash/sh's `ulimit` commands), they will be created in this directory as `core.pid`.
dev/	Files that represent various devices.
etc/	System configuration files.
lost+found	Orphaned files discovered by fsck.
mach	A symbolic link to the */mach.sym* file.
mach.sym	Kernel symbols.
mach_kernel	The Darwin kernel.
private/	Contains the *tmp*, *var*, *etc*, and *cores* directories.
sbin/	Executables for system administration and configuration.
tmp/	Temporary files.
usr/	BSD Unix applications and support files.
var/	Frequently modified files such as log files.

5. Different Kinds of Hidden Files

As with other Unix flavors, you can make a file invisible by prefixing its name with a ., as in */.vol*. This has the effect of making it invisible in the Finder, as well as when you issue an ls without the -a option.

Mac OS X also uses a file in the root directory (*.hidden*) to maintain a list of files that should be hidden from the Finder.

Also, HFS+ (the filesystem used by Mac OS) files and directories can have a hidden attribute set using the SetFile **[Hack #6]** command, as in SetFile -a V SomeFile. This setting won't take effect until you relaunch the Finder. You can log out and log in again or use the Force Quit option from the Apple menu. You can turn off the invisible bit with SetFile -a V *SomeFile*. See the manpage for SetFile for more details. (Note that invisible files set this way are invisible only from the Finder; you can still see them with ls.)

6. Aliases and Links

There are two ways to create links to files **[Hack #9]**. The first is to select the file in the Finder and drag it to a new location while holding down the Option and ⌘ keys (or select Make Alias from the File menu). This creates a Mac OS alias that Cocoa, Carbon, and Classic applications can follow. However, Unix applications will ignore those links, seeing them as zero-byte files.

You can also create a link with ln or ln -s. If you use this kind of link, Unix, Cocoa, Carbon, and Classic applications will happily follow it.

7. X11

Mac OS X does not come with the X Window System. Instead, it uses an advanced graphics system called Aqua. But if you want to run X11 applications, you're in luck: XFree86 has been ported to Mac OS X. You should first download and install XDarwin (*http://www.xdarwin.org*), which provides the X Server and essential tools. The next step is optional. OroborOSX (*http://oroborosx.sourceforge.net/*) is an X11 window manager with an Aqua look and feel. You'll be able to run X11 applications side-by-side with Mac OS X applications, and they'll look great.

 At the time of this writing, Apple has also released a beta of its own X11 system, which you can download for free from *http://www.apple.com/macosx/X11*.

8. Fink

Are there some Unix or Linux applications that you're missing? Check out the Fink project (*http://fink.sourceforge.net*), which modifies open source applications so they'll compile and run on Mac OS X. Fink **[Hack #58]** already includes an impressive array of applications, and more are on the way.

Other porting projects that you should explore include DarwinPorts (*http://www.opendarwin.org/projects/darwinports/*) and GNU-Darwin (*http://gnu-darwin.sourceforge.net/*).

9. /etc Is Not Always in Charge

If you've come to Mac OS X from another Unix OS, you may expect that you can add users and groups to the */etc/passwd* and */etc/group* files. By default, Mac OS X uses these files only in single-user mode. If you want to add a user or group, it will need to go into the NetInfo database, a repository of local directory information.

The quick way to add a user or a group is to feed a record in either the passwd or the group format into niload (commands you type are shown in bold; the ? is used by the here-document syntax that starts with <<EOF and ends with EOF):

```
% sudo niload passwd . <<EOF
? rothman:*:701:20::0:0:Ernest Rothman:/Users/rothman:/bin/tcsh
? EOF
```

After you've created the new user, you need to set the password, use the ditto -rsrc command (a copy command that preserves HFS+ resource forks when accompanied by the -rsrc flag) to create the home directory, and set permissions correctly:

```
% sudo passwd rothman
Changing password for rothman.
New password: ********
Retype new password: ********

% sudo ditto -rsrc \
/System/Library/User\ Template/English.lproj \
/Users/rothman

% sudo chown -R rothman:staff /Users/rothman
```

10. Shutdown Doesn't Really

At the time *Mac OS X for Unix Geeks* was written, we had indications that Jaguar (Mac OS X 10.2) would execute the shutdown actions in the scripts contained in */System/Library/StartupItems* and */Library/StartupItems*. As it turns out, it doesn't. So, if you are running a sensitive application such as a database server, be sure to shut it down manually before you shut down your computer. It's disappointing that Mac OS X does not include the facility to gracefully shut down daemons when the system is powered down. However, the infrastructure is present, and we hope it's switched on in a future update.

—Brian Jepson

Turning a Command-Line Script into an Application

What do you get when you combine the power of Unix scripting with the simplicity of the OS X GUI? A powerful droplet application limited only by your scripting prowess.

DropScript (*http://www.advogato.org/proj/DropScript/*), as the name suggests, is a little application onto which you can drop any shell, Perl, or other command-line script. It turns that script into a full-fledged, self-contained, double-clickable application capable of running on your desktop and doing interesting things with any files you feed it.

Perhaps an example is in order. I'll create a shell script to zip any files passed to it on the command line:

```
#!/bin/sh
gzip "$@"
```

I save it to *gzip.sh*, make it executable, and give it a whirl on the command line:

```
% chmod +x gzip.sh
% echo "something" > file1
% echo "something else" > file2
% ./gzip.sh file1 file2
% ls *.gz
file1.gz file2.gz
```

It works as expected, gzipping any files it's given.

Now I drag *gzip.sh* on to the DropScript application. Within seconds, a new application is created, called, suspiciously, Dropgzip (see Figure 5-23). This is a tiny application with all the functionality of my original *gzip.sh* shell script. Like its parent, it accepts files—only dropped onto it from the Finder rather than fed to it on the command line.

Figure 5-23. Creating a DropScript application, before and after

Yes, it's a simple example, but any script will work as long as it expects only files and folders as arguments.

Options

DropScript sports some simple options, embedded in the original script as comments. For example, while it makes sense that *gzip.sh* should accept any file or folder it's fed, *gunzip.sh* should accept only things that are zipped. To set this restriction in the script, you'd just add the following line:

```
# EXTENSIONS : "tgz" "tar" "gz" "Z" "zip"
```

Services

The most intriguing attribute of DropScript is that its applications can be made to export their functionality as services, appearing in the Services menu of just about any application.

To do so, specify a service name, like so:

```
# SERVICEMENU : "SomeService"
```

where *SomeService* is the name under which the service will be listed in the Services menu. You can even specify that a particular service live within a submenu by including a path in the option:

```
# SERVICEMENU : "SubMenu/SomeService"
```

Drop the script on DropScript and drag the resulting application to, where else but, your *Applications* folder. Log out and back in again and your new service will be right there in the Services menu, as shown in Figure 5-24.

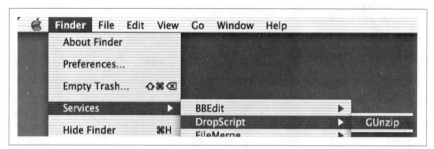

Figure 5-24. A DropScript application as exported service

I've only just scratched the surface of the sorts of applications you can build. After all, you have the power of all the built-in open source scripting languages (Perl, Python, Ruby, sh, etc.) at your disposal. You'll find some documentation and sample scripts (including a version of *gzip.sh*) in the *Examples* folder included with DropScript. These should be enough to get you started and experimenting.

See Also

- ScriptGUI (*http://homepage.mac.com/cnorris/ScriptGUI/about.html*), a similar Unix-script-to-GUI-application converter. It doesn't provide exported services, but does include a handy GUI window for running and inspecting scripts.

HACK #58 Installing Unix Applications with Fink

Apple's latest OS now gives you a wide range of software from two different worlds: our beloved Mac and open source. Thanks to utilities like Fink, installation is about as simple on the command line as it is in the GUI.

Fink appeared shortly after Mac OS X started picking up speed and, through constant development by the open source community, has become a powerful utility for installing other open source software. Fink itself is based on open source utilities that have been available under Debian: dpkg, dselect, and apt-get. Those utilities (installed with Fink) can be used seperately, or you can run them together through the made-for–OS X Fink utility. One of the nicer aspects of Fink is that it will install Unix code *only* in a root directory called *sw*, ensuring that you won't mess up your current OS X installation (or corrupt existing files).

Since a good portion of the packages available through Fink are shell-based, let's set about installing Fink through the shell as much as possible. These steps were written using Fink v0.40a, the latest release at the time of this writing:

```
% curl -LO http://us.dl.sourceforge.net/fink/fink-0.4.0a-installer.dmg
% open "fink-0.4.0a-installer.dmg"
% cd "/Volumes/Fink 0.4.0a Installer/"
% open "Fink 0.4.0a Installer.pkg"
```

The first command uses curl to download the file [Hack #61] into a local copy called *fink-0.4.0a-installer.dmg*. We then use open [Hack #54] to use the default Finder application associated with *.dmg* files (typically Disk Copy). Since mounted items are stored in the shell under */Volumes*, we move into that directory and then use open again to start the installation process. There's nothing special about the install, so run through this as you would normally. When the installer is finished, we need to prepare Fink's environment. To do so, in the Terminal, type:

```
% echo 'source /sw/bin/init.csh' >> ~.cshrc
```

This works under the default tcsh shell, but if you're using bash, add */sw/bin/init.sh* to your *.bash_profile*. When your respective line has been added, open up a new Terminal window so those changes take place, and enter the following (entering your normal password):

```
% fink scanpackages
% sudo dselect
```

Our final step to setting up Fink is to choose Update Packages at the dselect screen. If you recall, dselect is one of those Debian packages we mentioned earlier; it gives you the ability to choose the packages you wish to install from a console-based menu. Depending on your overall skill with console applications, dselect may be confusing, so this is how you'd update the packages through the Fink utility:

```
% fink selfupdate
```

The first time you run this command, you'll have the option of choosing whether you want to look at the CVS for package upgrades. If you're willing to have the latest and greatest, enter Y; if you're panicky about not-perfect-yet software, enter N. The selfupdate command will also check to see if Fink itself has any new updates available and will install them if need be. Depending on your Internet connection and decision concerning CVS, this could take anywhere from a few minutes to more than 20.

Once Fink has updated itself, you'll obviously want to check out the list of available packages for installation. To do so, enter the following, which will display a long list of packages, along with a short description:

```
% fink list
```

You can find more information about packages by using Fink's describe flag. Next, we ask for more information about the wget package, where we're rewarded with a few paragraphs, a web site for more information, and the current maintainer:

```
% fink describe wget
```

The wget description tells us it's a free network utility to retrieve files from the World Wide Web using HTTP and FTP. It has some advantages over another downloading utility named curl, which is shipped with Mac OS X. To install the wget package, enter the following:

```
% fink install wget
```

You'll see a progress report during installation, as well as a lot of output you won't need to understand, but you can add -v to any Fink command line to get even more dirt on what's going on. Software installed by Fink is always located in the /sw directory of your hard drive. Once installation is complete, you can immediately start using your new software. The following two commands will you give more information about wget, and a further example of its use is available in "Downloading Files from the Command Line" [Hack #61]:

```
% man wget
% wget --help
```

If you've installed something you don't like, it's just as easy to remove:

```
% fink remove wget
```

Mirroring Files and Directories with rsync

#59   With rsync, supplied by default on OS X, quick mirrors and backups are a command line away.

As its name suggests, rsync synchronizes files and folders from one location to another. That location could be another directory on your current machine, or any other rsync-enabled machine that you have access to. Using the rsync protocol, only differences between files are transferred; if you're transferring a 30MB text file that had only a few spelling corrections, you'll transfer only those corrections, not the entire 30MB. You won't believe how much of a time-saver this is until you turn your head back and realize it's finished.

I've always been fond of the learning-by-doing school of thought, so open up a Terminal and enter the following command:

```
% rsync -vaz ~/Library ~/Backups
```

Let's break that down: rsync is the name of our utility and -vaz are some flags we've passed to it. By issuing an rsync --help at the command line, we quickly find out what that means:

```
-v, --verbose  increase verbosity
-a, --archive  archive mode
-z, --compress compress file data
```

Archive mode is a special rsync configuration that is suitable for mirroring. As the manual suggests (see man rsync), archive mode is a quick way of saying you want recursion and to preserve almost everything. In this case, *everything* means permissions, ownership, file modification and access times, and so on. The -z flag, for compression, is more useful when you're handling mirrors or backups over a network (see later in this hack); it'll compress the data before sending it over your connection, further decreasing the amount of time the command will take.

The second part of the rsync command line is what we want to back up or mirror. In this case, we're saying "hey, take my entire *Library* directory and back it up to the third part of the rsync command," which is a location in our home directory called *Backups*. We can back up anything on our drive to anywhere else on our drive. The following command, for instance, backs up the movies in my home directory to another mounted hard drive (named *MouthWash*):

```
% rsync -vaz ~/Movies /Volumes/MouthWash
```

As mentioned, the best part of rsync is the protocol; once you do the initial backup, all future backups will be immensely faster than normal, since only the changed data will be acted upon. This is especially important when you start thinking about rsync over the network, like the following:

```
% rsync -vaz ~/Library 192.169.123.3:/Backup
```

This is almost the same as the first command, only this time we've added an IP address and a colon to our place to back up the files to. With this command (and rsync installed on the machine at 192.169.123.3), we'll be backing up the files over the network to a different machine entirely. If one day I delete my *~/Library/* directory accidentally, all I need to do is reverse the procedure:

```
% rsync -vaz 192.168.123.3:/Backup ~/Library
```

which takes all the files located in the *Backup* directory at 192.168.123.3 and sticks them into my *Library* directory on this machine. Thankfully, we can exclude certain files from a backup or restoration. In the following example, we won't back up any file or directory that has the word *Cache* in it:

```
% rsync -vaz --exclude=*Cache* ~/Library 192.168.123.3:/Backup
```

You can use as many excludes as necessary; here, we're stopping caches as well as our *Mail* directories:

```
% rsync -vaz --exclude=Mail/ --exclude=*Cache* ~/Library 192.168.123.3:/
Backup
```

By default, an rsync command is nondestructive, meaning that it will only add files to a mirror or backup, never remove them. This can be unwanted at times, as you don't want old files that you've deleted to continue to exist at the backup location. That's where --delete comes in:

```
% rsync -az --delete --stats ~/Library ~/Backup
```

In this case, we've removed the verbose option, added --delete, which will remove files in *Backup* that no longer exist in *Library*, and added a nice little ending report with the --stats flag. There are many more rsync options available, including inclusion or exclusion of patterns listed in an external file, throttling bandwidth, stopping after a large number of deletions, and so forth.

Probably the most confusing part of rsync is how it reacts to an ending slash character. The manual covers a bit of this confusion within the opening usage explanation. The following examples will hopefully make things a little clearer.

Either of these commands backs up the entire *Library* directory to *~/Backups/Library*:

```
% rsync -vaz ~/Library ~/Backups
% rsync -vaz ~/Library ~/Backups/
```

Either of these commands backs up the contents of the *Library* directory into *Backups* (i.e., *Backups/Application Support*):

```
% rsync -vaz ~/Library/ ~/Backups
% rsync -vaz ~/Library/ ~/Backups/
```

There have been many tales of users who have lost a backup (or worse yet, horrifically screwed up a restoration with the --delete command), all due to a little slash being in the wrong place. When in doubt and experimenting with new rsync commands, use -n:

```
% rsync -vazn --delete ~/Library/ ~/Backups
```

The added -n says "hey, this is only a dry run, so show me what you're going to do, but don't actually do it." Be sure to do this with verbosity (-v) so that you can see exactly what would be deleted and added.

Using CVS to Manage Data on Multiple Machines

Work with your data wherever you are without fear of getting out of sync with your home machine.

Here's the scenario: instead of just using one Mac, you regularly use two (a desktop and a laptop) and would like to keep up-to-date copies of all your data on all of your machines. After all, when working at home, you want to take advantage of the large monitor and dual processors of a desktop Power Mac, and when you are on the road, you want all the portability of an iBook or a PowerBook. Most solutions to this problem are haphazard and error prone.

However, a tool that software developers use can help you. It's called CVS. And with it you can work with all your data no matter where you are.

What Is CVS?

CVS is an open source tool that provides version control. Version control is the practice of maintaining information about a project's development by tracking changes and coordinating the development efforts of many programmers. CVS uses a centralized repository (sometimes called an archive or a depot) to store all the information about each and every file, as well as every change to those files, contained in a project. These kinds of systems are used in projects small and large, including the development of operating systems like Mac OS X.

Each and every developer of the project has a copy of these files on her own machine. As a developer makes changes, they are committed back into the central repository, allowing the other developers on the project access to the latest code. This allows many people to cooperate on the same source files with a minimum of fuss. If two developers make changes to the same file at the same time, CVS will defer the commit of the second file until the second developer resolves the conflict. Usually, these conflicts are dealt with easily, and development proceeds.

CVS supports all sorts of additional operations that are useful to large teams. However, for our purposes (which are much less demanding than software development), we can take the functionality that we've just described and use it to solve the problem of managing our own data on multiple machines. Even if you are the only person to use your data, CVS can help you maintain it easily on as many machines as your bank account can fund.

> CVS comes as part of Mac OS X's Developer Tools. In order
> to use it, you'll need to install the Mac OS X Developer
> Tools **[Hack #55]**.

Using CVS

So, how should we use CVS for the purpose of replicating our data on multiple machines? First, you need to identify a machine that can serve as the repository. If you have two machines, such as an iBook and a Power Mac, then you should use the Power Mac as your repository. If you are lucky enough to have a third machine that you use as a server for other purposes (maybe you are hosting your own domain or web site), then you should probably use that machine to store your repository.

Once the repository is set up, you can access it from the machine on which you set it up or from other machines. The first case, wherever both the repository and the working copy of your files are located, is an example of local usage. The second case—for example, when you check out your files onto your iBook—is called remote usage. In both situations, you use the same set of CVS commands, but you have to do a bit more setup work for the remote case.

Creating the Repository

Once you've decided on which machine to place the repository, you have to pick where on that machine you want your repository to live. You want to make sure it's in a location that you'll remember easily later. For my setup, I use the */Library/Depot* directory. Once you've decided where you want it, create the directory and then initialize your repository with the following commands:

```
[Mercury ~] duncan% mkdir /Library/Depot
[Mercury ~] duncan% cvs -d /Library/Depot init
```

The -d argument lets CVS know where the repository is located. init tells CVS to initialize the directory as a new repository. This blesses the directory as a CVS repository and installs a copy of the files that will control how it works.

The First Checkout

To make sure all is well, we are going to perform an initial check out of the repository. To do so, make an empty directory (on the same machine as the repository) and execute the following command in that directory:

```
[Mercury ~/tmp] duncan% cvs -d /Library/Depot checkout .
```

Once again, the -d argument lets CVS know the directory in which the repository is located. The checkout . (don't forget the dot) tells CVS to check out a copy of everything in the repository. You should see the following output from CVS:

```
cvs checkout: Updating .
cvs checkout: Updating CVSROOT
U CVSROOT/checkoutlist
U CVSROOT/commitinfo
U CVSROOT/config
U CVSROOT/cvswrappers
U CVSROOT/editinfo
U CVSROOT/loginfo
U CVSROOT/modules
U CVSROOT/notify
U CVSROOT/rcsinfo
U CVSROOT/taginfo
U CVSROOT/verifymsg
```

The files that were checked out are the administration files. By editing, and then checking these files back in, we can change how CVS works. Mostly, we will want to leave these alone for our use, but there is one file that we will need to modify.

Identifying Binary Files

In addition to several quirks, CVS has one major irritation: it wants to treat all files as text files and can't, by itself, tell the difference between text and binary. It wants to treat all files as text because then it can save space in the repository by storing only the difference between files. For HTML files, this is great. However, for binary files that we work with all the time, such as Microsoft Word files (*.doc*) or Excel files (*.xls*), this strategy falls on its face and will make a mess of your data.

To fix this, edit the *CVSROOT/cvswrappers* file to look like this:

```
# This file affects handling of files based on their names.
#
# The -t/-f options allow one to treat directories of files
# as a single file, or to transform a file in other ways on
# its way in and out of CVS.
#
# The -m option specifies whether CVS attempts to merge files.
#
# The -k option specifies keyword expansion (e.g., -kb for binary).
#
# Format of wrapper file ($CVSROOT/CVSROOT/cvswrappers or .cvswrappers)
#
# wildcard [option value][option value]...
#
```

```
# where option is one of
# -f from cvs filter value: path to filter
# -t to cvs filter value: path to filter
# -m update methodology value: MERGE or COPY
# -k expansion mode value: b, o, kkv, &c
#
# and value is a single-quote delimited value.
# For example:

# binary files

*.ai -k 'b'
*.doc -k 'b'
*.bmp -k 'b'
*.class -k 'b'
*.classes -k 'b'
*.dmg -k 'b'
*.eps -k 'b'
*.gif -k 'b'
*.gz -k 'b'
*.GZ -k 'b'
*.icns -k 'b'
*.jar -k 'b'
*.jpg -k 'b'
*.jpeg -k 'b'
*.nib -k 'b'
*.ofile -k 'b'
*.pdf -k 'b'
*.png -k 'b'
*.ppm -k 'b'
*.ppt -k 'b'
*.pqg -k 'b'
*.prj -k 'b'
*.ps -k 'b'
*.psd -k 'b'
*.sl -k 'b'
*.strings -k 'b'
*.tif -k 'b'
*.tiff -k 'b'
*.ttf -k 'b'
*.xls -k 'b'
*.Z -k 'b'
*.zip -k 'b'
```

This is not an exhaustive list, but it serves as the day-to-day list that I use in my repository. Make sure that any binary files that you plan on putting in your repository are on this list.

Once you have edited the file, you need to check it back in. To do this, issue the following command:

```
[Mercury ~/tmp] duncan% cvs commit -m "Sync"
```

This tells CVS to commit our changes back to the repository. The -m argument is the commit message that will be kept in the repository. When you execute this command, you should see the following output:

```
cvs commit: Examining .
cvs commit: Examining CVSROOT
Checking in CVSROOT/cvswrappers;
/Library/Depot/CVSROOT/cvswrappers,v <-- cvswrappers
new revision: 1.2; previous revision: 1.1
done
cvs commit: Rebuilding administrative file database
```

This output will tell you each and every action that is taken by CVS. In this case, it notices that we've modified one of the configuration files and rebuilds its administrative database.

You might notice that we didn't use the -d argument to CVS this time. We need to tell CVS where the repository is only if we haven't checked it out yet into the directory that we are working in. Once checked out, CVS leaves itself enough information to figure things out.

Checking Out on Remote Machines

To check out a repository on other machines, we are going to use the ability to run CVS over SSH. This requires two things:

- The SSH server is up and running [Hack #71] on the machine that the repository is located on.
- The CVS_RSH environment variable is set [Hack #52] on the client machine that we are going to check out the repository onto.

There are a few different ways you can satisfy the second requirement. You can set the environment variable on the command line with the setenv command. To do this, simply execute the following line:

```
[Titanium ~/tmp] duncan% setenv CVS_RSH ssh
```

Of course, this will soon become annoying, as you'll always have to remember to execute this command. You could always set it in your ~/.tcshrc file, but the better option is to set it in your ~/.MacOSX/environment.plist file. This will make sure that it is set for every application that runs, allowing programs that have built-in CVS integration, such as Project Builder, to use your repository seamlessly. All you need to do is create the ~/.MacOSX directory (if it doesn't exist) and save the following as your environment.plist file:

```
<?xml version="1.0" encoding="UTF-8"?>
<!DOCTYPE plist SYSTEM "file://localhost/System/Library/DTDs/PropertyList.
dtd">
```

```
<plist version="0.9">
<dict>
<key>CVS_RSH</key>
<string>/usr/bin/ssh</string>
</dict>
</plist>
```

This is by far the best solution, although you'll need to log out of your machine and back in for it to take effect.

Once you've done this, you're ready to check out the repository. To do so, we're going to use a variant of the cvs checkout command that we used before that will tell CVS that our repository is located on a different machine. This command is of the form cvs -d :ext:[user]@[machine]: [repository directory] checkout. On my machine, I execute the following:

```
[Titanium ~/tmp] duncan% cvs -d :ext:duncan@Mercury.local:/Library/Depot
checkout .
```

Once again, don't forget the dot at the end! If this is the first time that you've used SSH between your machines, you'll see some output asking if you are sure you want to connect. You will then be challenged for your password for the machine containing the repository. After that, the files will be checked out as before.

There is another way to access a CVS repository remotely (called pserver access), but it is more difficult to set up and not as secure for our purposes. If you'd like to set up a CVS pserver, consult a good CVS book (see the "See Also" section later in this hack).

Day-to-Day Use

Now that we've successfully checked out the repository onto two machines, we're ready to start using CVS for our files. The rest of this hack will give you the basic commands you need to work with your new repository.

Adding files. Let's say that we want to keep some pictures in the repository. To do so, we create a *Pictures* subdirectory in our checked-out copy of the repository, copy the images into it, and then add the files to CVS. The following commands illustrate how we do that:

```
[Mercury:~/tmp] duncan% mkdir Pictures
[Mercury:~/tmp] duncan% cp ~/Pictures/me.jpg Pictures/me.jpg
[Mercury:~/tmp] duncan% cvs add Pictures
Directory /Library/Depot/Pictures added to the repository
[Mercury:~/tmp] duncan% cvs add Pictures/me.jpg
cvs add: scheduling file 'Pictures/mejpg' for addition
cvs add: use 'cvs commit' to add this file permanently
```

```
[Mercury:~/tmp] duncan% cvs commit -m "Sync"
cvs commit: Examining .
cvs commit: Examining CVSROOT
cvs commit: Examining Pictures
RCS file: /Library/Depot/Pictures/me1.jpg,v
done
Checking in Pictures/me.jpg;
/Library/Depot/Pictures/me.jpg,v <-- me.jpg
initial revision: 1.1
done
```

To check out the file onto the other machine, we issue the cvs update command as follows:

```
[Mars:~/tmp] duncan% cvs update -d
```

The -d option to the update command tells CVS to check out any subdirectories that were added since the last time we performed an update. You should see the following output:

```
cvs update: Updating .
cvs update: Updating CVSROOT
cvs update: Updating Pictures
U Pictures/me.jpg
```

Voila! Your data is now mirrored and updated between multiple machines. Anything you add to one machine will appear on other machines. All you need to remember to do is to add files to the repository, commit any changes you make, and regularly run the cvs update -d command.

Removing files. Occasionally, you'll want to remove a file from the repository. To do so, simply remove the file from your local copy, then issue a cvs delete command. Here's an example:

```
[Mercury:~/tmp] duncan% rm Pictures/me.jpg
[Mercury:~/tmp] duncan% cvs delete Pictures/me.jpg
cvs remove: scheduling 'Pictures/me.jpg' for removal
cvs remove: use 'cvs commit' to remove this file permanently
[Mercury:~/tmp] duncan% cvs commit -m "Sync"
vs commit: Examining .
cvs commit: Examining CVSROOT
cvs commit: Examining Pictures
Removing Pictures/me.jpg;
/Library/Depot/Pictures/me.jpg,v <-- me.jpg
new revision: delete; previous revision: 1.1
done
```

Moving files is a pain with CVS. There is no cvs move command, so you have to delete the file from where it was and add it to wherever else you want it to be.

See Also

This hack gets you started with using CVS to manage your data. However, at some point you'll probably want to dig deeper into what CVS can do. The following resources can be of help:

- *CVS Pocket Reference (http://www.oreilly.com/catalog/cvspr/)* by Gregor N. Purdy (O'Reilly). This small and affordable guide gives you the complete list of CVS commands and options to those commands.

- The CVS web site *(http://www.cvshome.org/)* contains the source code for CVS, FAQs, and the 184-page official user manual for CVS by Per Cederqvist et al.

—*James Duncan Davidson*

HACK #61 Downloading Files from the Command Line

Few Mac users know of the utility named curl, shipped with every 10.2 Macintosh, or of the easily installed wget. Both allow you to download from the command line—and with a little magic to boot.

There are hundreds of ways to download files located on the Net—FTP, HTTP, NNTP, Gnutella, Hotline, Carracho, the list of possible options goes on and on. There is, however, an odd man out in these protocols, and that's HTTP. Most web browsers are designed to view web pages (as you'd expect); they're not designed to download mass amounts of files from a public web directory. This often leaves users with a few meager choices: should they manually and slowly download each file themselves or go out and find some software that could do it for them?

With OS X, your answer comes in the form of free software allowing you to download from the command line **[Hack #48]**—one installed by default, and one obtainable through Fink *(http://fink.sf.net/)* **[Hack #58]**. Investigating the preinstalled utility makes it sounds innocent enough:

```
curl is a client to get documents/files from or send docu-
ments to a server, using any of the supported protocols
(HTTP, HTTPS, FTP, GOPHER, DICT, TELNET, LDAP or FILE).
The command is designed to work without user interaction
or any kind of interactivity.
```

Further reading through its manual (accessible by entering man curl as a shell command or a slightly longer version with curl --manual) shows a wide range of features, including the ability to get SSL documents, manipulate authentication credentials, change the user agent, set cookies, and prefill form values with either GET or POST. Sadly, curl has some shortcomings, and they all revolve around downloading files that don't have similar names.

Almost immediately, the manual instructs you of curl's range power, so you can download a list of sequentially numbered files with a simple command:

```
% curl -LO http://www.example.com/file[0-100].txt
```

The -L flag tells curl to follow any redirects that may be issued, and the -O flag will save the downloaded files into similarly named copies locally (./file0.txt, ./file1.txt, etc.). Our limitations with the range feature show all too clearly with date-based filenames. Say I want to download a list of files that are in the form of *yymmdd.txt*. I could use this innocent command:

```
% curl -LO http://www.example.com/text/[1996-2002]/[000001-999999].txt
```

If you are patient enough, this will work fine. The downside is that curl will literally try to grab 900,000 files per year (which would range from 1996 through 2002). While a patient downloader may not care, that will create an insane amount of bandwidth waste, as well as a potentially angry web host. We could split the previous command into two:

```
% curl -LO http://www.example.com/text/[1996-1999]/[96-99][01-12][01-31].txt
% curl -LO http://www.example.com/text/[2000-2002]/[00-02][01-12][01-31].txt
```

These will also work correctly, at the expense of being lengthy (technically, we could combine the curl commands into one, with two URLs) and still causing a large number of "file not found" errors for the web host (albeit not as many as the first one).

Solving this sort of problem can be done easily with a freely available utility called wget, which used to ship with earlier versions of OS X (Apple replaced it with curl). You can install it again quite easily with Fink **[Hack #58]**. With wget, we simply enter the following:

```
% wget -m -A txt -np http://www.example.com/text/
```

We start off in mirror mode (-m), which allows us to run the command at a later date and grab only content that has changed from what we've previously downloaded. We accept (-A) only files that end in *.txt*, and we don't want to get anything from our parent directory (-np or no parent); this stops wget from following links that lead us out of the text directory. wget (as well as curl) will show you a running progress as it's downloading files. More information about wget is available by typing man wget on the command line.

Software Update on the Command Line

#62

Just like it's pretty GUI counterpart, the command-line softwareupdate checks for updates to OS X itself and other associated applications, installing them upon approval.

As Apple moves onward and upward in its efforts to synchronize what happens above and below the shiny Aqua desktop, some previously GUI-only bits have made their way to the Terminal command line. One such function is Software Update; just like its pretty GUI counterpart, softwareupdate (man softwareupdate) checks for updates to OS X itself and other associated applications, installing them upon approval.

Aside from simply appealing to Unix jocks, Software Update on the command line affords administrators (especially those with multiple Macs to keep in sync) the ability to log in remotely and perform updates without having to wander physically from machine to machine. A good admin can actually go so far as to automate the process.

Software Update CLI Walk-Through

Let's take a stroll through softwareupdate.

It's always advisable to close out of all applications except the Finder and Software Update or the Terminal in which you're doing a software update. This is the best preemptive medicine for avoiding complications and conflicts that might arise from updating the system beneath the feet of running applications.

The first step is to see if any updates are available. Launch the Terminal [Hack #48] application and type softwareupdate at the command-line prompt. Software Update calls home over your network or dial-up connection, returning shortly with a list of updates, if any.

Should your system be completely up-to-date, Software Update will simply tell you so:

```
% softwareupdate
Software Update Tool
Copyright 2002 Apple Computer, Inc.

Your software is up to date.
```

In this case, however, Software Update proffers a slew of updates, mostly having to do with language support:

```
% softwareupdate
Software Update Tool
Copyright 2002 Apple Computer, Inc.

Software Update found the following new or updated software:

- BrazilianPortugueseSU
Brazilian Portuguese Language Support (10.1.5), 5712K
- DanishSU
Danish Language Support (10.1.5), 6000K
```

```
- FinnishSU
Finnish Language Support (10.1.5), 5492K
- KoreanSU
Korean Language Support (10.1.5), 40640K
- NorwegianSU
Norwegian Language Support (10.1.5), 5592K
- SecurityUpd2002-08-02
Security Update 2002-08-02 (1.0), 5300K - restart required
- SimplifiedChineseSU
Simplified Chinese Language Support (10.1.5), 37580K
- TraditionalChineseSU
Traditional Chinese Language Support (10.1.5), 39060K


To install an update, run this tool with the item name as an argument.
e.g. 'softwareupdate <item> ...'
```

While installing any particular update is up to you and your particular system configuration, some, like the security update hidden among the others here, you'll want to install right away. To install a particular update, type softwareupdate, followed by the name—or names, since softwareupdate, like its GUI counterpart, can install more than one at a time—of the package you wish to install; you'll need to sudo **[Hack #50]**, since software updates invariably involve changing global system files and settings:

```
% sudo softwareupdate SecurityUpd2002-08-02
Password:
Software Update Tool
Copyright 2002 Apple Computer, Inc.

Downloading "Security Update 2002-08-02"... 10% 20% 30% 40% 50%
2002-08-05 13:52:48.941 softwareupdate[13686] File to verify:
/var/root/Library/Caches/a1028.g.akamai.net/5/1028/3093/1/
1a1a1a88ff63d249b72392f35785e656c63297c52897043397067
deb57c6278bfe2d82d504346a9bc8f8295a91c03867cb337bf347
8cf055960b71c5fd74a51258c53f99/SecurityUpd2002-08-02.tar
2002-08-05 13:52:52.207 softwareupdate[13686] File verification succeeded
2002-08-05 13:52:52.213 softwareupdate[13686] Verified file now to install:
/tmp/SecurityUpd2002-08-02.pkg.tar
2002-08-05 13:52:52.215 softwareupdate[13686] Returning 1 from VerifyFile

Unarchiving "Security Update 2002-08-02"... 50%
Installing "Security Update 2002-08-02"... 67% 70% 80% 90% 100% done.

You have installed one or more updates that requires that you restart your
computer. Please restart immediately.
```

Software Update downloads, verifies, unpacks, and installs the update. Notice the admonishment to "Please restart immediately"; when Software Update advises an immediate restart, take the advice and restart your Macintosh before doing much of anything else. While the GUI-flavored Software

Update won't let you out of Software Update without restarting when necessary, the command-line version leaves you, in true Unix style, to your own devices and peril.

What happens if you don't restart immediately? Bad things, no doubt. Perhaps you were editing the Apache configuration file, since updated beneath your feet by the software update. Or you've made some seemingly minor change via NetInfo that's incompatible with an updated system setting. While it's best to close down everything except the Finder before doing a software update, it's certainly strongly advised that you restart when told to do so.

Snooping About

Whether you're running Software Update from the GUI or command line, the mechanics are the same. While an understanding is in no way needed to use softwareupdate, the more inquisitive user might find the underpinnings well worth a quick gander.

There was some mention of verifying a file called *SecurityUpd2002-08-02. tar*. This is a compressed archive (often called a tarball [Hack #4]) containing all the files composing the update. The archive contains a signature for verifying that the archive wasn't damaged in transit and another tarball, the update package itself:

```
% tar tvf /var/root/Library/Caches/a1028.g.akamai.net/5/1028/3093/1/
1a1a1a88ff63d249b72392f35785e656c63297c52897043397067deb57c6278b
fe2d82d504346a9bc8f8295a91c03867cb337bf3478cf055960b71c5fd74a51258
c53f99/SecurityUpd2002-08-02.tar

-rw-r--r-- swupdate/wheel 543 2002-08-01 15:33:20 signature
-rw-r--r-- swupdate/unknown 5416960 2002-08-01 15:26:04 Security
Upd2002-08-02.pkg.tar
```

OS X keeps a record of installs and updates in */Library/Receipts*, the remnants of which may be found in each package's *Contents/Resources* directory.

```
% ls /Library/Receipts/SecurityUpd2002-08-02.pkg/Contents/Resources/
BundleVersions.plist VolumeCheck
Dutch.lproj da.lproj
English.lproj fi.lproj
French.lproj ko.lproj
German.lproj no.lproj
InstallationCheck package_version
Italian.lproj pt.lproj
Japanese.lproj software_version
SecurityUpd2002-08-02.bom sv.lproj
SecurityUpd2002-08-02.loc zh_CN.lproj
SecurityUpd2002-08-02.sizes zh_TW.lproj
Spanish.lproj
```

Of course, the actual files themselves have been installed into the appropriate places all over the filesystem. However, for a glimpse of all that was installed and altered, we turn to the *bom* (man bom), or bill of materials, file, viewable with the lsbom command (type man lsbom on the command line for more information):

```
% lsbom /Library/Receipts/SecurityUpd2002-08-02.pkg/Contents/Resources/
SecurityUpd2002-08-02.bom | more

. 41775 0/80
./System 40755 0/0
./System/Library 40755 0/0
./System/Library/Frameworks 40755 0/0
./System/Library/Frameworks/System.framework 40755 0/0
./System/Library/Frameworks/System.framework/Resources 120755 0/0 26
3302263027 Versions/Current/Resources
./System/Library/Frameworks/System.framework/System 120755 0/0 23
285767527 Versions/Current/System
...
./usr/share/man/man8/rotatelogs.8 100644 0/0 4150 1165073178
./usr/share/man/man8/sftp-server.8 100644 0/0 2087 1556173402
./usr/share/man/man8/ssh-keysign.8 100644 0/0 2375 3700322105
./usr/share/man/man8/sshd.8 100644 0/0 26471 342712072
```

HACK #63 Interacting with the Unix Shell from AppleScript

Via the do shell script AppleScript command or scripting the Terminal application itself, you can talk to the command line from inside AppleScript.

AppleScripters can use the Unix shell in two different ways with Mac OS X. The do shell script command executes a Unix shell statement without having to target a specific application. For example, type the following script into a Script Editor window; then compile and run it. It will issue three Unix shell commands, separated by semicolons:

```
do shell script "cd $HOME; pwd; ls -l"
```

The script then receives the return value as a string (a bunch of characters, like a written sentence, surrounded by quotes), which it can then process as needed. Here is a portion of the return value of the latter script:

```
"/Users/brucep
total 0
drwxr-xr-x 7 brucep staff 264 Nov 24 20:27 AllProps
drwxr-xr-x 5 brucep staff 126 Jan 4 19:57 Applications
drwx------ 17 brucep staff 534 Jan 18 10:24 Desktop
drwx------ 14 brucep staff 432 Jan 18 10:17 Documents
..."
```

You can also script the Terminal application, which is the command-line utility installed with Mac OS X. The following script will open a new Terminal window and launch the Apache Tomcat Java servlet engine and MySQL database server. Very useful!

```
ignoring application responses
  tell application "Terminal"
    activate
    do script with command " ⌐
    "/Users/brucep/bin/start_tomcat; /usr/local/bin/safe_mysqld &;"
  end tell
end ignoring
```

The ¨ character, a line-continuation character, is produced on the Mac by pressing Option-Return. The ignoring application responses / end ignoring block will prevent the AppleScript from stalling while it waits for a response from Terminal.

—Bruce W. Perry

HACK #64 Running AppleScripts on a Regular Basis Automatically

Automating tasks with AppleScript has always been a powerful feature of the Macintosh operating system; but, until recently, automating tasks repetitively required new software. With OS X, repetitious automation is built in.

AppleScript (*http://www.apple.com/applescript/*) is a wonderful piece of technology that has long been part of the Macintosh OS. Just about any application can become AppleScript-powered, allowing automated tasks to be written in a simple, English-like language. Because of this power and the ease with which it can be had, kazillions of ApplesScripts have been written, ranging from automating backups of emails, archiving data from network-enabled services, and Finder-based scripts that promote organization (make all these files lowercase), to plug-ins (type itunes to place the currently playing song on the clipboard).

What has been missing, however, is automation of the automation, repetitively running an AppleScript without user intervention. Take the following simple script, for example:

```
say the (current date) as string
```

Exemplar of AppleScript bluntness, this uses text to speech to enunciate the current day and time. Type it into Script Editor (in *Applications → Apple-Script*), click Run, and listen closely.

That's all well and good, but what if you wanted the time spoken each and every hour, on the hour? Under Mac OS 9 and earlier, you would have had to make use of a third-party scheduling application—or just clicked Run every hour on the hour.

Meet cron [Hack #53], a Unix shell program whose life revolves around running things every minute, hour, day, week, month, or year. Give it a command or script and a schedule and let it go. Of course, cron is available as part of the Unix goodness existing beneath the colorful OS X shell. Each user on the system can automate his own tasks with no restrictions: hear the date spoken every minute, have a backup performed every three days at 12:15, or automatically open his email every day at 7:00 a.m. and then again at 6:00 p.m. Whatever your scheduling needs, cron will satisfy them.

But cron is a Unix utility, and AppleScript traditionally lives above the GUI; how do we connect the two? A shell utility called osascript, which runs AppleScripts from the command line, can take our simple script and run right from the command line:

```
% osascript -e 'say the (current date) as string'
```

And, if you can run it from the command line, you can run it out of cron, as these examples show:

```
0 7 * * Mon-Fri osascript -e 'say "alright, time to go to work"'
0 18 * * Mon-Fri osascript -e 'say "whooo dawggy, time to go home!"'
0 12 * * Sat-Sun osascript -e 'say "maybe I should get up sometime soon"'
```

These three entries will speak veiled threats every weekday morning at 7:00 a.m., wonderful news at 6:00 p.m. the same day, and a questionable alarm clock at noon on the weekends. These are all parlor tricks, however; what you really want to do is run a complex operation with hundreds of lines of AppleScript, and you certainly don't want to include it all written out as part of a command line.

In that case, simply leave the -e option off osascript, and point to your AppleScript file:

```
osascript /Users/morbus/Scripts/Backup_Email.scpt
```

Merging the preceding osascript into your *crontab* will have your email backed up the 15th of every month at 9:32 a.m.—assuming *Backup_Email. scpt* exists, of course:

```
32 9 15 * * osascript /Users/morbus/Scripts/Backup_Email.scpt
```

Running Linux on an iBook

#65   This hack tells the story of a switch to Mac hardware without switching operating systems. It includes some handy hints and tricks picked up along the way while installing Debian Linux on an iBook.

It feels a bit like a homecoming. After years wandering in the cranky wilderness of mix-and-match PCs, I'm working again on a computer that feels like it has a soul. The reason I feel like this? I switched from an Intel-based laptop to an iBook.

However, this story is different from the recent Mac conversion you may have heard about (*http://www.macdevcenter.com/pub/a/mac/2002/03/05/ mac_community.html*). My day-in, day-out operating system of choice isn't Windows; it's Linux. To be precise, Debian GNU/Linux (*http://www.debian. org/*). And on my new iBook, it's still Debian. This hack tells the story of why I switched to Mac hardware and how the installation process went. It includes some handy hints and tricks I picked up along the way and, finally, my verdict on the hardware.

The Decision

As both a writer and programmer, my needs are pretty diverse. I spend quite a lot of time traveling to conferences and plenty of time working from my home office, too. For the last two years, my faithful companion in these activities has been a Dell Latitude CPiA laptop. Although not especially light, it's a compact, good-looking machine. For about a year and a half I've been using it with Debian GNU/Linux as its operating system; running the GNOME desktop gave me a good environment to work in, for both writing and programming needs. Unfortunately, the Dell developed an awkward fault that caused the screen to be unusable, so it was time to look for a new machine.

I spent a lot of time looking at options for replacing the ailing machine. Small size was an important factor, as was low weight. Unfortunately, it seems that to get that these days you must also pay through the nose. As a reasonable price was also very important, this made things difficult. One of the most frustrating things about current PC hardware is that it is overfeatured. Manufacturers are endlessly pushing the latest-greatest this or that into the machines, keeping the prices high and bundling stuff you will never need. For a Linux user, latest-greatest hardware is generally a bad sign: it more than likely means something won't work quite right for you.

I was complaining about how expensive small laptops were when a friend mentioned that he thought iBooks were cool. I'd never considered this before but headed over to the Apple site to check them out. I specced out a 12.1" screen 500MHz iBook with the sort of features I required, and it came out at a pretty favorable price compared to the Intel-based laptops I'd been looking at. There were several particularly attractive features: the small size, the long battery life, and Apple's sane approach to memory pricing.

My interest was piqued, but I was still a little skeptical. I spent some days researching whether Linux would run on iBook hardware. In particular, I was pleased to find that my current OS, Debian, ran just fine on an iBook. Eventually I was satisfied and decided to order the machine. Friends were definitely surprised.

After all, a lot of the fuss about the new Mac centers on the beauteous Mac OS X as much as anything. Did I intend to run Mac OS X? No. Isn't that a little odd? Well, umm, I guess... it just turned out to be the best and most economic decision. It seemed odd to people that buying Apple was purely a hardware-based choice.

Partitioning and Bootstrapping

It took seven days from ordering my iBook (12.1" screen, 384MB, 30GB disk, CD/DVD, AirPort card) until its arrival on my doorstep. I was slightly annoyed when it came, as it arrived at 3:00 p.m. and we had guests that evening. A lovely new toy and I wouldn't be able to play! Nevertheless, I switched the computer on that afternoon.

Before I could do anything, I had to feed the machine four system-restore CDs, which appeared to install a complete disk image onto the hard disk. That took about 45 minutes, after which I was free to start Mac OS X. As I knew I would shortly trash and repartition the hard disk, the wait was moderately frustrating. I had chosen to proceed with a network-based install of Debian. There are two other prominent PowerPC-based Linux distributions, Yellowdog and SuSE, but as I've been a Debian user for some years, it made sense to continue with a system I was familiar with.

I paddled around in Mac OS X awhile, not having time to do anything more. I could see why it is winning many converts. I was slightly amused by the vacuum-suction effect when you minimized a window, but in general found the system pleasant to use. It did what I needed—finding a network connection—quickly and without fuss.

When our guests had gone, I avoided going to bed and decided to make a start on the Debian install. The best resource for this is Branden Robinson's Installing Debian 3.0 onto an Apple iBook page (*http://people.debian.org/~branden/ibook.html*). Branden's page gives instructions for installing

Debian in a Debian-only; Mac OS X and Debian; or Mac OS 9, Mac OS X, and Debian configuration. I knew I didn't need Mac OS 9 but thought that it might be handy to have Mac OS X around, so I pursued the second option.

The first thing to do was repartition the hard disk. This meant junking the current setup and booting from the Mac OS X setup CD. You can then launch the disk configuration tool from the first screen of the install process. I set up a 20GB partition for Linux and a 10GB one for Mac OS X. The Linux partition is a placeholder—Mac OS X tools don't know about Linux filesystems, so you just set up a partition to delete later and fill it in properly. I made both partitions of type Mac OS X Extended. Branden suggests that using UFS for the Mac OS X partition might work too, but this caused problems for me later in the install process. Figure 5-25 shows the Debian login screen on my iBook.

Figure 5-25. iBook showing Debian login

The final step was to install Mac OS X into its new home. I reflected at this point how wonderful it was to have a full install CD for the operating system, in contrast to the current trend from PC manufacturers to give you some poxy restore disk–only solution. Apple should be thanked for not trying to lock you out of using alternative operating systems on its hardware.

Typical Debian installations proceed by means of a bootstrap floppy disk that loads enough to get your machine on the Net; from there, you can download the rest of the operating system. The iBook has no floppy disk. Instead, there's a nifty program called yaboot. You download the image of the boot floppy onto your Mac OS X partition, then you use the machine's Open Firmware to instruct it to start up from that image. I had no idea Open Firmware existed, but it can be entered by holding down a magic key combination at boot time. It reminded me of the boot managers of Sun Sparc workstations. Doubtless, there are many magical and strange things it can do, but I stuck to doing what I was told!

Once you've booted into the Debian install image, things proceed more or less as they do when installing on x86-based machines. The only real difference is in using the partition editor. Before you can install Linux, you need to create a boot partition, a swap partition, and as many Linux filesystem partitions as you need. Under Debian PowerPC, there's a specialized tool for this, mac-fdisk. As Branden notes, this is a cruel introduction to Debian. Happily, his installation notes enabled me to sail through this process.

The second quirk is that, rather than running the normal "make operating system bootable," you must drop into the command line to configure the yaboot boot manager for your machine. The effect of installing the boot manager is to give you a short menu screen when you switch your iBook on. You can press L to boot into Linux, X to boot into Mac OS X, or C to boot into a CD-ROM. If you press nothing, the machine boots into your chosen default (for me, Linux) after a few seconds.

Installing Debian

I won't document the ins and outs of a Debian install: they're described in detail in other places (*http://www.debian.org/releases/stable/powerpc/install*). I will describe, however, the quirks that are specific to the iBook.

Debian is often criticized as being difficult to set up. In part, this is due to the poor user interface at the package-selection stage. My personal policy is to select as little as possible for installation during the install process and install the software I need later. In particular, selecting the laptop-specific package isn't much use for the iBook, as it has a different style of power management and doesn't have any PCMCIA devices (even if you have an AirPort card, it does not use PCMCIA).

The machine booted the first time with a Debian 2.2.x series kernel. One of my first steps was to install a 2.4.x series kernel (Debian PowerPC currently has 2.4.16). I then proceeded to try and configure as much as I could. I had read that to get the most from the iBook you needed to compile your own kernel, but I intended to see how far I could get with the standard kernel as provided in Debian.

I had no problems at all with the built-in Ethernet port, screen, USB ports, or CD-ROM drive. They all worked just fine. Even configuring X Windows turned out to be easy enough: just run `dpkg-reconfigure xserver-xfree86` and answer the questions. Figure 5-26 shows the Debian desktop on my iBook.

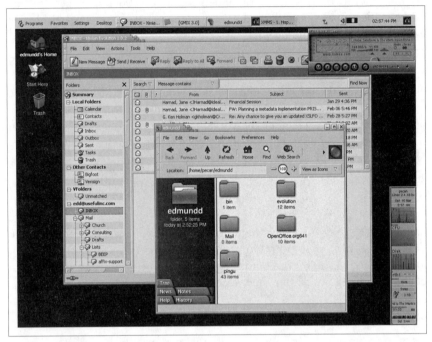

Figure 5-26. Debian desktop

Getting AirPort to take off. Setting up the AirPort wireless access was a little more difficult. For users accustomed to using wireless PCMCIA cards on Intel laptops, there are some differences. The main one is that there's no *wireless.opts* file that you can edit to set up your wireless network configuration, so when the machine enables the AirPort card, it can't find which network to join. I set up a simple workaround for this, after installing the wireless tools package.

In */etc/network/interfaces*, I added:

```
iface eth1 inet dhcp pre-up /usr/local/bin/inet_wireless.sh eth1
```

and created the */usr/local/bin/init_wireless.sh* script:

```
#!/bin/bash
IFACE=$1
iwconfig $IFACE nick MyMachineName mode Ad-Hoc
iwconfig $IFACE rate Auto
iwconfig $IFACE essid MyNetworkName
```

```
iwconfig $IFACE enc on
iwconfig $IFACE enc s:MyNetworkPassword
iwspy $IFACE 00:02:2D:02:9D:9D
```

It would be easy to adapt this script for your own needs and, indeed, write some housekeeping scripts so you can easily change between wireless networks. Note that I run an ad hoc network, rather than owning a base station. That iwspy line enables me to keep a log of the signal strength to the machine I'm using as a gateway to the rest of my network.

Support for the AirPort can be started either manually, by running modprobe airport as root, or by adding airport into your /etc/modules file.

As soon as the AirPort card worked, I breathed a sigh of relief: the rest of the configuration could take place from the comfort of my armchair!

Installing a new kernel. One major physical difference with the iBook is that the trackpad has only one button. To do the install, I plugged in a USB mouse to circumvent this problem. However, a more permanent solution needed to be found. Another issue was that I had no access to sound, either. Investigation on both of these scores led me to conclude that the time had come to compile a new kernel.

The hero of the PowerPC Mac Linux scene is Ben Herrenschmidt (*http://penguinppc.org/~benh/*). He maintains a version of the Linux kernel with all the latest toys in it, as well as some other useful tools. I followed the directions on his page to obtain a copy of his kernel. Compiling a new kernel for Linux isn't really that scary, and it went without pain for me. I was helped along the way by following the excellent instructions at iBookLinux:

> *http://www.ibooklinux.net/plain_page.php?caller=ibooklinux.*
> *php+record=79*

The only additional information I required to enable sound I found in a posting at iBookLinux:

> *http://www.ibooklinux.net/php/ibooklinux_g_h.php3?single=68+index=1*

This showed me which options I needed. I added i2c-core, i2c-keywest, i2c-dev, soundcore, dmasound_core, and dmasound_pmac lines to /etc/modules, rebooted, and was away.

Adding second and third mouse button emulation was quite simple. The latest "benh" kernel sets up an easy way to get Linux to interpret keyboard keys as mouse keys. I simply had to run these commands in order to make F10 work as the middle button and F11 as the righthand button:

```
% echo "1" > /proc/sys/dev/mac_hid/mouse_button_emulation
% echo "68" > /proc/sys/dev/mac_hid/mouse_button2_keycode
% echo "87" > /proc/sys/dev/mac_hid/mouse_button3_keycode
```

Every silver lining…. I got everything I've mentioned so far done within 24 hours, even managing a little sleep. However, there was one fly in the ointment. According to all the newsgroup posts I'd read, there should be no problems using the iBook's internal modem. However, I had no joy.

Further scouring of newsgroups turned up the suspicion that Apple had recently changed to using a software modem inside the iBooks, as they had done recently with the PowerBooks. Repeating the steps one of the posters had gone through confirmed that I, too, had a software-based modem. Resourceful though the Linux community is, it's highly unlikely that a driver will emerge for this modem for some time, if at all.

This left me with an obvious problem, as a modem connection while travelling is important to me. A search of the Linux USB hardware-compatibility charts (*http://www.qbik.ch/usb/devices/index.php*) turned up some likely options. I particularly liked the look of the Multi-Tech MultiMobileUSB modem (*http://www.multitech.com/PRODUCTS/MultiMobileUSB/*), as it was tiny. It is also quite expensive, so I had a quick look through eBay. I managed to find that modem's bigger brother (*http://www.multitech.com/PRODUCTS/MultiModemZBA/*) for a fraction of the price and settled for that. It's still smaller than an average paperback book, so won't add too much to my luggage—especially as it's USB bus–powered and doesn't need an external power adapter. The modem works fine with the iBook, using the ACM driver.

Handy Toys

To get the best from owning your iBook, you can install several useful packages.

Power management. The iBook uses a different power-management architecture from PC laptops. Whereas PCs use APM, iBooks use PMU. I installed the pmud and pmud-utils packages from Debian. Power management controls what happens when you close your iBook lid in order to put it to sleep and when to spin down the hard disk to save power. I was really happy with the way power management worked: sleep and resume were nearly instantaneous and a lot more reliable than with my old Dell laptop.

Special keys. The iBook has keys for adjusting the volume and screen brightness, as well as ejecting the CD. With a "benh" kernel install, the brightness keys worked but neither of the others did. Stefan Pfetzing has written a small program called ikeyd (*http://www.dreamind.de/ikeyd.shtml*) that makes the other keys work as advertised with a minimum of pain for the user.

Hot plugging. Since most of the devices I will plug into my iBook are USB based, I don't want to be manually configuring all the kernel modules I need to drive these devices. Instead, I installed the *hotplug* system. Hotplug implements plug-and-play and loads the correct device drivers when you plug in the devices. This also keeps your */etc/modules* file down to a short and manageable size.

So far, I've verified compatibility with a USB mouse, my Frontier NEX II MP3 player, and Kodak DC3400 digital camera; all work just the same as with the PC.

The Verdict

Buying the iBook for its hardware alone turned out to be an excellent decision. It is, however, a big change for PC laptop users. There are no mouse, parallel, serial, or docking ports. Instead, you get two USB ports, a FireWire port, a mini-VGA port for external monitor (adapter provided), and a speakers/headphone jack. The biggest difference is probably the lack of PCMCIA slots. This inevitably means that if you own any PCMCIA cards, this investment will be lost if you move to an iBook. This also puts you more at the mercy of whatever hardware Apple decides to put into the machine.

One of the iBook's best features is the screen, which is rock solid, bright, and very sharp. I was a little worried that such a small screen would be a problem, but my fears turned out to be unfounded, even at the maximum resolution of 1024×768 pixels. The keyboard is easy to type on and feels satisfying to use. The sound through the built-in speakers works surprisingly well: a lot less tinny than I had expected.

The iBook is very portable. Although not the world's lightest laptop, at just over 2kg it's eminently totable and appears pretty rugged in its construction. It also runs at a pretty cool temperature, so you can use it resting on your legs for prolonged periods. Putting the iBook to sleep by closing the lid works just fine, and waking it up again takes next to no time. Both Windows and Linux have problems doing this reliably on many PC laptops, so I was delighted to find how well it worked on the iBook.

Visually, the iBook is a winner. It has some great little touches, such as the LED indicator on the power cord that shows whether the battery is being charged. The machine's simplicity is very appealing. With other PCs, there's a trend to add many blinking lights and extra keys to the keyboard: Apple has chosen the minimalist route with great success. There are some cute surprises too: the first time I put the iBook to sleep, it was late at night and dark in my office. I nearly fell off my chair when I noticed the book breathing in its sleep with a little white light next to the lid clasp slowly pulsating.

There was one disappointment, however: Apple changed the modem inside the iBook to one that wouldn't work with Linux. As described earlier, I've got a remedy, but I'd love to see native support for the internal modem.

All in all, I'm exceedingly happy. The iBook feels, both inside and outside, as though it was designed to be a whole. It is a pleasure to work with: so much so, that I'm considering replacing the Windows PC on my home network with an iMac. Modem troubles aside, the iBook makes a fine platform for running Linux.

—Edd Dumbill

Networking

Hacks 66–78

Mac OS X is highly connected. It can attach to a veritable cornucopia of devices, as we saw in Chapter 3, *Multimedia and the iApps*. But, for my money, where OS X really shines is in its networking. It's the most network-savvy machine I've ever laid hands on; yet it's easy enough to get on the Internet just minutes after unpacking it from the box.

Communicate about as easily with Windows and Unix machines as with other Macs. Run Windows itself on and from your Mac's desktop. Connect to the Web, FTP sites, WebDAV shares, Windows (SMB) shares, networked printers—almost anything with an IP heartbeat. You can share your Internet connection via Ethernet, WiFi, or FireWire or connect one-to-one with another computer even when there is no network to be found.

This chapter highlights just some of the limitless possibilities for inter-networking with just about anything, just about anywhere.

HACK #66 · Anatomy of an Internet Shortcut

Under the covers, an Internet Shortcut is a perfectly ordinary text file with little in the way of magic.

Drag a Uniform Resource Locator (URL) from your browser's address bar to the desktop and OS X kindly creates an Internet Shortcut (Favorite, if you're coming from the Windows world), *something.url*, for you. Double-click or drag the shortcut back into your browser and you're returned to the URL you were visiting.

Under the covers, an Internet Shortcut is a perfectly ordinary text file with little in the way of magic. A shortcut to the Apple web site, for instance, looks like this:

```
[InternetShortcut]
URL=http://www.apple.com/
```

Editing an Internet Shortcut

Editing an Internet Shortcut is simply a matter of opening it up in your favorite text editor, altering the URL, and saving it. Introducing an extra space here or blank line there will render the shortcut inoperable, so tread carefully.

Creating an Internet Shortcut

Building a new Internet Shortcut from scratch is a simple affair. Fire up a text editor, type the requisite incantations, and save. Name it anything you like, but you should tack on a *.url* file extension **[Hack #6]**. The first line should read:

```
[InternetShortcut]
```

The second line is the URL itself, prepended with URL=. A shortcut to the O'Reilly Mac DevCenter would read:

```
[InternetShortcut]
URL=http://www.macdevcenter.com/
```

Any valid URL will do, whether pointing to a web site (*http://…*), FTP site (*ftp://…*), email address (*mailto:…*), or whatnot—just so long as your browser knows what to do with it. A shortcut to the *mailto: president@whitehouse.gov* email address would, via your browser, create a new email message to the president using your default mail application:

```
[InternetShortcut]
URL=mailto:president@whitehouse.gov
```

You can actually embed more complex addressing and a subject in a mailto: shortcut, like so:

```
[InternetShortcut]
URL=mailto:president@whitehouse.gov?cc=ex-president@whitehouse.gov ↵
&amp;subject="Transitions"
```

The URL..."Transitions" line was split for the purposes of publication; be sure to join them for your shortcut to work as expected.

Whether editing an existing or creating a new Internet Shortcut, you should be aware that each text editor has its own peculiarities when it comes to editing Unix and special files **[Hack #51]**. Some alter the line break **[Hack #5]** character; others, the Creator and Type codes **[Hack #6]**; and still others fiddle with both. The correct line break should be the Mac's preferred ^M. The file code should be LINK. The creator code should be that belonging to your default web browser (e.g., MSIE for Microsoft Internet Explorer).

You may find that your shortcut won't work because of line-break issues **[Hack #5]**. Also, you may need to bless the file as an Internet Shortcut and associate it with your preferred web browser **[Hack #6]**.

Renewing Your DHCP-Assigned IP address

On occasion, while ostensibly assigned an IP address by a local DHCP server, OS X doesn't appear to actually be on the network. Renewing your IP address often does the trick.

Getting your Mac to renew its dynamically assigned IP address is sometimes all that's needed to get stalled network traffic going again.

Launch System Preferences by either clicking its icon in the Dock or selecting System Preferences from the Apple menu at the top left of your screen. Select the Network control panel.

From the Network panel's Show menu, select the source of connectivity you're currently attempting to use, Built-in Ethernet for wired or AirPort for wireless connectivity. Select the TCP/IP tab. Using DHCP should already be selected in the Configure menu; if not, then you may well not be using DHCP, and this hack won't be of much help to you.

The DHCP Client ID field should be empty, unless you've used this hack before or your server uses client IDs (in which case this hack won't work for you). Type anything you like in the field—hack1 is as good a choice as any—and click the Apply Now button. You should see the IP Address field go blank for a moment, replaced by a shiny new IP address, as shown in Figure 6-1.

Close System Preferences and try out your new IP by pointing your web browser somewhere.

Sharing an Internet Connection

Turn your Mac into an Internet lifeline for those unwired systems around you.

I recently found myself at a meeting utterly surrounded by iBooks and PowerBooks, all connected by an invisible thread of 802.11b WiFi access. No Ethernet cables to trip over, no hubs taped to the tables, and no Internet access for the couple of poor souls running older Macs and Thinkpads without wireless access. In a valiant run at fairness, people started pitching in for a couple of WiFi PCMCIA cards and the group leader put on his heavy coat for the dash down the road to the local computer store.

Unfortunately, as such stories always go, one of the two disabled laptops didn't even have a PCMCIA card slot. There were mumblings about USB WiFi dongles and even one vote for buying an Ethernet hub; we had the cables.

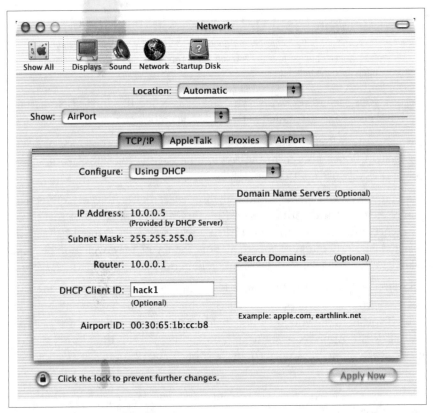

Figure 6-1. A shiny new IP address

Thank goodness all this scurrying was for nought. There were already at least 10 Ethernet hubs cum wireless bridges right beneath our very noses. Everyone had plumb forgotten about the Jaguar's ability to share Internet access.

Dongles and cables produced from various backpacks were used to plug each of the unfortunate laptops into a nearby iBook, and a few moments later everyone was wired—and happy.

Internet Sharing

As with all the coolest of features in Mac OS X, Internet Sharing is just a matter of clicking a Start button. Open the System Preferences → Sharing pane and click the Internet tab (see Figure 6-2). If it's not already on, click the Start button to start sharing Internet access with those in the vicinity less fortunate than you. This assumes, of course, that you're connected to the Internet in some manner; otherwise, all this is not particularly useful.

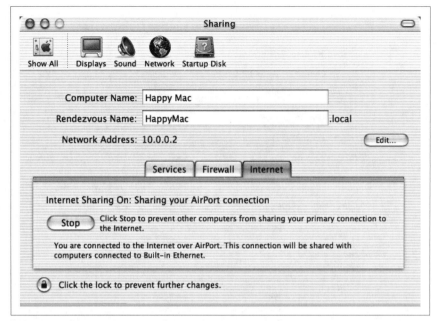

Figure 6-2. Internet Sharing over Ethernet

You'll notice that OS X is smart enough to figure out that since you're connected to the Internet over AirPort, it'll share Internet access over the only other available network port, Ethernet (see Figure 6-3). Conversely, if I were tethered to the Net by an Ethernet cable, OS X would notice that AirPort's free and turn my iBook into an AirPort base station.

Just like its hardware counterpart, your software base station has its own identity and can be configured to stick to a particular channel, remain open for neighborhood use, or be locked down using WEP encryption and password. The one thing you can't do is restrict by MAC, the hardware address burned into your wireless card.

Now take a look at the screenshot in Figure 6-4 and see if you notice anything out of the ordinary.

Where the heck did that second Ethernet adaptor come from? Remember, I have an iBook with only one Ethernet card and no room for expansion. OK, so there are USB solutions, but I have no need of them.

Give up?

I just turned on my FireWire network port, of course! Apple's recently announced IP over FireWire means that cable you usually plug into an external hard drive can also be used for network access. Simply install the preview

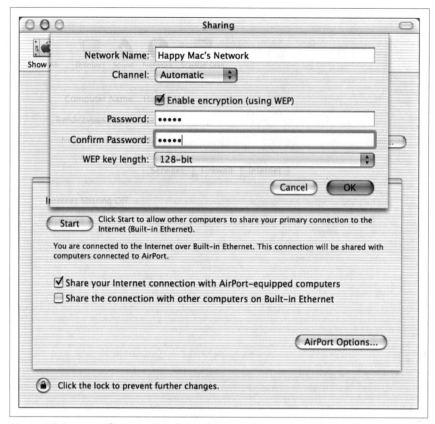

Figure 6-3. Internet Sharing as a software base station

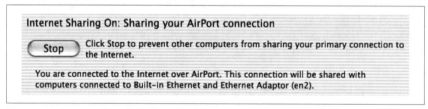

Figure 6-4. Internet Sharing with a second Ethernet adapter

release software (*http://developer.apple.com/firewire/IP_over_FireWire.html*) on both machines, plug them in to one another with a FireWire cable, and fire(wire) away! Figure 6-5 shows the FireWire Network port.

See Also

- "Creating a One-Wire Network" [Hack #69]

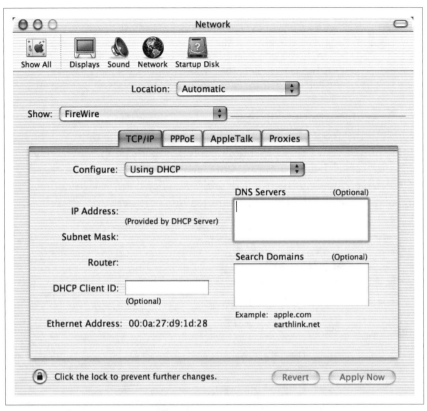

Figure 6-5. The FireWire Network port

HACK #69 Creating a One-Wire Network

A one-wire network can be a salvation when you're in need of a quick file transfer between laptops with incompatible parts.

You're on a plane and desperately need to pass a file to (or play Quake against) your coworker. You both have Ethernet jacks, but there's no network available to you. You both have wireless cards, but transmitter/receivers are a no-no aboard airliners. She has a floppy drive, but your iBook has never heard of these floppy things. You have a USB drive, but the file's massive. And you're fresh out of CDs, or you'd simply burn one and pass it across.

Oh, and she's running Windows.

If you have an Ethernet cable handy, you can plug one end into the Ethernet jack of each of your machines, open your System Preferences → Network pane, and select Built-in Ethernet from the Show pull-down menu.

If at least one of the computers is a Macintosh of recent vin-
tage (PowerBook G4, iMac 17", or iBook, at the time of this
writing), you don't even need one of those special crossover
Ethernet cables. Refer to the consummate list at *http://docs.
info.apple.com/article.html?artnum=42717.*

Wait.…Within a short while, you'll notice your system self-assigning an IP
address in the 169.254 range, as shown in Figure 6-6. The same will be happening on your coworker's Windows laptop. What's happening is that both
machines sense there's some network activity on the wire, yet there's no
DHCP server to assign them an IP address. They'll self-assign addresses in
the 169.254 range, establishing, in effect, a one-wire network.

Figure 6-6. Self-assigning an IP address

Now you can try and browse for any shares on the Windows laptop from
your Mac using Go → Connect to Server… or ⌘-K. You can also turn on
FTP Access [Hack #75] or Remote Login [Hack #65] on your iBook and SSH or
FTP in from the Windows side (see Figure 6-7).

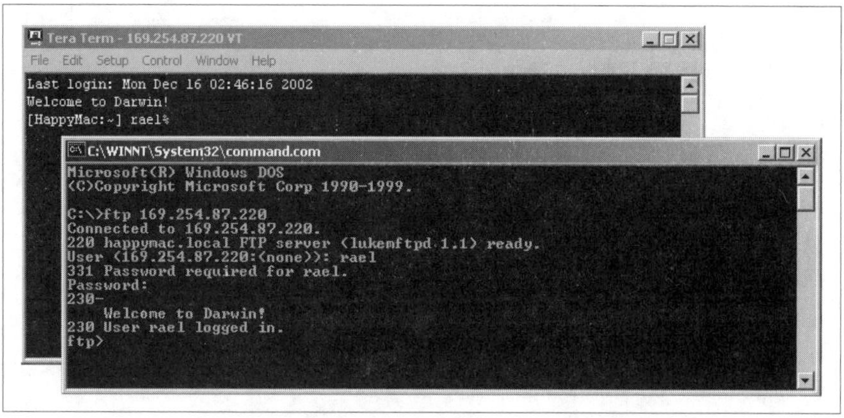

Figure 6-7. FTP and SSH from Windows to Mac over the one-wire network

Heck, you could fire up your Mac's Apache web server **[Hack #85]** and visit it from a Windows browser.

Go ahead and transfer to your heart's content via FTP or SSH (scp, if available on the Windows side). To disconnect, simply unplug the cable.

One-Wire Rendezvous

If you're both running OS X, you can actually let Rendezvous (*http://www.apple.com/macosx/jaguar/rendezvous.html*) take all the IP nonsense out of the equation. You should be able to browse each other's *Public* folders in the Connect to Server... dialog box and connect to each other using your machine's Rendezvous name (see System Preferences → Sharing). You can even chat and transfer files via iChat over Rendezvous; turn on Rendezvous in iChat with iChat → Log into Rendezvous or ⌘-Option-L.

One-FireWire Network

Apple's recently announced IP over FireWire (*http://developer.apple.com/FireWire/IP_over_FireWire.html*) (preview release at the time of this writing) means Rendezvous and all the joy it brings at FireWire speeds. Simply install the preview release software on both machines, plug them into each other with a FireWire cable, and fire(wire) away! Figure 6-8 shows the FireWire Network preferences.

—Inspired by Chris Stone and Brian Jepson

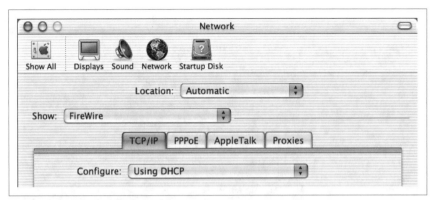

Figure 6-8. FireWire Network preferences

Secure Tunneling with VPN or SSH
HACK #70

Mac OS X's built-in Virtual Private Network client and SSH offer two secure ways to tunnel in to your company or organization.

Mac OS X 10.2 includes a Virtual Private Network (VPN) client for tunneling securely into your company or organization's network, authenticating yourself, and gaining access to shared resources otherwise available only to those on site. This works regardless of whether your connection to the Internet is dial-up, DSL, cable-modem, or what-have-you. You'll sometimes hear VPNs referred to as Point-to-Point Tunneling Protocol (PPTP). Whatever you call it, previous versions of the Mac OS didn't include a VPN client, leaving you to third-party software like DigiTunnel (*http://www.gracion.com/vpn/*).

> The endpoint of your VPN connection (i.e., your office) will need to be running a VPN server in order for this to work.

To initiate a VPN connection, the first step is to ensure that you're connected to the Internet in some form. Once you're online, launch *Applications → Internet Connect* or select Open Internet Connect… from the Internet Connect menu bar icon, as shown in Figure 6-9.

Select File → New VPN Connection Window or press Shift-⌘-P. Enter the server address, your username, and your password into the appropriate fields. Save the password to your keychain if you'll be using this connection often and don't feel like typing your password each time. Click Connect when you're ready.

Figure 6-9. Launching Internet Connect from the menu bar

One gotcha and quick fix: if you're logging into a Microsoft Windows–based VPN/PPTP server, you may need to provide the authentication realm in addition to your login. If so, tack the realm on before your login and separate the two with a \ (backslash), as shown in Figure 6-10.

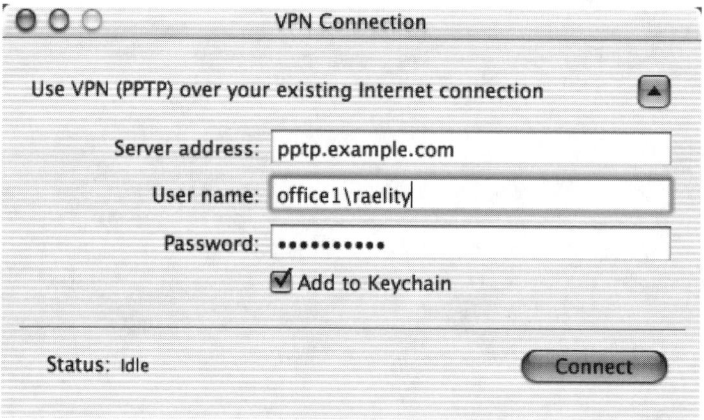

Figure 6-10. Making a VPN (PPTP) connection

Once established, all of your traffic will flow through the VPN connection. This may be a disadvantage if your home network is, for instance, faster than that running through your office; you'll be limited by the maximum throughput of both your connection to the Internet and your office's. Digi-Tunnel does have a workaround, sporting a split-routing feature that allows you to route requests directly to Internet sites while routing requests meant for your office via the VPN.

You may also need to fiddle with your PPTP Network settings (System Preferences → Network → PPTP), but most of the time you can just leave things as they were. Consult your local system administrator or Internet service provider if you're having trouble finding or reaching anything inside the destination network. Figure 6-11 shows the default PPTP Network settings.

Figure 6-11. Default PPTP Network settings

If all goes to plan, you should start seeing your office domains and shared drives showing up in the Connect to Server window (Go → Connect to Server or ⌘-K from the Finder).

When you're ready to leave the office behind, click the Disconnect button.

Tunneling Data Over SSH

SSH [Hack #71] isn't only for securing interactive remote sessions; you can piggyback just about any network traffic on it, adding a wrapper of ironclad security to anything you may be doing over the network: sending and receiving email, web browsing, backing up, synchronizing two computers—you name it.

This is called port forwarding. Think of ports as channels on a CB radio, with each service chatting away on its own channel. All web traffic communicates over port/channel 80, POP mail over port/channel 110, and SSH over port/channel 22. SSH can be set to handle data sent to a local port, performing encryption and sending the encrypted data to the remote end of the SSH connection. At the other end, it's decrypted and sent on to the appropriate port. For all intents and purposes, that remote port is masquerading as a local port.

Many a time I find myself in a strange locale without access to a mail server through which to send my outgoing mail. So, I simply tell Mail to direct all outgoing email to my local port 25 (that's the port or channel on which sendmail [Hack #82] usually lives) which, in turn, is forwarded over SSH to my mail server at work.

And it's all just a rather cryptic-looking, yet really very simple, command away:

```
% sudo ssh -l rael -N -L25:mailserver_at_work:25 mailserver_at_work
```

I (-l rael) am forwarding all traffic for local port 25 (-L25) to port 25 on my mail server at work (mailserver_at_work:25) via my mail server at work itself (mailserver_at_work). I could have routed the data via any machine that, in turn, is allowed to access the mail server at work, but since I have SSH access to the mail server itself, it only makes sense to cut out any further middlemen. The -N specifies that I'll not be running any remote commands, only forwarding the port.

You can add as many forwards as you wish to that one command line. I like to secure the mail I'm receiving as well as sending, so I can just as easily forward POP mail (port or channel 110) as well, like so:

```
% sudo ssh -l rael -N -L25:mailserver_at_work:25 -L110:mailserver_at_work: ⏎
110 mailserver_at_work
```

You'll notice that each time you do any port forwarding, you need to authenticate yourself to the remote machine; see "SSH Without Passwords" in "Remotely Log In to Another Machine via SSH" [Hack #71] for a workaround. Also, since ports 25 and 110 are privileged ports, accessible only by the root user [Hack #50], you'll have to use sudo to authenticate yourself before you're able to forward them. A simple way around this is not to use privileged ports on this side of the SSH tunnel. Just about anything above 1024 will do. Picking 5000 as the base, for example, I can forward all traffic for port 25 from 5025 and 110 from 5110.

```
% ssh -l rael -N -L5025:mailserver_at_work:25 -L5110:mailserver_at_work: ⏎
110 mailserver_at_work
```

That did the trick, allowing me to avoid sudo and local authentication.

For use of arbitrary unprivileged ports to work, the application you're using (Mail, in my case) must allow you to specify a port along with a hostname. Figures 6-12 and 6-13
show me configuring Mail to use localhost:5025 for SMTP
and localhost:5110 for POP mail.

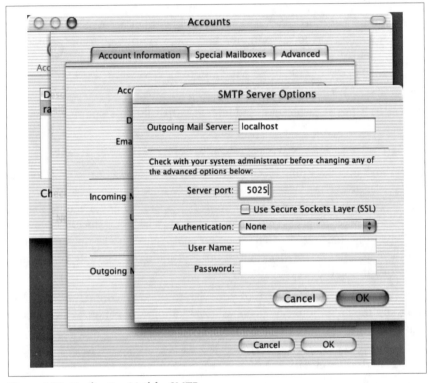

Figure 6-12. Configuring Mail for SMTP

Remotely Log In to Another Machine via SSH

HACK #71

Interact with a remote machine from the command line via SSH, the Secure
Shell.

Once you've acquired a taste of the Unix command line underlying Mac OS
X, it's hard to stick only to the machine at hand. You want to log in to that
old-but-upgraded PowerMac 7500 with G3 card in the closet to see how
your web server's faring. Your friend invites you to drop in on his X Server

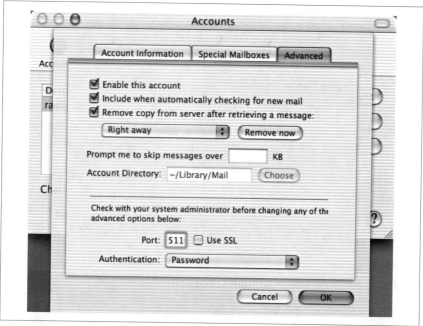

Figure 6-13. Configuring Mail for POP

across the country to check out his latest Perl hacks. The FTP server in your office doesn't appear to be allowing incoming FTP requests, despite being pingable (read: online and alive).

Forget remote screen-sharing applications; who needs a candy-coated graphical user interface to accomplish the remote administration tasks at hand? From the command line you can do most anything you can do locally—except play that addictive new fully immersive GUI game you left in your office machine's CD drive.

Introducing SSH

SSH, the Secure Shell, is a command-line utility for interacting with a computer over the network as if it were local, attached directly to your keyboard. SSH differs from other remote access options (e.g., Telnet) in its focus on security; all communication is encrypted, end to end. This means that anyone tapped into your network (called a man-in-the-middle attack) won't see much more than gibberish floating by. And it does this in a fast, safe, and intuitive way, making for some interesting and powerful hacks.

For everything you ever wanted to know about SSH, take a gander at O'Reilly's *SSH, The Secure Shell: The Definitive Guide* (*http://www.oreilly.com/catalog/sshtdg*).

Allowing Remote Login

Mac OS X, being a Unix-based operating system, comes with SSH remote-login capability baked right in. Before you can log into your Mac remotely, however, you do need to turn on SSH. Open the System Preferences → Sharing pane and select the Services panel. On the left is a list of services supported by OS X; along with Personal Web Sharing [Hack #88] and Printer Sharing is Remote Login. If it's off, start it up either by selecting it and clicking the Start button on the right or by clicking the associated checkbox. After a few moments of Remote Login starting up…, your Services panel should look something like Figure 6-14.

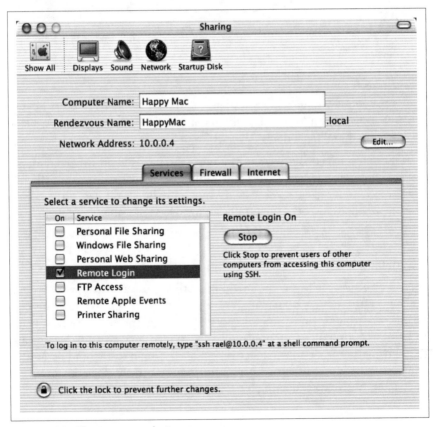

Figure 6-14. Allowing remote login

Of course, this does little good if the computer isn't accessible from wherever you need to be while accessing it. This usually isn't a problem when you're on the same local network in your house or office. If you intend to log in remotely from somewhere else on the Internet, check with your system administrator or Internet service provider about addressing [Hack #78] and reaching your machine.

Getting from Here to There

To log in to a remote machine, whether it be another Mac, Linux box, or anything else running SSH, open a Terminal [Hack #48] window and type:

```
% ssh -l username remote_machine
```

Substitute your login name on the remote machine for *username* and the name or IP address of the remote server for *remote_machine*. If, for example, I were logging into a machine called *foo.example.com* using the login raelity, my session would start out a little like this:

```
% ssh -l raelity foo.example.com
Last login: Thu Dec 12 10:34:03 2002 from 123.somewhere.isp.net
Linux 2.4.18.

raelity@foo:~$
```

If your remote login name is the same as your local one, you can forego the -l username bit, typing only:

```
% ssh remote_machine
```

That's all there is to it. You should now be on the command-line of a remote machine. Depending on the operating system running over there, it will look to some degree or another like your local Terminal command line.

Copying Files over SSH

It's just about as easy to copy files to and from an SSH-enabled machine as it is to copy them from one local directory to another on the command line, thanks to an SSH-based version of the cp [Hack #48] command, scp. It goes like this:

```
% scp login@remote_machine:/path/to/file .
% scp filename login@remote_machine:/destination/path
```

The first line copies a *file* from *remote_machine*, using the username *login* to your local current directory (.). The second line does the exact opposite. For example, to copy a file called *notes.txt* in the */tmp* directory on the remote machine, *foo.example.com*, as user *sam* to your local *Documents* directory, like so:

```
% scp sam@foo.example.com:/tmp/notes.txt ~/Documents
sam@foo.example.com's password:
notes.txt 100% |****************************| 22 00:00
```

scp works just about the same as cp, allowing you to copy multiple files (this works when copying files from here to there, not there to here), rename them during copy, and so on:

```
% scp image*.jpg sam@foo.example.com:~/images
% scp sam@foo.example.com:/tmp/notes.txt ./lecture_notes.txt
```

Port Forwarding

SSH isn't only for securing interactive remote sessions; you can piggyback just about any network traffic on it, adding a wrapper of ironclad security to anything you may be doing over the network. For an example of so-called port forwarding over SSH, see "Secure Tunneling with VPN or SSH" [Hack #70].

Remote Reboot

Your remote machine's stuck for some unfathomable reason, the screen frozen and mouse immobile (not that you can see it). Yet you still seem able to log in remotely. To remotely reboot that machine, SSH in and type:

```
% sudo reboot
```

Wait a short while and, assuming it comes up cleanly, all should be well.

Remote Screenshot

The combination of OS X's command-line screencapture utility [Hack #41] and SSH means being able to take a snapshot of a remote machine's desktop.

Simply log in remotely, type screencapture *filename.pdf*, and scp the file back over to your local machine.

This is a nifty way, by the by, to capture the Mac OS X Login screen.

SSH Without Passwords

When you're working with more than a few machines, having to type ssh *my.server.com* (followed by a password) is not only tedious, but it breaks one's concentration. Suddenly having to shift from "Where's the problem?" to getting there and back to "What's all this, then?" has led more than one admin to premature senility. It promotes the digital equivalent of "Why did I come into this room, anyway?"

At any rate, more effort spent logging into a machine means less effort getting your work done. Recent versions of SSH offer a secure alternative to entering a password endlessly: public key exchange.

To use public keys with an SSH server, you'll first need to generate a public/private key pair:

```
% ssh-keygen -t rsa
```

You can also use -t dsa for DSA keys, or -t rsa1 if the machine at the other end is using SSH Protocol v1 (Protocol v2, the default, is a better choice).

After you enter the preceding command, you should see this:

```
Generating public/private rsa key pair.
Enter file in which to save the key (/Users/rael/.ssh/id_rsa):
```

Just press Return to accept the default. ssh-keygen will then ask you for a pass-phrase; just press Return twice (but read the note on security later in this hack).

The results should look something like this:

```
Enter passphrase (empty for no passphrase):
Enter same passphrase again:
Your identification has been saved in /home/rob/.ssh/id_rsa.
Your public key has been saved in /home/rob/.ssh/id_rsa.pub.
The key fingerprint is:
a6:5c:c3:eb:18:94:0b:06:a1:a6:29:58:fa:80:0a:bc rob@localhost
```

This created two files, ~/.ssh/id_rsa and ~/.ssh/id_rsa.pub. Now you need to get those keys over to the destination machine; future SSH sessions will notice that you've got matching keys on both sides and not bother you for a password. Let's use SSH itself to copy the keys. The first command creates a remote .ssh directory, while the second copies the keys there:

```
% ssh server "mkdir .ssh; chmod 0700 .ssh"
% scp .ssh/id_rsa.pub server:.ssh/authorized_keys2
```

Of course, you should substitute the remote machine's name or IP address for *server*. It should ask for your password both times. Now, simply SSH in (e.g., ssh server) and you should be logged in automatically, without a password. And yes, your shiny new public key will work for scp, too.

If that didn't work for you, check your file permissions on both your local and remote ~/.ssh directories and the files within. Your private key (*id_rsa*) should be 0600 (and be present only on your local machine), and everything else should be 0655 or better.

Some consider the use of public keys to be a potential security risk. After all, one only has to steal a copy of your private key to obtain access to your servers. While this is true, the same is certainly true of passwords.

Ask yourself, how many times a day do you enter a password to gain shell access to a machine (or scp a file)? How frequently is it the same password on many (or all) of those machines? Have you ever used that password in a way that might be questionable (on a web site, a personal machine that isn't quite up-to-date, or possibly with an SSH client on a machine that you don't directly control)? If any of these possibilities sounds familiar, then consider that an SSH key in the same setting would make it virtually impossible for an attacker to gain unauthorized access later (providing, of course, that you keep your private key safe).

—Rob Flickenger

Running Windows on and from a Mac

HACK
#72

If you just can't do without running a piece of Windows software, there are a couple of options open to you: remote control and virtual PC emulation.

Sharing files between the Mac and the PC is good, but not enough for me. It would be better to be able to run my favorite PC applications on the Mac. While running a Windows application directly on the Mac is not technically possible, there are a couple of ways that come close to that. The first is to pump out the display of a PC to the Mac. Microsoft provides the Remote Desktop Connection (RDC) (*http://www.microsoft.com/mac/DOWNLOAD/MISC/RDC.asp*) for that purpose (see Figure 6-15). The second way (discussed in the next section of this hack) is to run a software emulator that emulates the Windows operating system.

Remote Desktop
Connection

Figure 6-15. Remote Desktop Connection application

The RDC allows you to hook up your Mac to the network and control your Windows system remotely. To test-drive RDC, I downloaded it and used it to connect to my Windows 2000 Advanced Server. To use RDC, you need to run Terminal Services on the Windows machine before the remote desktop software can connect to it.

In the RDC connection window (see Figure 6-16), you can specify the login information, screen size, key mappings, and so on. You can use the IP address, fully qualified machine name, or netBIOS name to connect to the Windows machine.

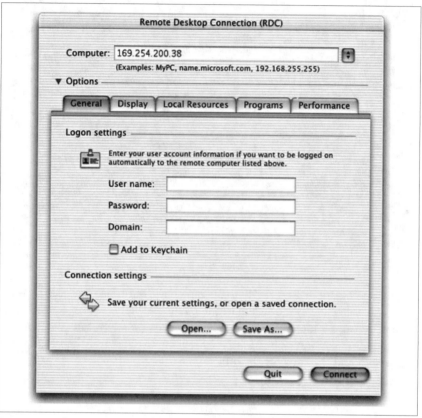

Figure 6-16. Remote Desktop Connection window

As RDC is dependent on Terminal Services, you can connect to all Windows versions that support Terminal Services, such as:

- Windows 2000 Server
- Windows 2000 Advanced Server
- Windows XP

If it connects successfully, you should see the familiar Windows screen, as shown in Figure 6-17.

Figure 6-17. Windows on Mac via Remote Desktop Connection

The nice thing about RDC is that you can create multiple instances of Windows using a single Windows machine. Although RDC will make only one connection at a time, there is a trick you can use: duplicate the Remote Desktop Connection application (see Figure 6-18) and use the original for one session and the copy for the other.

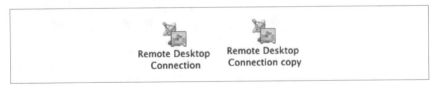

Figure 6-18. Duplicating the Remote Desktop Connection application

In Figure 6-19, I have two separate instances of Windows 2000 Advanced Server running. One is running Visual Studio .NET, and the other is running Adobe Acrobat.

Performance-wise, RDC is relatively fast. It translates keystrokes between the Mac and PC efficiently, and I have no problem in using my regular Control and Alt (using the Option key on the Mac) keys when controlling my Windows PC. Running CPU-intensive applications like Visual Studio .NET has no effect on the performance on the Mac, as all the processing is done

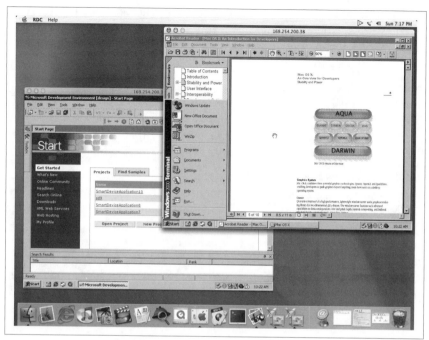

Figure 6-19. Two instances, two Windows machines

on the Windows PC itself. I also have no problems running regular applications like Word, PowerPoint, Adobe Acrobat, and so forth.

However, when two or more RCS instances of Windows are created, the
performance degrades drastically. But this is really the problem with the
Windows server, as multiple clients connecting to the Terminal Services
chalk up a lot of resources. Nevertheless, my notebook equipped with
512MB RAM and a 1GHz processor does not seem to digest the workload
well.

Virtual PC

If you don't have a spare Windows PC to connect to or if you are on the
road with only your Macintosh notebook, another option is Virtual PC from
Connectix (*http://www.connectix.com/*). Virtual PC emulates the PC's CPU
and hardware so that Windows, Linux, and other operating systems can run
on it.

Virtual PC is available in two flavors: with or without an operating system
(to be fair, the latter includes DOS). If you already have an unused license
for the operating system you plan to use, you can buy Virtual PC with DOS
for $129 from the Connectix store (*http://www.connectix.com/shop/*) and
install your own operating system. If you choose electronic delivery, you can

download it and install it right away (the disk image is about 12MB). After you download and install Virtual PC, you'll need to visit the Connectix support site to check for any updates. At the time of this writing, 6.0.1 was the most current version.

If you purchased an operating system with Virtual PC, you'll be able to start working with it right away. If you purchased the version that includes only DOS, you'll need to install Windows. For instructions on installing another operating system, see the documentation in the */Applications/Virtual PC 6/Extras/Installing Other OSes/* directory.

Windows XP runs well on Virtual PC (see Figure 6-20), but you need to optimize it heavily to get the best performance. Plenty of memory is suggested (256MB is good for Windows XP Professional), and you should consult the Optimizing Windows XP Professional and Home Edition For Connectix Virtual PC document, available at *http://www.connectix.com/support/library.html*. Aside from the tips in that document, we suggest aggressively diminishing the number of services you are running. TechSpot has a good article on this topic (*http://www.techspot.com/tweaks/winxp_services/*), as does ExtremeTech (*http://www.extremetech.com/article2/0,,5155,00.asp*).

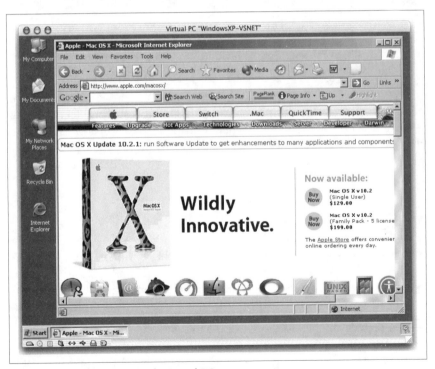

Figure 6-20. Windows XP inside Virtual PC

Virtual PC and RDC Performance

So how well does Windows XP run under Virtual PC and RDC? To find out, we chose a CPU and disk-intensive test: building Microsoft's Shared Source CLI (*http://msdn.microsoft.com/net/sscli*). We tested it on an 800MHz PC and a 600MHz dual-USB iBook running various Mac OS X versions and Virtual PC 5.0 (we weren't able to test 6.0 in time for this book).

Table 6-1 shows the results of our test.

Table 6-1. Virtual PC and RDC performance test results

CPU	MHz	Real RAM	VM RAM	Mac OS	Duration
Pentium III	800	256	NA	(RDC from 10.2.1)	0:15
Pentium III	800	256	NA	NA	0:15
G3	600	640	256	9.2.2	1:38
G3	600	640	256	10.1.5	2:02
G3	600	640	256	10.2.1 6D52	2:03
G3	600	640	128	10.2 6C115	3:09
G3	600	640	256	10.2 6C115	3:27

The CPU column lists the CPU of the machine running the test, and the MHz column shows its speed. Real RAM is how much memory is installed inside the system, and VM RAM is how much was allocated to the virtual machine (in the case of the Pentium running Windows XP, this was not applicable). The duration is shown in hours:minutes.

The abysmal performance under the initial release of Jaguar (10.2, build 6C115) is due to bugs that were fixed in the 10.2.1 release. So, if you're going to use Virtual PC with Jaguar, make sure you run the Software Update in System Preferences to bring your system up-to-date.

Our Verdict

From the times, you can see that running applications on a real PC is a huge win; 10.1.5 and 10.2.1 are very close, but running under 9.2.2 shaves about 25 minutes off the build. Still, the performance compared to a real PC is disappointing. And in everyday use, Virtual PC does not feel terribly snappy. For example, launching Visual Studio .NET takes 1 minute and 19 seconds before the start page appears using Virtual PC under Jaguar 10.2.1. Compare that to 28 seconds on the Pentium III machine. In fairness, once an application launches under Virtual PC, we've found that it performs adequately.

You can get by with Virtual PC, especially if you are willing to make some concessions. For example, instead of using Visual Studio .NET, you could use Notepad or another lightweight editor for editing .NET programs, and compile them with the command-line compilers (cl, csc, vbc, and jsc). With these kinds of adjustments, life under Virtual PC is not so bad.

Virtual PC is the best bet for people who want to take their Macintosh on the road with them. But as 802.11b access points become more prevalent, and 3G networking takes off, it would not be unreasonable to use a Virtual Private Network connection in conjunction with the Remote Desktop Client to access a Windows server on a home or corporate network.

—Wei-Meng Lee and Brian Jepson

HACK #73 Sharing Files Between Mac and Windows PCs

Apple has incorporated technologies into Mac OS X that allow easy file sharing across platforms.

Mac users often have to share files with Windows machines, both at work and at home. Occasionally, using portable media such as a ZIP disk or USB portable storage does the job nicely, but for daily use a cross-platform network is more robust. Apple has incorporated technologies into Mac OS X that allow easy file sharing among platforms. And with the release of Mac OS X 10.2, networking became even easier.

In this hack, we'll discuss how you can share files between your Mac and Windows machines. All the examples have been tested with Mac OS X 10.2.1.

Systems Configuration

I have an eMac and a Pentium 4 PC (an HP notebook). I used an Ethernet cable to connect the two machines directly. The nice thing here is that I can use a straight cable to connect both machines, and my eMac is able to automatically detect that it is connecting to a PC. There is no need for a cross cable here.

Viewing PC Files from a Mac

The first thing I want to try after connecting my two machines is to enable file sharing. On my PC, I create a folder and share it using the name *Macshare*. On my Mac, I want to be able to access that folder. To connect to the shared folder, select Go from the Finder menu and click Connect to Server.

You should be able to see the PC name displayed, as shown in Figure 6-21. Select the PC and click Connect.

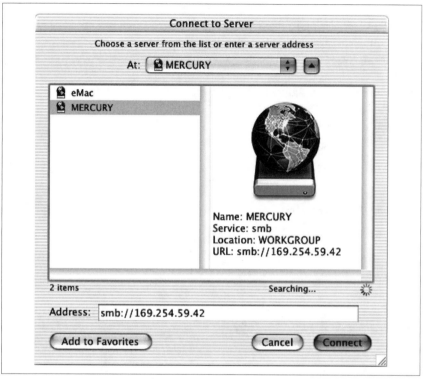

Figure 6-21. Connecting to a server

You will be prompted to enter the credentials to log on to the PC (domain/workgroup, username, and password).

If the connection is successful, you will see the share icon (see Figure 6-22).

Figure 6-22. The share folder on the Desktop

You can now browse the folder as though it is a local drive.

Viewing Mac Files from a PC

Because Mac OS 10.2 (Jaguar) contains a built-in SMB/CIFS server (Samba Version 2.2.3a), viewing Mac files on the PC is straightforward. You can use your Network Neighborhood to view the shared folders on your Mac. To do that, you need to turn on the Windows File Sharing on your Mac and check the "Allow user to log in from Windows" option, as shown in Figure 6-23. If the account you are setting is yourself, you need to type your password into the Current Password field before you can change the checkbox.

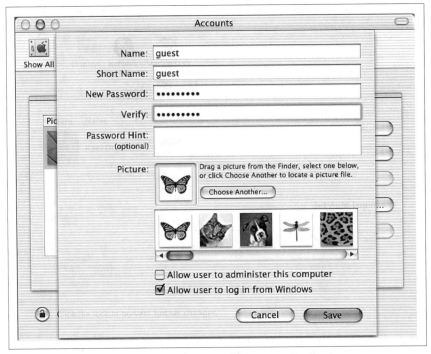

Figure 6-23. Allowing users to log in from Windows

SMB stands for Server Message Block. It's a lightweight protocol designed to allow the sharing of files and printers in a small network. SMB has since been renamed CIFS, or Common Internet File System. Mac OS X 10.1 contains only the SMB client, and thus you can only use SMB to browse for files on the PC, not vice versa. Mac OS X 10.2 contains both the SMB client and server, and hence PC users can browse for files on a Macintosh. For more information on SMB and Mac OS X, please see the Mac OS X and SMB HOWTO (*http://www.opensource.apple.com/projects/documentation/howto/html/osxsmb.html*).

Besides this method, two alternative ways to share Mac files with PC users are to use Web Sharing or FTP.

To use Web Sharing (using the built-in Apache web server), check the Personal Web Sharing item under the Services category in your System Preferences, as shown in Figure 6-24. Likewise, to allow FTP access, check the FTP Access checkbox. By default, the folder exposed by the web server is *~/Sites*.

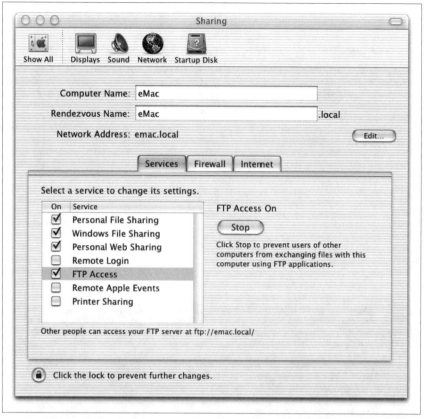

Figure 6-24. Enabling FTP access

The FTP services, though, expose the user's home directory, as shown in Figure 6-25. Hence, to share out any files on the Mac, you simply copy them to the respective folders, and they can then be accessed through FTP.

To access the Mac files using FTP, you can use the command window in Windows and issue the following command (see Figure 6-26):

```
C:\>ftp IPAddressOfYourMac
```

You can find out the IP address of your Mac in *System Preferences → Network → TCP/IP*.

For Web Sharing, you can use a web browser, such as IE, and enter the IP address of the Mac, followed by ~/username/ (see Figure 6-27).

—Wei-Meng Lee and Brian Jepson

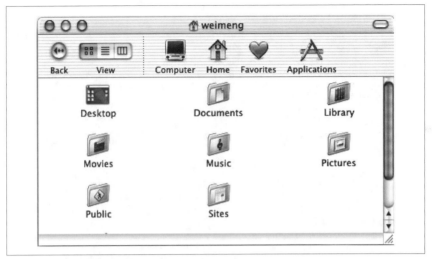

Figure 6-25. Home directory via FTP

```
C:\WINNT\System32\cmd.exe - ftp 169.254.253.106                        _ □ X
220 emac.local FTP server (lukemftpd 1.1) ready.
User (169.254.253.106:(none)): weimenglee
331 Password required for weimenglee.
Password:
230-
    Welcome to Darwin!
230 User weimenglee logged in.
ftp> ls
200 PORT command successful.
150 Opening ASCII mode data connection for 'file list'.
.CFUserTextEncoding
.DS_Store
.Trash
Desktop
Documents
Library
Movies
Music
Pictures
Public
Send Registration
Sites
226 Transfer complete.
ftp: 128 bytes received in 0.00Seconds 128000.00Kbytes/sec.
ftp>
```

Figure 6-26. FTP from Windows to Mac

 ### HACK #74 Mounting a WebDAV Share

Connect to a WebDAV-based network drive and work with remote content just as if it were on a local drive.

WebDAV, or Web-based Distributed Authoring and Versioning, allows you to share directories and files via your web server for remote editing of documents and other files. (See "Turning on WebDAV" [Hack #95] for more detail on WebDAV and WebDAV-enabled servers.)

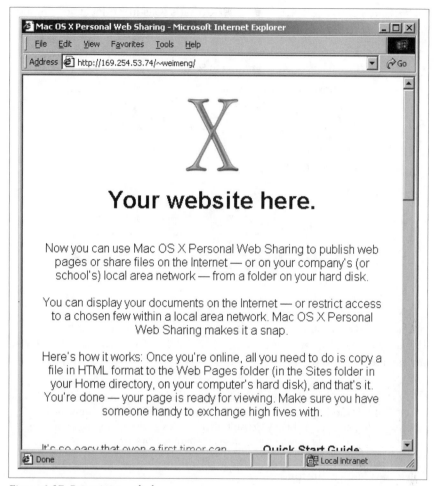

Figure 6-27. Browsing a web share

Mac OS X has support for WebDAV built right into the operating system and integrated seamlessly into the desktop environment. Simply point to a server, much as you would an AppleShare or SMB (Windows) share, log in, and bingo!, you have a new virtual drive right on your desktop. WebDAV is actually the technology behind much of iCal calendar publishing [Hack #30] and iPhoto sharing.

Connecting and Mounting

To connect to a WebDAV share, you'll need to start from the Finder. Click the Finder icon in your Dock or on any open space on your Desktop. Select

Go → Connect to Server... or type ⌘-K (that's K as in Konnect) to bring up the Connect to Server dialog box shown in Figure 6-28.

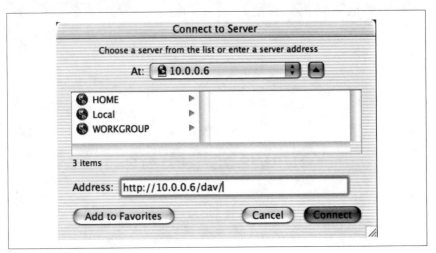

Figure 6-28. Connecting to a WebDAV server

Enter the URL of the WebDAV share into the Address field. In Figure 6-28, I've used a share created with "Turning on WebDAV" **[Hack #95]**, 10.0.0.6 on my private local network.

 You'll notice that the share doesn't show up in any of my local AppleShare and SMB (Windows) domain lists; unfortunately, WebDAV doesn't offer the same level of discovery of shared resources as with other sharing protocols.

Click the Connect button.

If the WebDAV server at hand isn't using SSL (Secure Sockets Layer) for secured, encrypted interaction, you'll be told as much (see Figure 6-29). If you're comfortable continuing (sending your username/password and content over the network in the clear), click Continue.

Next, if the WebDAV share restricts access (which it should), you'll be prompted for a Username/Password pair, as shown in Figure 6-30. Type in the appropriate authentication and click OK to mount the WebDAV share.

After a few seconds, a Finder window will appear with a view on the WebDAV directory you just mounted, *dav* in my case (see Figure 6-31). An icon for the networked drive will also appear on the Desktop.

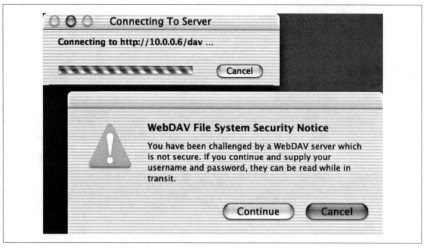

Figure 6-29. SSL security notification

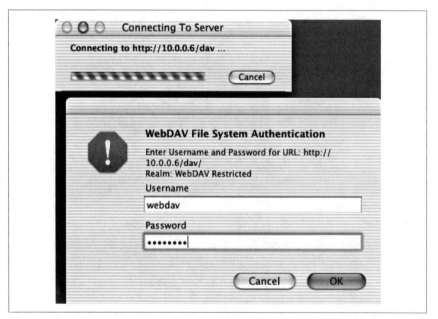

Figure 6-30. Authenticating yourself to the WebDAV server

You can browse around, add, update, and delete anything for which you have permission to do so, just as on any local drive. Of course, since the mounted share is treated just like any other drive, you can browse around and alter its content from the Unix command line via the Terminal (see Figure 6-32).

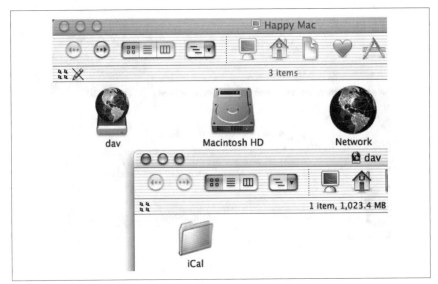

Figure 6-31. A mounted WebDAV volume in the Finder

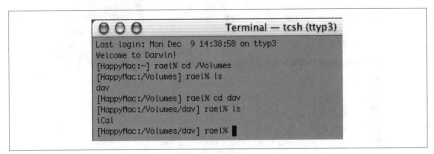

Figure 6-32. The WebDAV volume on the command line

Disconnecting

Unmount a WebDAV share just as you would any other removable media (CD, DVD, iDisk, etc.): drag it to the Trash can in your Dock—a little silly, if you think about it—or select the drive icon and press ⌘-E to eject it.

HACK #75 Mounting a Remote FTP Directory

Mount an FTP site right on your Desktop for perusal and easy downloading of files and turn on remote FTP access to your own Mac.

It used to be that just about any time you wanted to download something from the Internet, it was hosted on an FTP server. I've spent many an hour perusing FTP sites in search of some piece of open source software, a driver for my Linux box, or Perl modules. These days almost anything you download is made available to you via HTTP by clicking a link on a web site.

Still, sometimes a little FTP spelunking is in order. You can do it the old-fashioned way using ftp or ncftp on the command line. You can also open an FTP directory in your web browser. But if you're grabbing more than one file at a time, nothing beats a GUI FTP client. Nothing, that is, before OS X granted you the ability to mount remote FTP shares on your Desktop alongside AppleTalk, Windows **[Hack #73]**, and WebDAV **[Hack #74]** shares.

Mounting Anonymous FTP Shares

To mount an anonymous (read: open to all) FTP site on your desktop, you'll need to start from the Finder. Select Go → Connect to Server... or press ⌘-K to bring up the Connect to Server dialog box.

Enter the FTP URL into the Address field and click the Connect button. In Figure 6-33, I'm connecting to a mirror site for the Comprehensive Perl Archive Network (CPAN), the place to find Perl modules.

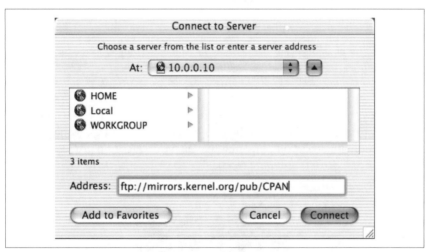

Figure 6-33. Connecting to an anonymous FTP site

The site will appear as a mounted drive on your Desktop. Peruse at your leisure, dragging files from the share to your Desktop to download them. You won't be able to drag anything into the mounted FTP drive, since you're logged in anonymously and don't have write access.

Mounting Authenticated FTP Shares

The technique is the same for mounting FTP shares requiring authentication. In Figure 6-34, I'm logging into the Mac in my closet. The only thing special is the addition of my login name to the URL, followed by an @ (at sign).

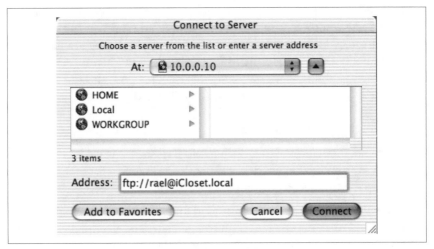

Figure 6-34. Connecting to an FTP site requiring authentication

 You'll notice, by the way, that I can refer to my computer by its Rendezvous name, *iCloset.local*; take a gander at the System Preferences → Sharing pane to find out and set your Mac's Rendezvous name.

After a few moments, you'll be prompted for authentication—a username/ password pair. Enter them into the appropriate fields and click the OK button. Once again, the FTP site mounts on your Desktop as just another (albeit remote) drive (see Figure 6-35).

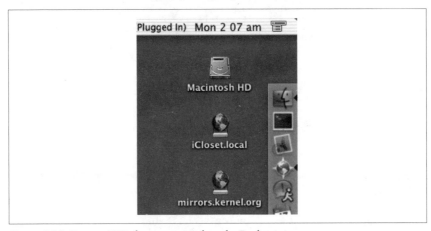

Figure 6-35. Remote FTP shares mounted on the Desktop

Depending on authorization set up on the FTP server, you may be able to upload files by dragging them from your Finder to the mounted share.

Disconnecting

To disconnect (unmount a share), do as you would any other removable media: drag the drive to the *Trash*, select File → Eject, or press ⌘-E.

Enabling Remote FTP Access

You can allow remote FTP access to your Mac by turning on the FTP Access service. Open the System Preferences → Sharing pane and select the Services panel. On the left is a list of services supported by OS X. If it's off, start FTP Access either by selecting it and clicking the Start button on the right or by clicking the associated checkbox. Your Services panel should look something like Figure 6-36.

Figure 6-36. Allowing FTP Access

If you intend to allow people to FTP in from the Internet, check with your system administrator or Internet service provider about addressing **[Hack #78]** and reaching your machine.

HACK #76   Exchanging a File via Bluetooth

Mac OS X 10.2's built-in support for Bluetooth wireless data means you have yet another way to exchange data with another Macintosh, PC, or mobile device.

If you're using WiFi (802.11b) wireless access, chances are you discovered it through Apple's fabulous AirPort base station and AirPort-enabled iBooks and TiBooks. The same is about to happen to an oft-dismissed technology called Bluetooth. Originally billed as a cable-replacement technology, Bluetooth is taking off as the standard for low-range, reasonable-speed, small-footprint connectivity between computers, PDAs **[Hack #32]**, cell phones **[Hack #31]**, modems **[Hack #77]**, cameras—any device with data to share.

Mac OS X 10.2 bakes Bluetooth (*http://www.apple.com/bluetooth/*) support right in, requiring only an inexpensive external USB dongle; in fact, by the time you read this, your iBook might just have Bluetooth onboard. Turn it on and you have yet another way to exchange your files with another Macintosh, PC, or other device.

The Bluetooth File Exchange application (*Application → Utilities → Bluetooth File Exchange*) is a drag-and-drop interface for sending and receiving files via Bluetooth.

Sending a File

To send a file to another machine using Bluetooth, simply drag and drop it onto the Bluetooth File Exchange icon, as shown in Figure 6-37.

The Send File dialog will appear (see Figure 6-38). Click the Search button to search for Bluetooth devices in the vicinity.

In my case, my Mac detected two Bluetooth devices: a Windows XP machine (MERCURY2) and an iPaq 3870 Pocket 2002 device (iPAQ PocketPC1). To send the file, select the destination device and click the Send button. It's just that simple!

Receiving Files

To receive files over Bluetooth, you need to ensure that Bluetooth File Exchange is running on your Mac. Double-click the application to start it.

Figure 6-37. Drop and send a file via Bluetooth File Exchange

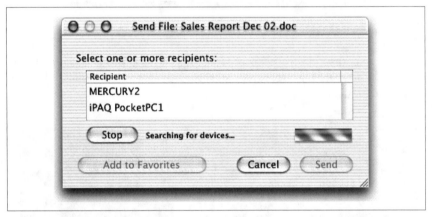

Figure 6-38. Finding Bluetooth devices in the vicinity.

Figure 6-39 shows a file being sent from my Pocket PC, prompting me for acceptance of the offer.

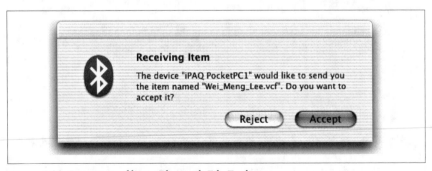

Figure 6-39. Receiving a file via Bluetooth File Exchange

Once the file's safely across, you'll be asked if you'd like to open it (see Figure 6-40). Click Open to do so. In this case, opening the proffered VCF contact file adds it automatically to my Address Book, where it belongs.

Figure 6-40. Opening a received file

You can, of course, do the reverse. Drag an address card from your Address Book to Bluetooth File Exchange and send it to a Bluetooth-enabled cell phone, as shown in Figure 6-41.

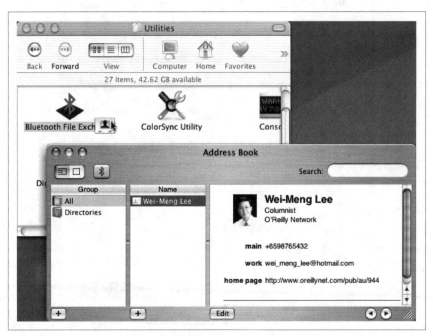

Figure 6-41. Sending an Address Book vCard to a Bluetooth-enabled cell phone

The odd part is that even if you've paired two devices in the recent past, Bluetooth File Exchange doesn't take this into account and still requires that you make the other device Bluetooth discoverable and scan the surroundings for it.

Ericsson Client for Phone

Jonas Salling Shareware's Ericsson Client (*http://homepage.mac.com/ jonassalling/Shareware/EricssonClient/*) ($10, shareware) is a cut above Bluetooth File Exchange for those of you with Sony/Ericsson Bluetooth-enabled cellphones like the T68i. Send files, images, text snippets, addresses, Palm Desktop or Entourage calendar events, themes, and ring tones to your phone simply by drag and drop, as shown in Figure 6-42.

Figure 6-42. Sending a text file to a Sony Ericsson phone

The application also supports grabbing a folder of vCards from the phone's contact manager or a vCal from the events manager or making a full backup to your Mac for restoring or transferring bulk information from one phone to another (via your Mac, that is).

—Wei-Meng Lee

Using Your Cell Phone as a Bluetooth Modem

Get online via your Bluetooth-enabled cellphone and AT&T's GPRS service with these comprehensive instructions.

With Bluetooth finally hailed as a strong buy, it's surprising how little detailed information there is on actually using your new Bluetooth-enabled phone with Mac OS X. When I went searching for instructions on setting up my Sony Ericsson T68i to allow my Mac to connect to the Internet via AT&T Wireless Services GPRS (a.k.a. mMode) service, I wasn't able to find anything comprehensive. I have been able to piece together instructions from other sites to form a working solution, though. This hack offers step-by-step instructions for getting online via Bluetooth and AT&T mMode.

This hack assumes you are running Mac OS X 10.2 (aka Jaguar) and have a Sony Ericsson T68i mobile phone and iSync via Bluetooth [Hack #32]. For the purposes at hand, make sure both Address Book and Internet Access are checked (as shown in Figure 6-43) and click OK.

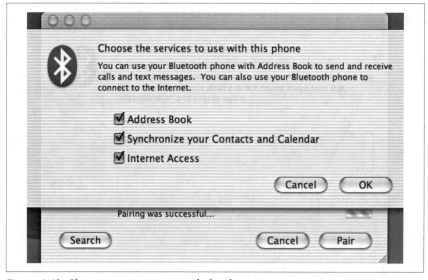

Figure 6-43. Choosing services to use with the phone

Now that your phone and Mac are able to talk to each other, we'll work on treating your phone as a Bluetooth modem. Click the Bluetooth menu bar icon and select Open Network Preferences, which will report New Port Detected. Click OK.

From the Location pop-up menu, select New Location..., name it Bluetooth, and click OK. From the Show pop up, select Network Port Configurations and uncheck all the boxes except for USB Bluetooth Modem Adapter, as shown in Figure 6-44.

Now we'll configure the Bluetooth adapter's network/modem properties. From the Show pop up, select USB Bluetooth Modem Adaptor. In the TCP/IP

Figure 6-44. Configuring the Bluetooth location

tab, select Using PPP from the Configure pop up. Leave the DNS Servers and Search Domains fields blank. Click the PPP tab. Type AT&T GPRS into the Service Provider field and proxy into Telephone Number, and leave the rest of the fields alone, as shown in Figure 6-45.

Click the Bluetooth Modem tab. From the Modem pop up, select Ericsson GPRS CID1, and click Apply Now. That's all for System Preferences; close it using ⌘-Q or System Preferences → Quit System Preferences.

Ready to connect? From the Bluetooth menu bar icon, select Open Internet Connect and click Connect. Your phone will display Connecting and after a few seconds, Internet Connect should show you as being connected to the Internet. To disconnect, click Disconnect.

See Also

- Ross Barkman's Mobile Phone Scripts (*http://www.taniwha.org.uk/*)
- GPRS, WAP Over Voicestream's iStream Service Using Bluetooth (*http://www.powerpage.org/story.lasso?newsID=9249*)

—Matthew Sparby

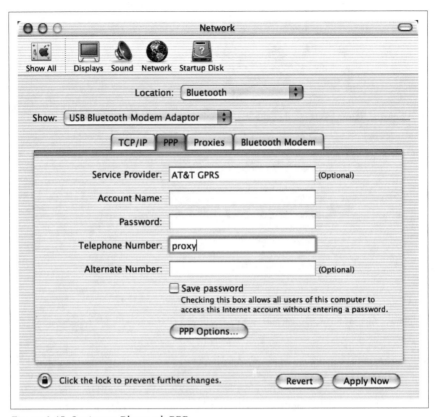

Figure 6-45. Setting up Bluetooth PPP

Setting Up Domain Name Service

#78   The most important step in bringing an Internet server online is making sure it can be found from the outside world.

Mac OS X, in addition to being a fabulous desktop machine, also has a full-fledged Unix server humming away beneath the hood. You can serve up web pages [Hack #88], send mail through your own sendmail [Hack #82] server, retrieve mail using IMAP or POP [Hack #82], and so much more.

Of course, bringing a server (particularly a web server) online isn't all that helpful unless you make sure it can be found and reached from the outside world.

Whether you are on a local intranet or on the Internet, an IP address is how people locate your computer. I'm not going to go into a lot of detail here, but when you register a domain name, you are required to point that domain to a name server, and that name server has an IP address.

The problem is that most DSL/cable companies give you a fat connection, but they don't include a static (nonchanging) IP address. They usually assign you a dynamic IP address that might change hourly, daily, or whatever. The problem is that you can't point to a domain name or locate your computer on the Internet if the IP address is always changing. It's like having your computer in the witness relocation program. Luckily, there is a solution.

Get a Static Address

Your first option is getting a static IP address from your DSL/cable provider. My DSL provider wants to charge me an additional $10 per month for that service, but I'm trying to cut down my costs, not increase them.

A Better Idea

Traffic on the Internet is simply routed from one IP address to another. No one can remember to type 102.0.43.23 when they want something like Yahoo!, so someone created a way of locating machines called Domain Name Service (DNS). When you type in *www.oreillynet.com*, DNS servers are able to resolve the proper IP address associated with it and take you to that location.

How Does This Help Me?

A number of organizations and companies provide what are called dynamic DNS services; for a fee, they will give you a DNS hostname. They do not redirect traffic to your IP address (which would involve traffic passing through their servers), but instead they point the computer requesting the domain name/DNS hostname of the correct IP location. Using a service like this ensures that whenever there is a request for your domain, it will always know where to point visitors.

If your dynamic address at home is always changing, how do they know what your current address is? Simple: you use a client application on your computer that pings your current local IP address, detects whether there has been a change, and updates the dynamic DNS service's database (see Figure 6-46). So, if my current IP changes from 215.23.0.34 to 64.23.123.3, the program takes that second number and sends the update to the dynamic DNS service. Easy as pie!

I use a service called DynDNS (*http://www.dyndns.org*). You can find a pretty good FAQ on this service at *http://support.dyndns.org/dyndns/faq.php*. If you use the service, you should support it by making a small contribution each year. The client I use is a carbonized freeware application called Mac

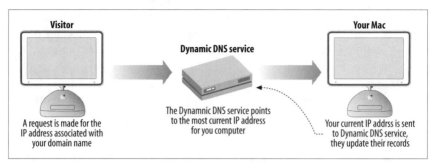

Figure 6-46. Dynamic DNS when you have a dynamic IP

Dynamic DNS, written by James Sentman. It has a number of features that allow for some pretty advanced scheduling and logging. It ain't pretty, but it does the job reliably. You can find the application on the DynDNS site.

Now, I want to point out that you don't have to register your own domain name to use this service. DynDNS has a number of existing domains that you can use. For example, you could create a domain name similar to *yourusername.homeunix.com*. This saves you the nominal cost of setting up a domain name and still gives you the ability to point people to your computer.

Go ahead and set up an account and make the donation. It may take up to 48 hours for confirmation from the donations department that your donation was received, so be patient.

Setting Up the Client

Go to the Network Preferences pane and make sure your network connection is set to DHCP so that your ISP will assign you an IP address properly.

A note about firewalls/routers: if your Internet connection travels though firewall software or a router, you may experience some trouble accessing your computer. Make sure it is set to accept inbound connections to port 80 (the default for HTTP requests). If you are using a DSL/cable router, make sure you've set up port forwarding properly (check your router's manual for instructions). Still having trouble? Check whether your ISP blocks inbound connections to port 80 (some have done this because of Internet worms). If this affects you, set up your HTTP server on a different port (for example, 8080).

Now, if you've made your donation and followed the DynDNS instructions to create your account, you need to add this account information to the Mac Dynamic DNS application. It has an easy-to-follow wizard that will walk you through creating the client account (see Figure 6-47). Set this as your master account, turn the account on, and click Check Now to update your IP address with the DynDNS service. When it has communicated with the service, it will show your current IP address in the window. Don't forget to set the application's preferences to update the address automatically!

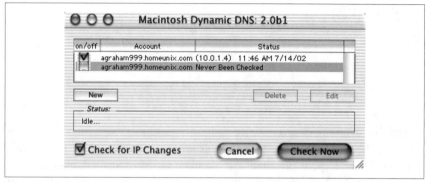

Figure 6-47. Macintosh Dynamic DNS regularly updates DynDNS.org

The *agraham999* account is on, displays my IP, and shows the last time it was checked. Hopefully, your IP address will look different. You can click Check Now to have it override the schedule.

Because I don't know how often my DSL provider updates my IP, I've set the Dynamic DNS application to check my connection every 15 minutes and notify *DynDNS.org* of any changes.

> Be sure that you set this application (and its background application) to launch at startup via the Login Preferences pane.

—Alan Graham

Email

Hacks 79–84

Just about everyone you know has an email address these days. But how many of them can truly customize their email environment? If you have a Mac, you're in luck. More than just a choice of excellent mail applications, OS X's powerful Unix underpinnings provide access to an array of the most popular and versatile mail servers and filtering systems on the planet.

Some of these, like the ubiquitous sendmail mail server, are built in and just need some configuration and switching-on. Others, like the UW IMAP server, are freely downloadable and ready to be built and installed.

This chapter takes you through setting up SMTP, POP, and IMAP servers, turning your Mac into a personal intranet mail server. We also teach you a little more about some of the mail applications you may be using and how to get the most out of them.

HACK #79   Taming the Entourage Database

Lurking beneath Entourage X's Aqua interface is a complex database handling all your mail and contact info. And, as with any other DB, you should back up and optimize on a regular schedule. Here's how to prevent email disaster on your Mac.

The first time I heard about an Entourage database crashing and leaving the poor user with neither mail nor contact info, I immediately dashed up to my hotel room and backed up my laptop. This wasn't going to happen to me.

The way I see it, we have two noteworthy alternatives for handling mail on Mac OS X. Choice number one is the Mail client that comes with the operating system. Apple's Mail is clean, stable, and pretty. It handles POP3 [Hack #81], IMAP [Hack #80], and secure mail transfer. The application is still evolving, getting stronger with each release of Mac OS X. But at the moment, it doesn't have all the bells and whistles some users want.

The other big name option is Entourage X (*http://www.microsoft.com/mac/ entouragex/default.asp?navindex=s4*), which is included with Microsoft's Office for Mac OS X. This version of Entourage is familiar to those who've used Office 2001 on Mac OS 9. Even though the look of the client has been updated to Aqua, it's still essentially the same concept under the hood, and that includes the database that drives the application.

Until recently, the maximum size for the Entourage database that manages all of your mail and contact info was 2GB. That should be more than enough room for all but the heaviest users, but if it isn't enough headroom for you, download Service Release 1 (*http://www.microsoft.com/mac/ DOWNLOAD/OFFICEX/OfficeX_SR1.asp*), which increases the database limit from 2GB to 4GB and also enhances Entourage's overall performance and stability. If you haven't updated your Office suite with Service Release 1, then I recommend you add it to your to-do list.

After installing the Service Release, choose About Entourage to double-check that you've upgraded (see Figure 7-1).

Figure 7-1. About Entourage

Beyond that, common sense says that you should take a few precautions with Entourage so that you don't end up living one of those horror stories you may have heard.

Back Up the Database

As with any other database, a regular backup schedule is essential. Your valuable information is located in your *Documents → Microsoft User Data → Office X Identities* folder. Inside the *Identities* folder you'll see a folder for each identity you've created in Entourage. Inside each of those folders, you'll see files for the actual database, database cache, signatures, rules, and mailing list.

I back up the entire *Identities* folder at least once a week and more often when possible. You can do this manually by dragging and dropping the folder onto a separate hard drive or CD-RW disk. Also, for about $50, you can buy Retrospect Backup Express (*http://www.dantz.com/index. php3?SCREEN=intro_mac_retrospect&sid=uMwlledDW2fgV5jB*) for Mac OS X. Dantz offers a free trial of this software, so you can try it out first to see if it's right for you. Either way, develop a regular backup procedure you can live with and will use regularly.

Thin Out and Delete

Chances are, you have lots of junk mail in your database that can be purged. When you highlight mail and press the Delete key or click on Entourage's trash can, you're simply moving the mail to the *Deleted Items* folder, not removing it from the database.

To really purge these messages, hold down the Control key and click on the *Deleted Items* folder. Select Empty Deleted Items from the pop-up window, and Entourage will remove this content from your database. This is not a speedy process, so save this task for when you have a few minutes to go get a cup of coffee.

If you ever have to restore your database from a backup copy, simply quit Entourage, replace the corrupted database in the *Identities* folder with the clean copy from your backup, then relaunch the application. If your restored information doesn't appear, try Switch Identities to jump-start the restored database.

Rebuild the Database

Once you've backed up and thinned out Entourage, you can optimize performance and regain some hard-disk space by rebuilding the database. It's quite easy.

First, check the current size of your database by using the Show Info command (⌘-I) on the *Office X Identities* folder. In my case, this folder was occupying 261MB of hard disk space. Then make sure you have enough hard disk space available for twice that amount. As part of the rebuilding process, Entourage creates a second database file. This means that I need 522MB to rebuild.

Then quit all Office applications (including Entourage). Now hold down the Option key and relaunch the application. In a few seconds you'll be greeted with a dialog box asking if you want the Typical Rebuild or the Advanced Rebuild (see Figure 7-2). Choose Typical. The Advanced Rebuild is only for emergencies and should not be used for maintenance.

Entourage will then compact your database and optimize it (see Figure 7-3). This normally takes less than 10 minutes for 300MB or less (your mileage may vary depending on your hardware).

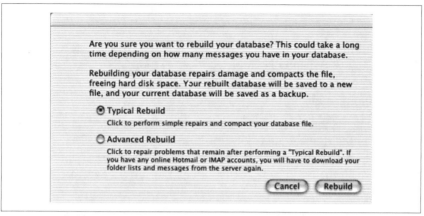

Figure 7-2. Rebuilding the Entourage database

Figure 7-3. Optimization notification

After optimization, run the application for a few minutes and check that everything is OK. If so, go back to your *Identities* folder and delete the Old Database and Old Database Cache files (see Figure 7-4), because you no longer need them.

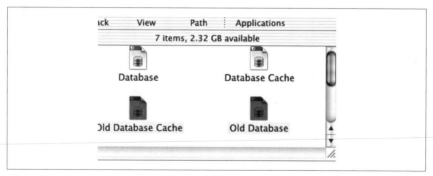

Figure 7-4. Deleting old versions of the database

If you use multiple identities, you'll need to rebuild those databases separately. Entourage will rebuild only the database for the identity that was last open. To rebuild a second database, switch to that identity, close the application, then hold down the Option key when you restart.

So how did things turn out? My database size was 261MB before optimization and only 180MB after I completed the operation.

Final Thoughts

By following the three steps of backing up, thinning out, and rebuilding, you should avoid all but the unluckiest of Entourage disasters. I have heard of one case in which the database corruption didn't manifest right away and was present in the backup copies as well as the current database. This was unfortunate, because the user lost all mail and contact information.

But I've uncovered only one such devastating incident. Chances are, if you follow the guidelines in this hack, you should be in good shape.

—Derrick Story

HACK #80   Using IMAP with Apple's Mail Application

Set up and use an IMAP-enabled mail account through Mac OS X's Mail application.

Most modern email clients, including Mac OS X applications such as Apple's own Mail, Qualcomm's Eudora, or Microsoft's Entourage, default to using the same mail transfer protocol: the venerable Post Office Protocol, more commonly known as POP. POP defines a simple set of instructions that lets users connect to a mail server account, download new mail, and then disconnect. Nearly every ISP's mail server supports POP, so it's a safe choice for mail-fetching client applications to support as well.

More recently, an alternative protocol known as the Internet Message Access Protocol (IMAP) has been steadily gaining popularity and support from Internet providers. IMAP contains a more sophisticated command set that allows users to store and organize mail on the server, instead of simply downloading and deleting it.

IMAP gives the most benefit to people who connect to a mail server using more than one computer, since an IMAP-enabled mail account will look the same on all these machines, from overall mailbox structure down to the status of individual messages, and any changes made to a mailbox on one machine become visible to the rest.

This hack will guide you through setting up and using an IMAP-enabled mail account through Mac OS X's Mail application, covering IMAP-specific concepts and terminology as they come up.

Checking for IMAP Service

Of course, before you can start having fun with IMAP, your mail server must support it! You can find out simply by asking your ISP or network administrator, or you could poke your mail server machine directly to find out, by launching the Terminal [Hack #48] application and trying this:

```
% telnet mail.server.net 143
```

Replace *mail.server.net* with the hostname of your mail server. If you've installed a local IMAP server (you've just arrived from "Setting Up IMAP and POP Mail Servers" [Hack #81]), use localhost. The 143 is the standard port number (think television channel) on which the IMAP server listens.

If you have an IMAP service at your disposal, you'll receive a response a little something like this:

```
Trying 127.0.0.1...
Connected to localhost.
Escape character is
'^]'.
* OK [CAPABILITY IMAP4REV1 LOGIN-REFERRALS AUTH=LOGIN] localhost IMAP4rev1
2001.315 at Mon, 29 Jul 2002 15:31:46 -0700 (PDT)
```

If so, you're good to go. If you instead receive a blunt "Connection refused" or something altogether different, check in with your service operator.

To end the IMAP session you just started, type foo LOGOUT and press Return.

Creating an IMAP Mail Account

Launch Mail (*Applications* → *Mail* from the Finder). To create a new account, you'll visit Mail's Preferences dialog, Mail → Preferences..., and select the Accounts tab. Click the Create Account button. Select IMAP Account from the Account Type menu on the resulting sheet (see Figure 7-5), and fill in the text fields with information appropriate to this account, just as you would for a POP account.

Specifying Account Options

Visit the Advanced tab to see Mail's IMAP-specific options, shown in Figure 7-6. (The controls that appear under this tab depend upon the type of account you've selected under the Account Information tab.) Mail will fill the "Connect to server using port:" text field with 143, the usual TCP port of a mail server's IMAP service. Change this value only if you know that your host runs its IMAP service on a different port. Activate the Use SSL checkbox if your host supports secure IMAP (a.k.a. IMAPS) and you wish to take advantage of it.

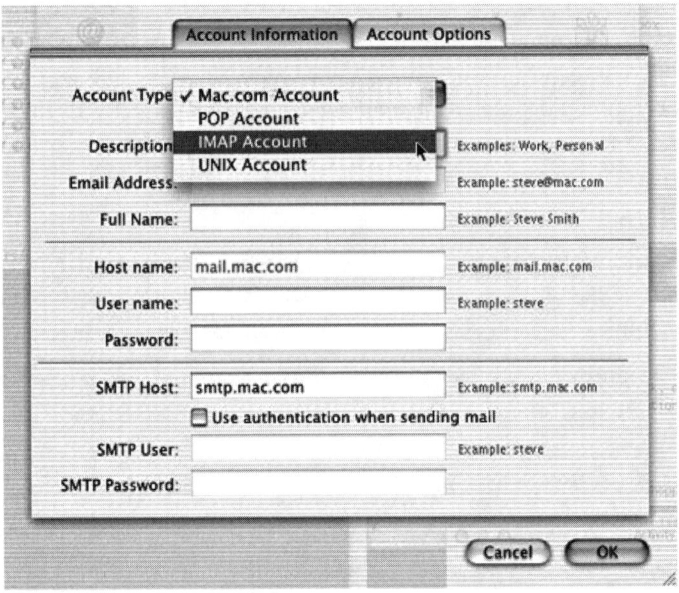

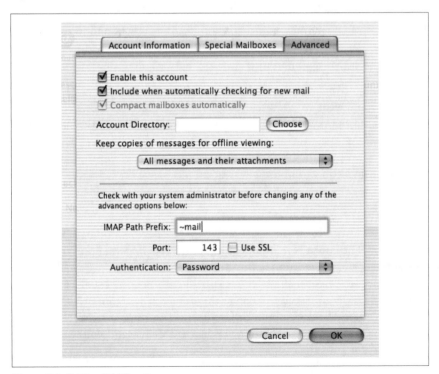

Figure 7-5. Creating a new IMAP account

Figure 7-6. Setting IMAP options

Check the "Compact mailboxes when closing" checkbox if you want Mail to purge your mailboxes of deleted messages when you quit the application; if left unchecked, deleted emails will remain within mailboxes, invisible to Mail but still accessible by other means.

Account directory. The Account Directory text field lets you specify the location of this account's cache folder on your local filesystem. Unless you have good reason to do otherwise, leave this field blank; Mail will use its default location of *~/Library/Mail/IMAP/account-name*, which should work just fine.

You'll notice that once you've started to use the account, this field becomes grayed out and uneditable, so choose wisely and type carefully.

IMAP path prefix. The Account Path Prefix text field specifies the path that Mail will prepend to all mailbox names when it's trying to locate them on the mail server. If you keep all your mailboxes in a directory called *mail* within your home directory, then you should put ~/mail here.

On the other hand, if you never log into your mail server machine directly, or are otherwise not sure what to put here, then you're probably safe putting nothing here at all and letting the server figure it out for you.

Message caching. To help keep things efficient, Mail keeps local caches of your IMAP accounts' content, even though the real messages reside on the server. By default, an account's cache lives in *~/Library/Mail/IMAP*, unless you specified a different location when you created the account. Every account gets its own folder there, named *IMAP/account name*.

Through the Message Caching pull-down menu, you can specify how much of your incoming email Mail should cache and when it should cache it:

Cache all messages and attachments locally
> This will direct Mail to download the entirety of every new message upon connection. This will allow you to read these messages and their attachments when you're offline, much as you can do through a POP account.
>
> This is the default selection for a new Mail IMAP account.

Cache messages' bodies locally
> When selected, Mail will cache all new messages' text bodies, as well as a list of any attachments for each, but not the attachments themselves (unless they're relatively small). If you specifically request to see a message's attachment (by clicking on the attachment's icon in the message view window), Mail will fetch a fresh copy from the server for you.

This is a good choice if you like the convenience of having all your textual email stored locally (which allows nice features like indexing and searching) but would like to avoid downloading large attachments you may not always want.

Cache messages when read

This directs Mail to hold off on any message caching when fetching new mail. It will display new mail in the message list as usual but doesn't actually fetch a message's content until you select one for reading. Once it loads a message, Mail places the body into the cache. Subsequent visits to this message will read from the cached copy (unless the server's version of the message changes).

Like the previous menu choice, this does not cache large attachments.

Don't cache any messages

Mail forgets about caching entirely. Every time you access a message, Mail will fetch its contents from the server anew, regardless of whether you've read it before.

While you'd think this a good idea if running a local IMAP server—after all, why have two local copies of every message—in fact, if you want to take advantage of Mail's searchability and indexing, you'll need caching on.

Mac.com Accounts

As testimony to the magical properties of IMAP, the Mac.com (*http://www. mac.com*) accounts that Apple provides to its customers as part of its .Mac package use IMAP as its protocol. This lets you consistently access and organize your Mac.com mail from any machine with an IMAP client—Macintosh or otherwise.

Setting up a Mac.com-flavored IMAP account is easy; just select Mac.com Account from Mail's Account Type pull-down menu, instead of IMAP Account. It's really just a shortcut that cues Mail to fill in the account configuration text fields to point to Apple's mail servers.

Organizing Mailboxes

In the mailbox list underneath an IMAP account's header, you'll find a list containing an inbox, any mailboxes you create, and any mailboxes Mail creates in order to support some of its own special features.

Inbox. An IMAP server abstracts all a user's new and otherwise unsorted mail into a single mailbox called Inbox, so you'll always have at least this mailbox available to you.

Creating and editing IMAP mailboxes. Mail's commands for creating and organizing mailboxes and folders, found under the Mailbox menu, remain consistent across all its account types, IMAP included. When you create, rename, and delete mailboxes through the commands in this menu or move mailboxes around by dragging their icons in the mailbox list drawer, Mail echoes these actions on your IMAP account's structure. Thus, all the changes you make in one session with Mail will carry across to any future connections you make to this IMAP account with any mail client.

Special mailboxes. While Mail takes full advantage of IMAP's ability to let you create and organize mailboxes any way you like, the application also has the ability to map its own functionality onto some special server-side mailboxes, if you let it. In all of the following cases, Mail will create these mailboxes on the server as necessary:

Drafts

By default, messages that you save as a draft (File → Save As Draft, ⌘-S, or the message window's Save As Draft toolbar button) stay in Mail's special Outbox mailbox, stored only on your Mac. If you wish, you can instead store unfinished messages on an IMAP mailbox, so they'll be available to choose and complete from other machines.

To do so, visit the Composing tab of Mail's Preferences panel (Mail → Preferences) and select one of your IMAP mailboxes from the "Save unsent mail in" pull-down menu.

Sent Messages

It's worth noting that Mail does not keep its Sent Messages mailbox on the IMAP server; it's only on your Mac. Mail stores copies of all the mail you send through all your accounts, IMAP and otherwise, here.

If you want to keep server-side copies of sent mail, choose an IMAP mailbox from the "Save sent mail in" pull-down menu found under the Preference panel's Composing tab.

Trash

If you have the "Move deleted mail to a folder named" checkbox set under the Viewing tab of the Preferences panel, Mail will create a folder on the server to serve as a trash can, where deleted mail will move itself.

You don't need to have a special folder for maintaining deleted messages, since IMAP lets you store deleted mail in any mailbox. However, Mail doesn't let you see any deleted messages except for ones in this special mailbox, and only if you have this checkbox activated.

Organizing Messages

An email message sitting in an IMAP mailbox can have some number of message flags set on it, recording the actions performed on this message, such as the user's reading, replying to, or deleting it. When you reply to a message on your office PC, for example, and then later connect to your mailbox at home, that message will remember the fact you already replied to it, and be able to report this to you.

Mail works with most flags in a fairly straightforward fashion, but it gets a little squirrelly when it comes to IMAP's Deleted flag.

There's nothing particularly magical about how message flags work; they exist simply as headers the IMAP server adds to the messages on its end as their status changes.

Message Flags

Mail displays IMAP flags through symbols in the Flag and Status columns of a mailbox's message list (see Figure 7-7).

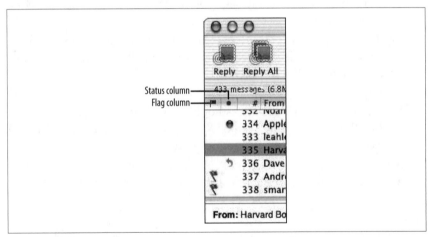

Figure 7-7. Message flags

Recent. A message gets a Recent flag if the current IMAP connection is the first to have seen it. Mail places a blue dot in this message's Status column, marking it as a new, unread message. Mail unsets this flag once the user reads a message.

Seen. A message with a Seen flag has been read.

Mail reacts to the absence of this flag; a message lacking a Seen flag (which all Recent messages do, by definition) gets a blue dot. Mail does not distinguish between unread mail that arrived since the current session started (and has a Recent flag) and unread mail carried over from a previous IMAP session (and therefore has no message flags).

Selecting Message → Mark As Unread (Option-⌘-M) removes this flag from selected messages, and Message → Mark As Read (Option-⌘-M) sets it. (One of these two commands appears in the Message menu, depending upon the status of the selected messages.)

Answered. Replying to an IMAP message prompts Mail to set its Answered flag. Mail displays such messages with a little U-turn arrow in its status column, unless the message lacks a Seen flag.

Flagged. The Flagged flag can mean whatever you want. Generally, it's meant to signal that a message requires urgent attention.

In Mail, you can toggle this flag for the selected messages through Message → Mark As (Un)Flagged (Option-⌘-G). Flagged messages receive little flag icons in the message list's flag column.

Draft. Mail sets a message's Draft flag if it's an unfinished, unsent message you're storing in an IMAP mailbox (see "Drafts" item in the previous "Special mailboxes" section).

Deleted. Mail gives messages Delete flags when you delete them (pressing the Delete key on your keyboard, selecting Message → Delete, or dragging them into your Dock's Trash icon). This seems fairly straightforward, and it does more or less what you want, but this flag's actual implications are convoluted enough that it's worth spending a little time on the subject.

Deleting Messages

IMAP uses a two-step process for deleting messages. Any message can set a Deleted flag on itself, which marks it as susceptible to actual deletion but doesn't actually get rid of it or even move it out of its original mailbox. A separate IMAP command purges a mailbox of all the deleted messages it contains.

Different mail clients have different ways of representing deleted (but not yet erased) messages to the user. Mail chooses to simply not show deleted mail at all, unless it's inside the designated Trash mailbox.

Mail's IMAP response to deleting mail changes depending upon how you've set the "Move deleted mail to a folder named" checkbox. If you've checked it, then deleting a piece of mail will cause Mail to move it to your chosen Trash mailbox, rather than setting its Delete flag.

If, instead, you've left that checkbox unchecked, Mail will set the message's Deleted flags but otherwise leave them be. Since Mail refuses to display deleted mail in mailboxes other than the Trash mailbox, this action will also make the message vanish from sight, even though it continues to exist on the server (and perhaps remain visible to other mail clients).

That same checkbox also dictates Mail's behavior with actually erasing Deleted messages. If checked, Mail gives you a Mailbox → Empty Trash Mailbox (⌘-K) command. This will have Mail send the IMAP EXPUNGE command to its Trash mailbox, and since it contains only messages with the Deleted flags set, they'll all go away (unless you've been weird and snuck other mail in there through sneaky means; those would stick around). Deleted messages in other mailboxes, however, simply remain present and invisible to you, at least as long as you use Mail as your client.

If you leave this box unchecked, then Mail instead offers the Mailbox → Compact Mailbox (⌘-K) command. This will simply expunge the selected mailbox, permanently erasing all its unseen deleted messages and seeming to shrink the mailbox's size without affecting any of its visible messages. (Compact, in this case, is Mail's positive way of spinning the fact that it doesn't have a way to deal with deleted mail in arbitrary IMAP mailboxes, and so they appear as so much deadweight.)

Note that both these commands share the ⌘-K keybinding, so pressing this combo will always erase deleted mail, one way or another.

—Jason McIntosh

HACK #81   Setting Up IMAP and POP Mail Servers

There's tremendous value in having all your email with you at all times. Unfortunately, this usually means being tied to a particular mail client. IMAP allows you to have this particular cake and eat it too. This hack focuses on IMAP but installs POP along the way, since it's just so simple to do.

Switching email clients can mean a pile of work and a plethora of less-than-great import/export/conversion functions and scripts. Wouldn't it be great to switch seamlessly between Entourage's gorgeous GUI, Mail's simplicity, Eudora's feature set, and the powerful, text-based Pine Unix mail app?

IMAP allows you to have this particular cake and eat it too.

IMAP (Internet Message Access Protocol) is usually considered a POP (Post Office Protocol) mail replacement. POP accumulates all of your incoming mail on your service provider's or enterprise's mail server, to be downloaded on a regular basis to your desktop or laptop and from there on saved and manipulated—filed in folders and such—locally. IMAP stores and manipulates all of your mail on the server, your mail client being fed the headers (To, From, Subject, etc.) and retrieving each message from the server on demand. Since everything's done on the server, you can switch mail applications on a whim, according to the functionality needed or just when the mood strikes.

But what if you're offline? Aye, there's the rub. Most mail applications can be set to keep a cache of messages locally for offline use, syncing with the server on occasion. This is hardly an efficient way to do things, messages being duplicated and needing ongoing synchronization between server and desktop—not to mention the fact that you don't have offline access to messages that just don't happen to be cached locally on your desktop.

What if you moved the IMAP server to your desktop or laptop? You'd have all of your mail right where you need it, yet not suffer the tax of being tied to a particular mail application.

Unfortunately, IMAP software doesn't ship by default on Mac OS X. Fortunately, it's easy to get, compile, and set up. We're going to use the University of Washington's IMAP server, but we'll need the Mac OS X Developer Tools [Hack #55] with optional BSD Software Developer's Kit (SDK) installed before proceeding.

Download and Build the IMAP Server

Downloading and building the IMAP server is a relatively straightforward process when you know exactly what to type. All you need to do is follow this script, typing the commands into the Terminal [Hack #48], and you will have a built and functional SSL-enabled IMAP server ready to be set up. As you type most of these commands, output on what is happening will scroll by, but as long as you don't make a mistake, everything should be fine:

```
% curl ftp://ftp.cac.washington.edu/imap/imap.tar.Z > imap.tar.Z
% uncompress imap.tar.Z
% tar xf imap.tar
% cd imap-2002.RC2/
% make osx SSLTYPE=nopwd SSLDIR=/usr SSLCERTS=/etc/sslcerts
% sudo mkdir -p /usr/local/bin
% sudo cp imapd/imapd /usr/local/bin/imapd
% sudo cp ipopd/ipop3d /usr/local/bin/ipop3d
```

There. That wasn't so bad, was it? You now have fully functional IMAP and POP servers just waiting to be used.

Configure the Servers

We need to do two things to configure the servers. The first is to set up SSL certificates that will be used by each server. The second is to enable the servers to handle requests.

To install a self-signed certificate (perfectly adequate for our needs), use the following commands. You will be asked a few questions as part of the process of making this certificate. The answers I used are highlighted in bold; yours will be different.

```
% sudo mkdir -p /etc/sslcerts
% sudo openssl req -new -x509 -nodes -out /etc/sslcerts/imapd.pem  -keyout ⏎
/etc/sslcerts/imapd.pem -days 3650
Using configuration from /System/Library/OpenSSL/openssl.cnf
Generating a 1024 bit RSA private key
.....................................................++++++
..........................++++++
writing new private key to '/etc/sslcerts/imapd.pem'
-----
You are about to be asked to enter information that will be incorporated
into your certificate request.
What you are about to enter is what is called a Distinguished Name or a DN.
There are quite a few fields but you can leave some blank
For some fields there will be a default value,
If you enter '.', the field will be left blank.
-----
Country Name (2 letter code) [AU]: US
State or Province Name (full name) [Some-State]: California
Locality Name (eg, city) []: San Francisco
Organization Name (eg, company) [Internet Widgits Pty Ltd]: x180
Organizational Unit Name (eg, section) []: Home Mail
Common Name (eg, YOUR name) []: James Duncan Davidson
Email Address []: duncan@x180.net
```

Now do the same for the POP server using the same values for the fields; only the command-line invocation changes:

```
% sudo openssl req -new -x509 -nodes -out /etc/sslcerts/ipop3d.pem -keyout ⏎
/etc/sslcerts/ipop3d.pem -days 3650
...
```

The last thing we need to do is configure Mac OS X to start up the IMAP server when it sees requests to the IMAP over SSL (port 993) and the POP server for POP SSL requests (port 995). This functionality is handed by inetd, the Internet daemon; it patiently listens for requests for particular services, farming them out to the appropriate applications for handling. Telling inetd about our new IMAP server is accomplished by editing [Hack #51] its configuration file, /etc/inetd.conf:

```
% sudo pico /etc/inetd.conf
```

Add the following lines to the very end of the file. If you want to enable one without the other, simply leave out the appropriate line (the first for IMAP, the second for POP):

```
imaps stream tcp nowait root /usr/libexec/tcpd /usr/local/bin/imapd
pop3s stream tcp nowait root /usr/libexec/tcpd /usr/local/bin/ipop3d
```

All that's left is to restart the inetd deamon, forcing it to reread its configuration file. The first command in the following code block finds out the process ID of the running daemon; the second sends a restart message to that process. Your inetd process ID will be different.

```
% ps -ax | grep inetd
323 ?? Ss 0:00.01 inetd
4798 std R+ 0:00.00 grep inetd
% sudo kill -HUP 323
```

Congratulations. You're done. Now it's time to set up your mail client to use it. This book provides information on using IMAP with Mail [Hack #80], but the settings should be similar across clients. Just be sure to turn on SSL security for your IMAP or POP account as we've set up your servers to use SSL.

—James Duncan Davidson

HACK #82 Getting sendmail Up and Running

sendmail is powerful, but at times it appears complicated too. Unravel the sendmail knot and you can configure this awesome mail server on your Mac OS X system.

sendmail is complicated software, no doubt about it. But sendmail is also the Swiss Army Knife of mail servers, and I don't mean one of those little keychain trinkets. Instead, it's the monster three-inch-wide kind with all the tools, most of which you have never seen before and have no idea what they do. However, with a little time and patience, you too can become proficient enough with sendmail to make it accomplish everything you need.

Here's what I'll cover in this hack:

- Dealing with Jaguar's permissions and sendmail's security precautions
- Working with configuration files
- The LUSER_RELAY
- How to set up aliases
- How to allow relaying from certain hosts
- Running behind a firewall
- Working with lame ISPs

Be warned, this is not a beginner's article. If you're uncomfortable performing shell commands as root on your system with sudo [Hack #50] and editing special Unix files [Hack #51], you may want to acquaint yourself with these first. However, if you do have a bit of shell experience, and I haven't scared you off by mentioning the word pico, then this should be just the quick reference you need to get your own mail server running under OS X.

Hacking the hostconfig File

First, we'll need to edit the `MAILSERVER` line in */etc/hostconfig* so that sendmail starts automatically:

```
% sudo pico /etc/hostconfig
```

The file will load. Use the arrow keys to navigate the file and edit the `MAILSERVER` line to look like this:

```
MAILSERVER=-YES-
```

If we lived in a perfect world, our next step would be to start sendmail. However, sendmail is a somewhat tricky beast to work with.

On Permissions and Blame

The number one trick to setting up sendmail on Mac OS X is dealing with the way that Apple has configured the permissions on the various directories of the filesystem. You see, in its quest to make Unix more Mac-like, Apple decided that it would be best to allow users, at least administrative users, to be able to move files in and out of the root directory with impunity. Apparently Apple doesn't want users to see a "You can't drag that file here!" dialog box.

This clashes heavily with sendmail's built-in paranoia. You see, sendmail really wants any directory that it is involved with to be modifiable only by the root user. This includes the / and */Users* directories. It will complain bitterly and refuse to start up with a statement that looks something like this:

```
/etc/mail/sendmail.cf: line 93: fileclass: cannot open '/etc/mail/local-
host-names': Group writable directory
```

There are two primary solutions to this problem:

- Change the ownership of the / and */Users* directories to something that sendmail prefers (`chmod g-w / /Users`).
- Configure sendmail to ignore its instincts and operate even though the permissions on some folders aren't exactly as it likes.

The first of these solutions is a bit more extreme, but it is the safest way to set up your server. It is the correct solution for the paranoid system administrator who wants to make sure that nobody, not even any of her users, can compromise the system. It does have the side effect that nobody, not even the administrator, will be able to use the Finder to copy files into the / and */Users* directories.

On the other hand, as long as you trust every person you give a user account to (or at least every user that you allow to administer your machine), there is a better way to go about this. This is to use the `DontBlameSendmail` configuration parameter with sendmail. Think of it as administering a small amount of medication to sendmail to reassure it that not everything in the world is a risk. For most people running Mac OS X (who aren't admins of systems serving hundreds or thousands of potential users and don't have untrusted or unknown users on the machine), this is the appropriate strategy to use.

In order to implement this solution, we're going to have to dig into how to work with sendmail's configuration files.

Working with Configuration Files

As soon as you decide to work with sendmail's configuration files, you'll find out that there is a lot of confusing stuff in there.

Take a look at the */etc/mail/sendmail.cf* file. The first thing you see is a header that says:

```
##### DO NOT EDIT THIS FILE! Only edit the source .mc file.
```

Scroll down a bit further and you'll see some stuff that could look friendly only to an old-time Perl hacker:

```
# hostnames ending in class P are always canonical
R$* < @ $* $=P > $* $: $1 < @ $2 $3 . > $4
R$* < @ $* $~P > $* $: $&{daemon_flags} $| $1 < @ $2 $3 > $4
R$* CC $* $| $* < @ $+.$+ < $* $: $3 < @ $4.$5 . > $6
R$* CC $* $| $* $: $3
# pass to name server to make hostname canonical
R$* $| $* < @ $* > $* $: $2 < @ $[ $3 $] > $4
R$* $| $* $: $2
```

So, if you're not supposed to edit this file, and really wouldn't want to even if you should, what are you supposed to do? The answer is to ignore it. Treat it like a binary file. You don't muck about in the */bin/sh* executable to use it do you? Take the same approach to */etc/mail/sendmail.cf*.

Instead, we're going to see how to edit the source code for this file. Take a look at the */usr/share/sendmail/conf/cf/generic-darwin.mc* file. The body of it looks like this:

```
VERSIONID(`$Id: generic-darwin.mc,v 1.3 2002/04/12 18:41:47 bbraun Exp $')
OSTYPE(darwin)dnl
DOMAIN(generic)dnl
undefine(`ALIAS_FILE')
define(`PROCMAIL_MAILER_PATH',`/usr/bin/procmail')
FEATURE(`smrsh',`/usr/libexec/smrsh')
FEATURE(local_procmail)
FEATURE(`virtusertable',`hash -o /etc/mail/virtusertable')dnl
FEATURE(`genericstable', `hash -o /etc/mail/genericstable')dnl
FEATURE(`mailertable',`hash -o /etc/mail/mailertable')dnl
FEATURE(`access_db')dnl
MAILER(smtp)
MAILER(procmail)
```

This is much more approachable than *sendmail.cf* ever could be. This is actually a script written in the m4 macro language. m4 has been around for a while and Mac OS X ships with GNU m4 Version 1.4. Luckily, it is simple enough to use without having to learn much about it. If you are interested in learning more, see the GNU m4 project page (*http://www.gnu.org/software/m4/m4.html*).

So, this is the source code we'll use to configure sendmail. Let's make a copy of it and put it where we will remember where it is:

```
% sudo cp /usr/share/sendmail/conf/cf/generic-darwin.mc /etc/mail/config.mc
```

We now have a copy of the source code for the sendmail.cf file in a place where we can edit it and keep track of its location. However, even if you have a copy of the source code, you still have to know how to compile the file. In our case, the set of commands to compile the *config.mc* file to *sendmail.cf* are:

```
% m4 /usr/share/sendmail/conf/m4/cf.m4 /etc/mail/config.mc ⏎
> /tmp/sendmail.cf
% mv /etc/mail/sendmail.cf /etc/mail/sendmail.cf.old
% mv /tmp/sendmail.cf /etc/mail/sendmail.cf
```

Yikes! That's too much to remember. It goes against my philosophy of keeping things as simple as possible (without being too simple, that is!). Luckily, I've written a little script that should help this part of working with sendmail's configuration files.

A Script to Simplify Your Life

The following script will compile *config.mc* into *sendmail.cf* and restart sendmail so that it will notice the configuration changes. You can put it anywhere you want; I happen to have placed my copy in the */etc/mail* folder so that I can find it easily. Fire up your editor of choice and type this in. Then, if you want to mirror what I've done, save it to */etc/mail/update*. Otherwise, you may want to save it as */usr/local/bin/sendmail-update* or some other fairly easy-to-remember location.

```
#! /bin/sh
if [ /etc/mail/config.mc -nt /etc/mail/sendmail.cf ]
then
echo Regenerating sendmail.cf
m4 /usr/share/sendmail/conf/m4/cf.m4 /etc/mail/config.mc > \
/tmp/sendmail.cf
mv /etc/mail/sendmail.cf /etc/mail/sendmail.cf.old
mv /tmp/sendmail.cf /etc/mail/sendmail.cf
/System/Library/StartupItems/Sendmail/Sendmail restart
fi
```

We're going to add a bit more to this script later. But for now, we're ready to feed sendmail that antiparanoia medicine.

Back to DontBlameSendmail

In order to use the DontBlameSendmail configuration parameter with send-mail, all we need to do is add one line to the *config.mc* file.

Edit it to match the following code. The line you need to add is boldfaced.

```
% sudo emacs /etc/mail/config.mc

VERSIONID(`$Id: generic-darwin.mc,v 1.3 2002/04/12 18:41:47 bbraun Exp $')
OSTYPE(darwin)dnl
DOMAIN(generic)dnl
undefine(`ALIAS_FILE')
define(`PROCMAIL_MAILER_PATH',`/usr/bin/procmail')
define(`confDONT_BLAME_SENDMAIL', `GroupWritableDirPathSafe')
FEATURE(`smrsh',`/usr/libexec/smrsh')
FEATURE(local_procmail)
FEATURE(`virtusertable',`hash -o /etc/mail/virtusertable')dnl
FEATURE(`genericstable', `hash -o /etc/mail/genericstable')dnl
FEATURE(`mailertable',`hash -o /etc/mail/mailertable')dnl
FEATURE(`access_db')dnl
MAILER(smtp)
MAILER(procmail)
```

Be careful to note that the quoting uses both the backtick (`` ` ``) and single quote (') characters around the arguments to the define statement. Save the file. Next, we need to compile it. Execute your update script. You may need to remember to give it execute permissions (chmod g+x /etc/mail/update) first!

```
% sudo /etc/mail/update

Regenerating sendmail.cf
Restarting mail services
```

After sendmail restarts, you can verify that it is running properly by trying the following in a Terminal window:

```
% telnet localhost 25
Trying 127.0.0.1...
Connected to dsl092-007-021.sfo1.dsl.speakeasy.net.
Escape character is '^]'.
220 dsl092-007-021.sfo1.dsl.speakeasy.net ESMTP Sendmail 8.12.2/8.12.2; Sat,
10 Aug 2002 00:43:35 -0700 (PDT)
QUIT
221 2.0.0 dsl092-007-021.sfo1.dsl.speakeasy.net closing connection
Connection closed by foreign host.
```

Simply type QUIT to end the interactive session. sendmail is now up and running. It will accept mail addressed to any user at the local host. For example, on my server, sendmail will accept any mail addressed to *duncan@dsl092-007-021.sfo1.dsl.speakeasy.net* (my ISP's address), but not *duncan@somehost.dyndns.org* (my personal web site I want to accept mail from). This is a good start and shows that the mail server isn't an open relay that will possibly spread spam, but we need to do a little more configuration to allow us to accept mail to our desired hostname.

Telling sendmail Which Hostnames Are Valid

To have sendmail accept mail sent to your machine's hostname, all you need to do is edit the */etc/mail/local-host-names* file. To do so, enter the following command:

```
% sudo pico /etc/mail/local-host-names
```

Simply add the hostnames that you want to receive mail for, one line at a time, to this file. For example:

```
somemachine.dyndns.org
66.92.7.21
```

For this to take effect, you'll need to restart sendmail. Instead of rebooting, we're simply going to stop and restart sendmail. Use the following command to do so:

```
% /System/Library/StartupItems/Sendmail/Sendmail restart
```

Setting Up the LUSER_RELAY

The next setting we are going to look at is the LUSER_RELAY. No, this doesn't mean a way to deal with those 14-year-old kids who hold their hands up to their foreheads saying "loooooos-errrr," but instead is a way of handling email that comes to your server that is not addressed to any user. The LUSER_RELAY setting will direct any piece of mail to your server without a user to a particular user's account.

This is particularly handy when you want to be able to hand out lots of different addresses, such as *im-a-geek@myhost.com* and *spam-target@myhost.com*, without having to set up anything on your server. I personally use this feature all the time when giving my email address out to stores that I'm interested in getting email from but fear that they will sell the address off or pummel me with too much information later.

So, to set this up, simply edit the *config.mc file* as follows (the bold line is where you will replace *duncan* with the name of the local user you want to get the mail!):

```
% sudo pico /etc/mail/config.mc

VERSIONID(`$Id: generic-darwin.mc,v 1.3 2002/04/12 18:41:47 bbraun Exp $')
OSTYPE(darwin)dnl
```

```
DOMAIN(generic)dnl
undefine(`ALIAS_FILE')
define(`PROCMAIL_MAILER_PATH',`/usr/bin/procmail')
define(`confDONT_BLAME_SENDMAIL', `GroupWritableDirPathSafe')
define(`LUSER_RELAY', `local:duncan')
FEATURE(`smrsh',`/usr/libexec/smrsh')
FEATURE(local_procmail)
FEATURE(`virtusertable',`hash -o /etc/mail/virtusertable')dnl
FEATURE(`genericstable', `hash -o /etc/mail/genericstable')dnl
FEATURE(`mailertable',`hash -o /etc/mail/mailertable')dnl
FEATURE(`access_db')dnl
MAILER(smtp)
MAILER(procmail)
```

Now, just run the update script:

```
% sudo /etc/mail/update
Regenerating sendmail.cf
Restarting mail services
```

Try things out. Use your mail client to send mail to all sorts of addresses that don't exist on your machine.

This all assumes you've already set yourself up with Domain Name Service **[Hack #78]** and have an mx (mail) record pointing at the Mac.

Allowing Relaying from Certain Hosts

sendmail doesn't like to relay mail that isn't sent from trusted sources. The designers of sendmail do this purposefully to try to alleviate the problem of spam. You see, spammers take advantage of mail servers that will relay mail from anyone in order to send mail to all of us while taking advantage of somebody else's bandwidth costs. It's truly heinous.

By default, sendmail's paranoia means that when we set up a server, we can relay through it only mail that originates on the local machine. In order to use it as a proper mail server, we need to let it know which hosts to trust to relay mail. For example, my mail sever is configured to accept email that comes from my private home network that is running behind a Network Address Translation (NAT) with a fixed IP address. In addition, I always want to be able to send mail, using my laptop, from my friends' houses that have known hostnames. To do this, you simply need to define these rules in the /etc/mail/access file, as shown here:

```
% sudo pico /etc/mail/access

192.168.123.2 RELAY
dsl-1-1-1-1.networkprovider.net RELAY
```

You can also allow blocks of IP addresses or partial domain addresses to relay through your server. For example, to allow anybody on a subnet, as well as let everybody at the *oreilly.com* domain use my mail server, I could edit this file to look like this:

```
% sudo pico /etc/mail/access

192.168.123.2 RELAY
dsl-1-1-1-1.networkprovider.net RELAY
192.168.145 RELAY
oreilly.com RELAY
```

This will let anyone with an IP address that starts with 192.168.145 or whose IP address resolves to the *oreilly.com* domain to use our server. We need to compile this file into a form that sendmail can use. To do this, use the following command:

```
% sudo makemap hash /etc/mail/access > /etc/mail/access
```

Yes, this is yet another command to remember, and I personally always have to look it up to use it. Don't fear; we can fix this problem.

Our Helper Script Expanded

Since I hate having to use the documentation to execute what should be simple commands, I have actually added all these commands (and more) to my update script. I gave you the short form earlier. Here's the long form (with the section we haven't seen before in bold type):

```
#!/bin/sh

if [ /etc/mail/config.mc -nt /etc/mail/sendmail.cf ]
then
echo Regenerating sendmail.cf
m4 /usr/share/sendmail/conf/m4/cf.m4 /etc/mail/config.mc > \
/tmp/sendmail.cf
mv /etc/mail/sendmail.cf /etc/mail/sendmail.cf.old
mv /tmp/sendmail.cf /etc/mail/sendmail.cf
/System/Library/StartupItems/Sendmail/Sendmail restart
fi

if [ /etc/mail/access -nt /etc/mail/access.db ]
then
echo Updating access
makemap hash /etc/mail/access < /etc/mail/access
fi
```

In short, this file checks to see if it should:

* Compile the *sendmail.cf* file
* Update the access database

When the source for any of these files is out-of-date, it will be updated. Easy huh? Now, all we have to do is remember to run the update script whenever we edit one of the configuration files and the right thing will happen.

Running Behind a Firewall

Running sendmail behind a firewall, especially if it's a NAT, can confuse it. You see, sendmail does its best to try and figure out what its hostname is. As long as your machine is a first-class citizen on the Internet (i.e., it has an IP address visible from the Internet at large), it can usually do a good job at this. However, when you are running behind a NAT or if your IP address doesn't resolve to any hostname, you'll need to give sendmail a little help. For example, if you are hosting mail for *domain.com*, you need to tell send-mail that its domain name is $w.domain.com. The $w part is an important part of sendmail trickery that means insert the local hostname here.

To configure sendmail to use a specific domain name, edit your */etc/mail/config.mc* file as follows:

```
% sudo pico /etc/mail/config.mc

VERSIONID(`$Id: generic-darwin.mc,v 1.3 2002/04/12 18:41:47 bbraun Exp $')
OSTYPE(darwin)dnl
DOMAIN(generic)dnl
undefine(`ALIAS_FILE')
define(`PROCMAIL_MAILER_PATH',`/usr/bin/procmail')
define(`confDONT_BLAME_SENDMAIL', `GroupWritableDirPathSafe')
define(`LUSER_RELAY', `local:duncan')
define(`confDOMAIN_NAME', `$w.domain.com')
FEATURE(`smrsh',`/usr/libexec/smrsh')
FEATURE(local_procmail)
FEATURE(`virtusertable',`hash -o /etc/mail/virtusertable')dnl
FEATURE(`genericstable', `hash -o /etc/mail/genericstable')dnl
FEATURE(`mailertable',`hash -o /etc/mail/mailertable')dnl
FEATURE(`access_db')dnl
MAILER(smtp)
MAILER(procmail)
```

As always, remember to run the update script:

```
% sudo /etc/mail/update
Regenerating sendmail.cf
Restarting mail services
```

Next, we'll take a look at one other common problem that people have that is introduced by their ISP.

Working with Lame ISPs

What do I mean by lame ISPs? Well, I mean ISPs that block all outgoing traffic on port 25. Instead of letting you have access to the Internet on port

25, they want you to use only their own mail server. They do this to try to stop spammers from utilizing open relays on their networks. However, this means that your personal mail server can't send mail to other hosts on the Internet.

Luckily, since sendmail is the Swiss Army Knife of mail servers, there is a configuration directive to fix this. To have all mail from your server go through your ISP's mail server, edit your */etc/mail/config.mc* file to match the following code:

```
% sudo pico /etc/mail/config.mc

VERSIONID(`$Id: generic-darwin.mc,v 1.3 2002/04/12 18:41:47 bbraun Exp $')
OSTYPE(darwin)dnl
DOMAIN(generic)dnl
undefine(`ALIAS_FILE')
define(`PROCMAIL_MAILER_PATH',`/usr/bin/procmail')
define(`confDONT_BLAME_SENDMAIL', `GroupWritableDirPathSafe')
define(`LUSER_RELAY', `local:duncan')
define(`confDOMAIN_NAME', `$w.domain.com')
define(`SMART_HOST' `mail.mindspring.com')
FEATURE(`smrsh',`/usr/libexec/smrsh')
FEATURE(local_procmail)
FEATURE(`virtusertable',`hash -o /etc/mail/virtusertable')dnl
FEATURE(`genericstable', `hash -o /etc/mail/genericstable')dnl
FEATURE(`mailertable',`hash -o /etc/mail/mailertable')dnl
FEATURE(`access_db')dnl
MAILER(smtp)
MAILER(procmail)
```

Once again, run the update script:

```
% sudo /etc/mail/update
Regenerating sendmail.cf
Restarting mail services
```

Problem solved.

Getting NetInfo Out of the Picture

Some of the Apple documentation on sendmail (notably, the */etc/mail/ README* file) implies that it's a good idea to set a few properties in NetInfo to ensure that the sendmail binary reads its configuration from */etc/ mail/sendmail.cf*. So far, I've not had a problem with this, but in the interest of making sure that we don't get bit by a modified sendmail binary from Apple in the future, we should go ahead and execute the commands that will modify the NetInfo database:

```
% sudo niutil -create . /locations/sendmail
% sudo niutil -createprop . /locations/sendmail sendmail.cf ↵
/etc/mail/sendmail.cf
```

—*James Duncan Davidson*

HACK
#83

Downloading POP Mail with fetchmail

You're running your own POP or IMAP mail server but don't have any way of
getting your mail from your ISP to your local machine. fetchmail, a popular
Unix utility, will fetch your mail for you.

In our ever-connected world, people are rabid about email. "Did you get my
email?" they clamor. "Did you read my message?" they beg. "I just sent you
an attachment!" they announce. Granted, Apple has thoughtfully included
its own nice email program with its latest OS, but you can also check your
mail via the Terminal [Hack #48] using a popular utility called fetchmail.

By itself, fetchmail does nothing more than fetch your mail. For those not
familiar with the shell, it does even this not so simply, as you've got to know
about mail directories and how things work together. Where fetchmail really
shines, however, is when it's used in combination with other hacks in this
email chapter—combining fetchmail with a local IMAP or POP mail server
[Hack #81] creates a powerful one-two punch for email independence.

Getting fetchmail running is easy when you have some hand-holding. The
first thing we've got to do is create our storage file; this is the place fetchmail will fetch our mail to. This, conveniently enough, is called a *mailbox*. In
OS X and most operating systems like it, this *mailbox* file is located under
the *var* directory—something you normally wouldn't see through the
Finder. To set up your *mailbox* file so you have adequate permissions, perform the following, replacing *username* with your own:

```
% sudo touch /var/mail/username
% sudo chown username /var/mail/username
% chmod 600 /var/mail/username
```

These commands will first create an empty file with the touch shell utility
and then modify the permissions and ownership until it's accessible only by
yourself. This ensures privacy as well as stopping a few warnings from various utilities you may use during your exploration. The file we've just created will be where our incoming mail will be saved, and messages will be
stored in plain-text format, where they can easily be imported or used by
other utilities.

Our next step is to actually use fetchmail. fetchmail is one of the larger utilities available and has an insane number of options—enough so that it's easy
to look at the manual and run away screaming in arcane tongues. Once you
have an example though, fetchmail is pretty easy. Take a look at the following command:

```
% fetchmail --check mail.example.com
```

This command is safe to run; it'll merely check (not download) the supplied mail server to see if there's any mail waiting for you. It'll automatically figure out what type of server you're running (POP3, IMAP, etc.) as well as prompt for your password, automatically assuming your current Mac OS X username as the POP3 username. But what if it's not? How about:

```
% fetchmail --verbose --check --protocol=pop3 --username=morbus ↵
mail.example.com
```

This command will spit out more information about what fetchmail is doing, as well as specifying the POP3 protocol (which should save a few seconds on your initial connection) and your preferred username.

With this command, we're only checking to see if we have new mail; we still haven't initiated any downloads. Let's swap out --check for --keep:

```
% fetchmail --keep --protocol=pop3 --username=morbus mail.example.com
```

After running this and filling in our password, we'll see some output telling us what mail is being downloaded and then delivered into our */var/mail/username* file. Again, even though we're downloading the mail to our local drive, that --keep flag will save the messages on the POP server until we're good and ready; removing the --keep flag will download and then remove the messages from the server.

Typing that long command line each and every time can be pretty pesky and, thankfully, fetchmail will read a configuration file that controls what fetchmail should do. To create one, start a file in your home directory called *.fetchmailrc* (it'll be invisible to the Finder because of the leading dot, but fetchmail will see it just fine). In this file, add the following, tweaking to your settings:

```
set postmaster "morbus"

poll mail.example.com
proto pop3
user "morbus"
password "xxxxxxx"
fetchall
keep
mda "/usr/bin/procmail -d %T"
```

We start off the file with set postmaster "username", which is really just a precaution; it says "if at anytime, fetchmail can't figure out where the mail should go, send it to this username." This option is primarily useful in multiuser systems (or servers).

The poll option is where the going gets good. This is where we start defining which mail servers we want to check. Until fetchmail sees another poll (or skip, but we won't discuss that here) line, it'll assume that all further directives are for the server we've just defined. That's fine with us, since this example shows only one server, using the protocol (proto) of pop3. This is the same thing as using -p or --protocol on the command line.

Our next two lines are obvious; they're the username and the password for the mailbox we want to check. Unlike the command line, we can set the password here (in plain text...be sure your file permissions are tight!) so that fetchmail will run without our input. If you're panicky about leaving your password in the open, just remove the password line and fetchmail will go back to prompting you.

The next three lines aren't required but merely tweak the way fetchmail is run. Here, we always want to fetch all the messages on the server (fetchall), as opposed to just new ones, and we want to keep them on the server after we've delivered them to our local box. We then set our mail delivery agent (mda) explicitly to procmail—something we won't be discussing in this hack (by default, procmail is configured correctly, so this line is harmless).

As mentioned, an insane number of options are available within fetchmail, and you can find out more by issuing a man fetchmail at the Terminal. This hack should give you enough to start downloading your mail, and later you can hook it up to more powerful environments.

H A C K #84 Creating Mail Aliases

Email aliases direct mail sent to webmaster@, me@, and so forth to the right email address.

A fancy bit of email functionality in common use, especially among those with their own domain, is having mail sent to so-called vanity email addresses delivered to a single email address. This is accomplished by creating aliases for a single email address. Perhaps you'd like *webmaster@* on your web site so that you can have your email application filter requests to another folder. *me@* is a popular one, though I can't quite fathom why. Others include *info@*, *support@*, *sales@*, and *godlike@*—OK, so that last one's not all that common.

This hack assumes you've already set up Domain Name Service [Hack #78] and have sendmail [Hack #82] up and running.

We'll use NetInfo Manager (*Applications → Utilities → NetInfo Manager*) to create email aliases (see Figure 7-8).

Figure 7-8. Setting up mail aliases in NetInfo Manager

 NetInfo was OS X's answer (prior to Mac OS X 10.2, Jaguar) to slicing, dicing, and otherwise managing both your individual local and multiple networked Macs. NetInfo Manager is a desktop application front end—albeit a thin layer providing little more than a hierarchical Finder-like view— to a comprehensive directory of users, groups, devices, and network services. Apple is slowly phasing NetInfo out in favor of the more esoteric yet more flexible text-based configuration files of OS X's Unix roots. Still, at the time of this writing, it's the simplest way to create email aliases.

Launch NetInfo Manager. Click the lock button ("Click the lock to make changes") at the bottom-left of the window to afford you the power to edit the current NetInfo configuration. When prompted to do so, enter your username and password and click the OK button.

Now that you're authenticated, you can get to work creating an alias. Click on the aliases entry in the center column; you'll see a list of current email aliases appear in the righthand column. Create a new entry, either by selecting Directory → New Subdirectory, typing ⌘-N, or clicking the "Create new directory" button—the folder labeled *New* on the left side of your toolbar. A new directory called, appropriately enough, *new_directory* appears in the bottom frame of the window. Double-click the new_directory value of the Name property and rename it webmaster (or your preferred alias).

Now that you've created a new alias, you'll need to associate a real email address with it. Create a new property, either by selecting Directory → New Property or typing ⌘-Shift-N. Rename new_property to members and new_value to your short user name [Hack #1]. Mine's duncan.

If all went to plan, the NetInfo Manager window should now look something like Figure 7-9.

Figure 7-9. Mail addressed to webmaster will be delivered to duncan

Save your changes (⌘-S or Domain → Save Changes). You will be asked to confirm your changes.

Now, any mail addressed to *webmaster* will be delivered to user *duncan*. Do the same for any more aliases you wish to create; you can add as many as you want.

—*James Duncan Davidson*

## CHAPTER EIGHT

The Web

Hacks 85–98

Mac OS X is a web powerhouse, both in terms of its web-serving capabilities and wide range of web browsers from which to choose.

On the server side, OS X's understated Personal Web Sharing is powered by the ubiquitous, flexible, and industrial-strength Apache web server. Just click the Start button (*System Preferences → Sharing → Services*) and you have a full-blown web server at your disposal. By the end of this chapter, you'll be serving up dynamic content, running CGI applications, scripting PHP pages, and putting together server-side include–driven pages with the best of them. We'll also show you how to control access to your web site, honing what visitors can and cannot see.

You want browsers? OS X has browsers splendid enough to put the 1990s Netscape/Internet Explorer browser wars to shame. Numbered among the top contenders are Microsoft's Internet Explorer, default browser through Mac OS X 10.2; Safari, Apple's brand new ultra-fast, super-sleek entry threatening to replace IE as OS X's browser-in-the-box; and the Mozilla variants, most notably Camino (formerly Chimera), built just for Mac. Then there are the microcontent browsers, catering to quick searches and syndicated news reading—daring to take content outside of the browser. This chapter introduces you to the pick of the litter.

HACK #85 Searching the Internet from Your Desktop

Thanks to a collection of freeware and shareware apps and a few clever hacks, you can weave Internet search into the fabric of your Mac computing experience.

Searching the Web—with Google in particular—has become such a part of our daily online lives that *Google* is now regarded as a verb and even the uber-literary *New Yorker* gets webby with Google-related cartoons. You're being Googled while on the phone with someone who can't quite remember who you are or why they asked you to ring them. Without Google close at hand, you're a day late and a dollar short.

Too bad web searching's so closely tied to the browser. For that matter, even choice of search engine is most often hardcoded into the browser and can't be pried loose without a modicum of hackery. Wouldn't it do wonders to be able to search from any application for the highlighted text right under your mouse pointer?

Thanks to a collection of freeware and shareware apps and a few clever hacks, all this and more is within reach. All of these solutions construct an appropriate query URL, much as you'd see in your browser's address bar after submitting a search directly (e.g., *http://www.google.com/search?q=hacks*).

Searchling

Michael Thole's Searchling (*http://web.ics.purdue.edu/~mthole/searchling/*) (open source donateware) embeds search functionality right into your menu bar for access from anywhere at any time (see Figure 8-1). Click the G— that's G as in *Google*—menu bar icon, type or paste your query in the fade-in search box, select your search engine of choice, and Searchling will bring up the results in your default web browser.

Figure 8-1. Searchling

Searchling ships with support for Google, Dictionary.com, and eBay. Beyond each engine's default search, a pull-down menu lets you home in on the type of search you're after. Search Google for web sites, images, or news; search Dictionary.com for a definition; or consult the thesaurus.

As one might hope, you're not limited only to the engines or types of searches Searchling offers out of the box. You can alter the offerings by editing Searchling's only mildly hairy *sites.xml* file. Perl maven Matt Sergeant added quick access to the vast array of Perl modules on the Comprehensive Perl Archive Network (CPAN), searchable by all, modules, distributions, and authors; his *sites.xml* is available at *http://www.sergeant.org/searchling_sites.xml*. Figure 8-2 shows a screenshot of it in action, along with the results presented in my browser. Note the generated URL in the address bar and appropriate search data in the web page itself.

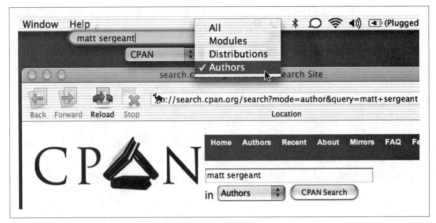

Figure 8-2. Searchling searching CPAN

Google Groups (*http://groups.google.com/*) sports a comprehesive archive of the past 20 years of Usenet news. Let's add it to Searchling's list of supported Google search types. Find Searchling on your drive (probably *Applications → Searchling*), Control-click its icon, and select Show Package Contents. Navigate down to to the *Contents/Resources* folder and open the *sites.xml* file in your favorite text editor. Add the wodge of XML called out in bold just below the piece defining the Google News search type:

```
...
<dict>
<key>type</key>
<string>News</string>
<key>url</key>
<string>http://news.google.com/news?hl=en&q=</string>
</dict>
<dict>
<key>type</key>
<string>groups</string>
<key>url</key>
<string>http://groups.google.com/groups?hl=en&amp;q=</string>
</dict>
</array>
...
```

Notice how you need to escape & as & in the search URL so that it sits well with the XML.

Alternately, if you prefer a more visual editing tool and have the Mac OS X Developer Tools **[Hack #48]** installed, open *Searchling/Contents/Resources/sites. xml* in Property List Editor (*Developer → Applications → Property List Editor*).

Save *sites.xml*, quit (Control-click the icon and select Quit Searchling) and relaunch Searchling. "groups" should now appear as a choice under Google Search Types.

Adding an entire site, as Matt did for CPAN and I for Meerkat: an Open Wire Service (*http://www.raelity.org/archives/2002/12/04#computers/ internet/www/search_engines/searchling*), is just as simple. Copy an existing site definition, paste it alongside its peers, and make the appropriate edits. Any valid query URL will do; just be sure the last variable= is the one to accept query keywords (e.g., q= for Google, query= for CPAN, and s= for Meerkat).

Huevos

Huevos provides multiple-search-engine support—it ships with 13—but is a little more obtrusive, floating about in a minimizeable window rather than tucking itself into the menu bar.

Huevos's major boon is the considerable ease with which you can add search engines to its stable. Select Huevos → Preferences, click New, edit the Name and URL and your search engine of choice appears in the alphabetical list, as shown in Figure 8-3. No need for XML editing or even restarting the application; changes take effect immediately.

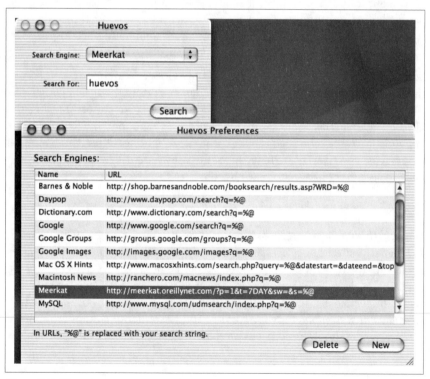

Figure 8-3. Huevos

> Have Searchling or Huevos available to you from the moment you log in by dragging its Finder icon into the System Preferences → Login Items Preferences pane.

SearchGoogle.service

SearchGoogle.service (*http://gu.st/proj/Searchgoogle.html*) (public domain donateware) adds "search Google" functionality to just about any OS X application's (Finder included) Services menu. Highlight a snippet of text and select Services → Search Google or press Shift-⌘-G to send the results to your default browser.

Installation is simple. Download the package, unstuff it, and drag *SearchGoogle.service* to *~/Library/Services* (create this folder if it doesn't already exist). Log out and back in and Search Google should appear in your Services menu.

I found SearchGoogle.service to function adequately, working from the Finder, iChat, Terminal, and various other applications. The service was grayed out in the two applications in which I would have most expected it to work: the Internet Explorer and Mozilla-based browsers. At times, the keystroke combo didn't work, cured seemingly by manually selecting the service for first-time use in the current application.

SearchGoogle.service, while supporting only Google search, does afford you the ability to change the default search engine. Edit its *SearchGoogle.service/Contents/Info.plist* with Property List Editor or a text editor, altering the URL in SgDefaultURL. The same rules as Searchling apply: the keywords are appended to the end. To change the key binding, alter the value of NSServices > NSKeyEquivalent. In both cases, you'll need to log out and back in again for changes to take effect.

Watson

Watson (*http://www.karelia.com/watson/*) ($29 single user, $39 household, $15-per-seat site license, 10–100; free trial), by Karelia Software, is a snazzy front end to a plethora of XML-based and HTML-scraped web services. Highlights include Amazon.com, movies, VersionTracker (*http://www.versiontracker.com/*), recipes, stocks, translation, a Google tool (*http://www.karelia.com/watson/plugins/google.html*), and a wonderful columnar interface for browsing Yahoo! (*http://www.karelia.com/watson/plugins/yahoo.html*).

Thanks to a comprehensive developers' kit (*http://www.karelia.com/developer/watson/*), new tools for Watson are popping up frequently.

Sherlock

Then, of course, there's Sherlock 3 (*http://www.apple.com/macosx/jaguar/sherlock.html*) (bundled with every Mac OS X 10.2 Jaguar installation). Sherlock, remarkably similar to Watson, provides a clean front end to various web services, including Internet search (shown in Figure 8-4). While the default lineup of underlying web search engines (About.com, Ask Jeeves, Looksmart, etc.) don't top the favorites charts of anyone I know, Apple has released a Sherlock 3 Channel SDK (*http://developer.apple.com/macosx/sherlock/*), everything a developer might need to build additional Sherlock channels. It took only a short while for a Google search plug-in for Sherlock to put in an appearance.

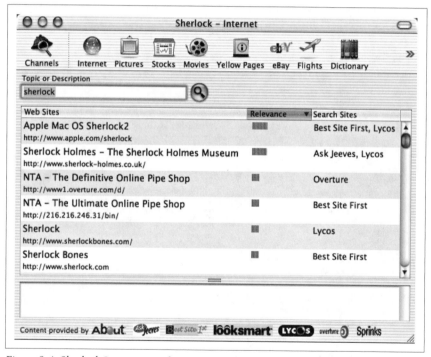

Figure 8-4. Sherlock Internet search

Everything required to develop a channel is provided in the Sherlock Channel SDK, including technical documentation, a sample channel, a Project Builder template, and an Interface Builder Sherlock palette.

Hacking Your Browser

Then again, perhaps the browser is the most appropriate place for a web search. That doesn't mean you have to type http://www.google.com/ and fill out the form each time. There are various hacks available for building in support for Google and other search engine searches right from the address bar.

By far, the most elegant is Mozilla's keyword searching (*http://www.mozilla. org/docs/end-user/keywords.html*). Simply bookmark a search-result URL, use %s as a stand-in for the keywords, and associate a keyword (I use g) with it. To search, type the keyword you specified, followed by an appropriate query (e.g., g mozilla keywords) into the address field and press Return for results. Create as many of these keyword searches as you like: a for Amazon. com, m for meerkat, and so forth (see Figure 8-5).

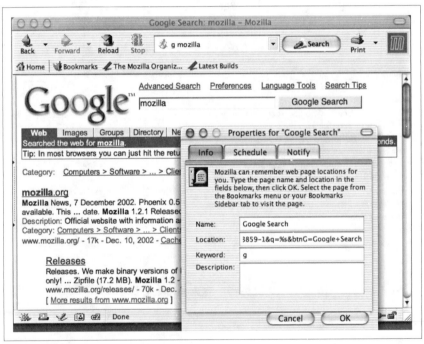

Figure 8-5. Mozilla bookmark with keyword

Google maintains a Googlify your Browser page (*http://www.google.com/ options/defaults.html*) with resources for making Google your default search engine and embedding search beyond the default Search button. For altering Internet Explorer's default search engine (triggered by typing ?, followed by keywords into the address bar), see *http://www.macslash.com/articles/01/10/10/1828238.shtml* and *http://www.macntalk.com/tips/googleie.html*.

How Lazy Can You Get?

True, it doesn't take much to launch your browser and browse to your favorite search-engine site. True, search results are usually returned in the browser anyway. But why take that one extra step and smidgen of mindwidth when you can click a menu bar icon, press Shift-⌘-G, or the like. It's all about integrating search into the fabric of your computing experience.

HACK #86 Saving Web Pages for Offline Reading

Save a single web page or even clusters of web pages in their entirety for reading on public transportation, at 35,000 feet, or anywhere else you happen to be.

There comes a time when we happen across a web page that is so uproariously funny, we simply must archive it forever. On the other hand, sometimes we want to save a few online transactions for proof of purchase. Even more commonly, we may run across a large site that we want to read in its entirety, but we don't want to tie up our phone line or incur bandwidth charges. Thankfully, OS X satisfies our offline-reading desires in a number of ways.

When we need to archive a web page or site quickly, a few options present themselves, depending on our goal. The quickest and closest opportunity is to use Microsoft Internet Explorer, bundled with Mac OS X. Within this popular browser lies a Scrapbook, as well as the ability to create Web Archives.

The concept of a Scrapbook harkens back to the pre–OS X days with a built-in system accessory called, conveniently enough, Scrapbook. With it, you could drop in files, text, sounds, movies, and pictures and then flip through the pages, viewing each item as part of a grander book.

A similar concept is built into Internet Explorer. At any time, you can take the web page you're currently looking at and save it into your the IE Scrapbook for later viewing. To do so, make sure the Explorer Bar is enabled (View → Explorer Bar) and click the Scrapbook tab to slide out its panel. To add the current web page into the Scrapbook, click the now-visible Add button.

You'll immediatley see the title of the current web page show up in the Scrapbook panel along with a camera icon, signifying that this is a snapshot of the current page. Now, or any time in the future, you can click an item in your Scrapbook and see an exact copy of what you were looking at, along with the time it was archived and its original URL. Just like bookmarks, you can organize your Scrapbook items into folders, rename and delete, and give them comments.

The Scrapbook excels at saving one page but doesn't do well at multiple pages; you'll need to create new entries for each page of the site manually. If you're looking to archive a whole site (the chapters of a book, news items in central Florida, etc.), you'll want to look at Internet Explorer's Save As feature, which has an easily-ignored Web Archive output.

There are a number of options available to a Web Archive, and all of them concern how much you want to save to disk. By default, a Web Archive does the same thing as a Scrapbook item, taking the current page (and all its images), wrapping it up into one proprietary file, and then saving it to your hard drive. The various options allow you to save sounds and movies but, more importantly, specify how many levels of other linked pages you want to archive, along with the current one.

Of course, the more things you want to archive, the larger the archive is going to become. The Save As → Web Archive option is certainly more powerful than the Scrapbook, simply because of its namesake: it's more an archive then a single page in a book. However, it does have two limitations.

Since the Web Archive feature creates a single, Internet Explorer–only file, it's not ideal if you're looking to collect and store only certain data, like the illustrations of your favorite artist; you're going to get the pages whether you want them or not, and there's no easy way for you to extract the images from the resultant single archive. The second limitation is how much you can archive; you can't choose more than five levels deep, which, granted, is probably enough.

If these limitations are deal breakers, then there are many other utilities for you to explore. The shareware Web Devil (*http://www.chaoticsoftware.com/ ProductPages/WebDevil.html*) has been around for years and provides a handy, powerful GUI for your web-sucking needs. If you prefer shell utilities, then look at GNU wget (*http://apple.com/downloads/macosx/unix_ apps_utilities/wget.html*), which provides a powerful, automated interface to downloading [Hack #61] and mirroring. Both utilities support filtering (i.e., save only *.jpg* and *.gif* files, etc.).

Reading Syndicated Online Content
#87
NetNewsWire is to syndicated content from weblogs, web sites, and online magazines as newsreaders are to Usenet news of old.

If you have been surfing the Web in the last couple of months, you undoubtedly have come across sites known as weblogs (also commonly referred to as blogs). Simply put, weblogs are like diaries of the thoughts and wanderings of a person or group of persons, pointing at and annotating things of interest on the Web. On the surface, a weblog looks no different than a conventional web page, but one salient feature of a weblog is that its content is usually exposed, in addition to the default web page view, as an XML document (RSS, to be precise) for syndication.

> Rebecca Blood's "weblogs: a history and perspective" (*http://www.rebeccablood.net/essays/weblog_history.html*) provides a nice overview of the emergence of weblogs. For more on the culture and practicalities of weblogs and blogging, may I suggest O'Reilly's *Essential Blogging* (*http://www.oreilly.com/catalog/essblogging/*).

News Aggregators

News aggregators are applications that collect all these RSS documents at regular time intervals. The advantage of using news aggregators is that you need not visit each individual site in order to know about the latest happenings. You can simply aggregate the news into one central location and selectively view the ones that you are interested in. Nowadays, a great number of online news sites and magazines have caught the syndication bug and are distributing news via RSS, which makes it all the more convenient for you to travel the world from the comfort of your Mac.

NetNewsWire

Ranchero's NetNewsWire (*http://ranchero.com/software/netnewswire/*) ($29.95 for the Pro version; the Lite version is free) is probably the most popular syndicated content reader for Macintosh. It sports a clean, intuitive Aqua interface (see Figure 8-6), not unlike those of Usenet newsreaders of the past.

On the left pane is the list of news, web sites, and weblogs to which you are subscribed. NetNewsWire comes presubscribed to a list of popular and Mac-slanted blogs, news sites, and online magazines. The top-right pane

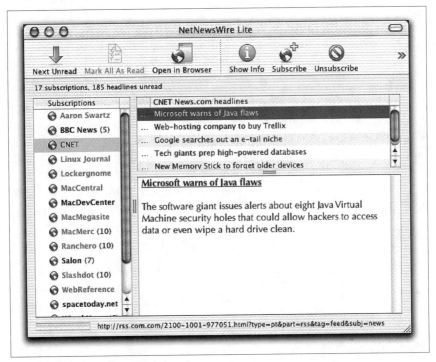

Figure 8-6. NetNewsWire Lite's interface

shows the list of headlines from the site that you have selected on the left. Select a headline and an abstract of the content appears in the bottom-right pane. Want to read the story in its entirety? Simply double-click the headline and your default web browser will fetch and display it for you, as shown in Figure 8-7.

Of course, with the proliferation of syndicated online content, the list of presubscribed feeds provides only a starting point. NetNewsWire comes with a list of well-known feeds, in addition to those in the default subscription list. You'll find them in the Sites Drawer (see Figure 8-8). Type ⌘-L or select View → Show Sites Drawer to open the Sites Drawer.

Feeds in the Sites Drawer are grouped nicely into categories for your convenience. Option-click on a feed and you're presented with three choices (see Figure 8-9): subscribe to the feed, open it in your browser for a quick taste of what it has to offer, or open the RSS feed itself in your default browser.

Another way of subscribing to sites is supplying the RSS URL yourself—perhaps you've copied it from a web page of interest. Select Subscriptions →

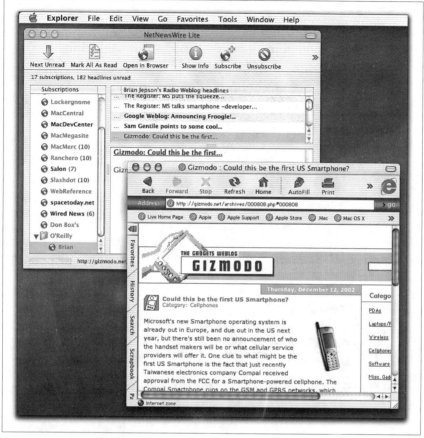

Figure 8-7. Loading the source of the news

Subscribe… or press ⌘-Shift-S. Type or paste in the RSS feed's URL and click OK to subscribe (see Figure 8-10). You'll notice the feed appearing and updating itself on the bottom-left.

> Many weblogs have a link to their RSS feeds right from the home page. These usually appear as easily recognizable orange XML buttons.

Housekeeping

With a long subscription list, it makes sense to organize feeds into groups—akin to keeping like with like in folders on your hard drive. Option-click the lefthand pane and select New Group (as shown in Figure 8-11) to do so.

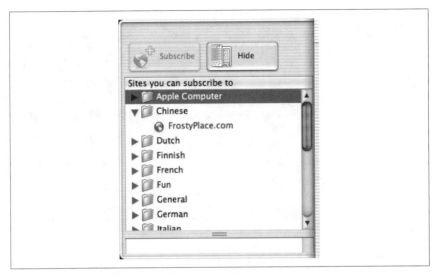

Figure 8-8. The Sites drawer

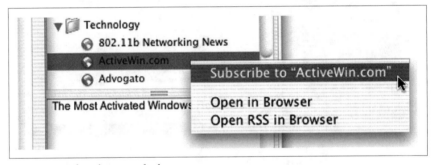

Figure 8-9. Subscribing to a feed

Another feature that you may want to configure is the rate at which subscriptions are refreshed and new stories dropped into your reader (see
Figure 8-12). The default refresh is manual. If you are pretty much always on
a network, you're better off setting it to refresh at regular time intervals so
that you're always reading the latest.

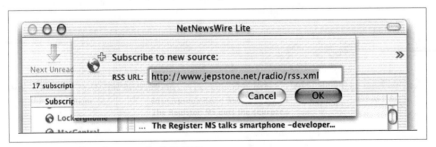

Figure 8-10. Subscribing via the RSS URL

Figure 8-11. Grouping subscribed feeds

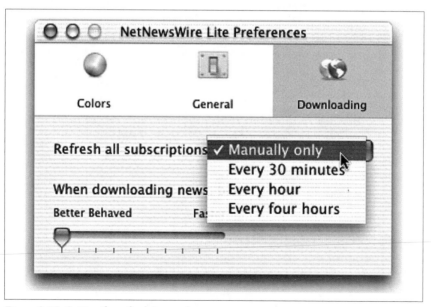

Figure 8-12. Setting the refresh interval

—*Wei-Meng Lee*

Serving Up a Web Site with the Built-In Apache Server

HACK
#88

With the Apache web server under the hood, OS X is a web powerhouse right at your very fingertips.

Apache is one of the most popular, if not the most popular, web server available today. It has support for literally anything you want to do. Jaguar ships with Version 1.3.26 of Apache, and all you need to do to start it up is to click a single button in your System Preferences application. Here's how.

Open up the System Preferences application. If it's not on your Dock, then you can find it in the *Applications* folder of your hard drive. Once launched, click on the Sharing button, then click on the Personal Web Sharing checkbox, as shown in Figure 8-13. Don't let the name Personal Web Sharing fool you. This is the full-strength Apache web server running, no matter how innocent or lightweight it sounds in the preference panel.

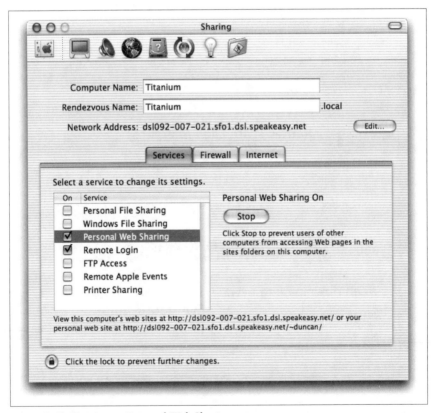

Figure 8-13. Turning on Personal Web Sharing

That's it. You can now point a web browser at your machine's IP address, hostname, or *http://localhost* and see the default Apache home page—yes, the one with the big "Seeing this instead of the Web site you expected?" caption. This rather bland default home page is located in */Library/WebServer/Documents*, the home of your web site on this machine. Easy huh?

User Sites

If you've ever had a web site hosted at an Internet Service Provider (ISP), you're probably used to having a URL that looks a little something like this: *http://www.myisp.com/~me*, where *me* is your login name. In addition to the main web site you now have running on your Macintosh, each user— remember, whether you're the only user or not, OS X is a multiuser system—also has his very own site.

The files for your user site live in the *Sites* folder in your home directory [Hack #1]. Point your web browser at *http://localhost/~me*, where *me* is the Short Name [Hack #1] associated with your user account. You'll be greeted with a friendly "Your website here" message, along with further instructions on building your own web site. That page is actually a file called *index.html* sitting in your *Sites* folder; edit it using your favorite text or HTML editor and reload the page in your browser to see the results.

Why use user sites when you have a perfectly good main site at *http://localhost* (*/Library/WebServer/Documents*)? Perhaps you share your computer with others and each of you wants your own web site. Maybe you want a space to experiment with content and functionality without reflecting that out to the world. I've configured my Apache server [Hack #89] such that, while my main site is readily viewable by anyone on the network, my user site is restricted only to viewing from my computer itself. This gives me a place to fiddle with all sorts of things without worry of anyone else stumbling across my experiments.

Behind the Scenes: the Configuration Files

But what's really going on here? Let's look behind the scenes and see what the Unix core of Mac OS X is doing.

When you click that innocent-looking Personal Web Sharing button in the System Preferences application, what happens is that a flag gets changed in the */etc/hostconfig* file. This file tells Mac OS X which services should be started. Mine looks like this:

```
% more hostconfig
##
# /etc/hostconfig
```

```
##
# This file is maintained by the system control panels
##

# Network configuration
HOSTNAME=-AUTOMATIC-
ROUTER=-AUTOMATIC-

# Services
AFPSERVER=-NO-
APPLETALK=-NO-
AUTHSERVER=-NO-
AUTOMOUNT=-YES-
CONFIGSERVER=-NO-
CUPS=-YES-
IPFORWARDING=-NO-
IPV6=-YES-
MAILSERVER=-NO-
NETBOOTSERVER=-NO-
NETINFOSERVER=-AUTOMATIC-
NISDOMAIN=-NO-
RPCSERVER=-AUTOMATIC-
TIMESYNC=-NO-
QTSSERVER=-NO-
SSHSERVER=-YES-
WEBSERVER=-YES-
SMBSERVER=-NO-
DNSSERVER=-NO-
CRASHREPORTER=-YES-
APPLETALK_HOSTNAME=Titanium
```

By looking at this file and seeing the line WEBSERVER=-YES-, Mac OS X knows that Apache should be on. If you are observant, you'll have noticed that in the System Preferences screenshot in Figure 8-13, I have my Remote Login service turned on, as well as Personal Web Sharing. This corresponds to the -YES- flag being set for the SSHSERVER entry. We'll be back to this file in "Getting sendmail Up and Running" **[Hack #82]** as we set up the mail services for our server.

The other file of interest is Apache's main configuration file, found at */etc/ httpd/httpd.conf*. The default file in Jaguar is sufficient for most people. But, if you need to do something with Apache that isn't enabled by default, all you need to do is edit this file **[Hack #89]** and restart the web server.

—James Duncan Davidson

Editing the Apache Web Server's Configuration

Wading through Apache's long configuration file isn't as hard as it seems when you know what to look for.

The standard Apache configuration file, located at */etc/httpd/httpd.conf*, is as large as it is well-documented. Take its introductory warning to heart:

> Do not simply read the instructions ... without understanding what they do. They're here only as hints or reminders. If you are unsure, consult the online docs. You have been warned.

For your own reference, the online docs are available at the Apache web site (*http://httpd.apache.org/docs/*).

Unlike the user configuration (later in this hack), this is the heart of Apache; everything in this file controls what features (modules) Apache loads at startup, as well as the default set of access restrictions, file types, and so much more. When searching through this file for something specific (say, how do I turn on CGI [Hack #92]), the quickest way to find and learn is to search for the feature you want to enable. In our case, we'll start looking for CGI. The first two matches we find are:

```
LoadModule cgi_module libexec/httpd/mod_cgi.so
AddModule mod_cgi.c
```

You'll see a number of these lines within the Apache config file. If you've ever worked with a plug-in-based program, you'll easily recognize their intent; these lines load different features into the Apache web server. Apache calls these modules, and you'll see a lot of module names start with mod_, such as mod_perl and mod_php. Lines that are commented out (that is to say, lines that are prefaced with a # character) are inactive.

On the other hand, if you're not interested in the specifics of how Apache configures itself, but rather about configurations specific to your web site (like *http://127.0.0.1/~morbus/*), then you'll want to look into user configurations. In most Apache installations, user-based web serving is handled generically; for every user on the system, be it 2 or 2,000, the same configuration applies. If an administrator wanted to change the capabilities of user mimi, she'd usually have to create a specific <Directory> block within the *httpd.conf* file.

Apple and Mac OS X makes this a lot easier by creating a config file for each user of the system; these files are located in */etc/httpd/users/*, take the form of *username.conf*, and are automatically merged into the main Apache configuration file at startup. If I open the *morbus.conf* in that directory, I see:

```
<Directory "/Users/morbus/Sites/">
  Options Indexes MultiViews
  AllowOverride None
  Order allow,deny
  Allow from all
</Directory>
```

These are pretty common default settings for directories under Apache; you'll see similar entries in the main configuration file for Apache's default document root (for OS X, that's */Library/WebServer/Documents*). Editing [Hack #51] either the user configuration file or *httpd.conf* involves authenticating as an administrative user [Hack #50] and then making your changes, such as this one, to block outside access:

```
<Directory "/Users/morbus/Sites/">
  Options Indexes MultiViews
  AllowOverride None
  Order deny,allow
  Deny from all
  Allow from 127.0.0.1
</Directory>
```

Restarting Apache

Each time you make alterations to any of Apache's configuration files and save your changes, you'll need to restart Apache by issuing the following command:

```
% sudo apachectl restart
httpd restarted
```

apachectl is a simple interface for controlling (starting, stopping, and restarting) Apache; type man apachectl for more information on the various command-line switches. Once Apache has restarted, your configuration changes will be active.

See Also

- Apache Web-Serving with Mac OS X: Part 2 (*http://www.macdevcenter. com/lpt/a//mac/2001/12/14/apache_two.html*)
- Apache Web-Serving with Mac OS X: Part 4 (*http://www.macdevcenter. com/pub/a/mac/2002/01/29/apache_macosx_four.html*)

Build Your Own Apache Server with mod_perl

Go beyond the capabilities of the Apple-supplied Apache web server, building your own version with mod_perl for scalable web applications built in Perl.

When Apple released Mac OS X, it included as part of the operating system one of the most powerful and most used applications on the Internet today: the Apache web server. This has been a boon for Mac users and dedicated Unix jocks alike, as the combination of Apache's simplicity and power and the legendary Mac OS ease-of-use has made for a robust Internet application development platform. Largely due to the inclusion of Apache, along with a host of other necessary Unix power tools, Mac OS X has rapidly become the Unix developer's platform of choice.

And lest anyone be concerned, the Apache that ships with Mac OS X is the genuine article. We're not talking about a weak, proof-of-concept port of Apache that runs under Windows. Mac OS X's FreeBSD underpinnings allow for the Apache web server to be as flexible and responsive as it is on any Unix-based operating system. See "Serving Up a Web Site with the Built-In Apache Server" **[Hack #88]** to get started web serving using Apache.

However, the version of Apache included with Mac OS X is arguably unsatisfactory in a number of ways. If you're like me and plan to do some serious mod_perl-based web development work on Mac OS X, you'll need to take the following issues into consideration as you begin working with Apple's Apache install:

- Although it includes support for mod_perl, it is as a dynamically loadable library (*dynlib*), which means that Perl can be dynamically loaded into the Apache binary at startup time. Unfortunately, a quick search of the mod_perl users mail list (*http://mathforum.org/epigone/modperl*) or the HTML::Mason users list (*http://sourceforge.net/mailarchive/forum. php?forum_id=5219*) archives reveals that the dynamically loadable mod_perl is notoriously unstable. As a result, most serious mod_perl users prefer to statically compile mod_perl right into the Apache binary.

- The version of Perl supported by Apple's Apache is the same as that included with Mac OS X: 5.6.0. Although Apple has provided instructions on how to compile the newer, more robust Perl 5.8.0 yourself (*http://developer.apple.com/internet/macosx/perl.html*), doing so won't automatically make mod_perl use Perl 5.8.0. You have to compile mod_perl yourself to get the latest and greatest.

- Although new versions of Apache are regularly released to fix bugs or patch security holes, Mac OS X users must wait for an OS update from Apple to enjoy the benefits of the latest releases. That time lag can leave OS X Apache users exposed to known security issues until Apple provides an update.

For those whose web-serving needs have exceeded the capabilities of the Apple-supplied Apache, and for those who need to develop scalable web applications built on Perl 5.8.0 and mod_perl, an important alternative exists: you can build your own Apache web server on Mac OS X. In this hack, I guide you through the steps necessary to build your own Apache server with mod_perl.

Preparation

Compiling your own applications means that you need a compiler. Apple kindly offers one with the Mac OS X Developer Tools **[Hack #55]**.

If we're to install Apache with mod_perl, the first thing we need to do is install the latest version of Perl. Fortunately, Apple has provided the aforementioned instructions for downloading and compiling Perl 5.8.0 (*http://developer.apple.com/internet/macosx/perl.html*). Although that article documents compiling Perl 5.8.0 on Jaguar, it should work reasonably well on Mac OS X 10.1.x, as well.

Next, we'll need to download the latest Apache 1.3 and mod_perl 1.x sources. You can find the Apache sources on the Apache HTTP Server Source Code Distributions page (*http://www.apache.org/dist/httpd/*) or at your nearest mirror (*http://www.apache.org/dyn/closer.cgi/httpd/*). As I write this, the latest version is 1.3.27, so that's what I'll use in the remainder of this article. The latest version of mod_perl is available from the mod_perl distribution page (*http://perl.apache.org/dist/*).

I also recommend that you grab the libapreq sources from their home page (*http://httpd.apache.org/apreq/*). The libapreq library provides some useful mod_perl-related modules for which I also include installation instructions. As of this writing, the latest libapreq version is 1.1, so that's the version you'll see in all the following examples:

```
% cd /usr/local/src
% curl -O http://www.apache.org/dist/httpd/apache_1.3.27.tar.gz
% tar zxvf apache_1.3.27.tar.gz
% curl -O http://perl.apache.org/dist/mod_perl-1.0-current.tar.gz
% tar zxvf mod_perl-1.0-current.tar.gz
% curl -O \
    ftp://ftp.cpan.org/pub/CPAN/authors/id/J/JI/JIMW/libapreq-1.1.tar.gz
% tar zxvf libapreq-1.1.tar.gz
```

Following Apple's example, I move into the *usr/local/src* directory and do all of the work there. I've used the handy curl utility to download the Apache and mod_perl sources right in my Terminal session. I then used the *tar* program to unpack the sources. The Apache sources will now be in the directory *apache_1.3.27/*, while the mod_perl sources will be in the directory *mod_perl-1.xx/* and the libapreq sources will be in the directory *libapreq-1. 1/*. As of this writing, the current version of mod_perl is 1.27, so I'll be working in the *mod_perl-1.27/* directory in the following examples.

Building mod_perl

Now, we're ready to start building the software. At this point, you should have downloaded, compiled, and installed Perl according to the instructions from Apple (with the source code still living in *usr/local/src/perl-5.8.0*) and followed the steps outlined earlier in this hack. Next, we'll build mod_perl.

Like most source-code installations, mod_perl offers a good number of configuration options. A quick perusal of the installation guide (*http://perl. apache.org/docs/1.0/guide/install.html*) reveals all. However, I'm going to recommend a relatively straightforward configuration that includes support for all of the mod_perl features you're likely to need, while allowing the flexibility to build other Apache modules into Apache later on. Here it is:

```
% cd ../mod_perl-1.27
% perl Makefile.PL \
APACHE_SRC=../apache_1.3.27/src \
NO_HTTPD=1 \
USE_APACI=1 \
PREP_HTTPD=1 \
EVERYTHING=1
```

The perl script Makefile.PL creates the Makefile that will be used to compile mod_perl. The APACHE_SRC option tells *Makefile.PL* where to find the Apache sources. The NO_HTTPD option, meanwhile, forces the build process to use this path but keeps it from compiling Apache before we're ready. The USE_ APACI option is what allows that flexibility, as it enables mod_perl's hybrid build environment, wherein we can later compile other modules into Apache. Meanwhile, the PREP_HTTPD option triggers the build process to set up the Apache sources for mod_perl by preparing the APACHE_SRC/modules/ perl/ directory tree. But we save the most important option for last. The EVERYTHING option enables *all* of mod_perl's features.

When this command runs, you'll be prompted to configure mod_perl with the APACHE_SRC sources. Do so by simply pressing the Return key. At this point, mod_perl's configuration will quickly take care of all of its tasks without further intervention.

Next, we'll build and install mod_perl. Fortunately, the tricky part is over. All we need to do is this:

```
% make
% sudo make install
```

These two steps build mod_perl and install it. But before we can take advantage of the newly installed mod_perl, we need to configure and build Apache.

Building Apache

The Apache configuration process offers a bewildering array of options, all of which are documented in the *INSTALL* file included with the Apache sources. Of course, I'll try to keep things simple enough to get the job done with the tools we need.

```
% ./configure \
--with-layout=Apache \
--enable-module=so \
--activate-module=src/modules/perl/libperl.a \
--disable-shared=perl \
--without-execstrip
```

Once again, the configuration is the most complex part of the process. The --with-layout=Apache option sets up Apache to be installed with its usual filesystem layout (i.e., in the */usr/local/apache* directory). The --enable-module=so option enables dynamically loadable library support, should you decide later to build and use any third-party modules as dynamically loadable objects. The --activate-module=src/modules/perl/libperl.a option activates mod_perl, while the --disable-shared=perl option forces Apache to compile in mod_perl statically, rather than as a dynamically loadable library. And finally, the --without-execstrip option is required on Mac OS X to prevent the Apache binary from being stripped (whatever that means).

After configure does its job, we compile and install Apache with the usual commands:

```
% make
% sudo make install
```

Testing Your New Apache Build

Now, Apache is completely compiled and installed with mod_perl. A quick test confirms that the installation was successful:

```
% sudo /usr/local/apache/bin/apachectl configtest
Syntax OK
```

This quick test confirms that Apache compiled properly and loads its default configuration file without error. But it's more interesting to actually get it to serve some web pages. First, make sure that Apple's version of Apache isn't running, by disabling Personal Web Sharing in the Sharing global system preference. Then, start up your newly compiled version of Apache:

```
% sudo /usr/local/apache/bin/apachectl start
/usr/local/apache/bin/apachectl start: httpd started
```

Now, fire up your favorite browser and type in your Mac's domain name ("localhost" should do the trick). If you see a page that starts with "Hey, it worked!" you're in business.

Testing mod_perl

As the final part of this process, we confirm to ourselves for the sake of our own sanity that mod_perl is functioning properly, too. Fortunately, this is rather simple to do, as mod_perl includes a module we can easily use for this purpose. The Apache::Status module is designed to display information about the status of your Apache web server, as well as mod_perl itself. To use it, simply edit the default Apache configuration file **[Hack #89]**, */usr/local/apache/conf/httpd.conf*, and add these lines to it:

```
PerlModule Apache::Status
<Location /perl-status>
  SetHandler perl-script
  PerlHandler Apache::Status
</Location>
```

Restart Apache so that it loads the new module:

```
% sudo /usr/local/apache/bin/apachectl restart
/usr/local/apache/bin/apachectl restart: httpd restarted
```

Now, hit your web server again, this time entering the *perl-status* directory name (e.g., *http://localhost/perl-status/*). You should see a page appear with something like this at the top:

> Embedded Perl version **v5.8.0** for **Apache/1.3.27 (Darwin) mod_perl/1.27** process **12365**,
>
> running since Thu Sep 19 01:05:43 2002

Building libapreq

Now that you have a fully working custom Apache installation, you might want to consider installing libapreq. This library includes Apache::Request and Apache::Cookie (*http://search.cpan.org/dist/libapreq/*), two convenient Perl modules that offer much more efficient processing than their analogs in the commonly-used CGI module (*http://search.cpan.org/dist/CGI.pm/*). As of Version 1.1 the libapreq library is fully supported on Mac OS X 10.2, although it requires a special installation process. (Mac OS X 10.1 users should read the *INSTALL.MacOSX* file for an alternative approach.) If you'd like to take advantage of libapreq's efficiencies in your mod_perl server, follow these steps to install it:

```
% cd libapreq-1.1
% ./configure --with-apache-includes=/usr/local/apache/include
% make
% sudo make install
```

Installing libapreq on Mac OS X is a two-step process. Here, we build and install the C library on which the Perl modules rely. The --with-apache-includes=/usr/local/apache/include option tells configure where to find the include files for our new Apache installation. Then, of course, make and make install compile and install the libapreq C library.

Next, we need to build the libapreq Perl modules. These follow the usual Perl module installation procedure:

```
% perl Makefile.PL
% make
% sudo make test
% sudo make install
```

The *Makefile.PL* script will ask a series of questions and then build the Makefile that will allow us to build the Perl modules. Be sure you enter the proper location for your new Apache server when prompted; *Makefile.PL* will most likely find Apple's Apache at */usr/sbin/httpd* and you'll need to enter */usr/local/apache/bin/httpd* instead. Of course, make compiles the modules, while make test and make install test and install Apache::Request and Apache:: Cookie. Be aware that make test will work only if you entered correct information when prompted by *Makefile.PL* and when the Perl modules LWP and URI have been installed from CPAN. The great thing about make test, in this case, is that it actually uses our Apache/mod_perl server to test the new Perl modules. This means that, if all the tests passed, Apache::Request and Apache::Cookie will be in complete working order and ready to use.

Apache Startup Bundle

Having a working Apache is all well and good but not worth much unless it's running. If you'd like your Mac OS X box to function as a web server all the time, you may want to create a startup bundle for it. Apple has documented a specification for startup bundles in its Creating System Starter Startup Item Bundles HOWTO (*http://www.opensource.apple.com/projects/documentation/ howto/html/SystemStarter_HOWTO.html*), but it's a simple matter to adapt Mac OS X's existing Apache startup bundle for our purposes.

Apple has created the */System/Library* directory structure for use by the Mac OS X operating system and the */Library* directory structure for use by third-party applications such as our new Apache server. All system startup bundles, including for Apple's build of Apache, go into the */System/Library/StartupItems* directory. The startup bundles for third-party applications go into the */Library/StartupItems* directory. So, to adapt Apple's Apache startup bundle, we'll first copy it to a temporary location. Later, we'll move the copy to its new home:

```
% cp -rf /System/Library/StartupItems/Apache ~/Desktop/
```

This command will copy the entire Apache startup bundle directory structure to the desktop where we can easily edit it. Next, using your favorite editor (TextEdit will work fine), open the *~/Desktop/Apache/Apache* file. The file should look like this:

```
#!/bin/sh

##
# Apache HTTP Server
##

. /etc/rc.common

StartService ()
{
    if [ "${WEBSERVER:=-NO-}" = "-YES-" ]; then
        ConsoleMessage "Starting Apache web server"
        apachectl start
    fi
}

StopService ()
{
    ConsoleMessage "Stopping Apache web server"
    apachectl stop
}

RestartService ()
{
    if [ "${WEBSERVER:=-NO-}" = "-YES-" ]; then
        ConsoleMessage "Restarting Apache web server"
        apachectl restart
    else
        StopService
    fi
}

RunService "$1"
```

This file is a Unix Bourne shell script and is executed whenever your Mac starts up and shuts down. There are essentially two changes we need to make to convert this script for starting our newly-compiled Apache server.

First, change the location of the apachectl startup script. Just calling apachectl will cause Apple's Apache server to start up. To get our new one to start, we need to change the location to */usr/local/apache/bin/apachectl*. Second, change the name of the variable to be checked in each if statement from WEBSERVER to APACHESERVER. The result of our changes to the startup script looks like this:

```sh
#!/bin/sh

##
# Apache HTTP Server
##

. /etc/rc.common

StartService ()
{
    if [ "${APACHESERVER:=-NO-}" = "-YES-" ]; then
        ConsoleMessage "Starting Apache web server"
        /usr/local/apache/bin/apachectl start
    fi
}

StopService ()
{
    ConsoleMessage "Stopping Apache web server"
    /usr/local/apache/bin/apachectl stop
}

RestartService ()
{
    if [ "${APACHESERVER:=-NO-}" = "-YES-" ]; then
        ConsoleMessage "Restarting Apache web server"
        /usr/local/apache/bin/apachectl restart
    else
        StopService
    fi
}

RunService "$1"
```

Next, add the $APACHESERVER variable to */etc/hostconfig*. This file contains all of the variables that are checked in the Mac OS X startup scripts, and we'll need to add ours here, since our new script checks for it. The simplest way to do this is to use the echo command on the command line to append it to the the file:

```
% sudo echo APACHESERVER=-YES- >> /etc/hostconfig
```

You can also edit the file directly using TextEdit, but you must open Text-Edit as the root user in order to be able to edit the file. You can use the sudo utility on the command line to accomplish this:

```
% sudo /Applications/TextEdit.app/Contents/MacOS/TextEdit /etc/hostconfig
```

Once you've added the line APACHESERVER=-YES-, save your changes and quit TextEdit. Now, move the entire startup bundle to its new home in */Library/StartupItems* and test it:

```
% sudo mv ~/Desktop/Apache /Library/StartupItems
% sudo /Library/StartupItems/Apache/Apache start
Starting Apache web server
/usr/local/apache/bin/apachectl start: httpd started
```

Point your browser to your local computer again and make sure a page loads. If it does, you're in business and the Apache server will be started whenever you boot into Mac OS X. If you ever want to prevent Apache from starting at system startup, simply edit */etc/hostconfig* again and change APACHESERVER=-YES- to APACHESERVER=-NO-.

—David E. Wheeler

AppleScript CGI with ACGI Dispatcher

It'd be a shame if you couldn't use AppleScript to automate web-serving tasks with Apache. 'Tis no shame; you can.

When Apple based OS X on a BSD kernel, they sought a way to combine the power of GUI scripting with the power of shell languages like Perl, bash, Python, and more. The result was osascript, a simple shell utility that could run AppleScript from the command line.

That was fine and dandy for interactive or timed usage, but it didn't immediately lend itself to using AppleScript as a CGI through the Apache web server. ACGI Dispatcher from James Sentman, on the other hand, gives that ability quickly, simply, and cheaply.

ACGI Dispatcher costs anywhere from $15 to $90, depending on your needs, and a 30-day trial download is available for testing. Installation is simple: extract, drag the dispatcher to your */Library/WebServer/CGI-Executables* directory, and double-click to finish the installation. You'll be asked for your administrator password so that the following lines can be added to your */etc/httpd/httpd.conf* file:

```
#BEGIN acgi dispatcher
Include /Library/WebServer/CGI-Executables/dispatcher.app/Contents/acgi.conf
#END acgi dispatcher
```

After those lines have been added by the dispatcher program, stop and restart Apache via your Sharing system preference (alternatively, use sudo apachectl restart from the shell). Once the web server has restarted, and with the dispatcher running in the background, you'll be all set to serve AppleScript-based CGI. Thankfully, you can test your new ability with the included *itunes.acgi*.

To control iTunes through a web browser, simply drag *itunes.acgi* into */Library/WebServer/CGI-Executables*, make sure the dispatcher is running, and load *http://127.0.0.1/cgi-bin/itunes.acgi*. Assuming that iTunes is running at the time of your request, you'll see a screen similar to Figure 8-14.

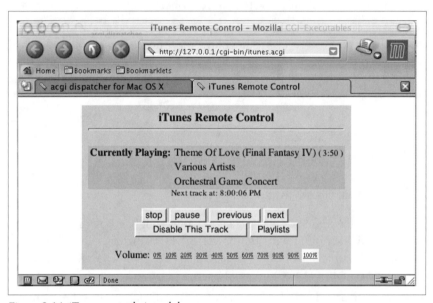

Figure 8-14. iTunes control via web browser

As the screenshot suggests, you have access to any playlists you've previously created (smart lists or otherwise), as well as the standard playback controls. The benefits of having one computer serving *itunes.acgi*, while you change the track from another computer or handheld in another room, are nicer than you'd think. Full source for *itunes.acgi* is provided so that you can modify the output of the page or learn how to create your own AppleScript CGIs.

If you're planning on using ACGI Dispatcher in a production environment, you'll want to make sure to register the software (after 30 days, it'll start displaying expiration warnings on the bottom of your results) and include the dispatcher as part of your Startup Items. Apache can't start the dispatcher automatically, so ensuring that it loads at login is important.

See Also

- ACGI Dispatcher (*http://www.sentman.com/acgi/*)
- Support Forums (*http://www.sentman.com/support/*)

Turning on CGI

#92

CGI scripts allow you to serve up dynamic content on your web site using a Unix-based scripting language like Perl.

It's now time to fiddle with the most commonly used way of generating dynamic content and serving it up on your web server. We're talking about Common Gateway Interface (CGI). Without getting overly esoteric, CGI allows us to install thousands of different scripts that can be accessed through a normal web browser. CGI scripts are most often written in a Unix scripting language like Perl, Python, or Ruby. They can allow users to access databases, use interactive forms, chat in bulletin boards, and so on.

Apache comes with two simple scripts that can verify CGI is configured correctly. Before we test them, however, we've got to poke around our *httpd. conf* file a bit. As mentioned earlier [Hack #89], the easiest way to find out more about a feature is simply to search for the term in question. These are all the relevant matches we'll find in our *httpd.conf* for CGI:

```
LoadModule cgi_module libexec/httpd/mod_cgi.so
AddModule mod_cgi.c

ScriptAlias /cgi-bin/ "/Library/WebServer/CGI-Executables/"

<Directory "/Library/WebServer/CGI-Executables">
  AllowOverride None Options None
  Order allow,deny
  Allow from all
</Directory>

# AddHandler cgi-script .cgi
```

We've already described the first two lines [Hack #89], but the ScriptAlias directive allows us to map a URL to a location on our hard drive. In this case, Apache is mapping *http://127.0.0.1/cgi-bin/* to the */Library/WebServer/ CGI-Executables/* directory. If you browse there now, you'll see the two CGI scripts I offhandedly mentioned earlier: *printenv* and *test-cgi*—we'll run those shortly.

Moving on, <Directory> isn't that important right now, so we'll jaunt off to our final search result, AddHandler. This is your first major decision concerning your Apache installation. When a certain directory has been

ScriptAliased (as our *CGI-Executables* directory has), the files within that directory are always executed as CGI scripts. If the files were moved out of that directory, they'd be served as normal text files.

By uncommenting the AddHandler, you're telling Apache to execute any file that ends in *.cgi*. This can happen from any directory and from any user and is often considered a security hazard.

In a default installation of Apache on Mac OS X, CGI scripts are allowed only within */Library/Webserver/CGI-Executables/*. Uncommenting [Hack #89] the preceding line (removing the # character) allows CGI scripts to be executed from any user directory, such as */Users/morbus/Sites*. It's really your choice, but if you're new to the world of web serving, your best bet is to leave this alone.

If CGI access is turned on already, we should be able to reach *http://127.0.0.1/cgi-bin/test-cgi* and see a happy result, right? If you went to that URL, however, you were probably greeted by a not so joyous response: "FORBIDDEN." Apache screams, "You don't have permission to access */cgi-bin/test-cgi*."

Huh? Why didn't this work? Now is a perfect time to prove how useful the Apache web-server logs can be. Apache's access file is located in */var/log/httpd/access_log*, so let's look at the very last lines of that file, easily reached with this command:

```
% tail /var/log/httpd/access_log
```

You'll see that the last line looks something like this:

```
...
127.0.0.1 - - [19/Nov/2002:21:59:46-0500] "GET /cgi-bin/test-cgi HTTP/1.1"
403 292
```

This line shows where the access request came from (127.0.0.1), the time the file was requested, the protocol used (HTTP/1.1), the response code (403), and the size of the response (292 bytes). This is all fine and dandy, but it doesn't tell us what went wrong. For this, we'll dip into our error log:

```
% tail /var/log/httpd/error_log
```

And we see:

```
...
[Mon Nov 19 21:59:46 2002] [error] [client 127.0.0.1]
file permissions deny server execution:
/Library/WebServer/CGI-Executables/test-cgi
```

Bingo! This tells us exactly what went awry: the file permissions were incorrect. For Apache to run a CGI script, the script in question needs to have execute permissions [Hack #55]. To give the *test-cgi* file the correct permissions, type the following on the command line [Hack #48]:

```
% cd /Library/WebServer/CGI-Executables
% chmod 755 test-cgi
```

After doing this, load the URL again, and you should be happily greeted with gobs of environment information. (To learn more about permissions and the chmod utility, see "More Terminal Tricks and Tips" [Hack #49].)

With the basics of CGI out of the way, you can now install CGI-based applications to complement your intranet. Need a content management system for the developers to keep everyone up-to-date on their coding progress and discussions? Try the Movable Type (*http://www.movabletype.org*) weblog application.

See Also

- Apache Web-Serving with Mac OS X: Part 2 (*http://www.macdevcenter. com/lpt/a//mac/2001/12/14/apache_two.html*)

Turning on PHP

PHP is a fabulous scripting language for beginners to try their hands at serving up dynamic web content.

Much like server-side includes [Hack #94], PHP code is included and interpreted into the actual HTML of your web pages. Here, we'll show you how to turn it on (it's installed by default on OS X), as well as how to certify that it's working properly.

As with the hacks on CGI and SSI, turning on PHP involves searching for the feature name (in this case, php) within the Apache configuration file [Hack #89]. The first entries we'll run into are:

```
# LoadModule php4_module libexec/httpd/libphp4.so

...

# AddModule mod_php4.c
```

These two lines enable (or disable, if commented out with a #) the loading of PHP on Apache web-server startup. Since they're commented out by default, we'll have to uncomment them in order to have the modules loaded and PHP functional. Do so, and the lines should now look like this:

```
LoadModule php4_module libexec/httpd/libphp4.so

...

AddModule mod_php4.c
```

Keep searching for php in the file and you'll find:

```
# For example, the PHP 3.x module will typically use:
#
# AddType application/x-httpd-php3 .php3
# AddType application/x-httpd-php3-source .phps
#
# And for PHP 4.x, use:
#
# AddType application/x-httpd-php .php
# AddType application/x-httpd-php-source .phps
```

 In some OS X installations (notably, 10.2 and higher), you won't see the preceding lines. That's alright; just add them in yourself.

In essence, these lines are saying that any file with the *.php* extension should be processed by the PHP module we just enabled. As we'll see soon enough, Mac OS X (Versions 10.1 and above) comes preinstalled with PHP 4, so go ahead and uncomment the two lines for PHP 4.x, like so:

```
# For example, the PHP 3.x module will typically use:
#
# AddType application/x-httpd-php3 .php3
# AddType application/x-httpd-php3-source .phps
#
# And for PHP 4.x, use:
#
AddType application/x-httpd-php .php
AddType application/x-httpd-php-source .phps
```

Save the Apache configuration file, and restart the web server:

```
% sudo apachectl restart
httpd restarted
```

We're going to return to our Apache error log for a second to illustrate a simple, yet helpful, bit of information. Each time you start Apache, it will spit out a single line telling you that everything has started successfully. With a plain-vanilla Apache server, it usually looks something like this:

```
[notice] Apache/1.3.20 (Darwin) configured -- resuming normal operations
```

When you add a third-party module or feature (like PHP, mod_perl, mod_ssl, etc.), Apache will graciously make mention of it in its startup line. If you just restarted the Apache web server now, take a look at the error log by typing:

```
% tail /var/log/httpd/error_log
```

You should see Apache wax poetic with:

```
[notice] Apache/1.3.20 (Darwin) PHP/4.0.6 configured -- resuming normal
operations
```

Apache tells us that PHP is enabled, but how do we really know for sure? Rather easily, actually. Create a file named *index.php* in your *Sites* directory using the following as its contents:

```
<html>
<body>
<h1>Gleefully Served By Mac OS X</h1>
<? phpinfo( )?>
</body>
</html>
```

Load *index.php* in your browser (*http://127.0.0.1/~morbus/index.php* for me) and you should see a long page full of PHP diagnostic information. PHP has been successfully configured for use.

HACK #94 Turning on Server-Side Includes (SSI)

Server-side includes (SSIs) allow you to include other files or dynamic content in your garden variety HTML document.

Commonly, SSIs are used to include things such as headers, footers, and "What's New?" features across an entire site. When you need to change the background color of your site, for instance, you can change the header file only, and the color will be reflected immediately wherever you've included that file.

This is done by Apache before the page is actually shown to the user; he'll never know what you've included or where.

SSIs, by default, are turned off; no worries, since it's quite simple to turn them on. Open your Apache configuration file [Hack #89] and search for shtml. You should find:

```
# To use server-parsed HTML files
#
#AddType text/html .shtml
#AddHandler server-parsed .shtml
```

Those simple Add lines tell us a lot. They continue a pattern based on what we already know about CGI. If you recall in our Turning on CGI [Hack #92] hack, we could have turned on the CGI feature for files ending in *.cgi*; in other words, any file you created with the *.cgi* extension (whether it was a CGI program or not) would be treated as an executable script.

Likewise, these lines tell us that we can turn on the server-side include feature for files ending in *.shtml*. Whether we actually use the SSI feature in these files doesn't matter; they'll still be treated and processed as if they did.

This is important. You may be thinking, if SSIs are so great, why not enable them for *.html* filenames? Ultimately, it's a matter of speed. If you have 3,000 *.html* files, and only 1,000 of them actually use SSI, Apache will still look for SSI instructions in the other 2,000. That's a colossal waste of resources. Granted, processing SSI incurs very little overhead, but if you're being hit 50,000 times a second, it can certainly add up.

For now, uncomment the AddType and AddHandler lines:

```
# To use server-parsed HTML files
#
AddType text/html .shtml
AddHandler server-parsed .shtml
```

This will turn on the SSI mojo power. But where? When we were learning about CGI, we saw a configuration setting that said our CGIs lived in */Library/Webserver/CGI-Executables/*. We need to tell Apache where we want SSI capability.

For now, we'll just assume anything in Apache's document directory, */Library/Webserver/Documents*, should be allowed to use SSI. Search your configuration file for /Library/Webserver/Documents/. We're after the following piece of configuration:

```
<Directory "/Library/WebServer/Documents">

    #
    # This may also be "None", "All", or any combination of "Indexes",
    # "Includes", "FollowSymLinks", "ExecCGI", or "MultiViews".
    #
    # Note that "MultiViews" must be named *explicitly* --- "Options All"
    # doesn't give it to you.
    #
    Options Indexes FollowSymLinks MultiViews

    #
    # This controls which Options the .htaccess files in directories can
    # override. Can also be "All", or any combination of "Options", "FileInfo",
    # "AuthConfig", and "Limit"
    #
    AllowOverride None

    #
    # Controls who can get stuff from this server.
    #
    Order allow,deny
    Allow from all
</Directory>
```

We're going to skip the brunt of what this entire configuration means, but for now, add the word Includes to the Options line:

```
<Directory "/Library/WebServer/Documents">
...
Options Indexes FollowSymLinks MultiViews Includes
...
</Directory>
```

Options is an Apache directive that can turn on or off different features for the <Directory> and all subdirectories beneath it. Subdirectories can override their parent configuration. Simply by adding Includes, we're allowing SSI in the main document directory.

Because we've made changes to Apache's configuration file, we now need to restart Apache:

```
% sudo apachectl restart
httpd restarted
```

To test that our SSIs are working properly, create an *index.shtml* file (because *.shtml* is the only extension we've enabled SSIs for) in the */Library/WebServer/Documents* directory, and edit to match the following snippet:

```
<html>
<body>
<h1>Gleefully Served By Mac OS X</h1>
<pre><!--#include virtual="/cgi-bin/test-cgi"--></pre>
</body>
</html>
```

Here, we're including a test CGI script into the contents of our main index page. When you load *http://127.0.0.1/index.shtml* (assuming you placed *index.shtml* in */Library/Webserver/Documents/*), you'll see our Gleefully Served message, as well as the output of the CGI script itself. We could just have easily created a static web page (say, *navigation.html*) and included that within our page instead.

SSI is configured and working, but what can you do with it? What if your marketing department wants to create an image gallery of the newest ads they've planned? Take a look at the SSI Image Gallery URL under "See Also" for one search engine–friendly way of doing it. Be sure to explore the Apache SSI documentation for more possibilities.

See Also

- Apache Web-Serving with Mac OS X: Part 2 (*http://www.macdevcenter. com/lpt/a//mac/2001/12/14/apache_two.html*)
- SSI Image Gallery (*http://evolt.org/article/Search_Engine_Friendly_SSI_ Image_Gallery/20/15882/index.html*)
- Apache mod_include Documentation (*http://httpd.apache.org/docs/mod/ mod_include.html*)

Turning on WebDAV

Share a space on your web server for remote file sharing and collaboration.

WebDAV (Web-based Distributed Authoring and Versioning, also called DAV) is a set of extensions to HTTP/1.1 (Hypertext Transfer Protocol, the protocol spoken by web browsers and servers) allowing you to edit documents on a remote web server. DAV provides support for:

Editing
> Creating, updating, deleting

Properties
> Title, author, publication date, and so on

Collections
> Analogous to a filesystem's directory or desktop folder

Locking
> Prevents the confusion and data corruption caused by two or more people editing the same content at the same time

WebDAV is platform-independent, both in terms of client and server. This means that Macintosh, Unix, and Windows users can collaborate on web content without all the usual conversion problems. Furthermore, it doesn't matter whether your documents are hosted on an Apache or Microsoft IIS server.

WebDAV is software agnostic. As long as your web-authoring tools are DAV-compliant, it makes little difference which particular product you're using.

WebDAV is (at least should be) seamless. Because DAV is simply a set of extensions to HTTP, it's easy for companies to build support into any product that already understands the Web. And, since DAV rides on top of HTTP, firewalls tend not to get in the way of accessing your web content remotely.

WebDAV makes use of the standard authorization and authentication methods built right into every web server. In the same manner as one restricts access to a portion (whether a file, folder, or entire site) of one's web site to a particular set of users or machines, so too can one finely tune WebDAV access to resources.

Mac OS X and WebDAV

While Mac OS X doesn't provide Apache support for providing WebDAV shares right out of the box, WebDAV functionality is available as a small downloadable module, easy to build and configure.

Install the Apache mod_dav Module

Download [Hack #61] the latest mod_dav module (*http://www.webdav.org/mod_dav/*) and extract it using Terminal [Hack #49]; I chose to use tar:

```
% curl -O http://www.webdav.org/mod_dav/mod_dav-1.0.3-1.3.6.tar.gz
% tar -xvzf mod_dav-1.0.3-1.3.6.tar.gz
mod_dav-1.0.3-1.3.6
mod_dav-1.0.3-1.3.6/sdbm
...
mod_dav-1.0.3-1.3.6/mod_dav.mak
mod_dav-1.0.3-1.3.6/autogen.sh
```

With the archive unpacked, it's time to build the module. It goes a little something like this:

```
% cd mod_dav-1.0.3-1.3.6
% ./configure
% ./make
% ./sudo make install
```

Between each command, the screen will fill with line after line of incomprehensible jibberish. I've left these out for brevity's sake; the only thing to watch out for is the process suddenly stopping with an error.

The module should now safely be installed in the right location (along with the other Apache modules) and DAV minimally enabled in the Apache server configuration. But there's more to do than simply making Apache aware of its new WebDAV functionality.

Configure WebDAV in Apache

Open [Hack #51] the Apache server's main configuration file [Hack #89], */etc/httpd/httpd.conf*, for editing. You'll need to authenticate yourself as an administrator using sudo [Hack #50] to do so:

```
% sudo pico /etc/httpd/httpd.conf
```

Zoom down to the end of the file and add the following text:

```
DAVLockDB /etc/httpd/dav/DAVLock
DAVMinTimeout 600
<Location /dav/>
  DAV On
  AuthType Basic
  AuthName "WebDAV Restricted"
  AuthUserFile /etc/httpd/dav/.passwd
  <LimitExcept GET HEAD OPTIONS>
    Require valid-user
</LimitExcept>
</Location>
```

The first line sets up a database file that WebDAV uses to track who's editing which file. It will lock a file to prevent something dangerous from happening, such as two people trying to update it at once. The second line tells the web server not to wait forever if the remote computer loses connection with it. The `<Location>` tags set the context of the WebDAV settings to be for the directory */dav*, which we will set up under the document root.

The security we're using is `AuthTypeBasic`, which requires a username and password to make modifications. The password will be stored in a file called */Library/WebServer/.passwd*, and the username required is webdav.

> There is a risk to using basic authentication. The username and password are weakly encoded, so it is possible that someone could listen to your network and steal the password. A few years ago, a new authentication scheme called *digest authentication* was developed for Apache. This scheme uses strong encryption to protect the password.
>
> Unfortunately, the digest-authentication module that ships with Apache Version 1.3 (the one that comes with Mac OS 10.2) is old and not compatible with most browsers and client software. My attempts to use it with iCal failed. There is a more recent version of the module, but it requires Apache Version 2.0, which is not trivial to set up and therefore out of the scope of this hack. Hopefully, Apple will upgrade Apache to a more modern version, but in the meantime, keep an eye out for an Apache v2 package that will compile on Darwin (perhaps from the Fink project).

The `<LimitExcept>` directive gives us some protection from malicious intent. First, it locks down all the actions that can be performed on WebDAV files except those that are read-only. Second, it limits the write privileges to one user, named webdav. This user will not have any other abilities on the system but to write files in this directory.

Setting Up Directories

First, you need to set up the realm of WebDAV documents. Based on what we put in the configuration file, this will be in a subdirectory of the document root called */dav* (that's */Library/WebServer/Documents/dav*). You'll need to create that directory yourself, as well as changing the permissions and ownership so that the web server can write to it.

```
% sudo mkdir /Library/WebServer/Documents/dav
% sudo chgrp www /Library/WebServer/Documents/dav
% sudo chmod 775 /Library/WebServer/Documents/dav
```

Next, you need to find a place for the WebDAV lock database file. For lack of a better place, I created a directory alongside the *httpd.conf* configuration file, */etc/httpd/dav*. Again, set the permissions so that the server can write files here:

```
% sudo mkdir /etc/httpd/dav
% sudo chgrp www /etc/httpd/dav
% sudo chmod 775 /etc/httpd/dav
```

Creating Users

While our configuration specifies that only valid users [Hack #97] are allowed to alter the contents of the *dav* directory via WebDAV, we've not yet created said users. We'll do so now.

Don't use an existing user's name and password. A malicious hacker sniffing your communications can grab that username and use it to sneak inside your system. The username we will create will be limited to WebDAV files only, which will be useless to a would-be intruder.

First, create a password file using the htpasswd utility. (Again, to keep everything related to DAV together, I used */etc/httpd/dav/*.) You'll simultaneously create a user account and password for webdav. You'll be prompted for a password. Invent something secure and save it someplace safe. Make the password unique (don't use one that you use elsewhere), because of the basic authentication risk I mentioned earlier.

```
% htpasswd -c /etc/httpd/dav/.passwd webdav
New password:
Re-type new password:
Adding password for user webdav
```

Restart the Server

An apache control script, apachectl, does away with the need to kill and restart the Apache server by hand. Simply issue a start, stop, or restart and apachectl will comply. In this case, you want to restart the server, so type:

```
% sudo apachectl restart
/usr/sbin/apachectl restart: httpd restarted
```

If Apache isn't already running, apachectl is smart enough to go ahead and start it up for you:

```
% sudo apachectl restart
/usr/sbin/apachectl restart: httpd not running, trying to start
Processing config directory: /private/etc/httpd/users
Processing config file: /private/etc/httpd/users/rael.conf
/usr/sbin/apachectl restart: httpd started
```

Your WebDAV server is now ready for use by anyone (with the proper authentication, that is) who can reach your Web server. Mac OS X has built-in support for mounting WebDAV shares **[Hack #74]** and treating them like just about any other hard drive.

Did you know that iDisk is WebDAV-based?

See Also

- "Publishing and Subscribing to iCal Calendars" **[Hack #30]**
- "Backing Up on the Go" **[Hack #3]**
- WebDAV Resources (*http://www.webdav.org*)

—*Erik T. Ray and Rael Dornfest*

Controlling Web-Server Access
#96 by Hostname or IP Address

It's easy as pie to get Apache serving something exciting, but at times, the joy of a running web server needs to be curbed by the stern eye of security. We'll take a quick look at how to enable hostname or IP access control, creating a set of acceptance or denial rules for content we want restricted.

While Apache can certainly handle authenticated access control, we're only going to touch on the location-based side of it for this hack (we get to user-names and passwords in our next one). To protect our Apache server, we're going to open *httpd.conf* **[Hack #89]** with our favorite text editor and modify (or define) the directory we want protected. In our example, we're going to protect the entire web server, so we'll look for our document root, which should look something like this:

```
<Directory "/Library/WebServer/Documents">
  Options Indexes FollowSymLinks MultiViews
  AllowOverride None
  Order Allow,Deny
  Allow from all
</Directory>
```

Quite simply, the Order Allow,Deny and Allow from all lines are the magic that will stop outside visitors from perusing our site. Right now, as these lines stand, we're wide open to the public. This is what we're going to end up with:

```
<Directory "/Library/WebServer/Documents">
  Options Includes FollowSymLinks MultiViews
```

```
   AllowOverride None
   Order Deny,Allow
   Deny from all
   Allow from gatesmcfaddenco.org
</Directory>
```

See what we've done here? The first thing we did was flip our Order directive. This tells Apache to process all Deny rules first, and then all the remaining Allow rules. Likewise, our first Deny is from all, meaning no one can come knocking. If we denied everyone, of course, no one would be able to see our site, so we add an Allow rule for a domain of our choosing. We can also Allow and Deny by IP, such as Allow from 209.204.146. This will allow access to anyone from within that block, but no one from without.

Once you've made these changes, restart Apache (type sudo apache restart) and you'll be protected nicely from the outside world, serving up pages only to allowed sites.

See Also

- Apache's mod_access documentation (*http://httpd.apache.org/docs/mod/ mod_access.html*)

HACK #97 Controlling Web-Server Access by Username and Group

Controlling access by hostname or IP is great when you want to ensure that only a network or machine you recognize is accessing your site or to block that pesky web spider that rudely ignores your robots.txt file. It is, however, used less often than user-based authentication.

To start the process, we're first going to create the user database. This database will contain all the usernames and passwords that will be authenticated against; they're not keyed to any specific directory, so you could use one database for 300 users spread across two dozen directories. To create the database, get into your Terminal and gaze blurry-eyed at the following command:

```
% htpasswd -c /Library/WebServer/.htpasswd morbus
```

It's nice and innocent, right? htpasswd is the name of the utility that creates and modifies the user database. The -c flag says if this database doesn't exist, create it. /Library/WebServer/.htpasswd is the full path to our database file, and you'll want to take special notice that it's outside Apache's document root (which, in OS X, is defined as /Library/WebServer/ Documents). Sticking the file outside the document root ensures that no one can view this database from the Web. Finally, morbus is the user that you want to add to the database. Here's sample output from this command:

```
% htpasswd -c /Library/WebServer/.htpasswd morbus
New password: ********
Re-type new password: ********
Adding password for user morbus
```

You'll want to make sure that when you add new users to an existing database file that you do not use the -c flag. Doing so will overwrite your existing file with a brand-new one. Adding a user is a simple matter (note the lack of the -c flag):

```
% htpasswd /Library/WebServer/.htpasswd imam
New password: *********
Re-type new password: *********
Adding password for user imam
```

If you look at /Library/WebServer/.htpasswd, you'll see the added users:

```
% cat /Library/WebServer/.htpasswd
morbus:Vcv7xTIIW6g7U
imam:3c4T6IdfWweU
```

Next, it's really just a matter of telling Apache which directory we want to secure. You can insert the following block of code into your *httpd.conf* file; it'll protect the entire web server:

```
<Directory /Library/WebServer/Documents>
  AuthName "Protected Directory"
  AuthType Basic
  AuthUserFile /Library/WebServer/.htpasswd
  require valid-user
</Directory>
```

AuthName will appear as the title or description in the password box that a visitor's browser will show, whereas AuthType is set to the standard basic authentication (a digest authentication exists but is outside the scope of this hack). AuthUserFile should be self-explanatory.

The require line affords some discussion. With it, you can tell Apache to allow any user in the AuthUserFile access (as we've done earlier), or you can tell Apache to allow only certain people. In the following example, only the users morbus and imam can authenticate to realms with the name Protected Directory. Any other users in the AuthUserFile will be denied:

```
  require user morbus imam
```

Users can also be defined by groups; for example, you could place dan, sbp, and morbus into a group called Marketing, and steve, geomisk, and sal into a group called Design. From there, you could restrict access by group instead of username. For these configurations and more about digest authentication, refer to Apache's authentication documentation (*http://httpd.apache.org/docs/howto/auth.html*).

Directory Aliasing, Indexing, and Autoindexing

A few more Apache configuration hacks involving creating an alias to a file outside the normal Apache document hierarchy and customizing the look-and-feel of directory listings.

When it comes to URLs that end in slashes and resolve to a directory on your web site, Apache can serve data two different ways. The most common is to serve the directory index, a list of filenames that can be used in place of the directory slash. The other possibility is to have Apache generate a bland list of filenames. In this hack, we'll talk about modifying the directory index to match your needs, as well as making that bland autoindex more attractive.

Aliases

Before we begin indexes, let's talk about aliasing. If you've read "Turning on CGI" [Hack #92], you'll know a `ScriptAlias` directive is a way to map a URL to a location on our hard drive. You can read more about the other capabilities of Apache's mod_alias at the Apache web site (*http://httpd.apache.org/docs/mod/mod_alias.html*), but here's a simple example of making */Users/morbus/Pictures/* accessible as *http://127.0.0.1/morbus/pictures/*:

```
Alias /~morbus/pictures/ "/Users/morbus/Pictures/"
```

When creating aliases like this, you want to be careful about permissions. Mac users have never had to deal with permissions before, so they can be an interesting thing to muddle through. We won't get into a detailed description here, but in a simplified nutshell:

- User directories like *Pictures, Library, Music,* and so forth are not normally viewable by the Apache web server; the permissions are too restrictive.

- Simply creating an alias probably will not work. Sure, you're telling Apache to serve files from that location, but that directory is still protected from other users (one of them is *www*, which Apache runs as). Again, the permissions are still too restrictive.

- In this case, to give Apache permission to access the */Users/morbus/Pictures/* directory, we need to say `chmod 755 /Users/morbus/Pictures` in our Terminal [Hack #48]. This loosens the permissions and allows Apache to read from, but not write to, files in that directory.

Here's another example of aliasing, only more powerful:

```
<Directory "/Developer/Documentation/">
  Options FollowSymLinks Indexes
</Directory>

AliasMatch ^/~morbus/docs/(.*) "/Developer/Documentation/"
```

Here, we're taking every file and directory accessed under */Users/morbus/docs* and instead serving them from */Developer/Documentation*. Accessing *http://127.0.0.1/~morbus/docs/Carbon/carbon.html* would serve */Developer/Documentation/Carbon/carbon.html*; likewise, *http://127.0.0.1/~morbus/docs/Carbon/* would return an index of the entire */Developer/Documentation/Carbon/* directory.

Directory Indexes

Why does Apache sometimes serve a listing of files in a directory, as it did for *Carbon/*, and other times serve an HTML document, often called *index.html*? The key is a directive within the Apache configuration file called DirectoryIndex. By default, on OS X it's:

```
DirectoryIndex index.html
```

What this means is that if a file called *index.html* is in a directory, Apache will serve that file instead of autogenerating a file listing. Remove the file, and Apache's back to spitting out what it can find: the contents of the directory itself.

We're not restricted to only one possible directory index. We could use *index.html* all of the time, *index.php* some of the time, and perhaps insomnia caused the rather suggestive *zzzdex.shtml*. Apache can be told to look for all of these, in order of preference:

```
DirectoryIndex index.html index.php index.cgi zzzdex.shtml
```

In this case, we're saying "Hey, if someone doesn't request a particular file in a URL, then look for *index.html*. If it's there, cool, display that. If not, try looking for *index.php*. If that's not there, try *zzzdex.shtml*. If that's not there, then yeah, I suppose you can automatically generate an index."

You can add as many entries as you wish to the DirectoryIndex, but you do want to try to keep the most common filename first. If you're serving thousands of pages a second, a properly ordered directory index will save you a tiny bit of time and processing.

Customizing the Directory Listing

There are times when we do want Apache to autogenerate a listing, and the mod_autoindex (*http://httpd.apache.org/docs/mod/mod_autoindex.html*) Apache module gives us a lot of power in customizing the autogenerated appearance. For instance, you can control the initial sorting order, the descriptions of the files shown, and even include headers or footers (in HTML with optional server-side includes or plain text).

Take the following example. This will add a descriptive element to all our JPEG images and a different description to all our PHP files. When Apache autogenerates the index, it'll display our blurbage for each matching file:

```
<Directory "/Users/morbus/Sites/">
  Options Includes Indexes Multiviews
  AllowOverride All
  IndexOptions FancyIndexing
  AddDescription "This is a short description" *.jpg
  AddDescription "This is a description of questionable quality." *.php
</Directory>
```

There's one problem, however, and that's length. With the look-and-feel of Apache's autoindex, the description is either cut off arbitrarily, or else the browser will scroll the data off screen. That's where HeaderName and ReadmeName come in. These directives tell Apache which files to use as the header (controlled by HeaderName) and footer (controlled by ReadmeName) of a directory listing. By default, these files are *HEADER.txt* (or *HEADER.html*) and *README.txt* (or *README.html*), respectively.

With that in mind, I'll create *HEADER.html*, like so:

```
<html>
<head>
<style type="text/css"><!--
pre { font-size: 14px; font-family: times, serif; }
--></style>
</head>
<body>
<h1>Smurferific Directory Listings</h1>
```

I'll also tweak the configuration a little:

```
<Directory "/Users/morbus/Sites/">
  Options Includes Indexes Multiviews
  AllowOverride All
  IndexOptions FancyIndexing SuppressHTMLPreamble DescriptionWidth=*
  AddDescription "This is a <u>short</u> description" *.jpg
  AddDescription "This is a description of questionable quality." *.php
</Directory>
```

Besides the fact that we've now added our own HTML header that makes the font smaller (via *HEADER.html*), we've also told Apache not to spit out its normal header code (with SuppressHTMLPreamble). Our descriptions will no longer be truncated, since we've given ourselves unlimited length via DescriptionWidth (they may still scroll off the end of the browser window, though).

You may also notice that we've added an underline to one of our descriptions. Including HTML within the `AddDescription` comes with no restrictions, but you do want to be careful about truncating. If you're not, the HTML code could be cut in half, distorting the rest of your page (in the previous code, there's nothing to worry about, since we've turned off truncating with `DescriptionWidth`).

There are many other options available. With a little ingenuity, a user wanting to offer a large collection of downloadable files could have a complete web site in 10 minutes. Think of it—thousands of MP3s sorted and described, using only two HTML files and some `AddDescription` lines. Need to add a new song? Just stick it in the directory, add a description, and you're done. No muss, no fuss, and you didn't need any database or programming knowledge.

Of course, you may not like the idea that millions of anonymous Internet users could leech your MP3 collection. With the tips described in "Controlling Web-Server Access by Username and Group" **[Hack #97]**, you'll be able to stop the tragedy of the commons and restore a little more order.

Databases
Hacks 99–100

Long the backbone of just about any open source–driven web site, the MySQL and PostgreSQL database engines are just as at home on your Mac as they have been in the more traditional Unix shop. With front ends like SQL4X and MacSQL, you needn't fear being restricted to a command line–only view of your data. And the combination of Apache web server, MySQL database, and web-scripting capabilities of PHP provide you all you need to build amazing, dynamic, content-driven web sites.

This chapter walks you through the installation and exploration of these two remarkable database applications, both on the command line and the desktop.

HACK #99 Installing the MySQL Database

Add the functionality of the most popular open source database server to the underpinnings of your Mac-powered web site.

MySQL is one of the most popular database servers, available for all flavors of Linux, Windows, and now Mac OS X. Due to its immense popularity, you'll often see web hosts and ISPs offering it as one of the default features for new accounts. It's a good database to get your feet wet with.

One of the drawbacks to its popularity, however, is the number of ways you can install it. There are various double-clickable packages available, as well as various ways to install and compile from source. We'll be focusing on the two I found best:

- Marc Liyanage's double-clickable MySQL 3.23.49 (*http://www.entropy. ch/software/macosx/mysql/*)

- MySQL's compilable MySQL 3.23.49 source code (*http://www.mysql. com/downloads/mysql-3.23.html*)

Before we go much further, we have to create a MySQL user. This is the account that our MySQL server will run itself as. (Whereas you may be the morbus user, and the administrative account would be the root user, our MySQL server will run as the mysql user.)

Creating this account is rather simple:

1. Click on your Apple menu.
2. Choose System Preferences.
3. Click the Users Preference panel.
4. Click New User.
5. For Name, enter mysql User.
6. For Short Name, enter mysql.

The Login Picture and Password can be anything you wish. Once you've got all the information filled in, click the OK button, and you'll see the mysql User entry in the User list. This step is required both for the double-clickable install and for compiling the source code—don't skip it.

Installing the MySQL Package

We're ready to move on with our double-clickable install, so download the MySQL 3.23.49 package from Marc's site (*http://www2.entropy.ch/download/mysql-3.23.49.pkg.tar.gz*). Once the download is complete, the install is much like any other OS X package; you'll need an administrative password, and a few button clicks later, the installer will be finished.

That's the extent of installing MySQL in package form—nothing fancy, really. There are a few more steps to configuring a properly working MySQL database, but since they're needed for both the packaged and compiled versions, we'll get to them after the next section. You can skim on down to "Post-Installation Wrap Up."

Compiling MySQL from Source

Compiling MySQL from source is relatively easy. In the next few steps, we'll create and install the MySQL database with the same configuration as the one available in the prepackaged form discussed earlier. To compile MySQL, you'll need access to your Terminal and an administrative password. Also, the latest OS X Developer Tools should be installed.

 If you've installed the packaged version of MySQL (discussed earlier), you do *not* need to do anything in this section.

The first thing, obviously, is to get the source code itself. You can find the closest mirror on the MySQL site (*http://www.mysql.com/downloads/mirrors. html*). Once the download is complete, get into your Terminal [Hack #48], create and move into the */usr/local/src/* directory:

```
% cd /usr/local
% sudo mkdir src
Password:
% cd src
```

When you're installing something new on a Linux-like system (such as Mac OS X), you really should keep most of your efforts and work environment centered around the */usr/local/* directory. This helps give a distinctive separation between software installed by the operating system and software installed by you. When you install the MySQL package (as shown previously), for example, it installs everything into */usr/local/mysql-3.23.49/*, including an alias (called a symlink in Linux terms) from */usr/local/mysql/*.

Next, we decompress our downloaded file (your path and filename will be different):

```
% sudo tar -zxvf /Users/morbus/Desktop/mysql.gz
```

We then move into the new directory (again, yours will probably be different):

```
% cd mysql-3.23.49/
```

At this point, you're going to use three commands that are very common when compiling source code. The first command is configure and, funnily enough, it creates a configuration file that is used by the other two commands. In most cases, this is where you choose how you want your program to act, where you want it installed, and so on.

The configure line for MySQL is simply:

```
% sudo ./configure --mandir=/usr/local/share/man --with-innodb
```

This line gives us an example of two things we can do with a configure statement. The first option, --mandir=/usr/local/share/man, shows an example of how you can override a built-in default. In this case, we're saying, "No, MySQL, don't install the documentation in the normal directory; install it over in this one instead."

The second option, --with-innodb, is an example of turning a feature on—one that normally is not. In this case, innodb is a way of adding foreign keys, transactions, and more to MySQL. Getting into what this really means is outside the scope of this hack; if you're interested, you can check out InnoDB's web site (*http://www.innodb.com/*) for more information.

After you run the previous command line, you'll see a decent amount of output, most of which probably won't make sense. That's OK, though;

configure scripts often check your build environment to make sure they know everything they need to do before you actually compile the source code. In essence, they're taking all the guesswork out of the eventual compilation. As long as there are no glaring errors (there shouldn't be), you can move on.

The next step is the actual compilation phase. This is where you take the source code you've configured and turn it into an executable program for OS X. To do this, simply enter the following:

```
% sudo make
```

make will take a look at the configuration you created (using that configure command) and go about creating a custom installation based on your whims and desires. Often, this can take minutes; it can also take seconds. (On my Dual 450 G4, it took a good eight or nine minutes, with three or four other programs open.) Either way, you're going to see a lot of stuff saunter by on your screen. You don't have to worry about reading or understanding it all; this is the art of a compile-in-progress.

Be careful that you don't get confused by the concepts of compiling and installing. Just because we're compiling our source code with make, there's no guarantee that we can use it to conquer the world. Our last command in our trio-of-temerity handles that aspect:

```
% sudo make install
```

This command simply takes all of the compiled code from our make and installs it in the places we've requested (said places being overridable using the configure command, if you recall). After you run make install, the code you've compiled is ready for your use. You can either begin using the program right away, or you can continue tweaking extra settings.

In MySQL's case, there are a few more commands we need to run—basic steps that ensure a properly running MySQL. Read on, stalwart traveler!

Post-Installation Wrap Up

Depending on how you installed MySQL (either as a package or by compiling the source code), certain files will be in different places under the /usr/local/ directory. This is normal and is covered in the install documentation, which I've excerpted later in this hack.

In the case of the package installation, your directory layout is shown here, with /usr/local/mysql/ being a symlink to /usr/local/mysql-3.23.49/ (note, however, that the client programs and server are also installed in /usr/local/bin/):

```
*Directory*                      *Contents of directory*
`/usr/local/mysql-3.23.49/bin'   Client programs and the server
`/usr/local/mysql-3.23.49/data'  Log files, databases
```

```
`/usr/local/mysql-3.23.49/include'    Include (header) files
`/usr/local/mysql-3.23.49/lib'        Libraries
`/usr/local/mysql-3.23.49/scripts'    `mysql_install_db'
`/usr/local/mysql-3.23.49/share/mysql' Error message files
`/usr/local/mysql-3.23.49/sql-bench'  Benchmarks
```

If you compiled from source, your directory structure becomes:

```
*Directory*                  *Contents of directory*
`/usr/local/bin'             Client programs and scripts
`/usr/local/include/mysql'   Include (header) files
`/usr/local/info'            Documentation in Info format
`/usr/local/lib/mysql'       Libraries
`/usr/local/libexec'         The `mysqld' server
`/usr/local/share/mysql'     Error message files
`/usr/local/sql-bench'       Benchmarks and `crash-me' test
`/usr/local/var'             Databases and log files
```

With the preceding hierarchy, your final steps are within walking distance.

For package installations:

```
% cd /usr/local/mysql/
% sudo ./scripts/mysql_install_db
% sudo chown -R mysql /usr/local/mysql
% sudo ./bin/safe_mysqld --user=mysql &
```

For source installations:

```
% cd /usr/local/
% sudo ./bin/mysql_install_db
% sudo chown -R mysql /usr/local/var
% sudo ./bin/safe_mysqld --user=mysql &
```

These orders will initialize the core MySQL database (which takes care of access control), as well as start the MySQL server in the background. If everything goes smoothly, you should see something similar to this (the pathname is based on which install you chose earlier):

```
Starting mysqld daemon with databases from /usr/local/var
```

Hello, MySQL!

If the foregoing steps went smoothly, it's time to make a quick PHP script to make sure database communication is possible. Copy the following code into your favorite text editor (like BBEdit (*http://www.barebones.com/*)), and save the file as *test.php* within a web-site directory (either */Library/WebServer/Documents/* or */Users/morbus/Sites*, for example).

> In order for this to work, you should have already turned on PHP [Hack #93] in your onboard Apache web server. If you've not already done so, do so first and then come right back.

```
<?
print "<pre>";

 // log into our local server using the mysql root user.
$dbh = mysql_connect( "localhost", "root", "" );


// select the 'test' database created during installation.
mysql_select_db( "test" ) or die ( mysql_error() . "\n" );
print "Connection to the database has been established.\n";


// create a simplistic table.
$table = "CREATE table wisdom ( ↵
id int(4) PRIMARY KEY AUTO_INCREMENT, ↵
wisdom char(255), author char(125) );";

 $response = mysql_query( $table, $dbh );
if ($response) { print "The table was created correctly!\n"; }
else { print mysql_error () . "\n"; }


// now, we'll add some data to our newly created table.
// to add different wisdom, just change the 'values'.
$INSERT_data = "INSERT into wisdom ( wisdom, author ) ↵
values ( 'Hello, World!', 'morbus' );";

 $response = mysql_query( $INSERT_data, $dbh );
if ($response) { print "The data was INSERTed correctly!\n"; }
else { print mysql_error () . "\n"; }


// and read it back for printing purposes.
$get_table_data = "SELECT * FROM wisdom;";
$response = mysql_query( $get_table_data, $dbh );
if ($response) { print "We successfully got all the table data.\n"; }
else { print mysql_error () . "\n"; }


// now print it out for the user.
while ( $one_line_of_data = mysql_fetch_array( $response ) ) {
  extract ( $one_line_of_data );
  print "#$id: $author sez: \"$wisdom\"\n";
}

 print "</pre>";
?>
```

We're not going to explore the syntax of the PHP script or the SQL commands that are used. Suffice it to say that this script will create a table in the MySQL test database, add some data, and then spit back the total contents of the wisdom table. If you need a brush-up on PHP or MySQL, be sure to check out ONLamp.com (*http://www.onlamp.com/*).

After you've saved the file, load it in your web browser. I saved my copy in */Users/morbus/Sites/test.php*, so I loaded *http://127.0.0.1/~morbus/test.php* in my browser. After the first run, this is what I saw:

```
Connection to the database has been established.
The table was created correctly!
The data was inserted correctly!
We successfully got all the table data.
#1: Morbus sez: "Hello, World!"
```

If I continue running the script, changing the INSERT line each time, my output will start to look like this:

```
Connection to the database has been established.
Table 'wisdom' already exists
The data was inserted correctly!
We successfully got all the table data.
#1: Morbus sez: "Hello, World!"
#2: Morbus sez: "Here is one more."
#3: Morbus sez: "And another."
```

This output certifies that our PHP-to-MySQL communication is working perfectly.

Two Minor Additions

When we turn on our web server (through the System Preferences → Sharing panel), OS X will happily restart Apache if our machine ever needs a reboot. Out of the box, MySQL doesn't restart automatically. Thankfully, there's a double-clickable solution (*http://www2.entropy.ch/download/mysql-StartupItem.pkg.tar.gz*), again from Marc Liyanage. Upon installing this startup item, MySQL will be at your beck and call after every reboot.

With the previous instructions, MySQL is woefully unsecured. Anyone can become the administrative MySQL user and wreak havoc with our data. This may not be an issue if you're using MySQL on a development machine, but publicly accessible servers need protection. Much as OS X has a root user with ultimate control over the machine, MySQL also has a root user that has ultimate control over the database server.

By default, the MySQL root user has no password assigned to it. If you take a gander back at our PHP script, you'll see that we connect to our database with that field blank:

```
...
// log into our local server using the mysql root user.
$dbh = mysql_connect( "localhost", "root", "" );
...
```

The simplest step in beginning to secure our database server is to set a password for MySQL's root user. To do so, enter the following in a Terminal:

```
% mysqladmin -u root password new_password_here
```

Once we do that, we'll have to modify our PHP code as well:

```
...
// log into our local server using the mysql root user.
$dbh = mysql_connect( "localhost", "root", "new_password_here" );
...
```

HACK 100 Installing the PostgreSQL Database

The PostgreSQL database has good third-party support from developers and passes the ACID (Atomicity, Consistency, Isolation, and Durability) test. What more could you want from an open source database?

Are you a longtime Mac user curious about working with databases in the past but scared away by prohibitive prices? Are you new to Apple and would like to put your prior database experience to use on the Mac? If you're either, read on. I'm going to walk you through installing PostgreSQL (*http://PostgreSQL.org/PostgreSQL.mp3*) on Mac OS X (I'm using 10.1.4), as well as using SQL tools with it and connecting to PostgreSQL with Java. The Java bit is at the tail end of this piece so that if programming (or Java itself) isn't your thing you can easily skip it.

I'm a new Mac user. I recently made the switch from Windows 2000 to Mac OS X and have become comfortable enough in my new environment to flex some of my database skills on this exciting new platform—having worked with everything from MS Access to Oracle in the past. I've kept up with some of the high-level news about what is going on in the open source DBMS realm. So when I pondered which DBMS I should install on my Mac, PostgreSQL was the rather quick answer. It has good third-party support from developers, and it passes the ACID test (*http://www.orafaq.com/glossary/faqglosa.htm*).

Installation

If you don't already have a current version of Apple's Developer Tools [Hack #55], now is the time to get and install them. We'll be using the compiler during installation of PostgreSQL.

All right, now let's get PostgreSQL. You can download PostgreSQL 7.2.1 via FTP (*ftp://ftp.us.PostgreSQL.org/v7.2.1/PostgreSQL-7.2.1.tar.gz*) or HTTP (*http://www.PostgreSQL.org/ftpsite/v7.2.1/PostgreSQL-7.2.1.tar.gz*). I saved the file to my Desktop, but you can save it wherever you wish. Use StuffIt Expander to extract the files.

To install PostgreSQL, open the Terminal [Hack #48] and navigate to the folder containing your newly unstuffed copy of the PostgreSQL source.

The first step is to configure the installation. configure will sniff out the proper system variables to set for Mac OS X (10.1 or later is required). Several files will be created in the build tree to record these customizations. To run the configure script, you must type ./configure at the command line. However, we are not ready to run the script just yet. First, let's discuss a few switches we can append to customize our configuration.

PostgreSQL will install into */usr/local/pgsql* by default. Since we're installing to Mac OS, we want to change this directory to something more appropriate. You can do this by specifying the command-line option --prefix=/Users/Shared/PostgreSQL.

Because I realize the audience for this hack is international, we're also going to include locale support. We do this by passing the argument --enable-locale. Additionally, if you plan to use your database with an interface that expects all strings to be in Unicode, you need to add the --enable-multibyte=UNICODE option. I'm turning on multibyte support because I plan to use PostgreSQL as the DBMS for some Java applications I'll be developing. If you're going to skip the Java portion of this hack, you can choose not to include this argument.

Some other interesting options are --with-openssl, --with-perl, --enable-syslog, and --enable-debug. I won't be covering these options, in order to be brief, but I do recommend you look into them.

Now is the time to run configure:

```
% ./configure --prefix=/Users/Shared/PostgreSQL --enable-locale `⏎
--enable-multibyte=UNICODE
```

You'll know configure is complete when you get back to a command prompt.

In order to actually begin building PostgreSQL, we need to execute GNU make from the command line by typing make (Apple has installed GNU make as the default make mechanism).

The build process can last anywhere between five minutes and half an hour, according to documentation provided by PostgreSQL. The build on my 600MHz iBook lasted seven minutes. Once the build is complete, type make install to begin installing PostgreSQL. If you plan to do server-side program development such as creating custom functions, replace install with install-all-headers. If your install was successful, you'll see the following output:

```
Thank you for choosing PostgreSQL, the most advanced open source database
engine.
```

Since we installed PostgreSQL to a location that is not searched for applications, we must add /Users/Shared/PostgreSQL/bin to our path. This can be handled by setting the appropriate environment variable [Hack #52] at the command prompt:

```
% setenv PATH ${PATH}:/Users/Shared/PostgreSQL/bin
```

You should type the following to reference the manual pages for PostgreSQL:

```
% setenv MANPATH ${MANPATH}:/Users/Shared/PostgreSQL/man
```

Setting Up a Database

In order to simplify things for the purpose of this hack, we're going to create the database as your own user, which should be set up as an administrator. However, for production systems, it is recommended that you create the database as a dedicated PostgreSQL user.

Initialize the database cluster by typing the following:

```
% initdb -D /Users/Shared/PostgreSQL/data
```

PostgreSQL will begin this task by displaying feedback similar to this:

```
The files belonging to this database system will be owned by user "steve".
This user must also own the server process.
```

It will then display the following feedback to indicate that it is finished:

```
Success. You can now start the database server using:

/Users/Shared/PostgreSQL/bin/postmaster -D /Users/Shared/PostgreSQL/data

or

/Users/Shared/PostgreSQL/bin/pg_ctl -D /Users/Shared/PostgreSQL/data -l ↵
logfile start
```

This is just what we want to do. The first command will start the database server in the foreground. The second command uses a shell script that automates the commands needed to start the database server in the background. Start the database with the second command.

Let's create our first database. Actually, PostgreSQL's first database (template1) was created when we initialized the database cluster. However, now we're going to create the first real database.

```
% createdb foo
```

Congratulations, you just created your first database! Its name is foo. That wasn't so hard.

Accessing the Database

Let's try accessing the database we just created. I'll touch on a couple of SQL tools for the Mac: ViennaSQL (*http://vienna.sourceforge.net/*) and SQL4X Manager J (*http://www.macosguru.de/*). I'll walk you through setting up ViennaSQL and connecting to foo with it. You'll also see a screenshot of the key-connection setup screen if you wish to use SQL4X Manager J instead.

First, download the Java Archive (JAR) file for ViennaSQL (*http://vienna. sourceforge.net/vienna.jar*). Then download the JDBC driver for PostgreSQL (*http://jdbc.PostgreSQL.org/download/pgjdbc2.jar*). I renamed *pgjdbc2.jar* to *PostgreSQL.jar* and placed it in */Library/Java/Extensions*. Now, add this JAR and the current directory to the classpath environment variable.

```
% setenv CLASSPATH ${CLASSPATH}:/Library/Java/Extensions/PostgreSQL.jar:.
```

You will need to edit [Hack #51] your *PostgreSQL.conf* file in order to activate TCP/IP sockets for PostgreSQL. The file is located in */Users/Shared/ PostgreSQL/data/*. You will see the following line near the top of the file, under the connection parameters section:

```
tcpip_socket = false
```

Uncomment the line by removing the pound symbol (#) and replace false with true. Open */Users/Shared/PostgreSQL/data/pg_hba.conf* in a text editor. Scroll to the bottom of the host-based access file and enter the following to allow access to all databases from any computer on the local network:

```
host all 192.168.0.0 255.255.0.0 trust
```

Restart the postmaster by issuing the following command:

```
% /Users/Shared/PostgreSQL/bin/pg_ctl -D /Users/Shared/PostgreSQL/data -l ↵
logfile -o -i restart
```

Be sure to specify the -o and -i arguments to turn on IP sockets.

OK, now start up ViennaSQL via its JAR file. Under File in the menu bar, select Configure. This will bring up the ViennaSQL Options window. Click on the Connection tab and create a new connection (see Figure 9-1). Fill in the Connection name with PostgreSQL. Type org.PostgreSQL.Driver in the Driver class text box. The URL should be jdbc:PostgreSQL:foo in our case. Then fill in the appropriate information for your current Mac OS user.

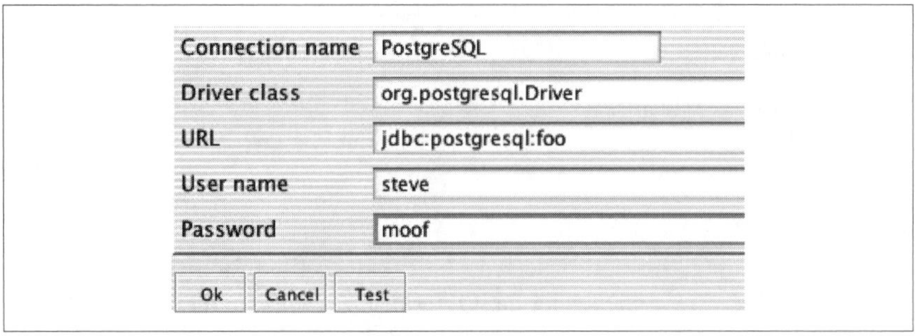

Connection name	PostgreSQL
Driver class	org.postgresql.Driver
URL	jdbc:postgresql:foo
User name	steve
Password	moof

Ok   Cancel   Test

Figure 9-1. Setting up a connection in ViennaSQL

Click the Test button to verify that your connection is working, dismiss the Connection Test window, then click on the OK button in the New Connection window and the ViennaSQL Options window. There is a combo box in the top-righthand corner of ViennaSQL's main window; select PostgreSQL from that box. This will connect you to the database. Type the following SQL into the lower pane of ViennaSQL's window:

```
CREATE TABLE books (
  code CHARACTER(13) CONSTRAINT firstkey PRIMARY KEY,
  title CHARACTER VARYING(40) NOT NULL,
  author CHARACTER VARYING(40) NOT NULL,
  price DECIMAL(4,2),
  kind CHARACTER VARYING(10)
);
```

Select Query and Execute from the menu bar. Then select Query and Commit from the menu bar. You've now created your first table. Congratulations again! Now, let's populate it with some sample data. Type the following lines of code in the lower pane, replacing what is already there:

```
INSERT INTO books (code, title, author, price, kind) ⏎
VALUES ('1-56592-846-6', 'Practical PostgreSQL', ⏎
'John C. Worsley, Joshua D. Drake', 44.95, 'database');

INSERT INTO books (code, title, author, price, kind) ⏎
VALUES ('1-56592-616-1', 'Database Programming with JDBC and Java', ⏎
'George Reese', 34.95, 'java');
INSERT INTO books (code, title, author, price, kind) ⏎
VALUES ('0-596-00160-6', 'Learning Cocoa', 'Apple Computer', 34.95, ⏎
'macintosh');
```

You'll need to execute and commit these statements just as you did the last one (see Figure 9-2).

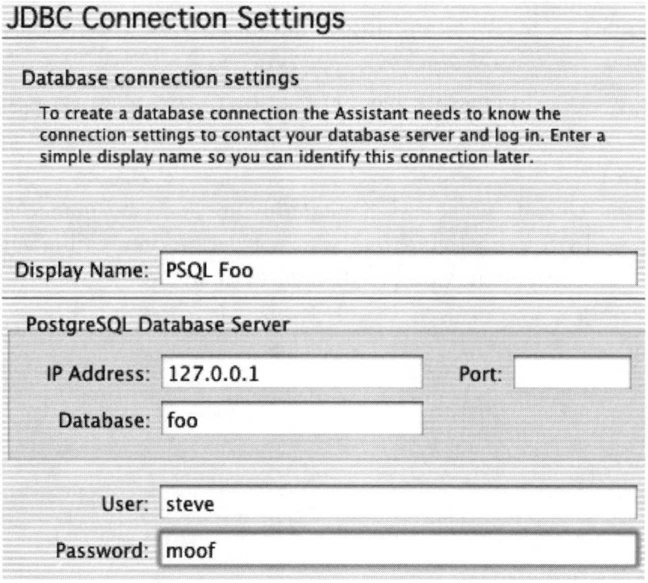

JDBC Connection Settings

Database connection settings

To create a database connection the Assistant needs to know the connection settings to contact your database server and log in. Enter a simple display name so you can identify this connection later.

Display Name: PSQL Foo

PostgreSQL Database Server

IP Address: 127.0.0.1   Port:

Database: foo

User: steve

Password: moof

Figure 9-2. Executing and committing statements

Now, in order to view the data we just inserted, let's check out some Java code! I've written some Java that will connect to our database and return some values from each row of the books table. Download *connectPostgreSQL.java* (*http://www.macdevcenter.com/mac/2002/06/07/ examples/connectPostgreSQL.java*) to your desktop. Now, in the Terminal, switch to your *Desktop* folder and compile the source. Then, run the resulting Java class. Here's what I had to enter into the Terminal to accomplish this:

```
% cd ~/Desktop
% javac connectPostgreSQL.java
% java connectPostgreSQL
```

After pressing Return on the third command line, you should see output similar to this:

```
Practical PostgreSQL costs 44.95
Database Programming with JDBC and Java costs 34.95
Learning Cocoa costs 34.95
```

And that's all I wrote. Well, almost. I've included some links in the "See Also" section for more information on PostgreSQL and some of the technologies that were touched on in this hack.

See Also

- How PostgreSQL Rose to Fame (*/pub/a/network/2000/06/16/magazine/PostgreSQL_history.html*).

- PostgreSQL SQL Commands (*http://www.us.PostgreSQL.org/users-lounge/docs/7.0/user/sql-commands.htm*).

- PostgreSQL's Interactive Documentation (*http://www.PostgreSQL.org/idocs/*) site has more information on what SQL is supported by PostgreSQL.

- *Learning Unix for Mac OS X* (*/catalog/lunixmacosx/chapter/ch04.html*) by Dave Taylor and Jerry Peek has information on creating a *.tcshrc* file to make environment variable changes permanent.

- Sun's JDBC pages (*http://java.sun.com/products/jdbc/*).

—*Michael Brewer*

Index

We'd like to hear your suggestions for improving our indexes. Send email to *index@oreilly.com*.

N

namespaces (speakable web services), 163
narration for movies, 66, 68–69
NAT addresses, sendmail and, 313
NetInfo database, modifying for sendmail, 314
NetInfo Manager, creating email aliases, 318–319
NetNewsWire, 164, 329
network traffic, 150
networking, 243–289
  creating one-wire network, 249–252
    FireWire, using, 251
    Rendezvous, using, 251
  Domain Name Service (DNS), setting up, 286–289
    dynamic DNS services, 287–289
    static IP address, 287
  file exchange via Bluetooth, 280–283
    receiving files, 280
    sending files, 280
  Internet connection, sharing, 245
  Internet Shortcuts, 243
  mounting remote FTP directory, 276–280
    anonymous FTP shares, 277
    authenticated FTP shares, 277
    disconnecting, 279
  remote login via SSH, 256–262
    allowing remote login, 258
  renewing DHCP-assigned IP address, 245
  secure tunneling with VPN or SSH, 252–256
    SSH, 254–256
    VPN, 252–254
  Sony/Ericsson cellphone, using as Bluetooth modem, 283–285
  WebDAV share, 272–276
    connecting and mounting, 273
    disconnecting, 276
news aggregators, 329
news sites, subscriptions to, 329–331
non-volatile RAM, modifying for verbose booting, 36
NTSC Video Standard, 68

O

Office for Mac OS X, 291
offline viewing, saving web page for, 54
one-wire network, creating, 249–252
  FTP and SSH from Windows to Mac iBook, 250
  IP over FireWire, 251
  with Rendezvous, 251
open command, using from command line, 203–205
  files without type/creator codes or file extensions, 204
  type/creator codes and file extensions, 203
Open Firmware password protection, 39, 237
open source software, Fink project, 211, 214–216
open_url( ), 101
operating systems
  booting from another device, 37
  line breaks, 17
OroborOSX (X11 window manager), 211
OrobosX, 106
OS X Server, running on older machines, 41
osascript utility, 100, 347
  running AppleScript from Terminal, 99
  running AppleScripts from command line, 233
Other World Computing (XPostFacto support), 42
Outbox mailbox, 299
output, piping via more command, 172
owner permissions, 182
  changing with chown, 183–185

P

packages, 30
  as folders, 30
  for Linux on iBook, 240
    hot plugging, 241
    power management, 240
    special keys, 240
Pager, VirtualDesktop, 141

W

Colophon

Our look is the result of reader comments, our own experimentation, and feedback from distribution channels. Distinctive covers complement our distinctive approach to technical topics, breathing personality and life into potentially dry subjects.

Brian Sawyer was the production editor and proofreader for *Mac OS X Hacks*. Norma Emory was the copyeditor. Mary Brady and Claire Cloutier provided quality control. Genevieve d'Entremont provided production support. Ellen Troutman Zaig wrote the index.

The tool on the cover of *Mac OS X Hacks* is an adjustable wrench. Wrenches are used to hold and turn nuts, bolts, and other threaded parts. While *fixed* wrenches have stationary jaws that are forged to fit a particular size of nut or bolt head, *adjustable* wrenches feature sliding jaws that open and close to suit many different sizes. For this reason, the size of a fixed wrench is always expressed as the capacity of its jaw, while the size of an adjustable wrench is usually expressed as the length of the tool. Adjustable wrenches vary in size from 4 inches to 2 feet in length, but 10-inch or 12-inch wrenches usually work well for most household tasks.

Fixed wrenches offer more precise control over specific tasks, since their stationary jaws always remain tight. Adjustable wrenches are ideal for jobs that call for a variety of wrench sizes in circumstances that limit the number of available tools.

Edie Freedman designed the cover of this book. The cover image is an original photograph by Edie Freedman. Emma Colby produced the cover layout with QuarkXPress 4.1 using Adobe's Helvetica Neue and ITC Garamond fonts.

David Futato designed the interior layout. This book was converted by Mike Sierra to FrameMaker 5.5.6 with a format conversion tool created by Erik Ray, Jason McIntosh, Neil Walls, and Mike Sierra that uses Perl and XML technologies. The text font is Linotype Birka; the heading font is Adobe Helvetica Neue Condensed; and the code font is LucasFont's TheSans Mono Condensed. The illustrations that appear in the book were produced by Robert Romano and Jessamyn Read using Macromedia FreeHand 9 and Adobe Photoshop 6. This colophon was written by Brian Sawyer.

By Rob Flickenger
1st Edition January 2003
240 pages, 0-596-00461-3

By Tara Calishain
& Rael Dornfest
1st Edition March 2003
352 pages, 0-596-00447-8

By Shelley Powers, Jerry Peek,
Tim O'Reilly & Mike Loukides
3rd Edition October 2002
1156 pages, 0-596-00330-7

From Power Tools to Hacks

The difference between computer "hackers" and ordinary users is that hackers are always trying something new, whether in solving an urgent problem, feeling the joy of pushing boundaries, or just, as the poet Wallace Stevens once said, "searching the possible for its possibleness."

I've always wanted to publish books that capture the essence of the hacker experience. I wanted a format that made it easy to present lots of small but useful tidbits—tips, tricks, and dare I say, hacks. Our first crack at it came with *Unix Power Tools*—a collection of tips that was both easy to search and fun to explore, harvested from the net and from a community of experts.

The books in our new Hacks Series pack the spirit of *Unix Power Tools* into smaller volumes on more narrowly focused topics. We chose the Hacks moniker for the new books because besides being an apt description of the book's content, we wanted to do our small bit to reclaim the term "hacker" from those who've redefined it to mean "unauthorized intruder" rather that the "computer equivalent of a great jazz improvisor."

Tim O'Reilly

O'REILLY®

To order: *800-998-9938* • *order@oreilly.com* • *www.oreilly.com*
Online editions of most O'Reilly titles are available by subscription at *safari.oreilly.com*
Also available at most retail and online bookstores.

How to stay in touch with O'Reilly

1. Visit our award-winning web site

http://www.oreilly.com/

★ "Top 100 Sites on the Web"—PC Magazine
★ CIO Magazine's Web Business 50 Awards

Our web site contains a library of comprehensive product information (including book excerpts and tables of contents), downloadable software, background articles, interviews with technology leaders, links to relevant sites, book cover art, and more. File us in your bookmarks or favorites!

2. Join our email mailing lists

Sign up to get email announcements of new books and conferences, special offers, and O'Reilly Network technology newsletters at:

http://elists.oreilly.com

It's easy to customize your free elists subscription so you'll get exactly the O'Reilly news you want.

3. Get examples from our books

To find example files for a book, go to:

http://www.oreilly.com/catalog

select the book, and follow the "Examples" link.

4. Work with us

Check out our web site for current employment opportunites:

http://jobs.oreilly.com/

5. Register your book

Register your book at:
http://register.oreilly.com

6. Contact us

O'Reilly & Associates, Inc.
1005 Gravenstein Hwy North
Sebastopol, CA 95472 USA
TEL: 707-827-7000 or 800-998-9938
　　　 (6am to 5pm PST)
FAX: 707-829-0104

order@oreilly.com
For answers to problems regarding your order or our products. To place a book order online visit:

http://www.oreilly.com/order_new/

catalog@oreilly.com
To request a copy of our latest catalog.

booktech@oreilly.com
For book content technical questions or corrections.

corporate@oreilly.com
For educational, library, government, and corporate sales.

proposals@oreilly.com
To submit new book proposals to our editors and product managers.

international@oreilly.com
For information about our international distributors or translation queries. For a list of our distributors outside of North America check out:

http://international.oreilly.com/distributors.html

adoption@oreilly.com
For information about academic use of O'Reilly books, visit:

http://academic.oreilly.com

O'REILLY®